Nixon on Stage and Screen

Nixon on Stage and Screen

The Thirty-Seventh President as Depicted in Films, Television, Plays and Opera

by THOMAS MONSELL

McFarland & Company, Inc., Publishers
Jefferson, North Carolina, and London

To
my parents
Amy Adele Prince Monsell
(1894–1978)
and
Harry Monroe Monsell
(1894–1969)

They had a sense of community

Frontispiece: Nixon's farewell to his staff, August 9, 1974
(a photograph that appears in virtually all documentaries).
"I spoke from the heart," he said afterward.

British Library Cataloguing-in-Publication data are available

Library of Congress Cataloguing-in-Publication Data

Monsell, Thomas.
    Nixon on stage and screen : the thirty-seventh president as
depicted in films, television, plays and opera / by Thomas
Monsell.
        p.   cm.
    Includes index.
    ISBN 0-7864-0163-X (library binding : 50# alkaline paper) ∞
    1. Nixon, Richard M. (Richard Milhous), 1913– — In motion
pictures. 2. Nixon, Richard M. (Richard Milhous), 1913– — In
literature. I. Title.
PN1995.9.N59M66   1998
791.43'651— dc21
                                     97-44651
                                        CIP

Manufactured in the United States of America

*McFarland & Company, Inc., Publishers
Box 611, Jefferson, North Carolina 28640*

Acknowledgments

I wish to thank the following people for helping to make this book possible: Angela D. Hughes for her constant encouragement; Eva and Gail Horton for their assistance on the manuscript; Christine Karatnytsky for being an excellent student and later an excellent researcher at the Lincoln Center Performing Arts Library; Mary and Peter Sternad for taking me to Whittier and Yorba Linda; Donald Pile and Ray Williams for taking me to the Eisenhower and Truman Libraries; my dear friend Josephine Hutchinson, the Nora of the Civic Rep's *A Doll's House*, who pointed out the many similarities between Richard Nixon and Ibsen's leading male characters; and Regina Hashim, Bob Gelman and Frank Trezza for being such good friends for over 40, 30 and 20 years, respectively, and John Simon, a critic whom I admire above all others, a man who loathed Richard Nixon but shares with him three of his best traits — courage, intelligence and a startling sense of the unpredictable.

I would also like to thank the East End Arts Council of Riverhead, Long Island, for giving me the grant that enabled me to go to California.

A note to the reader: A book that should prove helpful to anyone interested in the general topic of film and politics is the 538-page volume *A Political Companion to American Film*, edited by Gary Crowdus and published by *Cinéaste*.

Greenport, New York
July, 1997

"The cinema is for us the most important instrument of all the arts."
— Lenin, quoted in *Theory of Film*
by Siegfried Kracauer (1960)

Contents

"My interpretation is that there is in Nixon — as in many high achievers — a will to self-destruction that only becomes manifest at the point of total success."
— William Rusher, quoted in *Nixon: An Oral History of His Presidency* (1994) by Strober and Strober

"[Nixon] had a limited though real capacity to love and be loved, to trust and be trusting, as his relationships with his mother and grandmother showed."
— Stephen E. Ambrose, Nixon biography, volume I

"Addressing the nation the morning he left the White House after his resignation, Richard Nixon was overcome by reminiscences of his mother. Tears in his eyes, he said, 'She was a saint.' Media derision of this as Nixonian calculation surprised me: Italians do not find it ridiculous to speak of one's mother at peak dramatic moments. Italian soldiers lying wounded on the battlefield in two world wars called upon not wives or sweethearts but 'Mamma, Mamma.' At his moment of cataclysmic loss, a dissolution of the politically supreme male persona, Nixon underwent a voyage of Proustian memory from a sordid, self-befouled present into a mythical lost paradise of childhood. In the process, he summoned his mother...."
— Camille Paglia, *Sexual Personae* (1990)

"It's been a campaign since the day he was born. All his life I've been his campaigner."
— Hannah Nixon in *Presidents' Mothers* by Doris Faber (1978)

"This time, I couldn't help it. I said that I didn't think I was going to make it. [Pat] gripped my hand and said almost fiercely, 'Don't talk that way. You have got to make it. You must not give up.'"
— R.N., *In the Arena: A Memoir of Victory, Defeat and Renewal* (1990)

"The final verdict of history is not rendered quickly. It takes not just years but decades or generations to be handed down. Few leaders live to hear the verdict."
— R.N., *Leaders* (1982)

Introduction

In writing this book on Richard Nixon and how he is perceived by play-wrights and filmmakers, I have gained a greater understanding of the times I have lived through. Throughout this entire process, I was frequently exasperated by Richard Nixon's disastrous misjudgments, and I was often furious at the way he treated himself and his very appealing wife and children. But through it all, Richard Nixon remained absolutely fascinating to me, a figure of drama, of pathos even, because there was clearly an inexpressible hunger in his heart and soul. His was the "quiet desperation" that Thoreau wrote of. His was "the life lie," the self-delusion that Ibsen examined so vividly in his greatest plays. These words are not written in admonition but in harmony with Tom Wicker who titled his very worthy Nixon biography *One of Us*, using a perfectly chosen phrase from Joseph Conrad's cannily corresponding masterpiece *Lord Jim*. Wicker wrote: "Nixon ... with all his strengths and weaknesses, his virtues and deceits, his lack of grace in his self-willed ascent to the summit ... was 'one of us' and all the more to be embraced for that." Later in his introduction, Wicker said, "It seemed to me that no American of my time more nearly deserved study and reflection." Nixon deserves many studies, and he will have them. In Charles Krauthammer's words in the *New York Daily News* of April 28, 1994: "Richard Nixon was the most thoroughly psycho-analyzed President — perhaps public person — of our time."

Nixon on Stage and Screen contains, not psychoanalysis, but a great deal of "psychologizing" by the playwrights and filmmakers whose works are discussed. I doubt if more than half a dozen of them have degrees in psychology. Being cari-catured in cartoons and on editorial pages for almost fifty years has made Nixon easy prey for instant analysis by nearly everyone, qualified or not. As time passed there seemed to be a value in having an anecdotal record of Nixon as he was re-created by the playwrights and filmmakers of his own time, some with valid psy-chological points, most without.

Regardless of the nature of each work's psychological and political interpre-tations, the following annotated record is as inclusive as possible of all the the-atrical films and stage plays that feature Nixon as a character, have him edited in as a television image, or use him as an off-screen character referred to in a photo-graph in another character's home or office. The latter practice proved to be a rather frequent device, almost always leading to a wisecrack or some untoward

1

insinuation. Most major television documentaries are reflected herein as well because, after all, editing is an artistic process and statements are often implied through artful documentary editing. (Most of these documentaries are on video.)

Probably the greatest impetus for examining the theatricalized Nixon was Murray Kempton's statement in the April 21, 1994, issue of *Newsday*: "It is hard to think of a president since Lincoln who has exercised a command over the literary imagination as strong as Nixon's." This is true — even if we were to put Teddy, Eleanor and Franklin Roosevelt together, it would still come far short of this volume in the number of works cited because Nixon was a part of public life from 1946 until 1994, and in that time a lot of theatrical axes have been ground. In trying to find them, I have read dozens of books, seen dozens of plays and films and visited many of the sites associated with Richard Milhous Nixon. In the process, I have often been exasperated, never bored and sometimes elated.

Like Nixon, I come from a small town. I grew up in the 1940s on the east end of Long Island on the mercifully unfashionable North Fork, a bay away from the trendy Hamptons. I was 11 years old when the war ended, but I remember its effect on community life very well: The booming shipyards with over 2,000 defense workers, the sailors out for a good time and "all they could get," the hubbub when stars like Kate Smith or Lily Pons came to town to christen a mine sweeper, and the busy movie theater — my ticket to another world — with A pictures Sunday through Tuesday and Friday and Saturday and B pictures on Wednesday and Thursday. No matter what the night, it was always crowded in those pre-television days. Greenport was a lively, independent and very cosmopolitan little town with every kind of ethnicity and a general spirit of community pride with my parents as two of its best boosters. If a church, any church, white or black, Catholic or Protestant or the small synagogue, "had something going," my parents would, as they used to say, "stir their stumps" and be out the front door in that sense of civic-mindedness that was so much a part of small town life in the forties and fifties. This is not nostalgia spreading its gossamer wings. It is the reality of that time and place.

I lament many of the changes since those times. John Leo offered an insight in the *U.S. News and World Report* of October 20, 1995: "All that was swept away in the 1960s. The culture of the streets, the sidewalks and the porches were chased indoors by the arrival of television and air-conditioning. Technology and the market economy multiplied choices and helped loosen neighborhood ties, and the cultural revolution of the '60s, hostile to all rules and authority, produced the hyper-individualism and the narrow generational worship of 'rights' and 'choice.'"

It wasn't all gone, of course. It remained in many rural and suburban areas, and it was to be Nixon's key constituency in the squeaker election of 1960 and his two successful bids for the White House. For good or ill, this constituency let Richard Nixon leave his mark upon the country. More should be made of Nixon's positive record than is indicated by the high volume of Watergate material in the succeeding years. As *Time* writer Hugh Sidey noted on the David Brinkley television program of April 24, 1994: "In just one 16-month period, Nixon had the opening to China, the SALT talks, an air lift to Israel during the Yom Kippur War, the development of OSHA, the beginning of the end of the Vietnam War, the Supreme Court ruling on *Roe vs. Wade* and subsidies to the arts." Nixon had a good record on civil rights as well, and there were many other positive aspects of his administration in addition to those mentioned by Sidey.

The beginning student of Nixon's life and presidency would do well to consult the many excellent books that discuss all Nixon's plusses and minuses with varying emphases and enthusiasms. Stephen E. Ambrose's three-volume biography is the linchpin upon which much of the present work is dependent. It is richly detailed, filled with insight, sometimes admiring and often angry. It is a great achievement. Since both Pat and Richard Nixon were alive in 1991 when the last volume was published, I have often wondered what they thought of them. Roger Morris' *Richard Milhous Nixon: The Rise of an American Politician* is a superbly written social and political history. With his marvelous gift of language he takes us convincingly into Nixon's early Quaker world. Morris has a poet's eye as well as a poet's ear, neither of which ever obscure his tremendous political savvy. Herbert Parmet's *Richard Nixon and His America* is an authoritative but formal work by a respected academician. Jonathan Aitken's *Nixon: A Life* is an engaging and informative biography by Britain's Minister of State for Defense. More pro–Nixon than some biographers, Aitken nevertheless has a very good understanding of American life and politics. Joan Hoff's *Nixon Reconsidered* is another excellent book in which she (rather surprisingly) supports the idea found in the controversial *Silent Coup* that the attempt to cover up data on a call girl ring was the real reason for Watergate. She also — Messrs. Altman, Freed, Stone and Lees, take note — states that the "f word" was never used by the "president and his aides ... unless quoting someone else." Furthermore, there is no authentication in any printed source that Richard Nixon used the crude term for oral sex so frequently spouted by Anthony Hopkins in Oliver Stone's film and Gerry Bamman in Russell Lees' play on Nixon. John Taylor, executive director of the Nixon Library, called "a number of RN's aides, from Herb Klein to Charles Colson, and asked if they had ever heard him utter the word. None had, nor had [Taylor]."

In regard to Nixon books that are somewhat older, Garry Wills' *Nixon Agonistes* is a powerful work, one that the always politically aware Christopher Matthews continued to praise a quarter century after its publication. Matthews' own book *Kennedy and Nixon* is obeisance at the throne of John Fitzgerald Kennedy. His use of the Kennedy–Nixon dyad as a parallel to Mozart and Salieri is simply too pat and is as trite as calling the Kennedy years America's Camelot. Still the book is worth reading; Matthews is a good reporter and always gets his facts right — including the disclosure that LBJ was "the secret lover" of Helen Gahagan Douglas — even if his book is a little starry-eyed. Julie Nixon Eisenhower's *Pat Nixon* is a lovely book which includes a view of her father that many will not accept, but one reads the book, as one should, to learn about the pretty and extremely capable helpmate with whom he shared his life. Two of the three worst books are Fawn Brodie's "psychobiography" of Nixon, deservedly mocked by

Ambrose, and the gossipy and mean-spirited book on Pat called *The Lonely Lady of San Clemente* by Lester David, whose previous two books had been on Joan Kennedy and Ted Kennedy. Probably the most biased book is, ironically enough, one written for high school students entitled *The Great Stream of History* by Laurie Nadel. There is finger-pointing on every page. Reading it is like being told to stand in a corner.

With so much controversy, the verdict on Richard Nixon will always be coming in and always shifting slightly. In a *Newsday* interview (April 24, 1994), Roger Morris pointed to the eventual release of the Nixon tapes, "and from all that extraordinary legacy — from the thousands of hours of Oval Office tape recordings, from the tens of thousands of memos and documents — there will be no escape, no ultimate comeback campaign. It's in that ineluctable monument, and not in discreet funeral memories, that history will find the real Richard Nixon. It's there that he smears and intrigues, and brings to American politics the fatal curse of big money." Tough words — but Roger Morris was tough in *Haig: The General's Progress* and super-tough in his Clinton book *Partners in Power*, said by Hilton Kramer (*New York Post*, June 18, 1996) to "[go] further than anything yet published in nailing the Clintons, both of them, as shameless crooks, liars and impostors in every aspect of their personal and political lives."

Clearly, the drama of American politics did not end with Richard Nixon, although his tapes will be sharing headlines with his various successors for some time to come.

A fascinating aspect of my research has been sensing the growing dismay expressed by such able biographers as Ambrose and Morris as they re-live Nixon's course of self-destruction. The reader can almost see them wringing their hands at some ghastly Nixon misstep. Ambrose's despair is almost palpable as he progresses through the three volumes of the biography. For instance, in 1987, after the publication of volume I, Ambrose said in a *U.S. News and World Report* interview (May 4, 1987): "I like Nixon more now than when I started the biography. I've come to have an appreciation of him not unmixed with many of the feelings I had when he was an active politician, and I was a Nixon hater. Now I see him do things, chuckle and say, 'Go get 'em, Dick.'" By the end of volume III, however, Ambrose's dismay had turned to disgust as he cites all the beneficial things Nixon had projected — a free Vietnam, a comprehensive Middle East peace plan, welfare reform, a program providing health insurance for all Americans, an energy program, programs for student loans and at least half a dozen other salubrities for the American people that were all dashed by Watergate. A stupid campaign dirty trick perpetrated by a bunch of unscrupulous, opportunistic clowns, was allowed to convulse the country. That it happened was bad enough but that its charade continued and was lied about is doubly shameless. That is the emotion one feels at the end of Ambrose's last volume on Nixon. Like Ambrose, the reader wants to throw up his hands in disgust at the thought that so much that was good was thrown away. Ambrose's last words are, "When Nixon resigned, we lost more than we gained."

One of the character flaws that Ambrose points out in volume III was that Nixon was "a man who would not trust others, and had no real friends. Nearly everyone who worked with Nixon commented on this. Eisenhower told Ann Whitman [his secretary] that he could not understand how a man could go through life without friends.... Even with [Bebe] Rebozo and [Bob] Abplanalp there was a distance." Yet, it is a curious thing that Nixon always had the abiding love of many women of high moral character: Almira Milhous, Hannah (several authors have stated that Nixon changed after Hannah died), Pat, Tricia, Julie and Rose Mary Woods, who overheard "reporter Bill Lawrence make a crack about her boss [and] angrily poured a drink over Lawrence's head" (Ambrose, volume I). Is not such emotion a kind of love as well? As Morris described her: "Rather resembling her new employer, [Rose Mary] was both controlled and volatile; a mix, she would say, of 'my mother's cool head' and 'my father's temper.' It was the beginning of an intimate, fierce, sometimes tortured but lifelong loyalty to Richard Nixon.... Rose Woods was accepted by Pat with a kind of mutual respect, and the shared sorority of two working class professional women dedicated each in their own way to Richard Nixon." There had to have been something more to Richard Nixon than a familial bond or a weekly paycheck for such strong, decent, intelligent women to love him.

One of the reasons was surely his courage, but for all his courage, there was something vulnerable about Richard Nixon, a deep wound far inside, possibly arising from the anger of his father. (As Nixon's cousin, novelist Jessamyn West, said, "Frank saw only one side, his." Her brother Merle said that Frank could be "very punishing.") Possibly it came from Hannah's quiet but guilt-inducing reproofs since it was her love and approbation he had always sought. Possibly it was living in a home with little money, a great deal of hard work and the Quaker stress on rectitude and duty, and the early deaths of two other sons which left their marks on the entire family. There was a touch of self-dramatization, when Nixon titled one of his best books with a phrase from Teddy Roosevelt. *In the Arena* was clearly an allusion to his own life and the many "crises" with which he had struggled. As others have pointed out, it seemed Nixon's whole life was a struggle to prove that he was a worthy person, yet, through it all, he was also a needy person.

Murray Kempton's thoughtful essay "No Apologies for Liking Richard Nixon" (*Newsday*, April 21, 1994) captures my feelings too after spending five or six years reading and thinking about Richard Nixon and seeing him on the screen: "To meet the Kennedys was sometimes, through no fault of theirs, to feel like a social climber. To be met by Nixon was to sense how much he felt he was the social climber and that you were the distinguished person who, he would later boast, had treated him as an equal. He was in that way, as in so many others, so much kin to the rest of us that I have never felt the faintest impulse to apologize for liking Richard Nixon."

Richard Nixon, Arts Patron

A gifted amateur actor and musician, Richard Nixon gave more public support to the arts than any president of the United States prior to his term in office. Not only did he support the arts through government funding but when out of office and working as a New York lawyer, he and his wife, Pat, regularly attended Broadway plays and concerts. A little-known fact is that their initial meeting was at a tryout for the Whittier Community Theater production of *The Dark Tower*, a melodrama by George S. Kaufman and Alexander Woollcott in which they were both cast. On that very first night, Nixon told Pat Ryan that he was going to marry her.

Their tastes were wide-ranging, everything from *Bonanza* to the Bolshoi. They were also avid film fans. For instance, at the American Film Institute in Beverly Hills, Nixon presented the Medal of Freedom to John Ford and stated, "I've seen virtually all of the 140 Ford movies." As *Variety* noted (July 5, 1972), he was also "the only U.S. president ever to attend the Peking and Moscow ballets in their home theaters."

In an address before the Associated Councils of the Arts in Washington on May 26, 1971, Nixon stated, "Few investments in the quality of life pay so handsomely as the money spent to stimulate the arts.... As we look ahead ten, twenty, thirty years, we can chart the prospect of many great achievements. We have seen technological advance speed up by almost a geometrical progression; already we take Moon landings almost for granted. Computers, industrial advances, agricultural breakthroughs, all are multiplying the goods and services our economy can produce.... But by themselves these advances can never be enough. The engineers and the scientists can take us to the Moon, but we need the poet or the painter to take us to the heights of understanding and perception. Doctors are enabling us to live longer and healthier lives, but we need the musician and the dancer and the filmmaker to bring beauty and meaning to our lives."

Nixon's strongly held views in regard to the arts were so persuasive that continued support for the arts came to be regarded as one of his highest legacies. More than two decades later (December 26, 1994), *U.S. News and World Report* stated: "As Joseph Zeigler documents in his new history *Arts in Crisis*, arts funding grew 1,400 percent during the Nixon and Ford administrations — the most rapid growth ever."

Critics and Comedians: "Nixon to Kick Around"

Two emblematic quotations anent Richard Nixon and his many cartoonists and caricaturists: *Newsday* cartoonist Doug Marlette wrote (April 24, 1994), "Seldom has a politician's appearance so truthfully revealed his substance. Nixon looked like his policies. His nose told you he would bomb Cambodia." This is what passes for logic in some quarters of the press. Lloyd Rose (*Washington Post*, April 24, 1994) on Dan Aykroyd's "Nixon appearances" on *Saturday Night Live*: "There [was] a smug cruelty in Aykroyd's attack — his glee goes beyond smacking Nixon for his political sins and into the nasty, forbidden area of hurting someone *because* he's weak. Aykroyd and his contemporaries went after Nixon like playground bullies after the class nerd." Such are the hazards of being a politician in the United States, but the attacks upon Nixon were more virulent than those upon any other American president in the 20th century. (Let us not forget that during the 19th century Lincoln was often referred to as "the ape.") Nothing "stuck" to Reagan, but everything "stuck" to Nixon. Why is this so? A Walter Kerr essay of May 7, 1972, in the *New York Times* offers an answer:

> I speak of Mr. Nixon as an actor because, when I watch him on television, he seems to me to be one. (Reviewers are asked to review acting only when it takes place on a stage, which often leads to frustration while attending to men in public life.) He seems an *actor* to me in the sense that his gestures and inflections have an adopted rather than a reflexive air about them; he is conscious of the role he is playing and he has tried to train himself to its needs.

Nevertheless, Nixon had his fans as a television star. Among them was the witty, insightful critic of the *Washington Post* Tom Shales whose piece of April 26, 1994, was a contemplative analysis of this "maddeningly enigmatic" president. Shales wrote: "'Tenacious' is the word most often used to eulogize Richard Nixon. I prefer 'defiant.' His defiance was one of his saving graces, part of his makeup as a tragic hero, and it was at the heart of his first major TV appearance, the Checkers speech of 1952, undertaken in defiance of Republican Party bosses and Dwight D. Eisenhower. While Nixon never really mastered TV, it never mastered him either." Shales recalled Nixon and Pat on *The Jack Paar Show* (August 1960), which

9

"showed him in an uncharacteristically relaxed and convivial mood." Paar convinced Nixon to play one of his own compositions, "and Mr. Nixon engagingly complied. It was as close to charming as he ever got on the air." Shales noted that Nixon's 1968 appearance on the Rowan and Martin *Laugh-In* (when he said, "Sock it — to *me*?") "ranks as probably the most important five-second appearance in the history of political television. It changed his image as a stuffed shirt and helped him win the election."

Toward the end of his piece, before he took CBS newscaster Dan Rather to task for "mentioning again and again that Watergate 'involved criminal acts,'" Shales said, "One of the most unforgettable pieces of ... political theater ever seen on television [was] Nixon's farewell to his troops in the East Room, a rambling and nakedly emotional autobiography in which the president called his mother a 'saint.' ... I always wanted to meet Richard Nixon. I would have said, 'Thank you, Mr. President, thank you for all the great TV.'"

Nixon's leaving office meant, in the language of *Variety* (August 14, 1974), that "comedians lost their meal ticket." Celebrated Nixon mimic David Frye said in an interview, "I'm frightened on many levels. Nixon is someone I've been doing for years and years, living inside of, making a living off. It's a weird feeling, and a frightening one, knowing you can lose the guts of your act at any time. It's taken me years to get to know this man, to think like him.... You also become too close to the character and then to like the man. You start to feel sorry for him, for the tragedy of Richard Nixon." (A typical Frye routine would contain such lines as: "Pat and I this day have adopted two Vietnamese orphans — one from North Vietnam, one from South Vietnam. In America, anything is possible." Frye's Nixon also said, "My administration has taken crime off the streets and put it into the White House, where I can watch it.")

Other entertainers who "did" Nixon were Rich Little, Pat Paulsen, Alan King and Mark Russell, who regularly did Haldeman, Ehrlichman, Agnew and Checkers as part of his act. In another medium, Chevy Chase cut a comedy album called *The Missing White House Tapes*. In the comedy album *Nixorcism* (produced by Lou Adler), Nixon is wheeled in on a bed and tied down like Linda Blair in *The Exorcist* as Billy Graham and Henry Kissinger try and fail to expunge the devil from him. Another album was *The Honest to God! We Really Mean It! Very Last Nixon Album* from Earle Dowd, who also created the album *Welcome to LBJ Ranch*. Probably the best of the lot was David Frye's *Richard Nixon: A Fantasy* (Buddah Records), which also has Frye as Billy Graham, William F. Buckley and Hubert Humphrey.

Undoubtedly the most steadily employed Nixon imitator was James Laroe (sometimes spelled Leroe), who called himself Richard M. Dixon. Dixon played Nixon in well over a dozen films and appeared hundreds of times on television and in night clubs as the president. He also created a picture book called *Am I Your President?* with himself as Nixon. According to John Dean's *Blind Ambition*, "Haldeman requested an investigation of 'Richard M. Dixon,' the comedian who was seeking to capitalize on his striking resemblance to the President. [White

House investigator] Caulfield did a quick undercover investigation, but Haldeman lost interest when President Dixon faded."

The *New York Daily News* of May 15, 1978, called Dixon "a highly-paid freak attraction — before Watergate ruined both him and Nixon." Originally, Dixon had had hopes of becoming an actor, but after a screen test at 20th Century–Fox he was told, "You're a good actor, but you'll never get anywhere with a face like that." Ironically, it was his remarkable likeness to Richard Nixon that gave him at least five years of highly lucrative and visible employment. When his career as a Nixon look-alike began to fade, he opened a night club of brief duration called the White House Inn on Hicksville Road in North Massapequa, Long Island. He continued to make occasional appearances as Nixon, appearing several times on the *Conan O'Brien* show as late as the mid–1990s. In an interview in the *Christian Science Monitor* of April 13, 1977, Dixon stated that he refused "lots" of requests for appearances as Nixon because "they would not only have degraded the president but also the office of the presidency. 'Lots of people said thanks for *not* saying what you could have said,' he noted with an air of candor." In an interview for this book, Dixon stated that he was writing a book about his experiences playing the 37th president.

At the time of Nixon's death, one of his severest critics, political satirist Mort Sahl, was doing his one-man show in New York. Sahl was one of a group of comedians who talked to Stephen Williams of *Newsday* (April 24, 1994) about Nixon: "Nixon was smart, with no self-pity, and he had 'a lot of guts.' When Hubert Humphrey died, he went alone to the funeral — the only Republican among all those Democrats."

Even today, Nixon is with us. Don Imus, of the radio show *Imus in the Morning*, keeps him very much alive.

Nixon always said that a political leader should be "unpredictable." Two of the best-selling items at the Nixon Library and through their catalogue are Egil "Bud" Krogh's whimsical little book *The Day Elvis Met Nixon* and the T-shirt of Nixon the President and Elvis the King.

THE WORKS
ON STAGE AND
SCREEN

"A lot of Nixons have certainly appeared on stage and screen. And I'm sure the thought has crossed many minds that Nixon may well be the richest, most promising character the American theater has ever seen. His personality descends to almost oceanic depth, plunging from bright intelligence through piety, vulgarity, maudlinity and paranoia to the murky floor of violent criminality. His quivering cheeks and humped back are an actor's dream. And in the folk version that seems to be slowly emerging, he has become magnificently comic. His arms fly up in a v-for-victory gesture, his eyes peer suspiciously from an unshaven face, the jowls jiggle, and we can't help laughing."

— Paul Berman, *Village Voice*, September 27, 1983

The Checkers Speech (film, 1952)

30 minutes. NBC. Filmed without audience on stage at the El Capitan Theater, Hollywood, Tuesday, September 23, 1952. Funded by the Republican National Committee. Directed by John Claar with assistants from Batten, Barton, Dirstine and Osborne Advertising Agency. (In 1985, *The Checkers Speech* became a commercial release shown in tandem with Robert Altman's feature *Secret Honor.*) Cast: Richard and Pat Nixon.

In 1952, Richard Nixon was accused of having a secret financial fund. Almost immediately, widespread press and public censure forced him to make full disclosure of all his finances before a television audience of nearly 60,000,000 people, the largest audience for a single event in the history of the world.

Seated at a desk in a sparsely furnished "GI bedroom den," Nixon began simply and earnestly: "My fellow Americans, I come before you as a candidate for the Vice Presidency and as a man whose honesty and integrity have been questioned." The audience, he was sure, had heard the charge that he had taken $18,000 from "a group of supporters." He wished to discuss two points — whether it was "morally wrong" to do so and if the money had been "secretly given and secretly handled." He went on: "Not one cent of the $18,000 ... ever went to me for my personal use." The money was spent "to pay political expenses that I did not think should be charged to the taxpayers." He further pointed out that it was not "a secret fund," nor had any contributor benefitted through giving financial support.

Nixon asked several rhetorical questions. Who should pay for the publication of a speech? Who should pay for a television appearance? Who should pay for secretarial help? Nixon's Vice-Presidential rival John Sparkman had put his wife on the payroll. Would it be fair for Richard Nixon to do so as well? "Pat is a wonderful stenographer." The camera panned toward Pat, absorbed and tense, smiling faintly. "Pat has never been on the government payroll."

Also, since he had chosen not to accept any honoraria for speeches he had given, the so-called Nixon Fund was the only way these political, completely non-personal expenses could be met. His coming before the public was "the best way to expose this [the Truman] administration, the communism in it, the corruption in it." Furthermore, no contributor to the Nixon Fund had "ever asked me for a special favor." (Roger Morris's *Richard Milhous Nixon* states that Nixon's handwritten notes for the broadcast say "Six wrote me," but these words were not aired.) Nixon added that the Fund had been audited by the accounting firm Price Waterhouse and appraised by the law firm of Gibson, Sunn and Crutcher. Price Waterhouse found a correct accounting, and the law firm stated, "Senator Nixon did not obtain any financial gain from the collection and disbursement of the fund ... and Senator Nixon did not violate any federal or state law." Nixon concluded the reading of the two statements with obvious but restrained pleasure.

He gained confidence as he continued, knowing that Eisenhower was watching and that he must go to, as Eisenhower had told him, full financial disclosure, the public reaction to which would determine whether Eisenhower would keep him on the ticket or force him to resign his candidacy.

"And so now what I am going to do — and incidentally this is unprecedented in the history of American politics — I am going at this time to give this television and radio audience a complete financial history; everything I've earned; everything I've spent; everything I owe. And I want you to know the facts."

Nixon listed what he owned: A 1950 Oldsmobile; a $3000 equity in the California house in which his parents lived; a $20,000 equity in his Washington home; a $4,000 life insurance policy; "no stocks, no bonds, no interest in any other property or business." Then he listed what he owed: $10,000 on the California house; $20,000 on the Washington house; $4,500 to the Riggs National Bank of Washington; $3,500 to his parents; $500 on his life insurance.

Concluding his personal financial audit, he sought rapport with the audience, thinking, no doubt, that they would respond to a man who had little more than they: "Well, that's about it. That's what we have. And that's what we owe. It isn't very much. But Pat and I have the satisfaction that every dime that we have got is honestly ours."

He struck a further personal note: "I should say this, that Pat doesn't have a mink coat [an ironic reference to a minor scandal in the Truman administration] but she does have a respectable Republican cloth coat, and I always tell her she would look good in anything." The camera panned to Pat again.

A slight pause and on to the segment that gave the speech its name and set the tone for much of the Nixon discourse in succeeding decades. "One other thing I probably should tell you, because if I don't they will probably be saying this about me, too. We did get something, a gift, after the nomination. A man down in Texas heard Pat on the radio mention the fact that our two youngsters would like to have a dog, and, believe it or not, the day before we left on this campaign trip we got a message from Union Station in Baltimore, saying that they had a package for us. We went down to get it. You know what it was? It was a little cocker spaniel dog…. And you know, the kids, like all kids, loved the dog, and I just want to say this, right now, that regardless of what they say about it, we are going to keep it."

The Checkers reference was followed by what his critics would regard as a Uriah Heep-like humility: "It isn't easy to come before a nationwide audience and bare your life as I have done." Having drawn the cloak of humility around himself, he then introduced a note of class warfare. "Mr. Mitchell, the Chairman of the Democratic National Committee, made the statement that if a man couldn't afford to be in the United States Senate, he shouldn't run for the Senate. And I just want to make my position clear." Having shown that the rival Vice Presidential candidate had put his wife on the public payroll, Nixon went after the Democratic Presidential candidate: "I believe that it's fine that a man like Governor Stevenson, who inherited a fortune from his father, can run for President. But I also feel that it is essential in this country of ours that a man of modest means can also run for President, because, you know — remember Abraham Lincoln, remember what he said — 'God must have loved the common people, he made so many of them.'"

Nixon then challenged Stevenson and Sparkman to "come before the American people, as I have, and make a complete financial statement as to their financial history, and if they don't it will be an admission that they have something to hide."

There were ten minutes left. Nixon rose from the desk, dropped his notes and spoke extemporaneously as he looked directly into the camera.

His further defense was delivered with considerable strength. He had proven he had not taken any money for himself or Pat, and he was certain he had pointed out but not overplayed a certain hypocrisy he saw in his opponents, including the Stevenson

Fund about which the press had been virtually silent. Now he could score points with the voters and with Eisenhower, who had doubts about Nixon's being "mature" enough for higher office. As presented in Morris's biography of Nixon, Eisenhower, sitting with the Presidential campaign party in Cleveland, sensed a note of personal attack when Nixon mentioned "full disclosure" since Eisenhower himself "had been financed long and lavishly by private interests" and had received "a special tax dispensation accounting the royalties [of his memoirs] as capital gains rather than income." This may have been Nixon's way of blackmailing Eisenhower into keeping him on the ticket. Fortunately, their mutual distrust at this early point in their association was known only to a few.

Throughout, Nixon appeared as a man placed in a false position forthrightly defending his good name and his honor. His core audience, those to whom he referred as "the silent majority" in a famous speech on Vietnam nearly 20 years later, could not help but respond to a man not unlike themselves.

Nixon went on: "I know that this is not the last of the smears. In spite of my explanation tonight, other smears will be made. Others have been made in the past. And the purpose of the smears, I know, is this: To silence me, to make me let up.... I intend to continue to fight."

He blamed the Truman administration for the loss of 600,000,000 people to Communism "and a war which cost us 117,000 casualties." He wanted to get American troops out of Korea "just as fast as" he could. Warming to a finale, he said: "I know Dwight Eisenhower *will* do that, and that he [would] give America the leadership it needs.... In the Hiss case [the Communists] got the secrets which enabled them to break the secret State Department code." Nixon in effect was saying, "Yes, they tricked us before, but Ike and I know how to deal with them."

Time was running out. "And now, finally, I know that you wonder whether or not I am going to stay on the Republican ticket or resign. Let me say this: I don't believe I ought to quit, because I am not a quitter. And, incidentally, Pat is not a quitter. After all, her name was Patricia Ryan, and she was born on Saint Patrick's Day, and you know the Irish never quit." (In her highly unfavorable "psycho-biography" — a punning new *genre* devised no doubt expressly for her subject — *Richard Nixon: The Shaping of His Character,* Fawn Brodie quoted a disgruntled India Edwards, Vice President of the Democratic National Committee: "In the Checkers speech, Nixon told two unimportant lies, but lies nevertheless — [Pat] was born Thelma Catherine and on the sixteenth of March, not the seventeenth."

He made a final plea for public favor: "But the decision, my friends, is not mine. I would do nothing that would harm the possibilities of Dwight Eisenhower to become President of the United States." He stated that he was asking the Republican National Committee to decide his fate on the basis of this broadcast and the reaction to it. He urged the public "to drive the crooks and the Communists and those that defend them out of Washington." In closing, he added, "And remember, folks, Eisenhower is a great man."

Time was up. He did not have time to give the address of the Committee, but the phones started ringing immediately at the El Capitan Theater. Two million telegrams and two days later, Pat recalled, Eisenhower, "grinning all over," greeted the beleaguered candidate with "You're my boy." Nixon covered his face and began to sob.

Here's a sampling of critical opinion:

"One must mark 1952 as the date that Richard Nixon discovered how spectacular the influence of television could be, when, with his masterful and era-making Checkers speech, he reached for the first time, nationally, to stir the emotions of middle America and to over-ride the decision of the party masters for his dismissal." — Theodore H. White, *Breach of Faith: The Fall of Richard Nixon.*

"Such lachrymose appeals to an easily swayed public were not all that infuriated many in the huge audience — mostly those opposed to Nixon anyway. So did a certain holier-than-thou tone … that became a frequent presence in Nixon speeches." — Tom Wicker, *One of Us: Richard Nixon and the American Dream.*

"When Albert Upton [Nixon's acting coach at Whittier College] saw a picture of Nixon weeping on Senator William Knowland's shoulder after Eisenhower had forgiven him in the Checkers crisis, Upton exclaimed, 'That's my boy! That's my actor!' Nixon had learned to cry, but only as an actor." — Fawn Brodie, *Richard Nixon: The Shaping of His Character.*

"Three years later, Nixon acknowledged to the Radio and Television Executives Society that he had 'staged' the entire show. Pat had been as much of a prop as the American flag. The leading roles were, after all, being played by Richard Nixon, a veteran of Amateur theatrics, and Pat Ryan Nixon, a fellow thespian from Whittier days. She sat next to him as he spoke, the camera recording her tense but confident and admiring expression. Earlier, she had warned him that resignation and failure to fight back would be self-destructive. 'Your life will be marred forever and the same will be true of your family, and particularly your daughters.'" — Herbert S. Parmet, *Richard Nixon and His America.*

"Despite the flood of telegrams, a majority of the audience found the speech objectionable, if not nauseating. In the years that followed, one never heard Republicans bring it up, while Democrats quoted it to one another gleefully, and enjoyed heckling Nixon by calling out 'Tell us about Checkers.' What people remembered about the speech was Nixon's corny seriousness about a dog, … his awkward attempts at jokes, his use of that miserable little coat to make a political point, his threatening gestures at the end as he pledged war to the death with the Communists and the crooks." — Stephen E. Ambrose, *Nixon: The Education of a Politician 1913–1962.*

"Regardless of what party or cause the viewer championed, it was a brilliant feat in political journalism. It was, too, a major test of TV, demonstrating once and for all that with a good script, good casting and topflight production, you can't miss." — "Just Plain Dick," article in *Variety,* October 1, 1952.

"As a verbatim record, the Checkers speech makes the past and present startlingly meaningful." — *New York Times,* review of short political films at the Whitney Museum, May 24, 1974.

"After his emotional Checkers speech, [Nixon] received a phone call from Darryl F. Zanuck [producer of such classic films as *The Grapes of Wrath* and *All About Eve*] who called the Checkers speech 'the greatest performance I have ever seen.'" — Bruce Mazlich, *In Search of Nixon: A Psychological Inquiry.*

Richard Nixon was not the only presidential candidate to use the family dog as a major prop in an election campaign. Roosevelt's 1944 "Fala speech," however, was sarcastic and self-assured, not sentimental and pleading:"Franklin D. Roosevelt's Fala speech of 23 September 1944 marks a celebrated moment in American electoral history. Running for his fourth terms, President Roosevelt faced a surprisingly vigorous challenge from his Republican opponents. With World War II still raging and his health failing, the president had decided to limit his public appearances. After a disastrous speech in Seattle during the summer, Democrats began to worry that Roosevelt might lose the election. But in his rollicking address to the Teamsters Union convention that autumn night, the old master revived his campaign. The centerpiece of his comeback speech was a sarcastic defense of his Scottish terrier, Fala, from Republican attacks.

"Appealing as it may be to keepers of the Roosevelt myth, this scenario is not accurate. A closer look at the public reaction to the Fala speech reveals that the American people were not as charmed as Democratic partisans, and subsequent historians, claimed. In fact, many voters from both parties found the president's ribaldry offensive. Even Franklin D. Roosevelt, who had done so much to redefine the role of candidates in presidential campaigns, had to conform to the traditional notions of dignified behavior for the president of the United States." — Gill Troy, "'Such Insulting Trash and Triviality,' Franklin D. Roosevelt's Fala Speech Reconsidered," from the *Canadian Review of American Studies*, Volume 25, Number 1, Winter 1995, pages 45–72.

See *The Speeches of Richard Nixon* (1990), which contains *The Checkers Speech* and many other public addresses.

Report to Ike (film, 1952)

60 minutes. All networks. Election Eve, 1952. Produced by Arthur Pryor of Batten, Barton, Durstine and Osborne for the Republican National Committee. With Dwight and Mamie Eisenhower, Richard and Pat Nixon and various interviewees.

Report to Ike is an extremely skillful use of television techniques, a campaign film far in advance of any done previously and a model for later such films. The opening shot is a closeup of Ike. After a moment, the camera pulls back to disclose the Eisenhowers and the Nixons in an attractive living room (actually a studio set) watching themselves on television. What follows purports to be a "grass roots" "report to Ike" demonstrating the country's need for his even-handed guidance in the parlous times that had befallen it. The tone is that of benevolent paternalism, suggesting the temperament of a thoroughly decent man (Ike) who is "above politics" but who would respond to the needs of the country if called upon to do so.

After the opening shots, Ike says: "All we know about [the film] is that it's in the nature of a report to Pat and Dick, Mamie and me. The point of the show is that you share it with us. As we look on, you share it with us, as we sit here to take a look at what they're going to do, you look also. So in that way we'll all get to be together, all in your living room."

The overall development of *Report to Ike* is that while the two couples are sitting before a television set, various groups reveal their ideas on the state of the nation and the need for change. All areas of the country are heard from, as are all levels of society. This is a town meeting for all Americans to discuss the leadership needs of the country now that it is in the last half of the 20th century. It is a "report" *on what is needed*.

Three central issues recur in varying ways throughout the film: The economy, government corruption and the Korean War. All are presented in ways that reflected unfavorably on the Truman administration. Communism was not neglected. There are shots of Alger Hiss, the former Roosevelt administration figure accused of passing State Department secrets to the Soviet Union. Tried twice, he was convicted the second time, thanks to career-making moves by rabid anti–Communist Richard Nixon.

The film goes on to show that Ike's team had support everywhere, from Hollywood celebrities like Darryl Zanuck and John Wayne to housewives, veterans, blue collars, white collars, kids and a medley of ethnicities. Ike even had the support of such Democratic faithfuls as FDR's son John and FDR's granddaughter Sarah. According to the film, Ike and Dick support groups were springing up everywhere, and shots of typical gatherings (with plenty of "just plain folks" in evidence) were provided.

During this meeting of four friends who span two generations (the Nixons had just entered middle age and the Eisenhowers were about to attain Social Security status), they and the millions of viewers at home were treated to a very pleasing series of photographs — Ike's childhood home in Kansas, photos of his parents, Ike during the war and Ike with other iconic figures such as Churchill. The import is that clearly this is a small town boy who took his place in the great world without ever losing the common touch.

An artful device of the 1952 campaign used in the last minutes of *Report to Ike* was the "We Like Ike" bandwagon that was shot in several locations with enthusiastic volunteers joyfully flanking it. Attractive young women danced on its platform as it rolled along, gathering crowds wherever it went. These shots were intercut with the supposedly "live" shots of the Eisenhowers and the Nixons in a "family setting," not meant to be much better than the one the average viewer was in. In all the living rooms, the same basic message came through: "It takes regular guys like Ike and Dick to lead this country out of a bad economy, political corruption and war." The living rooms got the message.

One critic noted: "There were ... paid actors and staged scenes in the 'documentary,' although production notes said that the film was unplanned. Yet even critics acknowledged that the film was adeptly done.... '*The Nation* asserted [it was] a wonderful script [but] a monstrous patent fraud ... excellent propaganda.'"—Joanne Morreale, *The Presidential Campaign Film: A Critical History*.

House of Wax (film, 1953)

88 minutes. Warner Bros. Screenplay by Crane Wilbur. Based on a story by Charles Belden. Directed by Andre de Toth. Produced by Bryan Foy. In Warnercolor. Filmed in 3-D. Cast: *Prof. Henry Jarrod* Vincent Price; *Lieut. Tom Brennan* Frank Lovejoy; *Sue Allen* Phyllis Kirk; *Cathy Gray* Carolyn Jones; *Scott Andrews* Paul Picerni; *Igor* Charles Buchinski (Charles Bronson); *Bruce Allison* Philip Tonge.

Richard Nixon does not appear as a character in this cult film which was profitably re-released in 1983 and is a staple of late-night television. It is included here because of two related aspects: The striking physical resemblance between Frank Lovejoy and Richard Nixon (whom Lovejoy was to play successfully seven years later on Broadway in Gore Vidal's *The Best Man*) and the inclusion of a chapter called "Third Dementia" in Robert Coover's 1977 "metafiction" *The Public Burning*, which claims to be the memoirs of Richard Nixon and suggests a parallel between the mind of Richard Nixon and the grotesquerie of this horror film. Coover's iconoclastic satire fabricates Nixon's fascination with and sexual desire for Ethel Rosenberg, and the novel's epilogue contains a scene in which Nixon is sodomized by Uncle Sam. The spirit of the novel is very much that of the 1960s when protesters of the Vietnam War immolated themselves in public places. If there are any parallels here, in *The Public Burning,* we have the impending electrocution of the Rosenbergs; in *House of Wax,* several characters are boiled to death.

In many ways *House of Wax* is a typical Vincent Price shocker, but Coover uses it to show what he considers the bizarre quality of Nixon's mind. In 1953, film critic Bosley Crowther of the *New York Times* said that the film "was a raw, distasteful fable fit only to frighten simple souls with the menace of a crazy, fire-scarred sculptor embalming his victims in a waxworks of horrors." This is not too far from the way Coover views Nixon. The *New York Times* review of the novel on August 14, 1977, called *The Public Burning* "a destructive device that will not easily be defused," but Coover was not through with Nixon. He figures in a second bizarre Coover novel, *Whatever Happened to Gloomy Gus of the Chicago Bears* (1987).

For fuller considerations of *House of Wax* as it relates to *The Public Burning,* the reader may wish to consult:

Aaron, Daniel. "The Other Nixon Library. Portraits of the Ex-President as Literary Object." *The New York Times Book Review,* August 6, 1995. (A related Aaron piece appeared in the Fall 1995 *Raritan Review.*)
Anderson, Richard. *Robert Coover.*
Douglas, Wayne. "Tricky Dick: Richard Nixon as a Literary Character," *Lamar Journal of the Humanities,* Lamar State College of Technology, Beaumont, Texas, Fall 1981.
Fogel, Stan. "Richard Nixon by Robert Coover," *English Studies in Canada,* University of Toronto Press, Downsview, Ontario, June 1982.
Gallo, Louis. "Nixon and *House of Wax:* An Emblematic Episode in Coover's *The Public Burning.*" *Studies in Contemporary Fiction,* Washington, D.C.; Spring 1982.
Guzlowski, John. "Coover's *The Public Burning*: Richard Nixon and the Politics of Experience," *Studies in Contemporary Fiction,* Fall 1987.
Mazurek, Raymond. "Metafiction, the Historical Novel, and Coover's *The Public Burning,*" *Studies in Contemporary Fiction,* Spring 1982.

Darkness at Noon (TV film, 1955)

90 minutes. NBC, Producers Showcase, April 30, 1955, directed by Delbert Mann. Produced by Fred Coe. Arthur Koestler's novel adapted by Sidney Kingsley. With Lee J. Cobb (Rubashov), Ruth Roman (Luba) with commentary by Richard Nixon.

In the roles played on Broadway by Claude Rains and Kim Hunter, Lee J. Cobb and Ruth Roman movingly presented Arthur Koestler's modern classic of a purged Communist leader who admits to crimes he did not commit. This 1941 novel and 1951 play, winner of the New York Drama Critics Award in its year, was updated with commentary by Richard Nixon.

One critic noted: "Vice-President Richard Nixon offered *Noon* congratulations in a film clip for an effective document to combat Communism."—*Variety*, May 3, 1955.

Secret World of Kids (TV, 1959)

60 minutes. NBC. October 27, 1959. Directed by Dick Wesson. Written by Paul Henning. Host: Art Linkletter. Children discuss with celebrities various aspects of life. Guests: Vice President Richard M. Nixon, Vincent Price, Ann Blyth, Angela Cartwright. (Listed in *Television Specials* by Vincent Terrace, 1995.)

Kitchen Debate (TV, 1959)

A.k.a. *Nixon–Khrushchev Debate*. 18 minutes. Major networks, July 25, 1959, available through Library of Congress, printed text in *The Challenges We Face*, edited and compiled from the speeches and papers of Richard M. Nixon, McGraw-Hill, 1960.

Like the Checkers speech, the Hiss case and the later Nixon-Kennedy debates, the "kitchen debate" was one of the "six crises" Nixon described at length in his first book. It was correct that he should term it a "crisis" as he was able to turn an event of great uncertainty into one of personal enhancement and immense international prestige for the United States. Nixon's "standing up" to the Soviet leader was to become one of the highlights of his career since it was seen by millions of people in what were still the early days of television.

Nixon left Washington at 9:00 P.M., Wednesday July 22, 1959, accompanied by advisors Milton Eisenhower, Admiral Hyman Rickover, State Department officials and Nixon's staff on a flight planned by Howard Hughes to be the fastest Washington–Moscow link yet on record, further proof of the superiority of American aeronautics.

The plane arrived in Moscow at 2:50 on Thursday afternoon with Nixon's first meeting (essentially a courtesy call) with Premier Khrushchev scheduled for 10 A.M. on Friday in the Soviet leader's handsome office. The first meeting, which was highly belligerent, set the tone for the day, a day which included two further confrontations — one in a TV studio and the other during the exhibition of a model American home with a modern kitchen.

At the first meeting, Khrushchev excoriated Nixon for Congress's routine passage of the Captive Nations Resolution, a condemnation on the part of the United States of the Soviet Union's subjugation of other peoples in their quest of world domination. At the first meeting and throughout the day, Khrushchev would not leave this subject alone. Khrushchev said, "This resolution stinks. It stinks like fresh horse shit, and nothing smells worse than that."

Nixon, having done his homework as usual, remembered that Khrushchev had been a pig farmer. Nixon said: "I'm afraid you're mistaken. There is something that smells worse than horse shit. That is pig shit."

Khrushchev paused a moment and nodded assent but continued his attack, nor did he relent later on at the exhibition hall itself in Sokolniki Park. Quite by chance, Nixon and Khrushchev wandered into a color TV studio where the manager, as much surprised as they, asked them to say a few words. Khrushchev sensed a trap but when he saw many grinning Soviet workmen he decided he would not waste an opportunity to show off to his compatriots and to lambaste the United States. Nixon, feeling he might have lost the first round, took a firmer stand and went after the Soviet lack of "diversity" and "the right to choose."

Khrushchev, harping on the Captive Nations again, said that the Soviets "want to live in peace and friendship … [but the Americans] have churned the waters. What happened? What black cat crossed your path and confused you? But that is your affair, we do not interfere with your problems." Khrushchev wrapped his arms around a Soviet laborer and asked, "Does he look like a slave laborer?"

Nixon then pointed to an American workman, saying that Soviets and Americans had worked together to build the exhibition because that was "the way it should be." Nixon suggested that each leader should speak on the television of the other nation. Khrushchev agreed readily and the debate continued as they went to the model home and its soon-to-be-celebrated kitchen. The talk turned to military power and gave Khrushchev a chance to brag about Russian might.

> Nixon: "No one should ever use his strength to put another in the position where he in effect [faces] an ultimatum. For us to argue who is stronger misses the point. If war comes, we both lose."

> Khrushchev: "Who is facing an ultimatum? … We want to liquidate all bases from foreign lands. Until that happens we will speak different languages."

After more tough talk from Khrushchev, Nixon said, "Anyone who thinks our government is not for peace is not an accurate observer of America. In order to have peace … there must be sitting down at the table. There must be discussion."

> Khrushchev: "This is our understanding as well."

> Nixon: "The present position is a stalemate. Ways must be found to discuss it."

Khrushchev agreed, "the kitchen debate" was over, and Nixon had saved face. Two dramatic "debate" photos — one of Nixon poking Khrushchev in the chest — were printed throughout the world. According to Tom Wicker in his Nixon book *One of Us*, the finger-poking picture was "gold" and boosted Nixon's ratings in the pre-presidential polls a whopping 21 points.

One critic noted: "Popularly known as "the kitchen debate," this exchange took place unexpectedly at the American Television Exhibit in Moscow, July 24, 1959, when Premier Nikita Khrushchev challenged Vice-President Richard M. Nixon. Produced by Michael R. Gargiulo and Richard Gillespie, who recorded the event and smuggled it out within hours." — *Three Decades of Television,* Library of Congress.

Note: William Safire's *Before the Fall: An Inside View of the Pre-Watergate White House* (1975) presents much background for this episode since Safire was the press representative for the American builder of the model home, and it was Safire who took the much-reproduced picture of the two opponents leaning glumly on the kitchen railing.

Shortly after his Russian trip, Nixon had two consecutive half-hour programs on NBC and CBS, covered in a *Variety* article entitled "Nixon as TV Commentator."

Report to the Nation (TV, 1959)

NBC. Sunday, August 9, 1959. 7:00–7:30 P.M. Richard Nixon, narrator.

Variety noted, on August 12, 1959, "Diplomatic ice-breaker, Richard M. Nixon, back from Russia 'showed his pictures' to American television audiences … and demonstrated conclusively that as a commentator he'd rank with the best of them. NBC played down the Nixon role of narrator, putting too much emphasis on the film clips themselves."

What I Saw in Russia (TV, 1959)

CBS. Sunday, August 9, 1959. 7:30–8:00 P.M. Richard Nixon, narrator.

The *Variety* critic pointed out that *What I Saw in Russia* gave Nixon "the scope and format of presentation to distinguish himself as a reporter, commentator and analyst in recapping the highlights of his visit with Mr. K. and appraising its possible impact on the future…. CBS let [Nixon] talk, practically through the entire half-hour … as TV audiences witnessed the now-famous 'Nick and Dick' set-to at the American Exhibition; [his] visit to Leningrad, [his] tour of the steel mill; visits to Novosibirsk and Sverdlovsk and finally the overwhelming outpouring of friendship and affection in Poland. Nixon reacted as though a seasoned pro in TV, commenting as he matched clip for clip with sound, balanced judgment and reportage…"

For Soviet audiences only, Nixon's "A Talk to the Russian People," the television program promised to him by Khrushchev — an unprecedented television and radio event — was broadcast to the Russian people on August 1, 1959. Equally unprecedented was the fact that it was published in major Soviet newspapers. The text is available in English in *The Challenges We Face*. The American television material is there as well. It also appeared in the December 1959 *National Geographic*.

Jonathan Aitken's *Nixon: A Life* contains an interview with Boris Armanov, a prominent Soviet civil engineer who heard Nixon's 1959 Soviet broadcast on his mother's radio. "We argued about his talk and his speech for months afterwards … Most of us were fascinated by this American with his strength and openness. Do you know who brought *glasnost* to Moscow?

Richard Nixon! It's a joke of course, but there's just a bit of truth in it; in fact, there was a lot of truth in it if you think about what Nixon was saying and what life was like for us at the time of Stalin, Malenkov and Khrushchev."

Ambassador of Friendship (film, 1960)

Campaign film, 1960. 30 minutes. Filmac Productions (division of Paramount).
G. Wyckoff, producer.

Campaign films are usually of three types: Biographical films presenting the basic facts and personal qualities, the resumé film showing achievements and the visionary film dealing with the candidate's projections of an ameliorating future. Like Kennedy's 1960 *The New Frontier,* Nixon's *Ambassador of Friendship* was never aired on national television but had a vigorous career in small settings before audiences of the already committed. It was also televised in Nixon's home state.

Biographical films quite obviously can give a fuller portrait during a political campaign since "spots" can only address a single issue. Every major campaign uses both. Typically, the biographical film opens with the candidate demonstrating his own stability against a background of turmoil which he is surely the best choice to over-come for the good of all. Unfortunately for Nixon, *Ambassador of Friendship* is not the standard model biographical film but a poorly conceived résumé film which for virtu-ally its entire length addresses Nixon's foreign policy achievements to the exclusion of all other major issues. It was scheduled to pre-empt *The General Electric Theater* on November 6, but Nixon wisely canceled it in favor of another informal speech. In short, Nixon was shrewd enough to sense its mediocrity.

Ambassador of Friendship, by focusing on Nixon's foreign policy successes, sug-gested that Nixon had little regard for domestic problems, the problems that affect ordi-nary citizens. To give the producer his due, the original concept may have been to show that Nixon had successes of his own, and he was not riding on the coattails of Eisen-hower's period of relative calm and prosperity.

Ambassador of Friendship begins with stunning visual parallels to Leni Riefenstahl's classic propaganda film *Triumph of the Will* (1934) in which Hitler's plane comes down from the clouds. Here we have images of clouds, the sound of a motor and the shot of the plane's wing as it sparkles in the sun. In spite of the "lifted" opening, the film's assembled footage of foreign travels does not sustain interest. Such a film would win Nixon no converts and weary the already aligned.

In his book *The Image Candidates* (1968), the film's producer G. Wyckoff states that *Ambassador of Friendship* was made as a favor to Barney Balaban, a generous Nixon contributor and the president of Paramount Pictures from 1936 to 1969. According to Wyckoff, the film was "a dull illustrated lecture" that contained no reaction shots. Therefore, "stock" footage was needed; reaction shots were bought from a low-budget Universal film of 1932 entitled *Radio Patrol*. For a transitional device, shots of an air-plane's arrival and departure were taken from Paramount's 1958 *The Geisha Boy* with Jerry Lewis and Sessue Hayakawa. In the film, Nixon would arrive in each new coun-try on the "edited in" airplane, give a speech and be reacted to by various groups "edited in" from *Radio Patrol*. It did not matter that the fashions of 1960 did not match the fashions of 1932 since each country visited was far behind the United States in tech-nology and general advancement, reminding us all of how much better off we were than the rest of the world.

Ambassador of Friendship does nothing to deepen the portrait of Richard Nixon in human terms and presents little that would draw the public to him as a leader.

One critic noted: "Many of its images are not clearly related to the narration track or even of discernible content. There is little attempt to mythologize the candidate as a man of the people."— Joanne Morreale, *The Presidential Campaign Film.*

Note: Carroll Newton, vice-president of BBD & O, suggested two additional Nixon campaign films that were never made: *Khrushchev as I Knew Him* with an obvious propagandistic good vs. evil motif, and *For You and Your Family,* a film depicting the Nixon family as ordinary American citizens. Nixon rejected both ideas, probably casting aside the family film because of the claims of mawkishness that came down upon the Checkers speech in the press.

The Alamo (film, 1960)

United Artists. 192 minutes. Directed and produced by John Wayne. Written by James Edward Grant. Music by Dimitri Tiomkin. Songs by Dimitri Tiomkin and Paul Francis Webster. Second unit director: Cliff Lyons, Photography by William Clothier, Edited by Stuart Gilmore, Assistant producer: Michael Wayne, color, Todd-AO process. Cast: *Col. David Crockett* John Wayne; *Col. James Bowie* Richard Widmark; *Col. William Travis* Laurence Harvey; *Gen. Sam Houston* Richard Boone; *James Bonham* Patrick Wayne; *Angelina* Aissa Wayne; *Juan Seguin* Joseph Calleia; *Blind Nell* Veda Ann Borg.

This is obviously not a "Nixon film." Nevertheless, even 36 years later, the *London Review of Books* (May 9, 1996) called this October 1960 release by producer–director and conservative icon John Wayne a film "to help elect Nixon."

"I loved ... of course, John Wayne's two-hour-and-forty-minute epic, *The Alamo* with Davy Crockett, Jim Bowie, and Colonel Travis sacrificing their lives with incomparable gallantry for the cause of Texas independence."— Michael Medved, *Hollywood vs. America,* 1992.

At a March 3, 1973, White House gala honoring Vietnam POWS, "John Wayne got the biggest hand when he said to the POWS, 'I'll ride into the sunset with you anytime.' Just before he left the stage, he looked down at me sitting in the front row and said, 'I want to thank you, Mr. President, not for any one thing, just for everything.'"— Richard Nixon, *Memoirs,* 1978.

The Best Man (play, 1960)

A play in three acts by Gore Vidal. Presented by the Playwrights' Company. Directed by Joseph Anthony. Settings and lighting by Jo Mielziner. Costumes by Theoni V. Aldredge. Associate producer, Lyn Austin. Opened at the Morosco Theater March 31, 1960. Cast: *William Russell* Melvyn Douglas; *Art Hockstader* Lee Tracy; *Senator Joe Cantwell* Frank Lovejoy; *Alice Russell* Leora Dana; *Mabel Cantwell* Kathleen Maguire; *Mrs. Gamadge* Ruth McDevitt; *Don Blades* Joseph Sullivan; *Dick Jensen* Karl Weber; *Seldon Marcus* Graham Jarvis; *Senator Carlin* Gordon B. Clarke; *Dr. Artinian* Hugh Franklin.

The Best Man is essentially a political melodrama issuing a caveat for the 1960 electorate: "Don't vote for Richard Nixon," an obvious model for the symbolically named Senator Joe Cantwell. The play is also homage to two grand old men of the Democratic Party, Adlai Stevenson, the model for William Russell, and Harry Truman, the model for the snappy ex–President Art Hockstader. Cantwell's first name suggests echoes of Joe McCarthy, an enhancer of Nixon's early career, later ignominiously discredited. The symbolism of the last name is obvious. As the play progresses, Russell–Stevenson is the protagonist, Cantwell–Nixon is the antagonist and Hockstader–Truman is the raisonneur.

ACT I, SCENE 1—"A hotel suite in Philadelphia ... perhaps July 1960." William Russell is the current occupant, and he is anxiously awaiting the announcement of the name of the presidential candidate of his party, a party which remains unidentified throughout the play. The statement of former President Hockstader carries great weight, and Russell tells the assembled reporters that they must all wait for Hockstader's recommendation later in the day. (As a foreshadowing of Act III, Vidal introduces the off-stage character of Governor Merwin.) The opening scene does several things, but the most important is that it establishes Russell as a man above politics, an intellectual who uses irony as a not-unfriendly but often misconstrued shield against reporters. Hard-working committeewoman Sue Ellen Gamadge tells him his godlike serenity is off-putting to voters, especially women. In leaving the Russell suite, Mrs. Gamadge warns that Joe Cantwell, Russell's rival for the nomination, has a smear campaign in place that must be counteracted or Russell will be out of the race. Ex-President Hockstader enters and he and Russell reminisce about Russell's tenure as Hockstader's Secretary of State, a tenure with which Hockstader was somewhat displeased. The talk turns back to Cantwell, the Nixon figure, whom Hockstader calls "just plain naked ambition," a liar, a cheat, "a destroyer of reputations." Russell caps the Cantwell–Nixon discussion with, "He'll do anything to win."

ACT I, SCENE 2—The Cantwell suite. As the curtain rises we hear the voice of a TV commentator (Vidal during the two year Broadway run). After a scene with his bumptious wife Mabel, Cantwell shows his anti-intellectualism by a scornful reference to political pundit Walter Lippmann's endorsement of Russell. (The reference to Lippmann dates the play as a viable vehicle for revival, but it sheds light on the kingmakers of the late Eisenhower years.) Hockstader enters, and he and Cantwell have a verbal sparring match on J. Edgar Hoover, Joe McCarthy and the often reprehensible nature of politics — more specifically, Cantwell's theft of Russell's medical records, which reveal a nervous breakdown. Hockstader has a heart spasm during this exchange, Cantwell is so self-absorbed that he doesn't notice. They part angrily, but Vidal has obviously planted Cantwell's chicanery in the audience's mind.

ACT II, SCENE 1—The Russell suite. The next afternoon. Russell and Senator Carlin, "a ponderous politician of the prairies," discuss Russell's liberalism and his liberal constituency. Speaking of Cantwell, Russell says, "He may be the master of the half-truth and the insinuation, but we've got the facts." Later on, Jensen, Russell's campaign manager, says at the threat of a Cantwell smear, "Billy, you may have to pull a Nixon." Russell: "What does 'pull a Nixon' mean?" Jensen: "Go on television and cry on the nation's shoulder with *two* cocker spaniels." Dr. Artinian, a leading psychiatrist, joins the group and says that "apparently someone from Cantwell's office bribed one of our nurses to obtain the records of Russell's breakdown." As a countermeasure, some of the Russell forces introduce a former Army major named Marcus who claims that Cantwell engaged in homosexual acts while on duty in the Aleutian Islands during World War II. Hockstader, the practical man of politics, is willing to consider anything that will stop the unethical treatment it appears that Russell is about to receive from Cantwell.

ACT II, SCENE 2— Cantwell suite. A few minutes later, a press conference with the potential nominees' wives. Like the Nixons, the Cantwells have two daughters. However, Mabel Cantwell is clearly not modeled on Pat Nixon. She is from a southern state, heavier, much more talkative, completely lacking in refinement, much more aggressive and capable of the same kind of blackmail that Vidal assigns to Cantwell. For instance, Mabel Cantwell bullies Alice Russell into admitting that she worked for a birth control group 20 years before. Mrs. Gamadge, who is also at the "hen party," as Mabel Cantwell calls it, warns Mabel that the release of Russell's medical report will only backfire, and Gamadge and her followers pledge to work to overcome the dirty politics that the Cantwell forces are engaged in. After the women leave, Cantwell enters and receives a threatening phone call. The Russell forces will use Sheldon Marcus's claims of homosexual acts if they have to.

ACT II, SCENE 3— The Russell suite. Marcus now finishes his claims in regard to Cantwell's homosexuality. Since the bulk of the claims are stated in the *off-stage* action of the play — concurrent with the hen party — the charges remain deliberately ambiguous on the part of the author, as if Vidal is saying that guilt should be perceived but he will not codify it by any specific disclosure. In effect, it is a qualified smear. It is in this scene that the play's melodramatic elements are at their height. Not only do we have the two blackmail plots, one of which is delivered by the completely one-dimensional character Marcus, a mere convenience of the melodramatics of the plot, but Hockstader has a heart attack just in time for a big Act II curtain.

ACT III, SCENE 1— The Cantwell suite. The melodrama deepens. The first scene of the last act shows the two approaches to public life embodied by Russell and Cantwell. Cantwell is able to extricate himself from the charges brought by Marcus, but his treatment of Marcus is so vehement that the normally very measured Russell takes the copy of Cantwell's military records and decides to fight back because Cantwell would not "declare a moratorium on [the] mud [they could] both let fly." Toward the end of the scene, not able to break down the adamant, ego-driven Cantwell, Russell says, "You are worse than a liar. You have no sense of right or wrong. Only what will work." Russell holds up the court martial testimony referred to by Marcus. Cantwell, aghast, says, "But you're not going to use that now!" Russell replies, "Oh yes! Yes! I will use *anything* against you. I can't let you be President." Russell leaves. There is a pause and the sense of gathering of forces. Cantwell tells his campaign manager to release the psychiatric profile on Russell.

ACT III, SCENE 2— The Russell suite. The next afternoon. The psychiatric report has been circulated but has not done as much damage as expected. Reverting to his truer nature, Russell has had second thoughts and not released the material on Cantwell. Cantwell phones and requests a meeting. He wants Russell to be on his ticket as Vice-President. After Vidal inserts a theme-driven discussion, Russell states that Cantwell is unfit to be President, calls the convention chairman and asks him to release the Russell delegates to Governor John Merwin. Russell says, "Neither the angel of darkness [Cantwell–Nixon] nor the angel of light [Stevenson–Russell] … has carried the day. We canceled each other out." Stunned, Cantwell says, "I don't understand you." Russell gives another long theme-driven speech that begins, "I know you don't. Because

Frank Lovejoy as Joe Cantwell (Nixon) in Gore Vidal's Broadway play *The Best Man* (1960).

you have no sense of responsibility toward anybody or anything and that is a tragedy in a man and it is a disaster in a President." Cantwell calls him "a fool" and leaves. Russell and his wife are reunited. Ironically, "the best man" (Russell–Stevenson), did not win, but "a man without face," Governor Merwin, *did*, proving that politics is almost always a question of compromise. "Men without faces tend to get elected President, and power or responsibility or honor fill in the features, usually pretty well."

In a March 27, 1960, interview in the *New York Times*, Gore Vidal stated, "I'm not a private-minded writer. What I'm interested in is politics and philosophy." His interests are a result of his distinguished family background. He was born on October 3, 1925, at the United States Military Academy at West Point. His father was Eugene Vidal, an aeronautics instructor at the Point, and his mother was the former Nina Gore, daughter of Thomas Pryor Gore, the blind senator from Oklahoma whom the young Gore Vidal guided around Washington and to whom he read books and essays on politics including long selections from the Congressional Record. His mother and father were divorced in 1935, and his mother married Hugh Auchincloss, who was also the stepfather of Jacqueline Kennedy Onassis.

In 1943, after graduating from Philips Exeter Academy, Vidal enlisted in the United States Army. He became a first mate on an Army ship carrying soldiers and supplies throughout the Aleutian Islands. He wrote his first novel, *Williwaw*, while on duty. Released from the Army in 1946, Vidal devoted the rest of his life to writing. He has been successful in every genre he has worked in and there have been many, including mystery novels under the pseudonym of Edgar Box and films such as Visconti's *Senso* with Alida Valli. He wrote five Broadway plays, the first two of which, *A Visit to a Small Planet* and *The Best Man*, were very successful. His other plays were *Romulus*, an adaptation from Durrenmatt, and *Weekend*, a play some critics say is a not-too-flattering portrait of conservative pundit William F. Buckley. His *An Evening With Richard Nixon* will be discussed later in this text. In addition to novels (his favorite among his own works is *Myra Breckinridge*), plays, TV scripts, screenplays and essays, Vidal has also appeared on TV and in films. He played a small role in a TV script he wrote on his grandfather entitled *The Indestructible Mr. Gore* in 1959 and in Fellini's *Roma* in 1972. Vidal is extremely knowledgeable in history, politics and the arts. Never considered a major artist, he is nevertheless a tireless worker and an accomplished craftsman with a particular talent for self-promotion and good old-fashioned political ballyhoo such as Adlai Stevenson's "Address to Show Business on Why They Should Support Kennedy," which took place at the Morosco Theatre on October 17, 1960, with key supporters such as Tallulah Bankhead, Henry Fonda, James Thurber and Anthony Quinn in attendance. Mort Sahl delivered "an appropriate monologue." *The Best Man* and events it generated did what Vidal hoped it would do: It elected a Democratic president. It was a very well-crafted and effective piece of political theater. Nothing in nearly forty successive Broadway seasons has done anything like it. As Melvyn Douglas pointed out in his 1986 autobiography *See You at the Movies*: "My position as the title character evoked memories ... of the 1950 Nixon/Douglas campaign in California." By writing *The Best Man*, Vidal was not only shaping the future but righting what he thought were past wrongs.

Here's a sampling of critical opinion:

"[A] brilliantly slick job of upper-middlebrow political commentary, and its laughter-machinery works on you with high efficiency all through the evening; it's when you put your coat on after final curtain that you begin to look for something more substantial that isn't there."—Jerry Tallmer, *Village Voice*, April 6, 1960.

"In playwriting there's no mistaking craftsmanship. *The Best Man*, which opened last Thursday night (31) at the Morosco Theatre, is the best-written play of the season, an empathetic box office hit and an inviting prospect for films."—*Variety*, April 6, 1960.

"It is a play that is in every way absorbing, in many ways admirable, yet even when it is expressing lofty ideals and a genuine regard for decency in government and in human relations, it has a hollow ring. I think this is largely because Mr. Vidal is less interested in what he is saying than in the manner in which it is said. He has, however, constructed artfully and adorned with great style and wit and if it lacks inner conviction and fire, it does provide an evening of unflagging entertainment and for this we should be truly grateful." — George Oppenheimer, *Newsday*, April 6, 1960.

"[Vidal] uses the theatre not as a literary medium but as a sounding board for ideas and politics..." — Stanley Levey, *The New York Times*, March 27, 1960.

"A quarrel I have with Mr. Vidal's well-tailored play is that, consciously or not, he has borrowed some of his material from other skillful tailors. When the estranged wife of Russell finds herself booked into a hotel bedroom with her husband, she remarks, 'Politics makes strange bedfellows.' Certainly there is nothing sacrosanct about the line, which was coined by editor Charles Dudly Warner in the last century, but, in the greatly successful Pulitzer Prize play *State of the Union* by Howard Lindsay and Russel Crouse, the line is used in exactly the same situation — a candidate's wife forced, for appearance's sake, to share his room. Then too another situation — evidence uncovered pointing to a homosexual encounter experienced during the war by a politician, now married and above suspicion in this regard — seems to be lifted almost bodily from Allen Drury's best-selling novel, *Advise and Consent...*" — George Oppenheimer, as above (Note: In the July 1960 *Theatre Arts*, Vidal stated: "In our confused age, morality means, simply sex found out.").

"During the preliminary tour, [Vidal] has refused to identify the persons of the play. It is true that none of them coincides with the historical record, and that all of them are composite men. But one of the pleasures of *The Best Man* is the sardonic consistency with which it recalls characteristics of current politicians — the fastidiousness and wit of Adlai Stevenson, the belligerent political guile of Harry Truman, Richard Nixon's soap opera with wife and dog to convince the country of his honesty. Everyone on the stage has conspired with Mr. Vidal to get *The Best Man* acted boldly, in the broad style of a political poster. Frank Lovejoy gives an extraordinary portrait of a bigot and a charlatan who believes his own propaganda. There is something horribly plausible about his ethical obtuseness." — Brooks Atkinson, *The New York Times*, April 1, 1960.

"The villain, played by Frank Lovejoy so that the hilt runs right through the body, is one of the two principal contenders in the race for a Presidential nomination. This bristling fellow has put his career together out of the bits and pieces of his enemies' skins, and he has done quite a lot of it on television. 'I'm a very religious guy,' he says, shifting his nervous feet all over a hotel-room carpet as he announces the method he has chosen to slander his opponent. Our boy doesn't smoke, drink, philander or tell the truth. He can't tell the truth because he doesn't know what it is." — Walter Kerr, *The New York Herald Tribune*, April 1, 1960.

"This is a good election year show, and it won't influence your vote a damn bit..." — John Chapman, *New York Daily News*, April 1, 1960.

"Its characters may be a bit distorted, but they're fascinating to watch and hear in action." — Robert Coleman, *New York Mirror*, April 1, 1960.

"As soon as Kennedy was nominated, Vidal phoned his New York stage manager to make one script revision: The show's senator says, 'Let's try for a Catholic, Catholics are big this year — for second place.' The last three words were eliminated." — Leonard Lyons, *The New York Post*, August 8, 1960.

"Joseph Cantwell [marks] the first appearance of Nixon in a serious literary work." — Daniel Aaron, *New York Times Book Review*, August 6, 1995.

Meet the Press (TV, 1960)

60 minutes. NBC News. September 11, 1960. 10:30 A.M. Richard Nixon interviewed by Herb Kaplow.

Nixon was interviewed by Kaplow in regard to a statement made by Protestant minister Norman Vincent Peale dealing with Kennedy's Catholic faith. The Kennedy forces used the Peale speech as an example of a smear that placed the Democrats at a disadvantage. Nixon had intended to omit any discussion of religion in his campaign, and he "would not allow anybody to participate in [his] campaign who does so."

Kennedy followers stated that every time Nixon upbraided bigotry he was, in effect, making religion an issue. The Kennedys seemed to be playing the card of victimhood. "It is difficult ... to see what more Nixon could have done to keep the issue out of the campaign." — Ambrose, *Nixon*, Volume I.

Nixon–Kennedy Debates — First Debate (1960)

Alternate title *Kennedy–Nixon Debates*. The first televised live public debates between presidential candidates. Each program was produced by one network but aired simultaneously on all three. CBS, September 26; NBC, October 7; ABC, October 13 and 21.

The debates did not begin well for Nixon. His failures to articulate what he could bring to the presidency and what he had accomplished as vice-president were soon fixed in the public's mind and remained there, with brief exceptions, throughout the entire series.

Furthermore, Nixon's lack of energy, his appearance of illness, and gaffes in speaking such as his inability to remember his previous statements in regard to teachers' salaries (among others) suggested a man incapable of leading the nation.

Kennedy had his facts, illustrations and examples all at his fingertips. He was therefore capable of responding with cogency, authority and seeming conviction to virtually every question. An easy assurance suffused his every reply and gesture. On the debit side, the assurance contained a few over-reachings and a slightly melodramatic tone. Lincoln's question of 1860 ("Whether this nation could exist half-slave or half-free") Kennedy gave a 1960s spin with "Whether the world will still exist half-slave or half-free" as a counter to communist threat and the cold war period. The implication was that he was clearly the better choice as the world's savior. Kennedy also aligned himself rhetorically with Wilson, Truman and particularly FDR. As he peppered his responses with the names of the great figures of the past, the viewer was invited to see that he wore the same mantle. Such allusions recall Meg Greenfield's comments in *The Reporter* on "leadership by association" in regard to Nixon and Eisenhower. Here, in Kennedy's replies, were at least three great leaders, all of the highest stature, invoked to suggest Kennedy was fully their equal.

Nixon was overpowered and was unable to defend the achievements of the Eisenhower years, in spite of the widespread belief expressed in Ambrose's repeating Nixon's claim that "the '50s were the best years of the century," a statement which Ambrose said "was more or less true."

In summary, Kennedy's knowledge, humor and grasp of the necessity for leadership made Nixon a poor second to Kennedy's undeniable charisma — a political juggernaut whom no one could stop.

"My own recollection of the first debate — reinforced by watching it again in 1987 at the American Museum of Broadcasting — is that Nixon looked terrible but performed rather well." — Tom Wicker, *One of Us.*

Nixon–Kennedy— Second Debate

Nixon improved slightly in the second debate, which took place a week and a half later and dealt primarily with party labels. Nixon, although more assured and much more in control, was not able to convince the viewer that the party he represented was more responsible and humane. Kennedy was again able to give a roll call of notable leaders, all Democrats, with a portrayal of their political skills as more in keeping with the needs of their constituents. Overall, Nixon's performances were considerably smoother, but it did not dissuade viewers from the view that Kennedy represented a party that was there to nurture and guide its voters.

Principal topics were Kennedy's claim that the Republicans had been responsible for the loss of Cuba, Eisenhower's failure to apologize to the Russians for our spy flights over their territory, and the islands of Quemoy and Matsu just off the coast of Communist China (the topic that drew the greatest heat). There were several in the press who believed that Nixon had overcome his poor performance in the first debate when he was still in ill health. Unfortunately for him, the viewing public had dropped from 80,000,000 to 60,000,000.

Nixon–Kennedy— Third Debate

Prior to the presidential debates, Nixon's vice-presidential candidate Henry Cabot Lodge told Nixon (as noted by Ambrose) that it would be best for Nixon to rid himself of his "assassin image." Famous for his truculence in going after Alger Hiss (see *The Trials of Alger Hiss,* 1980), Nixon followed Lodge's advice perhaps too well.

By doing so, he had failed to define himself as presidential material. In this debate the speakers were 3,000 miles apart. Nixon was in Los Angeles, Kennedy in New York. The third debate was scrappier, and Nixon had regained some of his strength.

The first topic was the two islands off the Communist Chinese Coast, Quemoy and Matsu. The problem was that the United States agreement in regard to them was so vague (deliberately so) that one could take any position — to defend or not defend — and say that according to the treaty it was the right one.

Kennedy lambasted Nixon for not speaking up about the communist takeover of Cuba, the division and defense of Berlin, and the oil depletion allowance. The other topics (labor unions, social security, and health care) were dealt with animatedly on both sides, and Round III was something of a draw.

Nixon–Kennedy Debates— Fourth Debate

On October 20 Kennedy was interviewed to the effect that he advocated aid to the rebel (Castro) forces in Cuba.

Nixon was angry and in his opening statement at the fourth debate (which took place the next day) Nixon said that Kennedy's statements on Cuba were "the most dangerously irresponsible recommendations that he's made during the course of this campaign." In short, Nixon was saying that Kennedy's proposal risked war.

Nixon further maintained that Kennedy's programs were rehashes of those of the Truman administration. Kennedy contended that the Eisenhower administration was foundering, and it was time to move ahead. "Are we doing enough today?" Kennedy asked. Kennedy claimed the United States had lost prestige throughout the world.

The last major aspect of the fourth debate was moderator Walter Cronkite's furthering the dialogue on United States prestige. Kennedy went on the attack, and Nixon held his own.

"The best that could be said from Nixon's perspective was that the debates did not hurt him. But insofar as he had ignored Eisenhower's and his aide's advice to refuse to debate because he believed that he would slaughter Kennedy in a face to face confrontation, Nixon was the clear loser."— Stephen E. Ambrose, *Nixon,* vol. I.

Eleanor Roosevelt Diamond Jubilee Plus One (TV, 1960)

60 minutes. Directed by Dick Schneider. Written by Reginald Rose. NBC, October 7, 1960.

A tribute to Eleanor Roosevelt honoring her 76th birthday. Featured were George Burns, Carol Channing, Irene Dunne, Jimmy Durante, Bob Hope, Senator John F. Kennedy, Vice President Richard M. Nixon, Simone Signoret and Joanne Woodward.

Making of the President (TV, 1960)

90 minutes. NBC–TV. Produced and directed by Mel Stuart. Written by Theodore H. White from his book. Music by Elmer Bernstein. Narrated by Martin Gabel, Edited by William T. Cartwright. Broadcast Sunday, December 29, 1963, three years after the event, although the materials date from 1960, it seems more appropriate to place it in the earlier period. Sponsored by Xerox.

As Ambrose points out in the first volume of his Nixon biography, the first debate "was not a debate at all, but rather a press conference, with each candidate responding to questions each had already answered a hundred times and more on the campaign trail." Since the first "debate" took place in the first stages of the campaign (September 26), it was seen by the greatest number and contained Kennedy's most confident and best perform-ance; it also set the tone for the rest of the 1960 campaign and assured Kennedy's victory.

Nixon was at an extreme disadvantage during the first "set-to," as *Variety* called it. Even though Nixon was able to rally appreciably in the succeeding debates, an aura of illness and bad luck plagued the entire series. As White says in his book of the same title, "There was always an element of sadness about the Nixon campaign, from begin-ning to end, and a sequence of episodes that wrung sympathy for him even from his most embittered opponents. Of all the episodes, however, the very worst was his ill-ness. He had struck his kneecap on the door of a car on his trips to Greensboro, North Carolina. It had become infected. Two days after … he was informed by his doctors that this was no ordinary infection but one caused by an infection of such virulence that unless he were immediately hospitalized and the knee immobilized, the cartilage of the joint would be permanently destroyed — or worse. It was doctors' orders that no sane person could ignore, and so from August 29th to September 9th he lay ill at Wal-ter Reed Hospital — his leg held in traction by a five pound weight...."

As pointed out by many media critics and historians, another seemingly trivial matter that turned out to be crucial was Nixon's choice of attire. His advisors had sug-gested a light gray suit since the background was reported to be dark gray. This would afford a suitable contrast. However, the background, in spite of re-painting, remained light gray, having the psychological effect of making Nixon look inconsequential when contrasted with Kennedy in his crisp dark suit. Also, Nixon had lost a great deal of weight because of his illness and appeared in clothes that were now much too large on him. Kennedy projected the image of someone supremely in command, perfectly tanned, groomed and attired, a man in robust good heath with a razor-sharp intellect and high good humor — in short, a leader. Nixon, with his five o'clock shadow, a pasty complexion and baggy clothes could not compete with that.

Because of this internal drama and the chance the public had to relive a major public event, White's televersion of his well-regarded book, the first of an outstand-ing series, made excellent viewing. As *Variety* said (January 1, 1964), "Although the hour and a half special seemed more comprehensive than penetrating, it served a rare purpose in giving its viewers a better overall understanding of the shape and substance of a political campaign for the presidency. Above all it was a triumph in assemblage and construction of footage."

We'll Bury You (documentary film, 1962)

74 minutes (also released in a 77-minute version). Contemporary productions, distributed by Columbia Pictures. Produced by Jack Leewood. Written by Jack Thomas. Narrated by William Woodson.

We'll Bury You is a compilation of still photographs and newsreel footage tracing the rise of international Communism from Marx to the early 1960s. It includes shorts from the Russo–Japanese War, the power struggle before Trotsky, and Stalin's mass exe-cutions; Stalin's death, the rise of Khrushchev and "the kitchen debate" with Nixon. Although released commercially, it was primarily for use in schools. Clive Hirschhorn's *The Columbia Story: The Complete History of the Studio and All Its Films* (1989) states that *We'll Bury You* (words spoken by Khrushchev at the United Nations) was not one of "the half dozen of Columbia's documentaries to earn even a modest profit."

Political Obituary of Richard Nixon (TV, 1962)

ABC News. Sunday, November 11, 1962. Moderated by Howard K. Smith. Produced by William Kobin.

This alarmingly titled program was highly disputed and produced thousands of rude letters and phone calls. It occurred right after Nixon's gubernatorial defeat in California and was thought to be Nixon's "final" press coverage, at which he said, "You won't have Dick Nixon to kick around any more."

The telecast included an interview with Alger Hiss, who said in *The Christian Science Monitor* interview (Nov. 12, 1962), "I regard [Nixon's] actions as motivated by ambition, by personal self-serving, which were not directed at me in a hostile sense … He was responding to a situation in his country … and riding it rather than actually creating it, I think."

The content was put together in only hours, according to Howard K. Smith's statement in the *Newark Evening News* (Nov. 13), and had the approval of James Hagerty, President of ABC News and the White House press secretary under Dwight Eisenhower. "Controversy is a bad word in America these days, I'm afraid, and my program, I suppose, is controversial." In conclusion Smith said, "This was a matter of history and we treated it that way."

Nixon's then-recent defeats and the extremely negative title of this TV production set the tone for a violent political reaction from Nixon partisans, but in retrospect, the program seems more balanced with segments by such Nixon defenders as Murray Chotiner, his earliest campaign manager and colleague, as well as future President Gerald Ford.

Nevertheless, any positive elements did not come through at the time.

"Even *The Los Angeles Times* used the following headline above a column on what it all meant: 'Nixon's Rise, Fall, Warning for Americans.'"— Herbert Parmet, *Richard Nixon and His America*.

The Best Man (film, 1964)

102 minutes. Released by United Artists. Screenplay by Gore Vidal, based upon his stage play. Directed by Franklin Schaffner. Produced by Stuart Millar, Lawrence Turman and Schaffner. Costumes by Dorothy Jeakins. Art direction by Lyle Wheeler. Photography by Haskell Wexler. Cast: *William Russell* Henry Fonda; *Joe Cantwell* Cliff Robertson; *Mabel Cantwell* Edie Adams; *Alice Russell* Margaret Leighton; *Art Hockstader* Lee Tracy; *Sue Ellen Gamadge* Ann Sothern; *Dick Jensen* Kevin McCarthy; *Oscar Anderson* Richard Arlen; *Sheldon Bascomb*

Shelley Berman; *Tom* George Furth; *T.T. Claypoole* John Henry Faulk; *Mrs. Claypoole* Penny Singleton; *Mahalia Jackson* Herself; *Howard K. Smith* Himself.

As noted above, Vidal did his own screen adaptation that resulted in a few minor changes such as the use of integration as a key social issue, the introduction of several non-essential minor characters such as the Claypooles, changing the locale to Los Angeles and the verisimilitude induced by showing what appears to be an actual convention in progress. The greater mobility of film art and film resources, superior casting (with the exception of Shelley Berman) and a sharper focus in the writing actually improved upon what was already an accomplished piece of commercial theater. The creation of the screenplay has a few stories of its own.

In his "American Dream" autobiography *The Name Above the Title*, master film director Frank Capra discussed his projected stint as director of the screen version of *The Best Man*: "Playwright-author Gore Vidal is a caustic intellectual, a possessor of an eloquent bitchiness that I found entertaining. One would never expect him to be a dedicated evangelist with a life-long mission. But he was. It was during the incredible previews of *A Pocketful of Miracles* that Vidal checked into my Paramount office with a first draft screenplay of his Broadway hit *The Best Man*, a funny but biting probe of how the tortuous politics of smoke-filled rooms make or break Presidential candidates at our national conventions. I called Vidal's attention to the queer coincidence that all the main characters … were confirmed atheists. 'No coincidence,' he said. 'I'd like to convert the whole damn world to atheism. It's my vocation.'" After telling Vidal it wasn't *his* vocation, Capra departed the project.

A bit more light is shed on the script's problems in Joseph McBride's *Frank Capra: The Catastrophe of Success* (1992): "The Capra-[Myles] Connolly script for *The Best Man* invents a new protagonist: the hero is no longer the man who refuses to blackmail his opponent … but the dark horse of the title, who receives the nomination when the two leading candidates cancel each other out … (a) guileless young mixed-race governor of Hawaii, their muddled notion of a John Doe for the 1960s."

After a week of consultations with Capra, Vidal realized that Capra "was absolutely the worst director in the world for this project." Vidal delivered an ultimatum: "Frank, this is a different era, different politics. I'm the author of *The Best Man*, and it's going to be done my way or not at all." Capra was dismissed and replaced by Franklin Schaffner, and the film was directed from Vidal's own screenplay.

Shortly before the film's New York opening, Vidal wrote a piece for the *Times* (April 5, 1964) entitled "Primary Vote for a 'Best Man'" in which he said: "In the screen version of *The Best Man*, the contenders now seem to resemble Goldwater and Rockefeller. The original characters were meant to be political archetypes; to the extent that they were, today's candidates could resemble them. But I did bring the politics up to date. Integration is a key issue in the film, as it is in this year's election. In the play, I had no very urgent issue; neither did Kennedy and Nixon…" In fact, Vidal had discussed this very matter before in an interview with Murray Schumach of the *Times*: "The trouble with the play was that it had no real political issue. There were no real issues between Nixon and Kennedy." Vidal's second thoughts were generally considered to be correct. The film has a sharper bite than the play, captures the backrooms of politics trenchantly and is filled with spirited, yeasty performances like those of Lee Tracy and Ann Sothern as well as the two leads, Fonda and Robertson.

Here's a sampling of critical opinion:

"*The Best Man* has come to the screen, considerably improved in the process of transition. The original casting imbalance ... has been righted somewhat by the substitution of Henry Fonda and Cliff Robertson in Stevenson-Nixon roles. Fonda and Robertson not only act more subtly than Douglas and Lovejoy; they are richer in associations.... Robertson can serve double duty in 1964 as an approximation of both Dick Nixon and Bobby Kennedy, on record as two of Gore Vidal's lesser enthusiasms. To round out the analogies, Fonda portrayed young Abe Lincoln more than a quarter century ago, and Robertson young Jack Kennedy less than a year ago [in *PT 109*]."— Andrew Sarris, *Village Voice*, August 20, 1964.

"Dirty politics, the double-crossing, blackmailing that go on at a national party convention, are hung out on the line for the world to see in *The Best Man*, a devastating drama that is also scandalously amusing."— Wanda Hale, *New York Daily News*, April 7, 1964.

"What is not expected is Cliff Robertson's portrayal of Cantwell, the totally amoral villain whose primary villainy is his inability to identify right and wrong. Mr. Robertson, as a frighteningly human dynamo of evil, dominating the screen with a ferocious and righteous passion, provides ample proof that he can be something more than the pretty boy that Hollywood has hitherto made of him. Political neanderthals and idealistic daydreamers alike may find *The Best Man* strong medicine."— Judith Crist, *New York Herald-Tribune*, April 7, 1964.

"We being a democratic people and this being a Presidential election year — which means the season is open for slinging political mud — it is appropriate that Hollywood should send us one of its occasional melodramatic, gloves-off films about the ferocity and fascination of the great American game of politics.... As [Fonda's] rigid and ruthless rival, Cliff Robertson is excellent — a fair reflection of a type of opportunist that has been all too evident on our political scene. The drama goes almost out of the window in the crucial confrontation scene when the aspirant played by Robertson is brought face to face with an informer who accuses him of past degeneracy. In the first place, and, in the second place, the role of the informer is atrociously played. Shelley Berman, a stand-up comedian, plays it as though he's struggling for laughs, which is what you don't want in this most sordid and agonizing scene."— Bosley Crowther, *The New York Times*, April 7, 1964.

"*The Best Man* was released in a presidential election year, just as the Broadway version had debuted in an earlier election campaign time. However, it was not a major box office hit. *Variety* predicted one of the reasons for its lack of general appeal, 'There will be those who will be offended by some of its points-of-view.' Another factor was that the feature films dealing cynically with politics ... generally fail to attract the mass market of filmgoers, who want more traditional screen fare. *The Best Man* received one Oscar nomination: Best Supporting Actor (Lee Tracy). However, Peter Ustinov (*Topkapi*) won."— James Robert Parish, *Gays and Lesbians in Mainstream Cinema*, 1993.

Tsar to Lenin (documentary film, 1966)

90 minutes. A Herman Axelbank Associates release. Produced by Axelbank. Written by William Hepper and Cyril Jones. Narrated by Valentine Dyall.

This documentary narrated by noted British actor Valentine Dyall was released originally in 1966 and re-released in 1972. A generally worthy documentary, it features the pleasures of the court of Nicholas and Alexandra, the anarchy of Kropotkin, the 1917 revolution, the triumph and death of Lenin, the rise and death of Stalin and Khrushchev and Nixon in "the kitchen debate."

"At first glance, the Herman Axelbank production ... seems to be just another newsreel, but excellent narration and a fine musical background lift this documentary above the ordinary." — Ann Guarino, *New York Daily News*, May 27, 1966.

"Mr. Axelbank's long assemblage of documentary materials is both visually and historically impressive. And it is this that dominates his choppy but often gripping history of the Russian Revolution." — David Sterritt, *Christian Science Monitor*, January 17, 1972.

Made in U.S.A. (film, 1967)

90 minutes. Screenplay by Jean-Luc Godard, from *The Jugger* by Richard Stark. Directed by M. Godard. Produced by Georges De Beauregard for Rome–Paris Film/Anouchka Films/S.E.P.I.C. of Paris; distributed in the United States by Pathe Contemporary Films. Cast: *Paula Nelson* Anna Karina; *Richard Widmark* (a name chosen as a spoof on American *film noir*) Laszlo Szabo; *Donald Siegel* Jean-Pierre L'eandas.

A standard film noir plot: A young girl on the trail of her sweetheart's killer grafted onto a pseudo-philosophical treatise on life's meaning. "Un film politique, c'est Walt Disney plus le sang" (A political film, Walt Disney plus blood), Godard said of it in *Jeune Cinéma* (*Young Cinema* No. 21) upon its release in France.

Two TV-type killers named Richard Nixon and Robert McNamara are main characters in a bluntly anti–American exercise in existential despair and cynicism.

"The film, in color, is decorated with pop art bloodstains and bodies ... 'This is like a Disney film but one that stars Humphrey Bogart, so it must be political,' [Anna Karina] observes at one point. And that is about the best summary of all." — Richard Shepard, *New York Times*, September 28, 1967.

Richard Nixon: A Self-Portrait
(TV and campaign film)

Film on videotape. Interviewer: Warren Wallace. Executive Producer: Frank Shakespeare. Nixon Presidential Materials, division of National Archives, Alexandria, Virginia.

"Television elected Richard Nixon to the presidency. If the medium did not exist, he simply would not have won." — R. Gilbert, *Television and Presidential Politics*.

Nixon's 1968 campaign has been covered in depth in Joe McGinnis's *The Selling of the President 1968* which, curiously enough, became the basis of a Broadway musical in 1972. The McGinnis book also contains some of the scripts for the spot commercials of Nixon's 1968 campaign.

Nixon's biographical campaign film *Richard Nixon: A Self-Portrait* was a series of interviews together with still photographs re-shot with zooms and pans in order to create a sense of movement. The target audience was women, since for the most part, Nixon was out of favor with that voting block. Therefore, the showings were more frequent during the day than the more usual "prime time" hours of the evening. However, it was shown in the evening on two occasions, October 27 and November 2. The "self-portrait" was a relaxed and dignified film, but not without the proper sense of urgency at key points. The attempt was to show Nixon as an average American who had a vision for a better America and was willing to work hard to achieve it. The many close-ups and the conversational tone helped to produce an intimate effect so that it was a thoroughly professional film that avoided slickness.

Like the "G.I. bedroom den" set for the Checkers speech, the sets were chosen to suggest a self-made man of the people. The three sets were a study that contained leather chairs with a great deal of wood and a number of strong angles, the porch of Nixon's summer home with Nixon dressed casually as the sounds of nature were heard in the background, and a window above Mission Bay, California, as pleasure boats sailed by below. The settings were perfectly chosen to show Nixon as a strong man, very much at peace with himself and capable of leading a foundering nation to stability, if not prosperity.

The still photographs of the family store and people and places associated with Nixon's youth and young manhood were obviously chosen to strike a chord of familiarity with the essential American values Nixon's advisors wanted the campaign to project. Nixon's story, like many a persuasive political story, was that of a small town boy who made good; it is a story that played well in small town America in the 1960s when so many of the cities were being torn apart.

Nixon described his hard-working father, long-suffering saintly mother and his dignified Quaker grandmother and their devotion to hard work, thrift and civic-mindedness. His forebears were poor, but they never refused a person in greater need than they. They were a close-knit family that had known tragedy and some deprivation: one brother had died very young, and Mrs. Nixon had spent three years in Arizona nursing another son who died of tuberculosis. At the same time, in order to earn money for his treatment, she nursed three other tubercular young men, and Richard joined her in Arizona and worked as a barker in a carnival in order to earn money for the family. Nixon said he had learned from his experiences, even the bad ones. He had learned the value of hard work and competition. Competition made one excel, and competition was what had made America great. "Whenever you take the competitive spirit out of a people, or run to take it out of an individual, you lose something in a country," Nixon said.

Toward the end of the interview, Nixon stated that "the United States faced a responsibility," and that was "to lead the world." Nineteen sixty-eight was a very troubled year and the calm Eisenhower-like manner with which he now projected himself suggested that he was the best man to lead the world out of chaos. In this half-hour and in all his previous endeavors he had striven to prove himself equal to that mighty task. He had proven that a man with a humble background could overcome adversity and accept whatever challenges the world would offer him.

Duke Ellington at the White House (short subject, 1969)

Produced by the United States Information Agency.

Duke Ellington at the White House "was made on April 29 [1969] when President Nixon invited the famous jazz pianist to the White House to celebrate Mr. Ellington's 70th birthday and to present him with the Medal of Freedom, the nation's highest civilian award."—*New York Times*, January 30, 1970.

The Bearding of the President (film, 1969)

Produced and directed by Rip Torn. With: Geraldine Page and Rip Torn. Unreleased; shown as a benefit for *Realist Magazine* in February 1976 at the Elgin Theater on New York's Lower East Side.

Produced in 1969, this low-budget spoof of Shakespeare's *Richard III* was shelved although work continued spasmodically until ten days before Nixon's resignation. It never had a commercial release.

"Torn plays Nixon as Richard III sitting in the White House TV monitoring room, with a backdrop of screens that constantly play back, depicting all the atrocities of the Nixon Era. Some of the screens showed actual news footage (various assassinations, riots by armed personnel, put-downs of demonstrations, as well as Vietnamese massacre tableaus, etc.) while some were acted out—as in the murder of Clarence who looks and talks a lot like [Robert Kennedy]—all serving as Richard's ghosts and ceaseless nightmares, hounding the moral hunchback.... It's good theater but not the kind of thing I go out of my way to see these post-amnesty days."—Art Gatti, *SoHo Weekly News*, February 5, 1976.

The United States vs. Julius and Ethel Rosenberg (play, 1969)

A Cleveland Playhouse production of a three-act drama by Donald Freed, based in part on *Invitation to an Inquest* by Walter and Miriam Schneir and *The Judgment of Julius and Ethel Rosenberg* by John Wexley; staged by Larry Tarranto. Opened at the Cleveland Playhouse Brooks Theatre March 24, 1969. Cast: *Julius Rosenberg* Stuart Levin; *Ethel Rosenberg* Elizabeth Lowry. (Produced shortly after with well-known actors at the Music Box Theatre, New York.)

Note: The release of 49 decoded Soviet intelligence messages on July 11, 1995, by the National Security Agency was a stunning blow to the defenders of Julius and Ethel Rosenberg for as Walter and Miriam Schneir, the principal Rosenberg apologists, stated in the August 14, 1995 *Nation*, "[T]he Venona intercepts [the term for the United States decoding program] reveal that during World War II Julius ran a spy ring composed of young fellow Communists, including friends and college classmates whom he'd recruited. The group gave technical data from their jobs—information on radar and airplanes is mentioned in the documents. Julius passed this material to the Soviets. The K.G.B. awarded cash bonuses to the group."

However, from the day of Julius's arrest, July 17, 1950, until the day of their execution, June 19, 1953, the Rosenbergs inspired violent partisanship which continued with great intensity until the release of the Venona intercepts.

Here's a sampling of critical opinion:

"The atmosphere of the turbulent McCarthy era is established by a narrator and newsreel clips. These film vignettes of the Rosenbergs during their Federal court trial in 1951, and aped voices of their original defenders are shrewdly fused with stage and film re-enactments of the celebrated case."—*Variety*, April 2, 1969.

"It is a badly organized play ... but with the depiction of an execution ... with silhouettes of the victims in the electric chairs, no less—even the stones might wimper a little. But the play—while moving because of the subject matter—is by no means a success.... [I]t has about as much real drama as a rigged boxing match. There is a certain self-congratulating liberalism about the play that sets my teeth on edge."—Clive Barnes, *New York Times*, April 27, 1969.

"[A] crude melodrama of villains and heroes, obviously slanted in the Rosenbergs' favor."—Julius Novick, *Village Voice*, April 30, 1970.

Spiro Who? (play, 1969)

A social comedy by William Meyers. Music composed by Phil Ochs. Produced by Robert Steelse at Tambellini's Gate Theater, Second Avenue. Directed by Bernard Barrow. Scenery by Eldon Elder.

It is midnight. A college apartment. On the eve of graduation three very typical 1960s collegians have a highly personal and very amusing bull session in which hope, self-pity and post-adolescent angst ring startlingly true as each self-absorbed hobbledehoy presents his "take" on the state of the world with political references thrown in.

Here's a sampling of critical opinion:

"The scatter-gun method employed by the author militates against cohesive dramatic impact. The three students, each representing a distinct type, are shown in their room on the eve of graduation, and one of them, a would-be playwright, imagines a short scene in which each is supposed to be examined and explained."—*Variety*, June 11, 1969.

"*Spiro Who?* is by turns perceptive, witty and despairing. Although the peripheral characters are caricatures, the three students are viable, as types and as people. Meyers has written a piece of theater that swells with honesty. The humor, for the most part, is clever and current."—*The Villager*, June 16, 1969.

"To a rock beat ("Love me, love me, love me, I'm liberal!") the rush of consciousness skitters, stops, takes off again jaggedly: the boys (a homosexual, a radical wannabe playwright and an overweight nerd) swim in memory of nudes, beer, nudes, ham, nudes, Neapolitan ice cream, nudes (and) the model men of our time — Nixon and others." — Walter Kerr, *New York Times*, June 15, 1969.

Law and Order (TV documentary, 1969)

Osti Films for Public Broadcasting Laboratory of National Educational Television and Radio Center. 81 minutes. Distributed by Zipporah Films. B&W. Producer–director–writer–editor Frederick Wiseman. Photographed by David Martin.

An examination of the procedures of the Kansas City, Missouri, Police Department, *Law and Order* won an Emmy as the best news documentary of the 1968–1969 season. In an interview in the *New York Times* of February 1, 1970, Wiseman said, "I started it a few weeks after the Democratic convention in Chicago and I saw it as a chance to do in the pigs. But after about two days of riding around in police cars, I realized … the cops did some horrible things but they also did some nice things. We liberals frequently forget that people do terrible violence to each other, against which the police form a minimal and not very successful barrier. I understand now the fear that cops live with."

Among the scenes presented were those of a policeman choking a young prostitute, the aiding of a victim of a purse snatching, the apprehension of a youth who had vandalized three cars, the arrest of three young robbers of a clothing store, and officers playing with a lost child at a police station. Both the rough and the smooth were shown in an intelligent, informative way.

"Against the police routine, Wiseman inserted a clip of Richard Nixon as he campaigned in Kansas City on the 'law and order' issue, and the new President's proclamations seemed indeed specious within this documentary." — *Variety*, March 5, 1969.

In the Year of the Pig (documentary film, 1969)

101 minutes. Pathe Contemporary Films, Cinetree. Produced and directed by Emile De Antonio. Photography: John F. Newman. Music by Steve Addiss. Assistant director: Albert Maher.

In the Year of the Pig is composed of news material from many sources and filmed interviews with dozens of major and minor figures from the Vietnam War and earlier. It covers the French influence from the 1940s until the fall of Dien Bien Phu and American support of the domino theory of the 1950s through the American commitment in the 1960s. Some of the figures shown and heard are David Halberstam, Daniel Berrigan, Harrison Salisbury and Arthur Schlesinger, who were among the doves. Among the hawks were Presidents Eisenhower, Kennedy and Johnson and Vice-President Nixon.

Here's a sampling of critical opinion:

"Clips of speeches by Lyndon Johnson, President Nixon, Hubert Humphrey, Gen. Curtis LeMay, Madame Nhu and an array of politicians and soldiers are intercut to demonstrate the war's contradictory aspects and the claimed gulf between what officials say and do."—*Variety*, March 12, 1969.

"There are glimpses of wartime savagery on both sides, and there is even some comic relief, as when Madam Nhu announces, 'About that question of the rubber stamp parliament: I have repeatedly said, "But what's wrong to rubber the laws we approve?"'"—*Time*, November 14, 1969.

"One detailed sequence with a clutter of expressionless natives being firmly shepherded by American soldiers is a microcosm of the Vietnam war. But it is the almost unbroken flow of personal testimonies that will jolt the viewer, ranging from that given by combat soldiers to those of former President Lyndon B. Johnson and President Nixon."—*New York Times*, November 11, 1969.

The Silent Majority (short subject, 1969)

15 minutes. Produced by the United States Information Agency. Producer–writer–director Bruce Herschensohn.

Here's a sampling of critical opinion:

"Richard Nixon began to harness [the] 'Silent Majority' in 1968…"—Joanne Morreale, *The Presidential Campaign Film*.

"I thought that America needed a new sense and spirit of positive pride, and now that the Vietnam War was over, I felt that I could be instrumental in creating it, I felt that the silent majority of Americans, with its roots mainly in the Midwest, the West and the South, had simply never been encouraged to give the Eastern liberal elite a run for its money for control of the nation's key institutions."—Richard Nixon, *Memoirs*.

"A 15 minute film hastily prepared and released to over a hundred countries late in 1969 triggered a major controversy. Inspired by Nixon's Vietnam speech of November 3, 1969, Bruce Herschensohn … compiled the film in such a way as to suggest that despite the widespread demonstrations of the fall of 1969 most Americans agreed with the Administration's Vietnam policy. The film … was criticized for indulging in partisan policies, expressly forbidden under the USIA's charter…"—*Current Biography*, September 1970 (biography of Frank Shakespeare, then director of the USIA).

"The Nixon Administration has carried to potential television audiences in 104 countries a message suggesting that the President's Vietnam policies are backed by a 'silent majority' of Americans. Since last Monday, the United States Information Agency has shipped abroad 200 prints of a 15 minute television film, *The Silent Majority*, showing scenes from last week's antiwar demonstrations in Washington interspersed with comments appearing to support Mr. Nixon's stand and emphasizing the importance of the 'silent' citizens. *The Silent Majority* was produced in 12 days of intensive shooting and editing under the supervision of Bruce Herschensohn, the USIA's director of motion pictures and television."—*New York Times*, November 20, 1969.

"*The Silent Majority* shows Nixon opening up letters and telegrams which supposedly support his policy of 'Vietnamization' of the war. Also included is an interview with Dr. Gallup who summarizes the results of his poll which followed the Nixon telecast in which over 80 percent of those sided with the President..." — *Take One*, Volume II, number 6, 1969–70.

From the script of *The Silent Majority*:

> NARRATOR: The 'silent majority' — these are Americans from almost all segments of the populace. They include people of all ages, occupations, religions, people from every level of the community, people from every region.

> PRESIDENT NIXON: As President of the United States, I would be untrue to my oath of office to be dictated by the minority who hold that point of view and who try to impose it on the nation by mounting demonstrations in the street.

"No matter what the outcome of this controversy, demonstrations of support and opposition on many issues will continue to take place in Washington and throughout the land. What I have found, however, is that the loudest sound is not the only one that should be listened to." — Richard Nixon.

Making of the President (TV, 1969)

90 minutes. CBS–TV. From the book by Theodore H. White. Narrated by Theodore H. White and Joseph Campanella. Executive producer: Buc Rufkin. Production director, Mel Stuart. Script by Theodore H. White. Aired Tuesday, September 9, 1969, 9:30 P.M. Sponsored by Xerox.

This perceptive overview of all the aspirants for the top nominations was up to Theodore White's to-be-expected very high level. Chief among the aspirants were Humphrey, Romney, Muskie, Agnew, Wallace and Nixon, all presented in broad but telling strokes.

"A conventional reprise of filmed highlights of the year would be of only mild interest at this date, but White's version was strengthened by first-rate production values, skillful editing and astute commentary. It was of great interest to watch now, and one suspects the fascination will grow as time elapses.... Practically every scene that belonged in a documentary on the '68 campaign was there — including Richard Nixon at the piano in Miami Beach singing 'Home on the Range' the day after being nominated." — *Variety*, September 17, 1969.

"The snarl and self-pity which coated [Nixon's] campaigning of 1960 were gone; the years had mellowed him; what was left was genuine and authentic, true to the inner man. And the message, though the same as in 1960, was reaching an audience living in a country that violence, discontent, adventure and war had changed." — Theodore H. White, *The Making of the President*, 1968 (published version).

Christmas at the White House (TV, 1969)

30 minutes. A Metromedia production. Pat and Tricia Nixon interviewed by Bonnie Angelo of *Time* magazine. Produced by Neal Jones. Directed by Tom Vardaman. Aired Thursday, December 18, 1969, at 8 P.M.

"Metromedia managed to get an exclusive just-us-girls White House interview with the First Lady and her oldest daughter. And the resulting film has been slotted for airing on the chain's outlets and was being syndicated to about 50 stations plus Armed Forces Radio and the Voice of America. In addition, from the point of view of publicity, the interview won women's page space in a number of newspapers. Bonnie Angelo ... ably handled the Red Room interview. Her big plus was a genuine interest in all the White House angles with femme appeal. The interview is definitely a holiday good cheer session..."— *Variety*, December 24, 1969.

The Statue (film, 1970)

84 minutes. Directed by Rod Amateau. Produced by Anis Nohra. Written by Alec Coppel and Denis Norden from a story by Coppel. Music by Riz Artolani. Cast: David Niven, Virna Lisi, Robert Vaughn and John Cleese. Cinerama release.

The Statue is an unsuccessful comedy in which David Niven is concerned about the size of his genitals as sculpted by his wife (Virna Lisi) on a statue that honors him as the creator of a new European language. In other words, Niven's head has been stuck on another man's more heroic body. But whose? The film is developed through Niven's estimating the size of the genitals of each man who has visited his wife's studio. At the end, we learn that the genitals are those of Michelangelo's David. Nixon is an off-screen character because Robert Vaughn, as the American ambassador in London, the site of the statue, "confers frequently with the President — with Richard M. Nixon's photograph behind his desk — on the red phone over the statue which the U.S. State Department commissioned at a cost of $50,000. Vaughn's best lines are in his telephone seshes with the President."— *Variety*, January 28, 1971.

White House Conversation: The President and Howard K. Smith (TV, 1970)

60 minutes. Produced by Everett H. Aspinell. Directed by W.P. Fowler. ABC–TV.

"[Smith's] questions were largely based on issues raised by writers and politicians opposed to the President. But, either because of his own amiability, or agreement, or fear of embarrassing his notable companion, he had little success in following up Nixon's somewhat roundabout answers — evasions.... [E]ven when talking about domestic affairs, Smith seemed less tough than interview requirements might demand." — *Variety*, March 24, 1971.

Inquest (play, 1970)

A play in one act by Donald Freed, presented at the Music Box Theatre in New York City on April 23, 1970. Directed by Alan Schneider. Special projections by

Karl Eigsti. Lightning by Jules Fisher. (28 performances) Cast: *Ethel Rosenberg* Anne Jackson; *Julius Rosenberg* George Grizzard; *Emanuel Bloch* James Whitmore; *Irving Saypol* Mason Adams; *Roy Cohn* Mike Burnsten; *Judge Kaufman* Michael Lipton; *David Greenglass* Jack Hollander; *Tessie Greenglass* Sylvie Straus; *Harry Gold* Phil Leeds; *Ruth Greenglass* Hildy Brooks.

The prologue begins with a projection of Justice Felix Frankfurter and voice-over ("history has its claims") and a projection and voice-over of Albert Einstein. ("From the viewpoint of restoring sanity to our political climate, one must not let this case rest.") Other very brief projections follow. They are mainly of the early stages of nuclear technology and the scientists and political figures associated with it. This series ends with a projection entitled "the gods of the twentieth century" and we see shots of Marx, Freud and Nietzsche.

Projection: "EVERY WORD YOU WILL HEAR OR SEE ON THIS STAGE IS A DOCUMENTED QUOTATION FROM TRIAL TRANSCRIPTS AND ORIGINAL SOURCES OR A RECONSTRUCTION FROM ACTUAL EVENTS." Projections of J. Edgar Hoover and Richard Nixon follow. Nixon says, "If the President says the American people are entitled to know all the facts, I feel the American people are entitled to know the facts about the espionage ring which was responsible for turning over information on the atom bomb to the agents of the Russian government." The heads of the members of the reputed atom spy ring appear together with another projection of Hoover. All are supplanted by Nixon who says, in part, "The Communists are nibbling us to death in little wars all over the world." Other shots of spy ring figures and government officials are projected as well as footage of the Rosenbergs being arrested. The latter complete the prologue.

Acts I and II begin with projection: "UNITED STATES DISTRICT COURT, SOUTHERN DISTRICT OF NEW YORK. The United States of America v. Julius Rosenberg and Ethel Rosenberg, et al. Before Hon. Irving R. Kaufman, D.J., and a Jury, New York, March 6, 1951, 10:30 A.M." The projection of an American flag washes slowly away across the area. After procedural matters, the clerk reads the indictment:

"On or about June 6, 1944, up to and including June 16, 1950, at the Southern District of New York, and elsewhere, Julius Rosenberg, David Greenglass [note: Ethel Rosenberg's brother], the defendants herein, did, the United States of America then and there being at war, conspire, combine, confederate and agree with each other and with Harry Gold and Ruth Greenglass, named as co-conspirators but not as defendants…"

In his introduction to the trade edition of the play (Hill and Wang 1970), Freed, seeking to give weight to his approach to the material, quotes Lincoln in a manner which some might consider rather opportunistic: "We must disenthrall ourselves" by which Freed means his attempt to dispel accepted visions of history for newer, more perceptive ones. "So the play is anti-myth; it means to disenthrall," he concludes.

The play progresses in two acting areas: Stage A for the legal proceedings and Stage B for domestic scenes and "reconstructions." The trade edition is in two long acts running to 119 script pages with 20-some pages of additional material. The Broadway version was cut considerably and played as one long act in order to enhance the play's intensity. Other than the prologue, Nixon is not quoted, although what Freed feels Nixon represents is criticized throughout.

Here's a sampling of critical opinion:

"Those who've long been animated by the myth that Julius and Ethel Rosenberg were victims of a McCarthy-era, FBI-orchestrated frame-up suffered a major setback last week. Walter and Miriam Schneir, the only proponents of this thesis who've ever been regarded as remotely serious, acknowledged in an article in *The Nation* that recently released Venona intercepts had, at last, persuaded them that 'Julius Rosenberg ran a spy ring composed of young fellow communists, including friends and college class-mates whom he had recruited…. [T]he Venona intercepts make it abundantly clear that Rosenberg and his Los Alamos-based brother-in-law, David Greenglass, were deeply involved in passing Manhattan Project secrets to the Soviets. In fact, the Venona files that have been released deal only with atomic espionage. Moreover … Soviet intel-ligence archives demonstrate that Rosenberg and his confederates played a highly significant role in advancing Moscow's effort to build its own A-bomb." — Eric Brein-del, *New York Post*, August 10, 1995.

"Though the [communist] party's links with the K.G.B. were certainly not known to most rank and file members, there seems little doubt that top C.P. officials were aware of the espionage connection. A fragmentary but astonishing message from Moscow dated April 5, 1945, refers to information that was 'reported by LIBERAL [Julius Rosenberg's code name] himself to the leadership of his FELLOW COUN-TRYMEN. This is not a pretty story. We know that our account will be painful news for many people, as it is for us. But it is the duty of a writer to tell the truth." — Wal-ter and Miriam Schneir, *Nation*, August 14, 1995.

"*Inquest*, at the Music Box, cannot be judged — and it is not intended to be judged — solely on its merits as a play; if it were to be so judged, it would have to be given very low marks, being by calculation as well as ineptitude almost wholly devoid of any of the devices by which our interest is ordinarily aroused and manipulated in the theater. Given its tragic theme and the fact that it is cast in the form of a court-room drama, it is uncannily dull; the author Donald Freed has subtitled it 'A Tale of Political Terror,' but he has not succeeded in making the terror manifest on-stage, and the few glimpses that he offers us of the minds of his hero and heroine are so conven-tionally timid-lower-middle-class-domestic-amorous that the exemplary courage with which they eventually go to their deaths strikes us, in our ignorance of their motives and emotions alike, as a mere anomaly…. Mr. Freed is as clumsy a polemicist as he is a dramatist; his special pleading is as unconvincing as his scenes with the Rosenbergs *a deux*— which he defines as 'reconstructions'…" — Brendan Gill, *New Yorker*, May 2, 1970.

"Even if they were [guilty], however, their trial was a monstrous farce, and to that point the play speaks with ample eloquence." — John Simon, *New York*, May 18, 1970.

"Mr. Freed's play is not reopening the case: it is arguing the case from the basic premise that there is absolutely no question about the Rosenbergs' innocence. The point is that *Inquest*, while righteously paranoid about the political emotionalism that festered in the Rosenberg trial, indulges itself in an emotionalism from the other extreme, no less suspicious, no less damaging." — John O'Connor, *Wall Street Journal*, April 27, 1970.

"A form of moral pollution has seeped into the drama in recent years. It has adopted the totalitarian tactic of rewriting history. The latest entry is *Inquest*, a turgid, shrill and sob-sisterish courtroom polemic that glorifies Julius and Ethel Rosenberg as homey, humanity-loving innocents hounded to the electric chair by 'political terror.'

The Rosenbergs were convicted on March 29, 1951, of conspiracy to commit espionage in connection with supplying atomic-bomb data to the Russians. In the next 26 months, there were at least 14 appeals and reviews of their case. Justice may be blind once. It is not likely to be blind that often. Playwright Donald Freed makes the Rosenbergs like harmless and bewildered children made to pay with their lives merely for playing with a toy balloon called Communism…. Unconscionably and irresponsibly, the play trades on the emotions of the large New York Jewish theater-going audience by implying that the Rosenbergs were racial martyrs in a kind of mini-pogrom."—*Time*, May 4, 1970.

From a review of a West Coast production somewhat later:

"What [Freed's] really doing, with inelegant structuring, and hamhanded writing, is to confuse the issues and thus make us wonder all the more about the accused spies and why they behaved the way they did. There is probably a good play that could be written someday about the Rosenberg case — one that would permit the audience to come to its own conclusion about the anti–Communist hysteria of the early 1950s and the damage to the Constitution it caused — but this one by Freed is not it."—*San Francisco Chronicle*, February 24, 1989.

Tricia White House Tour (TV, 1970)

A twenty minute TV segment. CBS, May 26, 1970. Harry Reasoner, Mike Wallace and Tricia Nixon (*60 minutes*).

"Tuesday, April 28, 1970. P[President] worked me over on the phone about CBS filming of "Tricia White House Tour," which was set as a 20 or 30 minute segment on *60 Minutes* show. P feels she have full hour, or nothing. Really mad, and said so, chewed me out worse than he ever has as P. Basically a release of tensions on the big decision, but potentially damaging if he starts flailing in other directions. Think this one is under control."—*The Haldemen Diaries*, 1994.

The *New York Times* reviewed Tricia Nixon's tour of the White House most enthusiastically:

"Tricia Nixon, the President's 24-year-old daughter, proved a charming, lively and poised hostess last night in a televised tour of the family living quarters on the second floor of the White House. As seen in the segments of *60 Minutes*, presented by the Columbia Broadcasting System, the blonde Miss Nixon radiated a videogenic quality as she escorted Harry Reasoner and Mike Wallace through the upstairs of the Executive Mansion…. [T]he most lasting impression was that of a most attractive young woman in a white lace dress not taking herself the least bit seriously in such a distinctive setting. In effective use of TV, the President's most serious competition is Tricia."—*The New York Times*, May 27, 1970.

Nixon's Long March (TV documentary, 1970)

90 minutes. With Julian Pettifer (BBC), Solon Gray, Doug Ramsey. Produced by Carol Moore. Directed by John Coleman. Written by Pettifer, Brown, Moore and Ramsey. WPIX–TV, New York.

"[A] fascinating picture of the Chinese at work, learning and play — all dedicated to the greater glory of China and Chairman Mao. Commentary, which was interspersed during the film, was no better or worse than that which has appeared in newspapers and magazines and on TV since President Nixon announced that he would go to China. But it was thoroughly done and smoothly produced." — *Variety*, September 29, 1971.

Interviews with My Lai Veterans (short documentary, 1970)

Produced, written and directed by Joseph Strick. Photographed by Haskell Wexler and Richard Pearce. Tuesday, March 22, 1971, WNET, New York. (22 minutes on TV, 27 minutes as a commercial release.)

Background: On March 16, 1968, a unit of the United States Army commanded by Lt. William L. Calley killed more than 300 civilians in My Lai, a South Vietnamese hamlet reported to have been a Viet Cong stronghold.

"Although Calley and the infantrymen he led had gunned down unarmed Vietnamese civilians in March 1968 while Johnson was still president, Nixon had to contend with the fallout in part because the Department of Defense had been investigating the incident since April and the president had known about it since at least August [1969].... [His advisors] differed on how to handle the uproar over Calley, especially after he began to be lionized in the South (with a little help from such different southern governors as Jimmy Carter and George Wallace)." — Joan Hoff, *Nixon Reconsidered*.

"On March 31 [1971] the court martial sentenced Calley to life in prison at hard labor. Public reaction to the announcement was emotional and sharply divided. More than 5,000 telegrams arrived at the White House, running 100 to 1 in favor of clemency.... By April 1974, Calley's sentence had been reduced to ten years, with eligibility for parole as early as the end of that year. Three months after I resigned, the Secretary of the Army decided to parole Calley." — Nixon, *Memoirs*.

The general release of *Interviews with My Lai Veterans* was held up because it was thought it might influence the trial of Lt. Calley. Shown first to the members of the American Academy of Motion Picture Arts and Sciences, it won the Academy Award as the best documentary of 1970. Following its first public showing on WNET New York, this film by Joseph Strick, known for his adaptations of literary works such as Genet's *The Balcony* and Joyce's *Ulysses*, became a commercial release in 1972.

Plot: Five veterans tell their versions of a search-and-destroy mission to an obscure village where they took part in the killing of hundreds of defenseless people. They do not defend their actions, but they are uneasy when they discuss the rape and mutilation that took place there.

"Strick claimed that the [soldiers'] accounts indicated that Americans are as capable of genocidal acts as the Nazis, which may be stretching the point, but his sobering film, surprisingly unstatic despite its reliance on the 'talking heads' close-ups, is most assuredly a strong supportive exhibit of his admitted anti-war stance." — *Variety*, March 24, 1971.

Anatomy of Welfare (TV documentary, 1971)

60 minutes. Produced, directed and written by Ernest Pendrell with Frank Reynolds as host/narrator. ABC–TV, Wednesday, April 20, 1971.

Nixon's "family assistance plan" was eloquently defended by commentator Frank Reynolds, but the documentary's overall presentation did not "in itself justify the President's plan, even if it in reality might be worthy."—*Variety*, April 21, 1971.

Million Dollar Duck (film, 1971)

92 minutes. A Buena Vista (Walt Disney) release in Technicolor. Produced by Bill Anderson. Directed by Vincent McEveety Screenplay by Roswell Rogers. Based on a story by Ted Key.

Dean Jones, an impecunious scientist, takes home a duck that has been radiated accidentally. Thanks to the radiation and the pectin in wife Sandy Duncan's home-made apple sauce, the duck starts to lay eggs with golden yolks. Then, of course, good old-fashioned greed takes over, including the Treasury Department, get-rich-quick lawyer Tony Roberts, and Richard M. Dixon (in his usual role of Richard Nixon), who barks at the Treasury Department: "Now just let me say *this* about *that. Get that duck!* *Understand?*" They do, and Dean and Sandy and son Lee Montgomery are happiest when they realize that they just want the duck as a pet, not as the provider of a bank account.

"It's played for laughs until the soppily sentimental conclusion…. Also on the plus side are some low-key but mildly funny parodies on the anti-establishment hot-rod set and on what is depicted as a very pompous United States Treasury Department."—*Christian Science Monitor*, July 30, 1971.

Is There Sex After Death? (film, 1971)

97 minutes. Produced, directed and written by Jeanne and Alan Abel. Photography (Eastmancolor 16mm blown up to 35mm): Gerald Cotts. Released by the Abels.

A sex spoof that opens at Grant's Tomb, home base of the Bureau of Sexological Investigation, from which Dr. Harrison Rogers begins a country-wide tour in quest of sexual arcana. Among his interviewees is Richard M. Nixon (Jim Dixon), who discusses sex in the White House. In a favorable review, *The New York Times* (October 25, 1971) listed some of the other topics such as dildos, penis size and X-rated animal pictures.

This sexual phantasmagoria ends with the International Sex Bowl, a sporting event in which contestants from various nations compete to prove their sexual prowess.

Tricia's Wedding (short subject, satire, 1971)

30 minutes. Written and directed by Mark Lester with the San Francisco drag troupe, the Cockettes.

This controversial film spoofs the wedding of Tricia Nixon and Ed Cox in the White House Rose Garden on June 12, 1971, "the social event of the season in Washington" (Ambrose, Volume II). Among the guests were such Nixon friends as Billy Graham, Ethel Waters, Norman Vincent Peale and Red Skelton. Made during the early days of gay liberation, *Tricia's Wedding* contains many typically campy scenes: Mick Jagger making out with Prince Charles under the Queen's nose, gun-toting Lady Bird Johnson singing "If I'd Known You Were Comin' I'd-a Baked a Cake," Mamie Eisenhower nipping on a bottle of Gallo and Pat Nixon and Martha Mitchell squabbling over who should do the catering — Stouffer's or Colonel Sanders.

[Lester's] "treatment of the Nixon-Cox wedding ceremony is irreverent enough to make any newlywed hide in shame. Yet there is a strange poignancy to it — a feeling for the ritual as ritual perhaps only achievable by a homosexual, one who will never participate in such a performance." — Stuart Byron, *Village Voice*, August 26, 1971.

"There was ... a secret screening of *Tricia's Wedding*, a pornographic movie portraying Tricia Nixon's wedding to Edward Cox, in drag. Haldeman wanted the movie killed, so a very small group of White House officials watched the cavorting transvestites in order to weigh the case for suppression. Official action proved unnecessary; the film died a natural death." — John Dean, *Blind Ambition*, 1976.

Our Gang (novel, 1971)

Named after the Hal Roach comedies of the '30s and '40s. A novel by Philip Roth, primarily in monologue and dialogue form (it has been staged in part in various venues). Published by Random House.

Our Gang is notable for the uncanny way Roth captured a Nixon whom he detests and whom he has been able to sustain — a creepy, malevolent, obsequious, ruthless, self-serving charlatan — over a length of 200 pages. Roth sets the tone early: Nixon is called Trick E. Dixon and his alma mater is Prissier College. In the exact middle of this blistering lampoon there is an extremely clever parody of the Checkers speech. However, much of the book is labored with such sophomoric touches as referring to Secretary of Defense Melvin Laird as Secretary Lard and respected journalist Eric Severeid as Erect Severehead. Toward the end of this riveting screed, Dixon proclaims "the highest regard for [Satan] and his long and distinguished record as a liar."

Here's a sampling of critical opinion:

"*Our Gang*, published just before the Watergate break-in, is more passionate and cuts deeper than the lighter anti–Nixon spoofs, for Mr. Roth really loathes Nixon. The drowning of President Trick E. Dixon in a water-filled Baggie after an operation to remove the sweat gland from his upper lip exhales a merciless rage and disgust, and so do the other ghoulishly ebullient parts of the novel." — Daniel Aaron, *The New York Times Book Review*, August 6, 1995.

"*Our Gang* is almost insultingly sloppy and inane; it is devoid of the tiniest political or psychological insight, and since Nixon has seduced Roth into being less intelligent than he is, one closes his book knowing less about Nixon than when one began. The book is, stylistically, almost entirely indebted to standard TV skit comedy and in fact never moves beyond that level."— Stephen Koch, *World (Saturday Review)*, August 1, 1972.

Note: See *Watergate Classics*, 1973, in this volume.

Selling of the Pentagon
(TV documentary, 1971)

60 minutes. With Roger Mudd and others. Produced and written by Peter Davis. Tuesday, March 1, 1971, CBS–TV.

Here's a sampling of critical opinion:
"[A]n inquiry by CBS–TV into the public relations activities of the Defense Department became an attack on the Nixon administration and the conduct of the war."— Richard McCann, *The People's Films: A Political History of the U.S. Government Motion Pictures*, Hastings House, New York, 1973.

"[A]n outstanding piece of work."— Alan Rosenthal, *New Challenges for Documentary*, University of California Press, Berkeley, 1988.

A Visit with the First Lady
(TV documentary, 1971)

60 minutes. With Pat Nixon, Richard Nixon and Virginia Sherwood (interviewer). Produced and directed by Gary Herman. Sunday, September 11, 1971, ABC–TV.

What follows is a sampling of critical opinion:
"The hour spread itself from the opening session at the White House to the concluding one at the western White House in San Clemente, California, with film clips and comments in between concerning Tricia's wedding, Pat's trip to Peru and sundry activities on a cross-country journey. But through the hour, it also became clearly apparent that Mrs. Nixon is a highly polished political performer on a par with her husband, ever poised and cool in her adroit fielding of questions of varied ilk. The best part of the show was the San Clemente finale, with its intimate shots of the home and grounds. Here, Mrs. Nixon made a strong case against the media misinterpretation of her as a shy person and the President paid tribute to her poise and stamina as his helpmate in the political arena."— *Variety*, September 15, 1971.

"Pat Nixon was greatly maligned by the press... What a pity and what a distortion that was. Pat was bright, friendly, very well read, and always beautifully dressed.

Because Nixon made that speech in the 1950s about his wife not having a mink coat but only a good Republican cloth coat, Mrs. Nixon acquired the image of a frump. The image wasn't the reality, and the reporters knew it, but didn't bother doing anything to correct the public's impression of her. I got to know her pretty well. Pat used to come and see me whenever I sang at the Chandler Pavilion in Los Angeles.... She always brought me a basket of flowers and strawberries.... [W]e'd sit in my dressing room and talk for about 20 minutes before my performance, chatting about our children, our homes, people we knew — girl talk, really. She liked watching me do my makeup. I didn't find her shy. I think Pat felt there was a formal protocol that went along with being First Lady. She had certain duties to perform, and she performed them very well." — Beverly Sills and Lawrence Linderman, *Beverly: An Autobiography* (1987).

Millhouse: A White Comedy (film, 1971)

93 minutes. Produced and directed by Emile de Antonio. Edited by Mary Lampson. Photography by Ed Emshwiller, Mike Gray, Bruce Shuh and Richard Kletter. New Yorker Films release, B&W. Available from MPI Home Video; 15825 Rob Roy Dr., Oak Forest, IL 60452.

In an interview in *The New York Times* (October 17, 1971), de Antonio exasperatedly explained the deliberate misspelling of Nixon's middle name as the title of his merciless satire on the 37th president: "I wanted to be h-e-a-v-y; *Millhouse* is heavier than *Milhous*. And I wanted to make it clear that the film approaches fiction, despite its use of documents. But you don't have to be a student of *explication de texte* to get it: white comedy ... black comedy ... white Protestant ethic ... White House ... Political Mill ..."

Always an iconoclast, this son of a wealthy Pennsylvania doctor, a Marxist at Harvard and a classmate of John F. Kennedy, said he made *Millhouse* "to reveal the terrible comic theater that is America." Priding himself on his individualism, de Antonio went on to say, "I've never made a film with the audience in mind ... I'm not primarily interested in money, I'm interested in working things out." His dedication to the film as social criticism is to be found in other political documentaries such as *Point of Order* (1964) on Senator Joe McCarthy and *In the Year of the Pig* (1969). De Antonio is also the star of Andy Warhol's 20-minute short subject *Drink* (1966) in which he drank a quart of whiskey in 20 minutes. A marathon drinker, de Antonio said he would never give an interview without drinks. He died of a heart attack in his Lower East Side Manhattan apartment in December 1989.

In a 1982 interview in *Cinéaste*, de Antonio described his vision of Nixon: "Of course I use him as a comic figure, but I wasn't laughing at him. There's a difference. I'm not unsympathetic to that poor, wretched, clumsy, mixed-up man. I wouldn't want him for a friend, but I understand the drive he must have had from the first moment of his life. What I wanted to show in that film is that the souring of the Horatio Alger myth is almost a necessity in our culture."

One of the points de Antonio made in several interviews was that most of his films have been financially successful because "they're cheap to make." In fact, de Antonio's

A shot from Emile de Antonio's satire *Millhouse: A White Comedy* (1971).

financial and critical success caused quite a stir in the White House. As Fawn Brodie pointed out in her 1981 Nixon biography, "When Emile de Antonio tried to find a copy of the Checkers speech for inclusion in his anti–Nixon film *Millhouse* ... in 1971, he had great difficulty. Neither Republican National Committee, nor the White House, nor the networks had the film. When he finally found one, and featured the Checkers speech along with several other shorter clips, his film, opening in a small art theater in New York in September 1971, caused consternation in the White House.... H.R. Haldeman asked 'Could we stop it?' An IRS audit was recommended on de Antonio and the distributor Daniel Talbot. An FBI dossier on de Antonio was sent to the White House, apparently showing some left wing sympathies. 'We planned to leak it,' John Dean said, 'if the movie became a hit or if the Democratic Party sponsored showings. Neither occurred." The film did become a hit in its way. By preaching to the converted in major cities and on selected campuses, it hit its target audience and also garnered much lively press.

De Antonio's thrust is not so much an attack on Nixon — although he succeeds royally in that department — but to create an overview of how democracy failed in the last half of the 20th century when a mediocre man with limitless powers of manipulation could become president. In short, the government can easily fail the electorate and often does. To de Antonio, Nixon represents the greatest late 20th century manipulation of a system that is supposed to be fair to everyone.

To be sure, de Antonio uses many clever manipulations of his own in developing the film. *Millhouse* portrays Nixon as an opportunist whose lack of ideals is the very reason, according to the film, he can achieve political success. Without true convictions he is free to float with whatever policy wins the public.

The opening shot features a wax head being put on a torso at Madame Tussaud's Museum in London. Military music, always a favorite with Nixon, accompanies this less-than-reverent moment in Nixon legend-building. From then on, the film progresses with clever scatter-shot rather than a straightforward narrative or chronological development. The focus is always politics, but principally it's the loopy chameleon offered up by de Antonio who fascinates us. From the waxworks we cut to the famous 1962 "You won't have Nixon to kick around anymore" screed to the press which opens the door to a highly selective series of *faux pas* and de Antonio's view of Nixon's false pieties, his early years of Communist chasing and his Ike idolatry.

The major portion of the film is the Checkers speech, the tremendously effective self-defense that kept Nixon on the 1952 vice-presidential line. It was one of the first real evidences of the power of TV to promote an already persuasive speaker. The famous later "crises" which became a best-selling book are highlighted in carefully chosen shots, which all become grist for de Antonio's satiric mill: the riot in Caracas in which Nixon and Pat turned a horrible event into a victory, the crisis of Ike's heart attack and the kitchen debate in which Nixon waxes a little too enthusiastically about the ease of American housekeeping.

Millhouse also contains commentary by two chief Nixon critics, Jules Witcover, author of *The Resurrection of Richard Nixon*, and Joe McGinniss, author of *The Selling of the President*, which was soon to become a Broadway musical. "Inside" shots of public relations and image-creation techniques reinforced de Antonio's satirical approach. We also have glimpses of the Nixon "spins" on inflation, Vietnam and "The Silent Majority." In short, every aspect of Nixon's career and personality is placed, through astute editing, in the most self-condemnatory light. In *Millhouse*, Nixon is both a fool and a charlatan.

Here's a sampling of critical opinion:

"The film concludes with the jolly gaffe, made at the Inauguration Ball, when the new President recalled having saved his money so that he and his wife could celebrate V-J Day with Guy Lombardo at the Roosevelt Hotel and hoped that the orchestra leader would be around to play at the end of the next war…. *Millhouse* is anything but subtle…"—Vincent Canby, *New York Times*, September 29, 1971.

"[W]hen it works, de Antonio's sense of juxtaposition can be lethal. News film of 1968 nomination acceptance speech ['Let's win this one for Ike'] is intercut with the footage of Pat O'Brien in *Knute Rockne* advising his lachrymose squad to 'win one for the Gipper'—their hospitalized teammate, who with an anachronistic irony, was portrayed by Ronald Reagan … Subtitled 'a white comedy,' the film is hardly likely to win praise for fighting fair."—Jay Cocks, *Time*, October 18, 1971.

"Whatever the film's intentions, the all-too-sketchy portrait that comes through shows [Nixon] as disciplined, cautious, hard-working, devoid of wit, increasingly aware of his TV image, but less an object of derision than the kind of political Horatio Alger that could appeal to the average public."—*New York Post*, September 27, 1971.

"The film is sluggish at times because of the repetitive nature of the material and a tendency to linger too long over certain segments. Some of the editing, of both footage and sound, is heavy-handed and too obviously 'forced' in partisan zeal. Furthermore, de Antonio's disregard for chronological order, although often useful to his loaded purposes, occasionally makes the film confusing."—*Variety*, October 10, 1971.

"[De Antonio] wings some cheap shots: it proves little simply to juxtapose a Nixon speech on Law and Order with scenes of police subduing black rioters in Miami.

The footage of Middle Americans stammering about the 'new Nixon' comes off more as a sneer about 'bumpkins' than as a comment on Nixon's mutability.... [W]hat is on the line in movies like this is the filmmaker's own sensibility of what offends him — and if that in itself becomes offensive, then the point of the whole exercise is lost."— *Newsweek*, November 15, 1971.

"This rapid-fire revue format of *Millhouse* ... invites us to see Nixon primarily as a buffoon. This is certainly not the sole impression de Antonio seeks to convey, but his more serious purpose — to suggest that Nixon's stealthy phoenix-like ascent to power makes him a man as much to be feared as reviled — is partially sacrificed to the film's funhouse hatchet work."— *Boston After Dark*, October 19, 1971.

"The technique is to intercut clips of old newsreels with television interviews; the effect is devastatingly funny and profoundly depressing. We see a ham actor giving a series of public auditions which win him the world's most prestigious role.... Nixon is very aware of camera positions and angles. He likes to be cued five seconds in advance of each switch from one camera to another so that he can avoid being caught shifting his eyes to look directly into the lens."— Ronald Hayman, *Times* (London), October 27, 1972.

Nixon Recession Caper (screenplay, 1972)

Unproduced screenplay by Ralph Maloney and Robert Allan Arthur from the novel of the same name by Maloney. A projected production of Alfred Crown Enterprises with direction by Arthur.

The film "will deal with the comic adventures of a banker, an advertising account executive, a TV personality and a cloak-and-suiter who all band together to rob a bank and then use the profits to start a legitimate business. And this caper will also poke some good-natured fun at such diverse organizations as the F.B.I. and the Mafia."— *New York Times*, March 19, 1972.

Cool Breeze (film, 1972)

101 minutes. Written and directed by Barry Pollack. Produced by Gene Corman. Based upon *The Asphalt Jungle* by W.R. Burnett. MGM. With Raymond St. Jacques, Margaret Avery.

Cool Breeze was a successful medium-budget re-make of John Huston's classic 1950 *film noir The Asphalt Jungle*— with a difference. Except for a few minor white characters, it now had an all-black cast and the up-to-the-minute *angst* of a disillusioned Vietnam veteran. Pollack's film follows the original script closely, retaining and heightening its violence in order to capitalize on the vogue for black action films which peaked around 1970.

The core of the plot is the planning and execution of a jewel robbery, the ostensible reason for which is to use the re-sale money to open a bank in a black section of

Los Angeles. However, the participants deceive one another and the robbery is botched. Along the way, some attention is paid to the plight of the Vietnam veteran and how race is a factor in society's judgments of individuals. A strong anti-establishment touch is the distribution of the robbery's paraphernalia which includes rubber masks of Nixon, Agnew and George Wallace, a gimmick repeated in 1991's *Point Break*. (Note: This is the fourth time MGM filmed Burnett's novel. Number Two was the Western *The Badlanders*, set in Arizona, and Number Three was *Cairo*, not only the same story but the same title as an old Jeanette MacDonald–Ethel Waters comedy.)

What follows is a sampling of critical opinion:

"Its contrived 'blackness' ... is something of a distraction; but it comes over successfully and entertainingly..."—*Punch*, June 21, 1972.

"The film is essentially humorless, not to mention confusing, with the single exception of the long-awaited and disappointingly swift robbery episode. Having provided themselves with a city bus to get to and from the scene of the crime, the trio of crooks disguise themselves with rubber masks caricaturing George Wallace, Richard Nixon and Spiro Agnew. There is a chilling and droll poetic justice in this little gimmick, and it is the best scene in a film that is otherwise dreary and exploitative."— John Koch, *Boston After Dark*, April 18, 1972.

Richard (film, 1972)

83 minutes. Produced, written and directed by Lorees Yerby and Bertrand Castelli. Additional dialogue: Harry Horowitz. Cast: *Richard M. Nixon* Richard M. Dixon; *Pat Nixon* Lynn Lipton; *Plastic Surgeon* John Carradine; *Guardian Angel* Mickey Rooney; *Washington Doctors* Vivian Blaine, Paul Ford and Kevin McCarthy; *Ma and Pa Nixon* Imogene Bliss and Tyrus Cheeney; *young Nixon* Dan Resin; *Richard M. Nixon* Richard M. Nixon.

A satiric "take" on the life of Richard Nixon, *Richard* is an independent film that did not have wide distribution in spite of mildly favorable reviews. *Richard* splatters through Nixon's career until 1972 using film clips of the real Nixon and "re-enactments" played by Richard M. Dixon and an over-the-top cast.

Early on Nixon answers a newspaper ad to run for a congressional seat. The ad was placed by three political hacks who represent stereotypical constituencies — Italian, southern fried and Irish. These three advisors help Nixon along until and through the Checkers crisis. In the film, Nixon's failures are overcome because of the new face (Dixon's) created for him by mad plastic surgeon John Carradine. After his transformation, Guardian Angel Mickey Rooney guides Nixon through his new-found success.

Richard parodies other films such as *Here Comes Mr. Jordan* with the Rooney character and *A Clockwork Orange* as the three Broadway veterans Blaine, Ford and McCarthy brainwash the new Nixon with actual newsreel clips of bygone and then-current politicians and movie stars such as Ronald Reagan, Adolphe Menjou, Robert Taylor, Marlon Brando and Marilyn Monroe. Sample dialogue (Nixon): "I thought you knew I was of the Quaker persuasion ... but I'll point out the direction the Japs are coming from."

Producer Bertrand Castelli was an immigrant who, not knowing a word of English, was marvelously entertained by a rather solemn and stiff-jointed comedian whom he saw gesturing oddly on American television. The "comedian" was in reality Vice-President Nixon, although Castelli did not know that at the time. Several years later, Castelli, by now a confirmed New Yorker, married the successful off–Broadway playwright Lorees Yerby (*Save Me a Place at Forest Lawn*) and the idea of spoofing the squeaky-clean persona of Richard Nixon fed their appetites eager for the kind of funky satire that was typical of the late 1960s and early 1970s. No doubt to the dismay of many Nixon-scoffers, *Richard* did not do well in what proved to be a landslide Nixon year.

Here's a sampling of critical opinion:

"The finished work, a Hollywood-style comedy about the man who becomes the 37th President, is mildly amusing and sophomorically disrespectful at the same time. It makes tremendous use of old TV newsreel clips which have been cleverly juxtaposed with new footage aimed at giving Nixon the needle. Yet in lampooning the President, the filmmakers, perhaps unintentionally, make him appear very human."—Ann Guarino, *New York Daily News*, August 1, 1971.

"It's a grand collection of film clips (theatrical and documentary) and wonderful fantasies, presenting its hero as a dogged believer in what he believes. Light-handed and light-hearted, it is skillfully acted with Dan Resin, Richard M. Dixon and Nixon himself portraying the hero."—*New York*, August 1, 1972.

"It tends to run down, thus allowing those with any lingering sympathies for Nixon, the victim, to feel that he is being maltreated."—*New York Post*, August 1, 1972.

"*Richard* is skillful, impudent, kind when it should be and hilarious when it needs to be—a refreshing drink of water in a summer movie dry spell."—*New York Daily News*, August 4, 1972.

I'm Glad You Asked Me That Question (satiric revue, 1972)

Written and produced by Joanne Joseph. Directed by Timothy Hayes. Designed by Tim Ward. Washington Square Methodist Church, New York City, August 1972. Cast: David Baker, Joseph Nydell, Elaine Chartoff.

"With such a wealth of source material at her disposal (any daily newspaper, for example), it seems incredible that Joanne Joseph has written and produced such a dull and witless so-called political satire on the Nixon debacle. *I'm Glad You Asked Me That Question* could be considered well-meaning, but it's ineffective and an imposition on its audience."—*Show Business*, August 10, 1972.

An Evening with Richard Nixon and ... (satiric collage, 1972)

Compiled from the writings and speeches of Richard M. Nixon by Gore Vidal. Directed by Edwin Sherin. Character masks by Jane Stein. Produced by Hillard

Elkins. Opened April 30, 1972, at the Shubert Theater, 225 West 44th Street, New York (closed Saturday night, May 13, 1972, after 16 previews and 16 performances). Trade edition — Random House, 1972. Cast: *Pro* Gene Rupert; *Con* Humbert Astredo; *George Washington* Stephen Newman; *Dwight Eisenhower* Philip Sterling; *John F. Kennedy* Robert King; *Richard M. Nixon* George S. Irving; *Jessamym West, Martha Mitchell* Susan Sarandon; *Gloria Steinem* Maureen Anderman; *Pat* Dorothy Dorian James; six other actors in a script with 55 speaking parts.

There were considerable hopes for this political satire because Vidal's *The Best Man* had had such a terrific success and producer Hillard Elkins had produced nothing but hits: *Oh! Calcutta!*, the erotic revue; *The Rothschilds*, the musical on the banking family, and a successful Ibsen repertory starring his then-wife Claire Bloom. Bloom, along with such luminaries as Paul Newman, the director William Friedkin and the librettist Joseph Stein, was an investor in this highly anticipated and politically correct production.

In a *New York Times* interview (April 28), Vidal stated that *An Evening* was a "small and cheerful contribution … to the decline of the American empire." Presiding over Nixon's theatricalized decline are the shades of three presidential icons: Washington, Eisenhower and Kennedy, the latter two coming off surprisingly badly. Two other major characters are Pro, who "may or may not be" Vidal's old nemesis William F. Buckley, and Vidal himself, who "may or may not be" Con. Vidal calls the script an "act of politics" because he is "not interested in theater, only "politics." Vidal's lack of concern about trying to make the piece more theatrically vibrant was later cited as one of the reasons for its short Broadway run.

During the last week of performances, Vidal revealed that he had received death threats and that was the reason he had dropped plans to appear as Con, a character who, in spite of Vidal's somewhat artless hedging, is an obvious self-portrait. In a *New York Post* interview, Vidal stated that after talking to producer Elkins and the theater owners, the Shuberts, they all concluded, "It's not very good business to have … rifle shots in the theater." However, it should be noted that since the play closed only four nights later, this shocking but no doubt true disclosure may have been a last-minute attempt to gain some much-needed publicity.

The play begins as George Washington introduces himself and his father asks him who chopped down the cherry tree. Washington says, "Later, father." We then hear a voice-over of Richard Nixon "saying whatever it is that he has been saying the day of this particular performance." Eisenhower enters holding a golf club, which occasions a lame joke about Ike recognizing Washington as the face on the dollar bill. Shortly after, Kennedy arrives and Ike refers to him as "that smartass kid." Washington blusters on — he has a "directive" to "explain" Nixon "to the people still living." From then on, the events of Nixon's life are presented in capsule form, the first of which is Frank Nixon threatening the president-to-be with a leather belt. We are led to believe that Richard Nixon's self-discipline was imposed upon him by a tyrannical father who did not hesitate to beat his son if he did not achieve the goals his father set for him. Hannah Nixon is presented in the more or less standardized rendition — calm, deeply religious but deceptively controlling in her passivity. The completely contrasting natures of his parents lead the young Nixon to iron self-control and acute social estrangement, making hard work and politics, high and low, the arena in which he could become a leader.

The piece rehashes many of Nixon's personal grievances — not being invited to the Eisenhower White House or the Gettysburg country home, not playing football in spite of not sparing himself in practice. Vidal then goes on to show the "arena" itself during which most of the other actors hold masks to their faces in playing notable figures in Nixon's life (such as his cousin Jessamym West) and many of his adversaries and associates (including Helen Gahagan Douglas and Murray Chotiner, Nixon's "evil genius"). At key moments, "the American people," a row of stuffed dummies, are wheeled out to show how submissive the American electorate is, whether offered Nixon, Kennedy or Eisenhower. Every major event in Nixon's life prior to 1972 is presented: childhood, college, the navy, early elections, Alger Hiss, Stevenson, the *meleé* in Venezuela, *Six Crises* and Nixon's telling Ike "to piss or get off the pot" when the latter was dallying in his choice for vice-president. Virtually all of the major figures and many of the minor ones are included, even Martha Mitchell, played by Susan Sarandon in her Broadway debut.

The cavalcade ends with the answer to "who cut down the cherry tree": Kennedy promptly replies, "Nixon did." Finally, Ike says: "Now we gotta be fair about that one. We ... uh, we all did!"

The grace note that ends the play does not overcome the all-enveloping aura of excoriation that preceded it. Choosing Nixon's own words to self-incriminate succeeded in making Nixon sound pompous and fatuous, one of Vidal's intentions to be sure, but pomposity and fatuity can make a tedious evening.

What follows is a sampling of critical opinion:

"As diversion for pros and cons, *An Evening with Richard Nixon* possesses two principal flaws. The first is that it goes on too long, like an overextended revue sketch. The second is that Mr. Vidal has failed to learn from Shaw that sprightly debate demands well-matched protagonists." — John Beaufort, *Christian Science Monitor*, May 5, 1972.

"It merely seems petty. We already know [Vidal] doesn't like Nixon, Kennedy or American foreign policy, and he simply restates it without forcefulness." — Richard Watts, *New York Post*, May 1, 1972.

"[The] work is charged with the non-energy of a very simple assumption: that Nixon is a silly mediocrity, a contemptible figure of fun, absurd. Intoxicated with that disdain, [the] work goes wrong, badly wrong. Vidal's play falls limp with a vapid sneer." — Stephen Koch, *World (Saturday Review)*, August 1, 1972.

"Satire was invented to give polemics entertainment value. Otherwise, an argument would have no value in moving from the rostrum to the stage. Gore Vidal seems to have forgotten this in writing *An Evening with Richard Nixon* instead of writing satire, he has mounted a diatribe, humorless, relentless, abusive. In the end, it is not theater but a harangue." — Martin Gottfried, *Women's Wear Daily*, May 2, 1972.

"Blame television for *An Evening with Richard Nixon* because the talk shows encouraged author Gore Vidal to become the William Buckley of the liberals. Yet what works on David Frost — an impressive grasp of facts, an air of polished superiority, a skill at putting down — doesn't necessarily work on the stage.... [T]his lawyer's and debater's game, where facts are used to score points rather than to seek truth, has limits in the theater, particularly when you're dealing with a man like Nixon who plays it himself.... After the first act, I left, having had enough of its prissy, mean spirit. To bridge the gap between gossip and theater, [Vidal will] have to create some perspective." — Dick Brukenfeld, *Village Voice*, May 11, 1972.

"[Nixon] is, after all, part of history's comedy, and history is serious. I therefore found all he said in Gore Vidal's transcription fascinating and frequently funny. The historical content from the man's green youth through to his present high estate is rapidly processed, the montage witty, the staging by Edwin Sherin sufficiently deft and George Irving's impersonation amusing. The total account is summary, based — the basic attitude disheartened, but the picture on the face of it befits the facts. Contemporary politics in general is a self-made mockery — to some a comedy, to others a tragedy. In any case, for all its frivolity, *An Evening with Richard Nixon* has more substance than most of the 'art' Broadway now has to offer." — Harold Clurman, *Nation*, May 22, 1972.

"[A] Broadway that sorely needs political theater here takes a necessary if unsteady step in the right direction ... [George S. Irving] gives us a Nixon that goes beyond brilliant impersonation into great acting: caricature carried to the depths of insight. At least Vidal has explained Nixon: the suitably styleless boss of a nation of shopkeepers." — John Simon, *New York*, May 15, 1972.

"[T]edious ... an almost resolutely non-theatrical piece ... Vidal's entertainment, if you can call it such, is designed to present the man as a buffoon grown increasingly dangerous.... [W]hen Vidal says, as he did in an interview that he's not interested in theater, I'm inclined to take him at his word ... [this play] is like riffling through a stack of old newspapers, a political satire lacking bite." — Douglas Watt, *(NY) Daily News*, May 1, 1972.

"Actor George S. Irving's brilliant caricature of the President is hilarious; even Spiro Agnew wouldn't vote for this Richard Nixon. With his masterful exaggeration of the President's mannerisms, Mr. Irving can make the audience laugh a dozen times just while reading a list of the cities visited on a campaign tour. But as hard-hitting satire, Mr. Vidal, bad intentions are not enough." — Roger Ricklefs, *Wall Street Journal*, May 2, 1972.

"Vidal's avowed purpose is to prove that Nixon 'is a conscienceless fraud'; but his charade of press clippings only proves that anyone can become president. What finally emerges is hardly a satire on a small President, but rather a dark but effete arraignment of a big system. The demoralization of an intelligent man like Vidal is the most significant thing about his play." — Jack Kroll, *Newsweek*, May 15, 1972.

"Gore Vidal is a dramatist who wants to look daring without daring much. Like Emile de Antonio and Philip Roth he has produced an anti–Nixon polemic whose effect — at best — is to make anti–Nixonites feel better about themselves. The result is an ungainly, superheated pageant..." — Stanley Kauffmann, *New Republic*, May 27, 1972.

"Gore Vidal has written a needle-sharp and exceedingly funny pasquinade ... I share most of [Vidal's] political opinions, and the result is that his incessant savaging of Nixon gave me great pleasure. In Vidal's view, Nixon is a man devoid of any principle — or even motive — save that of running for public office and winning by whatever means happen to be in his grasp. A terrible indictment." — Brendan Gill, *New Yorker,* May 6, 1972.

"[Vidal] offers a nonstop diatribe, vitriolic and at times caustically amusing. Nixon is so one-sided that it has the curious effect of creating a certain sympathy for its leading character. George S. Irving does a superb imitation in the role. Vidal vows that he will now abandon playwriting. Thanks for small favors." — T. E. Kalem, *Time*, May 15, 1972.

"The piece has a heavy-handed manner despite a lot of smart aleck cracks, no

one of which seemed to amuse more than a half-dozen spectators. Ed Sherin directed
... as though it were a malicious high school pageant."— William Glover, *Associated
Press*, May 1, 1972.

"It may seem odd to object to the startling lack of *seriousness* in this comedy. But
there is in it a depressing political complacency, a giggling underestimation of the man,
a painfully familiar smugness for which we — all of us — have to pay a heavy price. We
are not talking about the buffoon in Roth's cute cartoon, or the Nobody Vidal wishes
us to snobbishly brush away beneath the TV lights. We are talking about an endlessly
shrewd and deeply troubled human being who has made himself the most powerful
man in the world."— Stephen Koch, *World (Saturday Review)*, August 1, 1972.

On May 22, 1972, columnist Leonard Lyons (*New York Post*) stated that *An
Evening with Richard Nixon* would be a TV special just prior to the election; the *Daily
News* (April 16, 1972) reported that Ode Records would record the play; *Variety* (June
20, 1973) stated that Vidal had re-written parts of the play and that Hillard Elkins
would present the new version in the fall. None of these things happened. It closed at
a loss of its entire $180,000 capitalization.

The Nixon Years: Change Without Chaos (resume campaign film, 1972)

Produced by David Wolper for the November Group. Directed by Alex Grasshoff.
Narrated by Richard Basehart.

The Nixon Years: Change Without Chaos did not take partisan positions because
it was aimed at those who might split their tickets. As usual, documentary footage was
used together with scenes created for theatrical effect. Grainy black-and-white footage
of social unrest gives way to vital color shots of Nixon speaking about law and order.
To create a well-rounded portrait, he is also shown playing the piano for Duke Ellington at the White House. Other scenes show Nixon's vision and compassion, and the
film gains strength from the resonant voice of screen actor Richard Basehart and a
forceful script filled with well-chosen verbs and the pinpointing of specifics such as
the treatment of minorities and the state of the economy. Thus, *The Nixon Years:
Change Without Chaos* is both a resume and an agenda. It showed what Kenneth
Jamieson in his 1984 *Packaging the Presidency* said a campaign film must show: courage,
vision, engagement, decisiveness and a willingness to look at all major issues in all their
particulars.

A 15-minute version played at the Republican convention; a half-hour version
played on CBS–TV on October 14 as paid programming. (Film on videotape at the
National Archives, Alexandria, Virginia.)

Richard Nixon: Portrait of a President (biographical campaign film, 1972)

Produced by David Wolper for the November Group. Directed by Ed Speigel.
Originally entitled *Nixon, the Man*.

Nixon advisors Haldeman and Erlichman told Wolper what to include in both 1972 campaign films. Since it is a biographical film, *Richard Nixon: Portrait of a President* deals with the President on a more personal level than most campaign films. There are interviews with Tricia, Julie and such Nixon associates as Leonard Garment, Robert Finch and Erlichman. We hear about Nixon as a poor boy growing up and learning about life through adversity, hard work and championing American freedoms. Essentially it is a film in which Nixon enthusiasts do all the talking for him. (Film on videotape at the National Archives, Alexandria, Virginia.)

Pat Nixon: Ambassador of Good Will (TV film, 1972)

30 minutes. With Pat Nixon and Fay Gillis Wells (writer and interviewer). Produced by Storer Broadcasting. WJBK–TV Detroit and WPIX–TV New York, April 1, 1972.

Mrs. Nixon recounted "her travels as a goodwill ambassador to Ghana, Liberia, Peru, China and Russia — with graphics from those forays in the form of clips from newscast footage. Mrs. Nixon was predictably diplomatic and gracious in her references to the peoples of the countries she visited..." — *Variety* December 6, 1972.

The Making of the President, 1972 (TV documentary)

80 minutes. Produced by Al Wasserman for General Mills. Written by Theodore H. White as adapted from his 1973 publication of the above title. Broadcast Sunday, May 25, 1975, at 9 P.M., WNEW–TV, New York. (Note the telecast date).

"It is amusing to reflect that only a couple of years ago the networks were afraid to air this soft and superficial telementary on the Nixon-McGovern campaign of 1972 based on Theodore H. White's prizemaking book series."
It took a couple of years to find a sponsor for this by-then unpromising TV documentary on what *Variety* called "this final curtain assessment of the most venal Administration in American History."
"White is a pop journalist of *Reader's Digest* stripe and in no way could a viewer expect a deep and hard look at ... so incredibly corrupt a Chief Executive." — *Variety*, May 28, 1975.

The Selling of the President (musical comedy, 1972)

In two acts. Written by Stuart Hample and Jack O'Brien. Music by Bob James and lyrics by Jack O'Brien. Based on the book of the same name by Joe McGinniss.

Costumes by Nancy Potts. Musical direction by Harold Hastings. Special effects by Mort Kasman. Produced by John Flaxman and Harold Hastings. Shubert Theatre, New York, opened March 22, 1972. Cast: *Senator George Mason* Pat Hingle; *Grace Mason* Barbara Barrie; *Irene Jantzen* Karen Morrow; *Ward Nichols* John Glover; *Johnny Olson (M.C.)* Johnny Olson.

"The medium is the message and the masseur gets the votes." — Joe McGinniss.

Accompanying the libretto of *The Selling of the President* at the New York Public Library Lincoln Center is a note from co-author Jack O'Brien: "I enclose a copy of the rehearsal script for *The Selling of the President* with my apologies for not responding to your gracious request sooner. I suggest no restrictions on access, and must add, somehow that since I can not foresee a considerable interest in this sadly maligned project, such restrictions seem somewhat needless in any event." In an interview for this book, O'Brien's collaborator Stuart Hample also revealed his disappointment at the show's reception as revised by two later authors. As it is, the rehearsal script has virtually nothing to do with the musical's source, a slash-and-burn satire of the same name by journalist Joe McGinniss, best known as the author of several controversial non-fiction best sellers. Other than the title and the facts that, like Nixon, the presidential candidate has a two-syllable name with the same last syllable (Mason) and the overall theme of ruthless media manipulation, the book's "hilarious and gruesome" spirit (Joseph Heller) is entirely missing in this Broadway adaptation.

McGinniss's original intention was to show the image-making technique of both the 1968 presidential candidates, but Hubert Humphrey's advisors, perhaps smelling journalistic opportunism, warned against it. Eager for any coverage possible, Nixon's staff agreed and the result for Nixon and his media consultants (including such savvy telecasters as Frank Shakespeare and Roger Ailes) is that they appear as anything-to-win zealots. After the book's publication, McGinniss was accused of deceiving the Nixon camp for the harsh portrait he had presented. The 26-year-old author had followed the Nixon group for five months, and his journalistic instincts for the telling phrase, gesture and incident form a riveting volume re-enforced at the end by some of the manipulative campaign scripts that had been in the process of creation in the scenes McGinniss had re-created in the earlier sections of the book.

In October 1969, the slim but potent work began a seven-month tenure on the best seller list, for four of which it was the most popular book in the country. Its "inside take" on the politicians' latest stratagem, enlisting television as the major source of "selling" a candidate, fascinated the public. With the book's name recognition and phenomenal commercial track record, the idea of a Broadway musical seemed daring and very much a part of the unrest to be tapped by the Vietnam era when government had become more and more an object of criticism, even scorn; such a show was a very "now" thing to do.

The show began promisingly enough in April 1971 at San Francisco's Geary Theater, produced by the American Conservatory Theatre and directed by Ellis Rabb. The time frame was jumped ahead to 1976. In the original script, Mason won the election but was assassinated by a pistol hidden in a TV set. (Death by television?) His vice-president Kenesaw Mountain Dixon then becomes president. Stanley Eichelbaum of the *San Francisco Examiner* pronounced it "a sorry mishmash" and said there was "little hope for its future." However, Daine Knickerbocker of the rival *Chronicle*, much more encouraging, enthused that it was "satiric, sardonic and surprisingly funny as it

Karen Morrow as a political advisor and Pat Hingle as Senator Mason (Nixon), who is vying for the White House, in *The Selling of the President*, a 1972 Broadway musical (Martha Swope photo).

turns an unblinking light on television's selective hypocrisy." In short, what is called "a money review."

  After some revision, the show began a pre–Broadway tour with a three-week stand at Philadelphia's Shubert Theater with Pat Hingle and Barbara Barrie as the Masons and Karen Morrow a hard-driving advertising executive. *The Philadelphia Inquirer*, formerly

McGinniss's home paper, was also encouraging: "The effect looks eminently worthwhile, for the show has an original structural concept and an impressive amount of talent on the stage."

An announcement in one of New York City's neighborhood papers, *Our Town* (January 28, 1972), called it "an electronic vaudeville," a term very much of the moment: the cynicism of the book coupled with the dazzle of state-of-the-art Broadway technology, the new kind of show Broadway was waiting for. But it did not happen. Instead, almost total rejection ensued and the bubble burst to a ringing chorus of disapproval. Decades later, Stuart Hample and other members of the creative team were still smarting.

A look at some of the reviews should suggest some of the reasons. For one thing, there was no play to speak of. As *Variety* said (March 1, 1972) in its "shows out of town" review, "*President* spends over two hours trying to show how a presidential candidate is marketed by an ad agency in much the same manner as deodorants, detergent or any other product. At times it almost succeeds, but not very well, considering there is no other action or thrust in the play.... [I]t is a one-gimmick, and basically one-joke show."

Martin Gottfried's review in *Women's Wear Daily* (March 23, 1972) is more to the point: "The [writers] have not even adapted the book in the simplest sense of making the show about Nixon" as McGinniss described him: "grumpy, cold and aloof." Gottfried went on, "[Nixon] could claim privately that he lost elections because the American voter was an adolescent whom he tried to treat as an adult. But if he treated the voter as an adult, it was an adult he did not want for a neighbor." But such a musical comedy portrait prior to such dark-hued shows as *Sweeney Todd*, *Evita* and *Assassins* and other on-the-edge, breakthrough "concept musicals" would have been unthinkable in 1972.

One of the points commented upon by every critic was the fact that none of the three principals ever sang, even though Barbara Barrie and Karen Morrow were excellent singers and Pat Hingle could more than get by. As *Variety* pointed out, "the members of the chorus sang well. They have to, since this is a musical in which the principals do not sing at all"; and virtually every musical number was a commercial, not one of which is relevant to the slim story or character revelation. Nor did the songs make sufficient satiric points because they were not presented wittily enough. Furthermore, satire must be rooted in some kind of truth or it does not succeed. Until that point and for decades after, other than campaign songs such as Irving Berlin's "I Like Ike," no presidential candidate was ever so desperate a hawker of his presidential qualifications that he made singing commercials.

This concept, stretched over two hours, led to serious problems, upon which reviewers commented freely. (Note: The opening night performance was an hour and three quarters, but, according to *Variety*, "seemed longer.")

The problem as George Melloan saw it (*Wall Street Journal*, March 24, 1972) was that "*Selling* falls into [a] trap as a satire of TV advertising. *A musical must sell itself* (italics added) to its audience. But if the audience is first warned that the big chorus numbers they are to hear are part of a phony sales pitch, how can they be expected to be receptive to the numbers as entertainment? *Selling* becomes a satire of itself. It's not a very promising formula. Finally, and perhaps most serious of all, a great flaw ... is its lack of any sense of humanity."

A problem that Douglas Watt of the *Daily News* (March 22, 1972) discussed was the musical's inconsistency of tone. The audience could not tell what was supposed to be funny and what was not. Many of the commercials were "undeniably slick," but "they get out of hand" and some numbers are "not meant to be satiric." The audience is further disquieted when the subject is patriotism; even in 1972, middle-class and middle-aged Americans were not quite ready to laugh at patriotism, especially since Mason is not the Nixon of the book but a comfortable old shoe kind of guy with a sweet and pretty wife. In conclusion, Watt said the show clearly "strikes a sour note. I don't know that this is exactly the moment ... for a derisive musical about our highest office."

As co-author Stuart Hample said to the present author (who, incidentally, was one of the few people to see *The Selling of the President* during its brief Broadway run): "Nobody really had the guts to try to make it good, and we had litigation involving a real commercial about a pest control spray stuck into the show in order to meet the backing the producers needed. That caused a lot of anger."

But worse was to come. George Oppenheimer (*Newsday*, March 23, 1972) called it "a parody of a parody" and Walter Kerr (*New York Times*, April 2, 1972) called it "a musical of staggering ineptitude." One of the few critics who defended it did so by saying it "opened at the Shubert last week and promptly closed again after five performances; but it was not really that bad" (Julius Novick, *Village Voice*, March 30, 1972). Novick's major point was that "we need political satire, we need all we can get ... [T]he failure of *The Selling of the President*—a failure of talent and courage, as well as a failure at the box office puts a fine opportunity to waste." The death blow was the last paragraph of the *Variety* review after it insisted on beating a dead horse: "Under circumstances like this, it's sometimes considered sporting to omit the names of the leading players. They presumably read the script and heard the numbers, however, and nobody forced them to become accomplices. Also, they're being paid, however briefly." This is an extremely harsh criticism for the three leading performers who acted to the very best of their considerable abilities characters that, unfortunately, by design were almost impossible to act. As George Melloan observed, "A fairly strong case could be made that television and other mass media are more successful at exposing the foibles and failures of politicians than in promoting their careers or strengthening their power. There is nothing wrong with taking the contrary view, but in order for such a view to make good theater it has to be presented in at least a partly convincing way.... To the extent that it is possible the characters treated most sympathetically are [Mason] and his bumbling wife. The rest is all charade."

Sensing failure very early on, the producers opened a week early because the previews were so poorly attended that, if need be, the closing notice could be posted the first weekend, rather than the second, thereby saving a week's expenses. The show closed at a $600,000 loss on a $500,000 investment.

In sum, the show failed because it deserved to fail, but, if nothing else, it contained an unforgettable performance by Barbara Barrie as someone clearly meant to be Pat Nixon, performed as winningly as any talented actress could possibly perform an under-written character. Her rendering of Grace Mason, who is almost a transparency in the writing, deserves one of the highest places in the theatrical realizations of the Nixon family. It almost justifies this entire ill-conceived venture. As Leo Mishkin said in *The Morning Telegraph* (March 24, 1972), "I think I would vote for Barbara Barrie for the highest office in the land... She seems much more sensible and is certainly much more appealing than anybody else around."

Watergate (music suite, 1972)

Music by Ernest Bacon (1898–1990), libretto by John Edmunds, performed on Station KPFA, Berkeley, California on November 2, 1972. There are two versions of the script in the Bacon papers at the Music Library at Lincoln Center. Selections are entitled "Nixie's Party," "Nixie's Circus," "Nixie," "Watergates" and "Waterbuggers." Bacon was a respected composer, pianist, conductor and teacher whose obituary appears in the March 18, 1990, issue of *The New York Times*.

Sleeper (film, 1973)

88 minutes. Directed by Woody Allen. Written by Woody Allen and Marshall Brickman. Produced by Jack Grossberg. Released by United Artists. Color. Cast: *Miles Monroe* Woody Allen; *Luna* Diane Keaton; *Dr. Orva* Bartlett Robinson.

Sleeper is a spoof on futuristic films. Woody Allen plays an ordinary New Yorker who enters St. Vincent's Hospital for "a lousy operation." When he wakes up after the operation it is 200 years later — 2173. His body has been frozen, and he is engulfed in aluminum foil. The time lapse allows for some lively jabs at the social life and customs of the 20th century such as dietary habits, sexual mores and politics. The 22nd century physicians barrage Allen with questions. They show him a picture of Richard Nixon because they have not been able to identify him. "We have a theory," says one of the doctors, "that he might once have been the President of the United States, but that he did something horrendous."

Kathleen Carroll of the *New York Daily News* said that this successful medium-budget comedy had moments "to be cherished if only because we have so little to laugh about these days."

The Devil and Dr. Noxin (satire, 1973)

Satire by B.H. Wolfe, based on Marlowe's *Doctor Faustus*. A "Lone Wolf Original," published by the Wild West Publishing Company, San Francisco, 1973.

The Devil and Dr. Noxin is apparently a "vanity publication" with no known production history and no body of criticism relating to it. It is the work of a political enthusiast or "junky" whose style lacks grace, wit or insight. Yet, it shows the lengths to which the "voiceless" will go to make their views public. The text is 218 pages, a jumble of various bits of Satanic literature including *Rosemary's Baby*, but it has no illuminating synthesis. Failing that, it remains a kind of pseudo-intellectual diarrhea. For diehard Nixon popular culturists, a (selected) cast list follows with the briefest content analysis of its 14 scenes. The author's word on naming his hero: "The name 'Noxin' first appeared in the San Francisco *Chronicle* during the Kennedy–Nixon campaign of 1969. One of the loyal readers of Herb Caen, the *Chronicle*'s highly popular society columnist, wrote to him suggesting that Nixon's name backwards sounded like a poison and the Democrats could make some use of the circumstance in the political campaign."

Partial cast: Lucifer, Jehovah, Dr. Ralph H. Noxin, Scarlett O'Hara, Good and Evil Angels, Jay Gould (GREED), Jane Austen (PRIDE), Nietzsche (ANGER), W.C. Fields (GLUTTONY), Mae West (LUST, with muscle men), Porky Pig, Jesus Christ, Happy Schmidt a.k.a. Howard K. Smith, Kerry Lampton a.k.a. Murray Kempton, Soviet Premier Nikolai Boobikov, Alton Crankshaft a.k.a. Walter Cronkite, of the Society of Satan and others *ad infinitum*.

What follows is a summary of scenes:

ACT I, SCENE 1— To a burst of Handel's "Hallelujah Chorus," Jehovah appears and talks to Dr. Noxin, who has "a dread of death."

ACT I, SCENE 2— Alone in his study, Noxin craves power. He wants to call up the Devil in order to gain it.

ACT I, SCENE 3— Jehovah tells us Noxin has given up his practice to study the black arts.

ACT I, SCENE 4— The office of banker Simon Greenstone, who is talking to his public relations man Peter Klingle. (They are meant to be played by imitating Sydney Greenstreet and Peter Lorre.) Greenstone and Klingle are to assist Noxin in his campaign against Congressman Lavoris (Jerry Voorhis), who is called a "mouthwash liberal."

ACT I, SCENE 5— Noxin is alone in his study eating cottage cheese as Lucifer appears. Lucifer tries to make Noxin yield to temptations of the flesh by summoning Helen of Troy and Scarlett O'Hara. Noxin is not interested, but he does want to meet Martha Washington. However, Martha, Lucifer says, "is up there...makin' fudge forever." Noxin has "no thoughts of impropriety."

ACT I, SCENE 6— The Seven Deadly Sins appear, including Jane Austen as PRIDE who kicks her Mammy and says "a little prejudice is a good thing." Noxin is particularly drawn to ENVY. "My life would've been a lot different if the coach of the football team hadn't resented my intelligence. He made me third string because of that. He hated cultured people." Obsessed with ENVY, Noxin says, "I hope to meet him again."

ACT I, SCENE 7— An illustration of how one's name influences the life that is to follow.

ACT II, SCENE 1— A litany to Satan.

ACT II, SCENE 2— Press conference, meant to ridicule Nixon's press conferences. Wolfe's note: "Most of Noxin's lines are taken from transcripts of statements of Richard Nixon."

ACT II, SCENE 3—"The Spot Speech," a spoof of the Checkers speech. Wolfe's note on this scene: "I have no idea what Richard Nixon's true feelings about dogs may be, any more than anyone knows his true feelings about anything ... maybe he likes dogs. He owes his political life to that one."

ACT II, SCENE 4— The bathroom debate. Many of the lines in this scene are clearly derived from the famed "kitchen debate."

ACT II, SCENE 5— An exaggerated rendering of the arguments of the 1960s Nixon-Kennedy debates.

ACT II, SCENE 6— A consideration of Noxin's psyche in prurient terms. Author Wolfe says, "A President who never goes to the bathroom, plays with himself, or makes love, is not even real."

ACT II, SCENE 7—Noxin fails as a Satanist and as a Christian. In Wolfe's view, Noxin (Nixon) "will not save himself until he learns how to reconcile his dualistic nature and become an integrated human being."

As literature or thought, *The Devil and Dr. Noxin* has very little to offer. What it really shows is the self-indulgence that passed for political commentary during a time of great civic unrest. *The Devil and Dr. Noxin* will remain on a few library shelves as a shrill, cacophonous echo of its time. To be successful, satire must have a unity of vision and be much more than a diatribe.

Hail to the Chief (feature film, 1973)

(A.k.a. *Hail*). Directed by Fred Levinson. Original story and screenplay by Larry Spiegel and Paul Dusenberry. Produced by Roy L. Townshend. Music by Trudi Martin. Released by Cine Globe. Cast: *President* Dan Resin; *Secretary of Health* Richard B. Shull; *Attorney General* Dick O'Neill; *Vice President* Willard Waterman; *Reverend Jimmy Williams* James Sirola; *First Lady* Patricia Ripley; *Tom Goodman* Gary Sandy.

The satiric *Hail to the Chief* starts in imitation Billy Graham-style with a pompous eulogy for a Supreme Court judge who has recently been assassinated by young demonstrators. We cut immediately to a second assassination—that of the President of the United States by his best friend, following which, in *Citizen Kane* retrospection, we discover why.

Fred Levinson's satire, according to Jay Cocks in his *Time* review (September 24, 1973), "is structured rather cleverly, as a send-up of John Frankenheimer's *Seven Days in May* (1964), in which a sometimes violent plot was enacted within hailing distance of the White House. Here, the President (Dan Resin) is turning the Secretary of Health's cherished VISTA camps into prisons for political dissenters. 'Not concentration camps,' the President has to reassure his Secretary (Richard B. Shull). 'Detention camps—this is America.'"

The Health Secretary is astounded as the President quickly mutates into a home-grown fascist who attempts to cease all free elections "just this once." The Secretary and the Vice President (played by Willard Waterman, well known at the time for his portrayal of the small town political buffoon on a radio show) join the President's foul-mouthed religious guru Reverend Jimmy Williams and other self-serving political frauds in a plot to literally blast the President out of office. From then on the plot careens on like an out-of-control paddy wagon driven by the Keystone Cops, braking only when the President, during late-night poker games, orders pizza and anxiously adds, "You can't miss it. It's the only house on the block. It's all lit up" or when "Henry" calls from Paris and wants a rush order of cheesecake.

This irreverent farce was made by Wylde Films, a division of Twentieth Century–Fox, more than two years before its release, but in 1971, the impact of Watergate had not been realized and America was not yet ready for a comedy showing the President of the United States as a paranoid dictator. As Watergate began to unravel, the political climate changed, but by that time, Twentieth Century–Fox had sold the rights to another distributor, CineGlobe, a division of TransAmerica. For some, the release of the film turned director Levinson into a prophet. "I don't want the feeling that I exploited Watergate," Levinson told Kathleen Carroll of the *New York Daily News* (July 21, 1973), but the truth is that without Watergate the film never would have been released.

In spite of eventually finding distribution, the film did not do well. Perhaps the humor was too rough, such as the sight of the President walking around with toilet paper stuck to his shoe; the Billy Graham character saying, "In times of distress, prayer is a powerful laxative"; Pat Nixon smoking a cigar and saying, "I wish you'd do something about getting Cuba back"; the President choosing Nazi storm trooper boots for his special police force. But probably the most unsettling of all is the thought that the President and his "good old boys" would consciously create civil unrest in order to turn the country into a dictatorship. It was all too much for a mass audience.

Here's a sampling of critical opinion: "Although the over-all design of their satire is hardly grand, some individual moments are most congenial ... [such as] when someone reminds [the President] of the intentions of the founding fathers when they wrote the Constitution. 'What did Benjamin Franklin know about nuclear capability?' the President asked. 'He had a hard time just getting his kite up.'" — *New York Times*, July 28, 1973.

"It seems to fall somewhere between poor taste and topicality. Moral: for some movie makers, it is safer to be accused of quickie exploitation than of insight or prophecy." — Jay Cocks, *Time*, September 24, 1973.

"Mr. Levinson tends to sacrifice depth for momentary effect, as one might expect from a man with 2,000 television commercials to his credit. The result is tacky and sometimes distasteful." — *Christian Science Monitor*, October 26, 1972.

"The limitations imposed upon him by a low budget are very evident on the screen. The pacing is off. And the satire has a tendency to weigh a little heavy at times, particularly in the scenes showing the surprise attack of the President's police force on a junkyard filled with hippies." — Kathleen Carroll, *New York Daily News*, July 28, 1973.

"*Hail*'s occasional tackiness is certainly appropriate to its subject especially when it focuses on men aping small town Rotary Club camaraderie. One forgives the film its excesses partly because one admires its frequent perceptiveness, partly because we need the release afforded by a revenge fantasy. *Hail* is not quite as devastating as the Watergate hearings, but it had a relatively happy ending, which is more than one can reasonably expect of the real thing." — Howard Kissel, *Women's Wear Daily*, July 30, 1973.

National Lampoon's Lemmings (satirical revue, 1973)

Words and lyrics by P.J. O'Rourke, David Axelrod and others. Music by Paul Jacobs and Christopher Guest. Village Gate — Bleecker Street — Greenwich Village (New York City). Opened January 25, 1973, closed November 25, 1973.

This long-running revue contained a sketch called "Mission Impeachable" showing a Senate hearing in which a Senator asks a witness, "What did the President know and when did he stop knowing it?"

The Watergate Scandals of 1973 (cabaret)

A cabaret starring the Hot Peaches. Opened June 28, 1973, at Peach Pits, 200 West 24th Street, New York.

An amusing topical revue that was, according to Howard Thompson of *The New York Times*, "political camp, dominated by drag but surprisingly clean as such" (7/21/73). It contained "good-natured malice" and was vastly superior to the then-current "television series" (the Watergate hearings). Some of the characters were Zero Agnew, Martyr Mitchell and Tricky Niki who looked "like Ella Raines after walking through a door." There was much discussion of the Pentagon Papers under their new name "the Bent and Gone Papers."

Francis Levy of the *Village Voice* (8/2/73) particularly enjoyed Martyr Mitchell sitting on a toilet trying to call United Press during one of her attacks of acute telephonitis which was followed by her big number "I'm Going Back Where I Can Be Me at the Bonjour Tristesse Brassiere Factory." In a sketch called "Niki's Nursery," Nixon sang, "Caesar, Napoleon, Louis XIV and Me." Levy concluded, "One of the problems of satirizing Watergate is the utterly pathetic nature of the whole caper. It's on such a low level that there really isn't much of an issue."

Tragedy of Richard II (play, 1973)

A satiric stage play by Robert J. Myers modeled on Shakespeare's *Richard II*, apparently unproduced. Published by Acropolis Books, Washington D.C., 128 pages, out of print.

The Tragedy of Richard II, written by the former publisher of the *New Republic*, is a rather academic parody modeled on Shakespeare's *King Richard II*. Its sub-title is "The Life and Times of Richard II (1367–1400), King of England (1377–1399), compared to those of Richard of America in his Second Administration." It is a "conspiracy" play long before Oliver Stone made that element the *sine qua non* of at least two of the presidencies of the late 20th century. Unfortunately, it lacks the raucous irreverence and hard-edged wit of *MacBird*, Barbara Garson's LBJ lampoon (1966).

Characters: King Richard, Queen Pat, Princess Tricia, Duke Agnew, Lord Haldeman, Lord Ehrlichman, (Bill) Bishop of Graham, Sir John Dean, Lord Kissinger, Sir Victor of Gold, Sir George of Bush, Sir Charles of Percy, two gardeners, assorted soldiers and the Clangbird.

ACT I, SCENE 1— King Richard and his cronies, the Lords Haldeman and Ehrlichman, are chortling about their victory over Sir George McGovern, who is "a pool of curdled milk and rancid honey." King Richard assures his drooling lackey, Duke Agnew, that he will succeed him should he, Richard, be felled by an "assassin's arrow" or a bowl of spoiled cottage cheese. After some further gloating among his retainers, Queen Pat quits the Oval Office, saying: "Adieu, King Richard, for a while until / The noon repast is nigh. I hasten now / To set the catsup and the cheese / For just the temperature you please." Lords Haldeman and Ehrlichman throw down their gauntlets against

Duke Agnew, whom they accuse of having "a false and forked tongue." King Richard exiles Duke Agnew for "one year" for his "transgressions."

ACT I, SCENE 2 — A luncheon scene with King Richard, the Bishop of Graham, Sir John Dean and Lord Kissinger in which they discuss what to do with Duke Agnew, "who is threatening a rebellion." Suffused with admiration for King Richard, the Bishop of Graham soldiers on, calling Richard the "guard of morals of the world, a sure hand of justice." He adds, "If virtue slackens in the teeming mass. One knows the consequence. A fiery sword shoved up their ass!" There is much applause and the Bishop of Graham bows to all. Lord Kissinger speaks of his humble allegiance to King Richard: "I have / Forsooth made claim that my role / Doth stem in part from their perception of / My task as cowboy, lone and silent, riding into town. / It's me against the world." Talk turns to Watergate and Lady Graham of the *Washington Post* and her "sneering louts who urinize the news" (Woodward and Bernstein). Richard will take arms against these "sordid scribes." He counsels his counselors: "Harness now the power of my Administration for this o'erdue task. I'll make low who oppose me, leave / Them maimed and torn right where they fall. / Our patience is exhausted. Go!" Much stirred, the Bishop of Graham says: "Spoken like a Royal Christian, Prince of Peace!" Kissinger unctuously adds: "Your firmness is the strength downed guides us all." Sir John Dean tells Richard to seize Duke Agnew's "goods / On this fair earth, appropriate it by the CREEP." Sir John Dean says the traitor Agnew must be "like a suckling pig." Act I ends with Richard, plagued by Watergate, confessing "my sleep's impaired / By sounds of running water. / The plumbers must take prompt repairs."

ACT II, SCENE 1 — Duke Agnew is called a "noble Greek" who has been conspired against. He will march on to "face King Richard," urged on by Sir George of Bush.

ACT II, SCENE 2 — The palace. A mob demands Richard's abdication. Duke Agnew, wearing a mask, leads his fellow maskers, Sir Victor of Gold (named for a Nixon speechwriter) and Sir George of Bush, through a secret tunnel. They are halted by Lord Haldeman. Richard uses high-flown rhetoric to quell Duke Agnew's anger. He does not succeed because he has lost the support of the people. Duke Agnew says: "Well spoken, Liege, except for one, the mob / That now surrounds the Palace is that flower / I first grew in '68, / And watered by Watergate. It is / The cultivation of my time. I am its sum. / It will disperse and homeward wend content again / That this proud house has cleansed itself / Of perfidy." Richard is forced to read grave charges that are placed against him as the roar of the crowd escalates throughout the end of the scene. King Richard is forced to accept the exile he had plotted for Duke Agnew.

ACT III — In the palace rose garden... Two gardeners, Queen Pat and Princess Tricia. In a very short scene, typical of the "falling action" of a Shakespearean tragedy, Queen Pat and Princess Tricia bewail the fate of Richard. Queen Pat: "I make my lonely path / To Richard, ere his enemies begin / What evil action I know, but from / The looks of Agnew and his band, 'twill take / The fire of heaven no less to melt the ice / Around their hearts."

ACT IV — The Tower of London. A very short conclusion to the play. King Richard and Queen Pat are consoling each other. Richard speaks: "Dear Pat, my long and lovely Queen, / How has it come to this? We worked, we saved. / Collected strings and stamps. Yes, bottle tops. / I wore frayed cuffs and you a good cloth coat." Pat: "That Watergate and all its findings cast / Aspersions on your Grace. Once legal cards / Are all played out, the mob takes o'er the game." Sir Charles of Percy and Sir Victor of Gold announce that a "clangbird" "will be the carrier of [their release]," which one assumes, is an airplane about ready to explode going by the name of a creature of fable, thus sustaining the play's parodistic quality by paralleling a *deus ex machina*, a frequent element of Greek tragedy.

Werewolf of Washington (film, 1973)

90 minutes. Directed and written by Milton Ginsburg. *Cast:* Dean Stockwell, Biff Maguire and Clifton James.

A spoof about a presidential press aide who happens to be a werewolf.
"It contains a few isolated gems."—*Real Paper*, December 4, 1973.
"Dean Stockwell as the werewolf is visually perfect, a cross between a young Richard Nixon and David Eisenhower."—*Boston Phoenix*, December 4, 1973.

Watergate Classics (satiric revue, 1973)

Produced by the Yale Repertory Theatre. Sketches and songs by (among others) Robert Brustein, W.A. Mozart, Maury Yeston, Jules Feiffer, Kurt Weill, Cole Porter, Harold Arlen, Philip Roth. Directed by Isaiah Sheffer. Choreography by Carmen de Lavallade. World premiere at the Yale Repertory Theatre, New Haven, November 16, 1973. Cast: Sigourney Weaver, Robert Brustein, Norma Brustein, Frederic Warriner, Jeremy Geidt, Jerome Dempsey, Carmen de Lavallade, et al.

In an essay entitled "Nixon on the Delphi Road" in the *London Observer* of May 13, 1973, Robert Brustein describes a journey he and his wife took through the Greek countryside in order to see the ancient theater at Delphi. Part of their journey meant driving through Thebes, "past Mount Cithaeron and over the Triple Way" where legend has it that Oedipus pulled Laius from his chariot and murdered him after "his stranger-father" had whipped him across the face. There, in the actual settings of the great Greek tragedies, Brustein was struck by the undeniable permanence of their message and their relevance to modern times, specifically to the Watergate era. In *Oedipus Rex*, Oedipus, at the height of power and well-being, discovers that a plague is devastating Thebes. The plague will only be lifted when the murderer of Laius is found. As readers of the play know, he finds the murderer and brutal self-knowledge. Character is destiny. In Nixon's case, a plague of quite another sort had polluted the body politic. Nixon also was at the height of his powers, having won a tremendous victory in the last election. He promised to "take full responsibility" and root out the miscreants who were befouling the nation. "But," as Brustein says, "instead of starting a thorough investigation, he does everything within his substantial power to obscure the truth, probably because, like Oedipus, he may himself be the defiler of the land." Thus a parodistic rendering of *Oedipus Rex* and other great ancient and modern works such as *Hamlet* and *Krapp's Last Tape* formed in Brustein's mind to show the "disintegration of personal honor in American politics."

The Watergate Classics was published in its entirety in a *Yale/Theatre* special issue, winter 1974. The last sketch, Philip Roth's monologue "The President Addresses the Nation" with Robert Brustein as Nixon, had already appeared in the June 14, 1973, *New York Review of Books.* The two-and-a-half hour evening opened with a parody of the prologue to Shakespeare's *Henry V* with appropriate Nixon substitutions also delivered by Brustein: "Oh, for a muse of fire that would expose / The hidden horrors of the White House. / A nation for a stage, Congress to impeach / And judges to redeem the squalid scene! / Then should the sleazy Nixon, like himself / Consume the gifts of CREEP, while at his heels / Leashed in like hounds should Colson, Hunt and Liddy / Crouch for employment." This is followed by "Oedipus Nix," which Brustein admits is "somewhat labored." In it, Nixon refuses to resign or be banished. In an Aeschylus parody, Agamilhous must sacrifice his daughter Iphigejulia, but Agamilhous declares her death "inoperative." Other characters are Kissysseus and Iphigejulie's husband, 25-year-old Ickysauer. In *Samlet,* which includes such characters at Patrude, Claudickus, Ehrilichrantz, Haldenstern and Felonious, the stage "business" in the "closet scene" is not a comparison of two lockets, but two audio tapes "that thy father needs mended." Act II opens with a parody of the "Pirate Jenny" song from the Brecht-Weill *Three-penny Opera,* now transformed into "Pirate Martha," a solo for the Martha Mitchell character (known at the time as "the mouth that roared"). Her closing lyrics are "This is Radio Free Martha / And my ratings are climbing / And you guys are through." A parody of the Western classic *High Noon* appears as "High Shame" with Ms. Mitchie (Martha Mitchell) as the proprietress of the Long Snatch Saloon. She kills Tix (Nixon) for making her "Doc" (John Mitchell) "the laughing stock of our Georgetown block." As he dies, Nixon rolls over and says "Rosebud." In the monologue "Waiting for G," Alvin Epstein, the Lucky in the original Broadway production of Beckett's *Waiting for Godot,* does a jumbled Nixonite rendering of that theatrical milestone, ending in a state of hysteria when he cannot pronounce the name of Nixon's friend Bob Abplanalp. A re-write of Cole Porter's "Anything Goes" proclaims: "And Presidents who once lived by the law / Now openly defy the law, and it shows / Anything goes." "Dick's Last Tape," another Beckett clone, has Nixon fumblingly trying to insert "But it would be wrong" after agreeing to pay hush money to E. Howard Hunt. A parody of the Harold Arlen–E.Y. Harburg "Somewhere Over the Rainbow" was one of the hits of the show, Julie was Dorothy and Nixon was the Cowardly Lion. Julie sang: "Somewhere over the rainbow, way up high / There's a land that you dreamed of, now kiss that dream goodbye." Her song continues, but Nixon has the sketch's last three lines: "If all great Presidents can fly / Above the rainbow / Why oh why can't I?" As noted, the evening ends with Brustein doing a somewhat condensed version of Roth's monologue from the *New York Review of Books.*

The *Watergate Classics* was the work of many hands, all of whom could not be credited. The published version includes a "Watergate Spillover" section of the material that was considered for production but later dropped. As presented, the show was already lengthy, and satire, unless it is consistently clever, tends to lose pace. It is something of a miracle that the show evolved at all. The third production at Yale that season was to be a new translation of Moliere's *The Misanthrope,* but that was picked up for a commercial production instead. Yale Theatre had thought of substituting Brecht's *Arturo Ui* using Nixon and his circle rather than Hitler and company as parallels to the American gangsters who take over Chicago and Cicero, Illinois. The plan was dropped because of possible problems in dealing with the Brecht estate. Yale had already

Robert Brustein as Nixon in *Watergate Classics*, Yale, 1973.

done a satiric evening with Watergate elements under the title *The Bug Stops Here*. With that approach in hand, a full evening was planned. New ideas were gathered, and work began. Some of the country's best-known satirists were asked to contribute (among them Russell Baker, Woody Allen and Art Buchwald), although in the end, they did not participate. As the evening's material grew, Brustein realized that they had more than enough. One of the group's major concerns was whether "history would betray us, invalidating the whole undertaking before it had a chance to open.... As it turned out, Nixon decided to hang in there and let our show open; and since Congress proved too sluggish to impeach him, we couldn't have asked for a better press agent, since the President continued to dredge up revelations that kept the show not only fresh but popular."

The Watergate Classics was a "source of pride" to Brustein and Yale Theatre, brought about by a set of curious chances — his recall of his earlier trip over the Triple Way near Delphi and the sudden gap in his theater schedule, and the fact that he was able to create a new work that showed the validity of ancient themes through their application to modern life. *The Watergate Classics* contained at least one *coup de theatre*: After Brustein gave the Roth–Nixon monologue, the audience filed out under the watchful eyes of armed soldiers. This brought home the point of the play in a startling manner.

In an essay entitled "Can a Parody Be Parodized?", Walter Kerr wrote:

"Philip Roth couldn't do it in *Our Gang*, Gore Vidal couldn't do it in *An Evening with Richard Nixon*, and now a considerable assortment of competent hands haven't been able to do it with the Yale Repertory's *Watergate Classics*. What is 'it'? Parodying the present administration, of course. And it's admittedly a puzzle why subject matter so apparently ripe for a satirical right to the jaw should prove so intractable. Most of the people struggling for an answer will suggest that it's impossible to travesty what is already a travesty."—*New York Times*, December 30, 1973.

Other reviewers noted:

"*Watergate Classics* has something more than just the makings of good drama school entertainment.... [T]he contributors to this session of sass and satire have applied themselves enthusiastically to their appointed assignments. Result: generally refreshing diversion."—*Variety*, December 19, 1973.

"*Watergate Classics* has its ups and downs. There is too much repetition of characters (too many Marthas and Johns). It needs more music and better organization. But the actors (including the redoubtable Brustein) offer their own comic embellishments and the show is blessed with total irreverence. It is an entertaining antidote to the day's news."— Mel Gussow, *New York Times*, November 26, 1993.

Trial of Richard Nixon (play, 1973)

Written by Howard Koch. An unproduced play by the distinguished screenwriter of *The Letter, In This Our Life, Letter from an Unknown Woman* and co-screenwriter of *Sergeant York* and *Casablanca*. Blacklisted by the House Un-American Activities Committee and unable to work for many years, Koch may have used this unproduced play as his way of breaking through the anger of his forced inactivity. The play was announced for production in 1976 under the management of Alan King, the comedian.

Nixon Audio Tapes (1974)

Simulated tapes with Jerry Orbach as many of the voices and Will Jordon as Nixon. Books on Tape, P.O. Box 7900, Newport Beach, California. Announced in *Variety* May 22, 1974. In a telephone conversation in 1996, the company stated that the simulated tapes were contracted but never made.

Note: See the same title in 1996.

The Nixon Tapes (play, 1974)

Adapted and directed by Thomas Sharkey for the Village Players Studio Theater, 441 South Boulevard, Oak Park, Illinois. July 5, 1974. Cast: *Richard Nixon* Robert Tolman; *John Dean* Don Sladaritz.

A four-hour play based on more than a thousand pages of White House transcripts dealing with Watergate and done in a documentary style. A telephone call to the theater revealed that the play had no other productions.

"A cram course on Watergate."—*Chicago Sun-Times* July 8, 1974.

Emperor Nixonoff's New Clothes (puppet play, 1974)

A puppet play by the Poor People Puppets, 111 St. Mark's Place, New York City, April 1974.

"Nixon" is a hand puppet in a ghastly light green with a large nose and bushy black hair and eyebrows. To the delight of some viewers, the Nixon puppet also appeared nude. This is Greenwich Village, and socio-economics rule even in children's theater. This Nixon closed the day care center, the hospital and the toy store. True to the participatory democracy the Village is known for, audience participation was encouraged, and one little girl wanted to know about his noses. "Nixon" said, "I only have one nose, even though I may have two faces."

Very much in the afterglow of the 1960s, the *Village Voice* (May 2, 1974) said, "It's a puppet show for our time."

The Parallax View (film, 1974)

102 minutes. Produced and directed by Alan J. Pakula. Written by Lorenzo Semple, Jr. Adapted from the novel of the same name by Loren Singer. Photography by Gordon Willis. Production designed by George Jenkins. Assistant Director: Howard Koch, Jr. Technicolor. Paramount. Cast: Warren Beatty, Paula Prentiss, Hume Cronyn, Stacy Keach, Sr.

The Parallax View is a curious film that, as the London *Observer* (October 6, 1974) says "leaves us with precisely nothing." It is a grim peeling away of the secrets behind a group of assassins for hire. *Variety* (September 19, 1974) called it "entertaining but unsatisfying." Other critics were not so kind. The *New York Daily News* (July 20, 1974): "True terror and tension can only come when we can imagine ourselves experiencing the peril and frustration of the hero. This movie about a reporter's effort to discover a gang of political killers is so cold and sterile that it prevents any such involvement. The reporter [Beatty] is a loner, a cad and an opportunist. He's so hip he can barely speak a complete sentence." Like many Hollywood political films, it fiddles with conspiracy theories "but is too cowardly to make any direct accusations.... If you fear the American Nazi Party or the American Communist Party, the oil industry or the C.I.A., Henry Kissinger or Ralph Nader, any or all of them might be involved in the mysterious Parallax Corporation" (*New York Times*, June 9, 1974). The film, in essence, has no point of view. It was made simply to stir up an audience, to create paranoia and tap into their hidden fears.

Richard Nixon appears in the film at several points in a graphic five-minute montage which is used as a psychological test for anyone considered for the Parallax Corporation. Nixon is juxtaposed with images of social stability and instability. However, the majority of the photographs are negative; thus, all the photographs become negative. In such a context, the photos of Nixon are meant to have no other effect. The subtext seems to be: Nixon is either in league with such forces as the Parallax Corporation and its policy of murder for hire, or, if not, he should be a suitable target.

White House Madness a.k.a. *The Way He Was* (film, 1974)

A.k.a. *White House Wedding* in the planning stages; not to be confused with the short subject *Tricia's Wedding* from the same director. Directed by Mark Lester. Produced by George Caton. Written by "Sebastian." Released on a limited basis; none of the country's major film archives owns a copy.

In May 1995, GOP presidential hopeful Philip Gramm of Texas was revealed as one of the investors in a "sexploitation" film about Richard Nixon entitled *White House Madness*. Knowledge of Gramm's investment came about because in 1984 Gramm attacked his Senate rival Lloyd Doggett for accepting an unsolicited contribution from a gay political group. About the same time, Gramm's supporters, previously in the dark, learned of Gramm's attempted 1974 investment in the R-rated sex and violence melodrama *Truck Stop Women*. Gramm, wishing to preserve his mien of probity and purity, begged producer George Caton (his former brother-in-law) not to disclose Gramm's investment in a later production, *White House Madness*, a venomous attack on Richard Nixon and his family. By 1995, Caton was no longer willing to evade the truth.

In brief, in 1973, Gramm was anxious to invest in Caton's film *Truck Stop Women* which was already in production with the investment fully subscribed. Disappointed, Gramm asked to be cut into Caton's next project *Beauty Queens*. Caton: "It was a sexploitation of beauty contests, how all the beauty queens are screwing the contest judges to win. Phil had read the script and he loved it" (*New York Post*, May 18, 1995). Gramm invested $7,500 under a partner's name because he said he was considering running for office.

In the winter of 1974, Watergate became a very hot topic, and *Beauty Queens* was dropped and a feature-length sequel to *Tricia's Wedding*, entitled *White House Wedding*, was planned instead. Caton said that Gramm "was more excited than ever and wanted to put in more money." The film went into production with the $7,500 Gramm had hoped to invest in *Beauty Queens*. Caton stated that Gramm knew the new film would be a degradation of Nixon and his wife and children. When the film was released, the *San Francisco Chronicle* (March 1975) called it "a vilifying defamation." The film was a financial dud, and Gramm lost his entire investment which could not have been a small setback for Gramm since at the time he was a professor at Texas A&M.

Sidney Blumenthal, writing in the *New Republic* of June 19, 1995, called *White House Madness* "unspeakable, but [it] speaks (often profanely) for itself." Unable to contain himself, Blumenthal, who more usually writes for the *New Yorker*, goes on to say: "The movie Phil Gramm hoped to profit from is more than a nasty, puerile and relentless attack on the man he voted for and eulogized. It ridicules the office of the presidency, religion, the legal system and the military. It deliberately offends conservative sexual mores, shows marriage and parenthood to be hollow jokes and is filled with scenes of transvestitism and bestiality."

Blumethal is one of the few people who actually saw or will admit to having seen this misbegotten film, and from the tenor of his writing he did so with a missionary's all-purging zeal. His scorn for this enterprise takes no prisoners. A few of the "highlights" should give a sense of its squalor: Nixon keeps incriminating tapes hidden in the stomach of Checkers, now stuffed and hidden in a White House closet where he speaks to Nixon in taped messages, some of which are quite sexual. Bebe Rebozo kidnaps Checkers and puts him in the Watergate Hotel. Nixon is grief-stricken and instructs Haldeman, Ehrlichman and Mitchell to find Checkers. Meanwhile, Nixon gives a wild party with a drag queen in Carmen Miranda garb, and back at the Watergate Nixon's three emissaries send Checkers to doggie heaven. In other scenes, Kissinger and King Faisal of Saudi Arabia have a shoot-out in the Cabinet Room, Nixon opens a fast food restaurant called Dick in the Box, Billy Graham has Nixon tied to a bed, and Nixon speaks to a mummified Eisenhower. There are many other scenes of even more sophomoric grossness, but these vignettes should suffice. Blumenthal was quite right, *White House Madness* is "unspeakable," and all the more so because it was partially financed by a man who sought the nation's highest office himself.

The Tragedy of King Richard: Shakespearean Watergate (pastiche, 1974)

Written by Dana Glenn Bramwell, Survey Publishers, Salina, Kansas. Cast: Mitchell, Nixon, Haldeman, Dole, Dean, Grey, Kissinger, Inouye, *Washington Post* editor, *Washington Post* reporter, Satan, Ervin, Agnew, Cox, Ziegler, Jaworski, Sirica, St. Clair, Gerald R. Ford.

A clever parodistic rendering of Nixon's political life, Bramwell's play has no apparent stage history.

What follows is a summary:

ACT I, SCENE 1— The White House. Nixon's ambition as a parallel to that of Macbeth. Nixon's lines: "Plots I have laid, inductions dangerous / By hecklers, dirty tricks, libels and slanders" set the fast pace that follows.

ACT I, SCENE 2— Nixon says: "Haldeman, a word with you. [Draws him aside.] Ehrlichman hath sounded Dole in our business / And finds the man so honest / that we must replace him / As head of our Committee to Re-Elect the President. / See that it is done."

ACT I, SCENE 4—*Washington Post* office. A reporter prophesies that "this great nation [will] come to peace when Nixon is impeached."

ACT I, SCENE 5— Florida White House. Nixon is alone thinking of "legitimate charges I must have ... quashed."

ACT I, SCENE 6— The White House. In an odd pairing, Haldeman and L. Patrick Gray (acting FBI Director) become Hamlet and Polonius. Gray says Haldeman is "still harping on those letters." The first half of the scene ends with Haldeman saying, "These tedious old fools — if he did not burn the letters then all is lost." Kissinger and Nixon enter arguing over the Vietnam War. Nixon: "If on the tenth day, there be no peace we will bomb Hanoi, with you in it."

ACT I, SCENE 7—*Washington Post* office. The Editor says, "To be maligned by a fool [Agnew] is complimentary. Then when we attack Nixon our stature will be greater in the eyes of this nation after Agnew is removed."

ACT II SCENE 1— San Clemente. Nixon discusses Archibald Cox (first Watergate special prosecutor) using Macbeth's speech on Duncan. "This Cox hath borne his faculties so meek, hath been so clear in his office, that his virtues will plead like angels." Later in the scene, Nixon convinces Haldeman and Ehrlichman that Agnew is their enemy. Nixon concludes the scene by saying: "Agnew, thy honor's flight if it find heaven, must find it tonight."

ACT II, SCENE 2—Agnew has a press conference in which he wails, "Who are they that complain unto the people that I forsooth am dishonest and love them not?"

ACT II, SCENE 3—Haldeman's office. In a most oleaginous manner, Haldeman placates Agnew: "Tomorrow at ten o'clock, we can fit you in between the labor leaders and the Ambassador from Liechtenstein."

ACT II, SCENE 4—The White House. Nixon to Agnew: "Resign thyself to the fate which awaits you. From Nonentity I brought you, to Nonentity you go."

ACT III, SCENE 1—Camp David. A clever pastiche of *Richard II*, *Hamlet* and *Macbeth*. Nixon echoes Claudius' speech on his guilt ("My offense is rank"). It continues: "What if this hand were thicker than itself with payoff money?" Mitchell says: "His [Agnew's] absence, sir, lays blame upon him," but Agnew appears like Banquo's ghost and causes Nixon to register high octane paranoia. The entire assembly is dumbfounded as Ehrlichman says: "Sit, worthy friends, the President is often thus and hath been since the election." Continuing Lady Macbeth's lines, Ehrlichman says: "This is the very painting of your fear. This is the air-dawn lie which led you to dismiss Agnew." After witnessing the President's fit, John Dean says: "Good night and better health attend the President." In a murderous mood, Nixon says, "I will have revenge. They say dirt will have dirt. Tapes have been known to be erased, but speak again, Aides, … senators and prosecutors and newsmen … there's not one of them but in his house I keep a wiretap on."

ACT III, SCENE 3—Cox's office. Cox gains Dean's promise to testify against Nixon.

ACT III, SCENE 4—Pentagon. Nixon comes upon Ehrlichman, Dan and Haldeman who represent witches or tempter figures. They gloat at his fall from a once-great height. Nixon demands visions of the future because he is afraid that Kissinger will have a greater place in history.

ACT III, SCENE 5—The Senate rooms. Dean gives Polonius's lines on Hamlet's madness: "The President's mad. Mad I call it, for to define true madness but what is't to be nothing else but mad?" Ervin (Sam Ervin, Chairman of the Senate Watergate Committee) demands proof of Nixon's guilt. Dean promises it.

ACT III, SCENE 6—Florida White House. Haldeman speaks Lady Macbeth's lines recriminating Macbeth (Nixon) for showing fear. "My hands are of your color, but I shame to wear a heart so white. I hear a knocking at the south entry. Retire we to our chamber. A little lying clears us of these deeds."

ACT IV, SCENE 1—Prosecutor's office. Cox asks for evidence, but Haldeman says he has none. Haldeman and Ehrlichman use some of the equivocating lines of Rosencrantz and Guildenstern. Cox, tired of games, says, "Before you leave, you will be subpoenaed."

ACT IV, SCENE 2—San Clemente. A brief discussion of Cox's growing knowledge and power.

ACT IV, SCENE 3—Further Nixon chicanery is discussed by Ervin and Senator Inouye, a member of Ervin's committee.

ACT V, SCENE 1—The White House. Nixon says to Cox: "Do thy worst. You can never prove me guilty. Get out I say. Out! Out! Out!" After he leaves, Nixon says, "Now he must be fired."

ACT V, SCENE 2— Camp David. Nixon and his press secretary Ron Ziegler strategize the Cox firing.

ACT V, SCENE 3— Senate Committee Room. Ervin tries to ferret out the Haldeman secrets. (Lines from *Othello* are used.)

ACT V, SCENE 4— Washington. Ehrlichman and Haldeman discuss conscience. Ehrlichman says: "It is a dangerous thing — it makes a man honest."

ACT V, SCENE 5— Ervin accuses Ehrlichman of lying to protect Nixon.

ACT V, SCENE 6— Florida White House. With lines drawn from *Hamlet*, Leon Jaworski (second Watergate Special Prosecutor) says, "Refrain from fighting and that shall lend a kind of easiness to the next subpoena, the next more easy.... Assume a virtue if you have it not..."

ACT V, SCENE 7— San Clemente. Haldeman and Ehrlichman observe Nixon sleepwalking. Nixon drones, "Erase that tape, put on your clothes, go into the office. I tell you again, you cannot subpoena something that is not here."

ACT V, SCENE 8— Judge Sirica and Jaworski talk like admonishing fathers: Sirica with Polonius's "this above all" and Jaworski on Denmark (*any* nation) "soiling" its "addition" and "achievements."

ACT VI, SCENE 1—*Washington Post* office. Typical "falling action" of a Shakespearean play: "Evidence so damning."

ACT VI, SCENE 2— The White House. The falling action continues. Messenger: "I swear I saw a newsman with a tape."

ACT VI, SCENE 3— Court chambers, suggested by the second scene of *Hamlet*. Judge Sirica: "I'll go straight to listen to the tapes.... Foul deeds will rise though all the earth o'erwhelm them to men's eyes."

ACT VII, SCENE 1— Outside the court. Nixon's madness, the madness of Lear (III, 4).

ACT VII, SCENE 2— Courtroom. The last scene is drawn from *Richard III*, *Macbeth*, *Hamlet*, *King Lear* and *Othello*. Nixon: "My tapes! My tapes! My office for those tapes." Sirica: "Resign, Mr. President." Sirica signals that the tape player be turned on. The tapes are damning. Shock. Consternation. Dismay. Loathing. Nixon is forced to defend himself but to no avail. Filled with pity, the new president says, "Oh, wretched man to lose his position, power, fame" as Nixon is lead away. Ervin ends the play with: "And as the final die was cast / Events portrayed are now the past."

More successful that many satiristic parodies, Bramwell's work has a tighter construction and the benefit of many more sources with memorable lines that provide amusing surprises because of their fresh treatment. As has been so often the case, Nixon is once again the falsely humble, power-mad paranoid endlessly scheming to achieve malevolent, self-serving ends.

Dick Deterred (musical, 1974)

A musical parody of Shakespeare's *Richard III* in two acts by David Edgar. London credits of 1974 as noted in the text published by the *Monthly Review Press* in 1974: "*Dick Deterred* was first produced in February 1974, in a slightly shortened version of this script, at the Bush Theatre, and later moved to the Terrace Theatre, in London. The seven combination roles were played, respectively, by Gregory

Floy, Philip Jackson, Harry Ditson, John Grillo, Robert Bridges, Deborah Grant and Sharon Adair. The director was Michael Wearing, the musical director was Graham Field, the choreographer was Sue Lefton, the designer was Sue Plummer and the lighting designer was Chahine Vavroyan. The doubling plot for the seven actors is 1. Richard; 2. Edward IV, Buckingham, Dighton, Riot Cop; 3. Edward IV, 3, Rackenbury, Ely, Stanley; 4. Clarence, Citizen, Tyrrell, Catesby; 5. Hastings, Murderer, Forrest, Richmond; 6. Anne, Plantagenet, York, 1st Nun, Ghost; 7. Elizabeth, Prince, Martha, 2nd Nun, 2nd Ghost." NEW YORK CREDITS: A Merry Enterprises Theatre, Inc. production. Artistic director: Norman Thomas Marshall. Music by William Schimmel. Costumes by Marla Kaye. Set by Ted Reinert and Beate Kessler. Lighting by Leslie Ann Kilian. Choreography by Mary Pat Henry. Executive producer: Lily Turner. Directed by George Wolf Reily. Opened at the William Redfield Theatre, 354 West 45th Street on January 13, 1983 (a showcase run); remounted as a cabaret performance at the West Bank Cafe Theater, 407 West 42nd Street in late September. Cast: *Lady Anne, Martha (Queen of Washington), Singer* Mary Kay Dean; *Plantagenent, York, a Nun, Singer* Elf Fairservis; *McClarence, Citizen, Tyrrell, Forrest, Stanley* Malcolm Gray; *Lord Hastings, Man* Richard Litt; *Richard* Steve Pudenz; *Brackenbury, Wales, Catesby, a Ghost* Ted Reinert; *Buckingham, a Ghost* Sylvester Rich; *Woman, a Nun, Lady Jackie, Singer* Rhonda Rose; *Murderer, Dighton, Ely, Richmond* Carl Williams.

Songs, Act I: "Gotta Know the Score" (*Richard, Man, Woman*), "Gotta Win" (*Richard, Anne*), "Murderer, Murderer, Murderer" (*Murderer*), "How Many KKK's" (*Plantagenet, Richard*), "Don't Let Them Take Checkers Away" (*Richard*), "You are Bugging Me" (*Forrest, Dighton, Brackenbury*).

Songs, Act II: "Hostess with the Mostess of Them All" (*Martha [Queen of Washington, wife to Hastings]*), "The Buck Stops Here" (*Richard, Buckingham, Hastings, Ely*), "Everlasting Peace" (*Richard, Nuns*), "I'm Leaving" (*Richard, Anne*), "Ghost Song" (*Tyrell, Buckingham, John Dean*), "It's All Over Now" (*Richmond, Anne, Elizabeth, Plantagenent*).

The text was published in 1974 by the Monthly Review Press, 62 West 14th Street, New York, New York 10011 and 21 Theobalds Road, London WCLX 8SL, England.

Prolific British playwright David Edgar (born in Birmingham in 1948) attained international success with the Royal Shakespeare Company production of his eight-hour adaptation of Dickens' *Nicholas Nickleby*. This was a brilliant achievement, one he did not match through any of his own works or further adaptations, although he has had some success in documentary drama. (See *I Know What I Meant* elsewhere in this volume.)

Produced twice in London; *Dick Deterred* was also produced twice in New York, first in a proscenium theater, later in a cabaret. Both New York productions were the work of feisty off–Broadway producer Lily Turner, who was still producing plays at 90 in 1996. Her greatest success was *Jacques Brel Is Alive and Living in Paris*, but her strong suit was social drama starting with Sartre's *The Respectful Prostitute*, a play about moral depravity and racial injustice in the American South in which she cast Ann Dvorak, leading lady in many a Hollywood social drama in the 1930s and 1940s.

"Shakespearean parodies ... are rarely designed as attacks on Shakespeare; instead, his language — which has the authority of genius — is used as a weapon, turned against the follies of a later age." — Jonathan Bate, *Journal of Popular Culture*, Vol. 19, no. 1, Summer 1985.

"[Shakespeare] was writing tragedies — plays about great men destroyed by their own failings. In no case was he revealing anything his audience couldn't have known. And in one case, *Richard III*, he made a dramatically riveting play about the paranoia of power, based on the facts about that king which are almost certainly a pack of lies." — David Edgar, *Stage and Television Today* (Britain), April 16, 1981.

"I rang up the Bush [Theater] and said 'Watergate Richard the Third.' And they said 'wonderful,' and I went back to whatever I was doing. I didn't, in fact, actually read *Richard the Third*, check whether it was going to fit, until the statutory five weeks before the play was due. In fact, it does fit, and it was mainly a mathematical task of fitting the two components together. So essentially form preceded content there." — David Edgar, *Theatre Quarterly* (Britain), Spring 1979.

In *Dick Deterred*, the title character is a corporation lawyer who becomes President of the United States. When the lights come up, he is in the winter of his discontent as he makes moan:

> ...the days I strutted in the sun
> Before I lost the California governorship
> And before I told the gloating press, with quivering jaw
> They'd not have Dick to kick around no more.

Richard's aide Hastings, a self-important schemer, devises a strategy through a group called the Committee to Re-Elect the King (CREEK) to gain Richard another term in office. They are all determined to win by whatever means possible. Their campaign follows the philosophy of: "Fair is foul and foul is fair / There's no distinction anywhere." Their ruthless ambition leads them to the assault against the two boys, the Prince of Wales (the senator from South Dakota) and the Duke of York (the senator from Maine), in the tower of Watergate. The burglars attach electronic devices to various parts of the boys' bodies; they sing at their work:

> If it moves, then bug it
> If it leaks, then plug it.

From then on, a desperate cover-up begins which leads to the battlefield when Richard cries out, "A scapegoat! A scapegoat! My kingdom for a scapegoat!" After being defeated in combat, Richard's corpse is placed in a coffin and the Earl of Richmond gloats:

> You can lock the door
> Lie on the floor
> Swallow the key
> You can break the law
> But God I know
> You won't break me.
> You can mount a guard
> The military
> Take a last bow
> But Richard you see
> It's definitely
> All over now.

Richard rises from the coffin and says, as he grabs the crown, "Wanna bet?"

Mary Kay Dean as Martha and Steve Pudenz as Dick in *Dick Deterred*, Off-Broadway, 1983. Photo: Marvin Einhorn.

Here's a sampling of critical reception of the London production:

"David Edgar's *Dick Deterred* is, like the Shakespeare it parodies, good popular rather than political theatre, because this satirical musical that stars Nixon as Crookback Dick relies on a shared and unchallengeable mutual feeling. The play, which is well-written and witty all through, gets the most out of the incredible facts and two or three scenes — Muskie and McGovern as the princes in the tower, for example, being completely wired up with bugging equipment are unbeatable theatre. It needs to grow a bit more but it's bound to be a good evening out. Nice music too."— *Time Out*, March 1, 1974.

"[Edgar] turns Catesby — a court toady in the original play into an instantly recognizable Presidential press secretary, Ron Ziegler, who complains to his master, 'But, noble lord, I must myself have knowledge of the truth if I am to deny it.' ...In the title role, Gregory Floy looks like a harassed Prince Valiant. But he makes it perfectly clear what's foremost in King Richard's mind: 'Greater love hath none in time of strife, than laying down his friends to save his life.' He directs his henchmen to do a score of criminal deeds —'of which, of course, I am in total ignorance.'"—*Newsweek*, April 4, 1974.

"Mr. Edgar is able to make dramatically convincing the parallels between Shakespeare's anti-hero, with his megalomania and paranoia, and Mr. Nixon. He mixes, with devastating humor, his own Shakespearean parody ('To bug or not to bug, that is the question') and verbatim passages from the original."—*International Herald Tribune*, March 23, 1974.

"The plot fits so closely that it hurts. The waffly, other-worldly Clarence becomes a priestly, prevaricating Eugene McCarthy; Buckingham becomes the ill-fated Haldeman; Catesby a greasy Ron Ziegler. The dupe Hastings goes through successive fall-guy transmutations as Mayor Daly, Archibald Cox and John Mitchell. The wittiest translations of all are Elizabeth and Anne as two cheerleaders. Anne a simple-minded Democrat, and Elizabeth a betrayed Republican, whose sexy torch song 'I'm Leaving' is one of the most striking of the show's 14 numbers."—*Observer*, March 3, 1974.

The May 1, 1974, *Variety* announced that Hillard Elkins, the unsuccessful producer of Gore Vidal's *An Evening With Richard Nixon* two seasons before, planned an off–Broadway production of *Dick Deterred*. Elkins had a short life as a New York producer. It was nine years before Lily Turner brought *Dick Deterred* to New York where it received mixed but generally favorable press.

What follows are critical accounts on the New York production:

"Steve Pudenz is a remarkably good caricature of Mr. Nixon, down to voice and to the very familiar workings of the Presidential face. He leers and conspires expertly, so that the double duty of playing the Watergate figure and Richard III at the same time is executed strikingly."—Richard Shepard, *New York Times*, January 24, 1983.

"Steve Pudenz's King/President Richard is at times frighteningly real. Any physical dissimilarity is overcome soon enough by the marvelous impression and the trademark five o'clock shadow. All the other characters function excellently in their roles; most memorable are Malcolm Gray's Tyrrell (G. Gordon Liddy), who passes a cigarette lighter under his hand when he has nothing else to do, and Sylvester Rich as H.R. (Bob) Buckingham…"—*Clinton Community Press* (New York City), February 1983.

"[Pudenz] manages to suggest not only Nixon's mannerisms but even his face…. Most of the audience found the production hilarious. The one exception was a woman who told anyone who would listen that a great man was being maligned. The rest of those in attendance found her as funny as the parody."—*Backstage*, October 14, 1983.

"Steve Pudenz does an excellent job as Richard. Without actually looking like the character he's portraying, he has picked up remarkably on the facial mannerisms, the walk, the essence of the former President. He seems to have a great time doing so, and his impishness is delightful."—*New York Daily News*, September 26, 1983.

"And what preschooler could not recite a litany of Nixon's mannerisms? The fingers trilling in the air, the hunched shoulders, darting eyes, gravely monotone and five o'clock shadow. As Dick, Steve Pudenz is all this and more, a captivating-man-you-love-to-hate-slimeball. 'I ate at Alice's restaurant' he says, as he tries to ingratiate himself to a hippie."—*Village Voice*, October 4, 1983.

"Steve Pudenz gives the role of Nixon a vaudevillian comic charge. Constantly lurching his shoulders and shifting his eyes, his Richard Nixon impersonation suggests a politician who loves his own skullduggery."—Steve Holden, *New York Times*, October 2, 1983.

I Know What I Meant (TV drama, 1974)

45 minutes. Written by David Edgar. Based on the Watergate tapes and other public statements. Directed by Jack Gold for Granada TV (Britain). Broadcast in Britain Wednesday, July 10, 1974. ITV Network. Cast: Nicol Williamson (Richard Nixon), Bob Sherwood, James Berwick, John Bay and Shane Rimmer.

Nicol Williamson as Nixon in the television drama *I Know What I Meant* by David Edgar in 1974.

Variety (August 24, 1974) gave Nicol Williamson high praise for his Nixon performance, declaring: "Every unctuous inflection, every movement seemed just right, or at the least a socko job of imitating David Frye imitating the President, which is no small trick either."

The show also used the real Nixon on tape and reconstructions. As a result, the show lacked unity; as *Variety*'s review concluded, "By the end, it was hard to know what had been established, who implicated."

On August 15, 1974, a 12-minute segment of *I Know What I Meant* appeared on American television. "Good Night America" host Geraldo Rivera called the presentation "real living theater." Three short scenes were presented with Williamson as Nixon and other actors playing Haldeman, Erlichman, Dean and Ziegler. This was followed by footage of Chief Justice Warren Burger swearing in Gerald Ford as President.

Williamson, before he appeared in *I Know What I Meant*, was the only actor to play Nixon who had actually played in the Nixon White House. On March 19, 1970, Williamson was introduced by President Nixon as the actor described by Prime Minister Harold Wilson as "the best Hamlet in a generation, perhaps in this century." Williamson gave readings from Beckett, Benchley, e.e. cummings and Arthur Miller as well as speeches from *Hamlet*, *As You Like It*, *Richard III*, *The Tempest* and John Osborne's *Inadmissible Evidence*, which Nixon had seen in its film version. With a jazz band back-up, Williamson sang "Baby, Won't You Please Come Home" to a delighted audience of 300 guests in formal attire.

The President's Last Tape (TV drama, 1974)

Written by Philip Magdalany. Produced by BBC–TV; Saturday, June 29, 1974, at 10:25 P.M. Telecast in Britain. Cast: *Nicky, President of the United States* Alec McCowen; *Nicky's Mother* Elaine Stritch.

The British publication *Stage and Television Today* (July 4, 1974) expressed disappointment at the "weakness" of Philip Magdalany's script about an American President called Nicky who faces "imminent impeachment." The narrative thread is a reverie by Nicky's mother, a character who seems modeled on Rose Kennedy. In spite of having such larger than life models, "the characters had little life of their own.... [I]nterest in the play lay in [its] satirical relevance, but this was neither direct enough nor biting enough to hold us."

The point of the play seems not to portray Nixon or Kennedy in any telling way but to advance an attack on the office of the Presidency and "the pressures of America's life style." Nixon appears to have been relatively free of criticism, in spite of Nicky's saying he "tapped every room" in his mother's house. Nixon newsreel footage, headlines and quotations promise a treatment that is not forthcoming.

The Seventh Crisis: Nixon on Nixon (news special, 1974)

60 minutes. With Dan Rather. Produced by John Sharnik. Directed by Vern Diamond. CBS, 10 P.M., January 10, 1974.

Its title an update to Nixon's 1962 book *Six Crises* (to no doubt suggest that Nixon's life was a continuing crisis), this TV special began with shots of the landslide victory of 1972. It was pretty much downhill from there with shots of Nixon explaining and not explaining the convolutions of Watergate. Other topics were Nixon's real estate transactions and the resignation of Vice-President Agnew. The presentation was not skewed in its narration or editing, but all the topics were definitely on the down side.

The program also featured some very unflattering political cartoons including Herblock's showing Nixon crawling out of the sewer. Throughout, Rather, usually strongly anti–Nixon, tempered his feelings and let the topics do their own damage. Rather could not resist a final reference to Watergate's "Saturday Night Massacre" and Nixon's firing of Special Prosecutor Archibald Cox.

White House Transcripts (TV docu-drama, 1974)

90 minutes. Adapted from White House documents. Produced by Thomas P. McCann and Webster Lithgow. Directed by Webster Lithgow. Sunday, October 6, 11 P.M., WNEW–TV, New York. Cast: *Richard Nixon* Harry Spillman;

John Dean Russell Horton; *H.R. Haldeman* Jon Terry; *John Erlichman* Glenn Kezer; *Ron Ziegler* Scott Ricketson; *John Mitchell* Rudy Bond.

This unusual TV drama — a presentation in which, unbeknownst to the audience, the actors read their parts from monitors — received unanimously high praise. *Variety*'s review (December 9, 1974) was an unqualified rave, saying, among its high points, that in a series of "stunning portrayals ... the sustained performances of Spillman as Nixon and Horton as Dean [were] downright uncanny."

White House Transcripts was produced in Boston and first shown in Boston and Toronto in *Variety*'s view this "astonishing" production attained "the eerie reality of the desperate conversations taking place in the Oval Office and the President's executive office."

One of its artful devices was the use of "stop-action at points when the Judiciary Committee's interpretations differed from in the originals in the White House." In spite of the problems of bringing life to such over-exposed material, *Variety* concluded that this was "TV dialog drama at its best."

Here's a sampling of critical opinion (taken from undated press kit material):

"We urge you not to miss it; it will unquestionably be the conversation piece of the month." — *New York Daily News*.

"[A] most engrossing view of what life may have been like in the Oval Office ... it was very well done." — *Montreal Star*.

"[T]he more human side of Watergate ... intriguing. Scenes range from the astonishing to the amusing ... more vivid than ever before." — *Toronto Star*.

[T]he most dramatic use of the tapes ... it *is* educational. And more." — *Dallas Times Herald*.

"[E]xcellently done and one of the best presentations I have ever seen on television." — Al Pacino.

Brother, Can You Spare a Dime? (documentary film, 1975)

103 minutes. Written and directed by Philippe Mora. Produced by Sandy Lieberson and David Puttnam. Released by Dimension Pictures. B/W.

The title comes from a song popular during the Depression and, in essence, it is a portrait of the 1930s in the United States. It is not a traditional documentary because it has no narrative thread, its form being what Stanley Kauffmann in his July 20, 1975, *New Republic* review calls a "compilation film." The effect of such films relies very little on words but rather on its music and images. For the music, we have (among others) Bing Crosby, Rudy Vallee and Billie Holiday. Much of the film — such as the Stock Market crash of 1929, the Dust Bowl, well-remembered movie stars (Loretta Young, James Cagney), Communist infiltration, rioting strikers — works. Thus, as a once-over-lightly social panorama the film is fairly successful, but it falls short in really illuminating its imagery. For instance, in a segment on the CCC, the name behind the letters is never explained, and who but the most socially concerned among succeeding generations will ferret out that it stands for the Civilian Conservation Corps? Walter Reuther of the United Auto Workers is shown bloody and beaten after passing out leaflets at a Ford plant, but he is not identified. One wonders, if this is to be a true portrait of the era, how well is the era really served?

"Apparently, the makers of this film were trying to tell their audiences that history repeats itself, because occasionally clips of Richard Nixon and various fairly recent historical events are interpolated with those matching activities from the Depression."— Michael R. Pitts, *Hollywood and American History*, 1984.

Ain't That a Shame: The Saga of Richard Nixon (musical satire, 1975)

Written by Joseph Renard. Music by Henry Kreiger. Directed by Neil Flanagan. Choreography by Lisa Jacobson. Cubiculo, 414 West 51st Street, New York City, April 18, 1975. Cast: *Nixon* George Wolf Reily; *Kissinger* William Duff Griffin. Other characters depicted include Martha Mitchell, LBJ, JFK, Khrushchev, Checkers, Bob Haldeman, Maurice Stans and Sigmund Freud.

Cue (April 28, 1975) called it "a kicky cross between *An Evening with Richard Nixon* and *Marat/Sade*." This is a loopy Nixon retrospective featuring his early days in Congress, Alger Hiss, Checkers and the entire Watergate Gang as Nixon unburdens himself to Sigmund Freud in a "home for the mentally unusual."

The *Village Voice* critic was quite taken in with it, particularly its novel "take" on Richard Nixon: "George Wolf Reily brings humanity to the role of Richard Nixon, which is more than the man from San Clemente ever did, and that is the secret of *Ain't That a Shame: The Saga of Richard Nixon.* Happily both this superb performer and playwright Joseph Renard have avoided the overwhelming temptation to assassinate Mr. Nixon's character. If a show did nothing more than kick the man around, we would soon lose interest as we did with Gore Vidal's Nixon play…. While this is by no means the last word on Nixon, it's good light entertainment, and with a little work should be a winner."

Katherine (TV film, 1975)

100 minutes. Written and directed by Jeremy Paul Kagan. Produced by Gerald I. Isenberg. New World Video, color, ABC, October 5, 1975. Cast: *Katherine Alman* Sissy Spacek; *Thorton Alman* Art Carney; *Emily Alman* Jane Wyatt; *Bob Kline* Henry Winkler; *Elizabeth Alman Parks* Julie Kavner.

This TV film financed by ABC is an alarming look at the unrest of the 1960s. Its 29-year-old director/writer Jeremy Paul Kagan expressed his intentions in the *Filmmaker's Newsletter* of November 1975: "I did everything possible to tell the truth about the parents of the children of the '60s … I admired the guts of ABC to make this movie." But not for long. After an early viewing, ABC had second thoughts and, fearing controversy, planned to "bury" the film in "the most inconspicuous spot available." However, the arraignment of heiress Patty Hearst (clearly the model for the title character) as a member of a terrorist gang suggested a larger public and the date was changed to prime time.

The film covers the years 1964–1970 in an artful medley of cinema techniques: fast forward, flashbacks, documentary footage of Vietnam and Katherine's talking directly to the audience as she explains the fads and phases of her life. The film also has the benefit of a plot device used in Hitchcock's 1937 film *Sabotage* in which star Sylvia Sidney's younger brother is sent to deliver a time bomb; he is distracted and the bomb kills him. In *Katherine*, Sissy Spacek is chosen to deliver a time bomb set to go off at 9:00 A.M. As Katherine makes her way to the bomb site, a government agent follows her through the streets of San Francisco. She forgets to watch the time, and the bomb kills her. It is during this parallel time of delivery and pursuit that Katherine's life is recounted in flashbacks, punctuated by voiceovers and shots of the political figures of the day (JFK, LBJ and Nixon).

In spite of the fact that it is obviously a doctrinaire film, *Katherine* was considered a work of undeniable merit that, in swift strokes, captured many of the attitudes and catch phrases of a turbulent time as viewers witness the growth of a young terrorist who goes from being a social worker in Peru, a civil rights worker in the South and finally to complete radicalization. It is a spiral that goes from the early Katherine saying "I want to help people," after graduating from college, to the radicalized vehemence of inveighing "against the pig state and its corrupted institutions."

The film is an indictment of our national leaders and middle-class morality, the latter exemplified by Katherine's parents whom Jane Wyatt and Art Carney play as agreeable conformists. As John J. O'Connor pointed out in the *New York Times* (October 19, 1975), "The fact is that the compulsion of Katherine and her non-fiction counterparts to save America 'no matter what the cost' is usually rooted in childish arrogance, an exhibitionist performance of 'Look, Ma, I'm blowing up an institution.'"

Hearts and Minds (film, 1975)

110 minutes. Directed by Peter Davis. Produced by Bert Schneider and Peter Davis. Research by Brennon Jones. Cinematography by Richard Pearce. Edited by Lynzee Klingman and Susan Martin. Color. Warner Bros.

Hearts and Minds caused quite a stir at the 1975 Academy Awards when, after winning the Oscar as the best feature-length documentary of 1974, the film's producers read a telegram from the Viet Cong as part of their acceptance speech. Bob Hope, the master of ceremonies, was furious. Hope's anger was followed by a statement read by Frank Sinatra absolving the members of the Academy from any political statements made during the broadcast. Sinatra's statement was met with hisses and boos by the audience's anti-war contingent.

A few months later, the film's director Peter Davis told the *Christian Science Monitor* (July 24, 1975) that he "wanted to make a film that would be interesting to people whether or not they were for or against a given policy — that would be beyond the

THE WAR RESISTERS LEAGUE
Presents the second in their film series

Peter Davis'

HEARTS
AND
MINDS

It happened in Vietnam and it could happen again in Central America. HEARTS AND MINDS touches on many of the personal and political aspects of the Vietnam War, both in Vietnam and in the U.S. Through interviews with Vietnamese people and U.S. policy makers (including five presidents), a sharp contrast is made conveying the war experience of the two countries.

The illegal arms and "humanitarian" aid the U.S. is funneling to Central America follows the same path that our country took in the intervention in Vietnam.

Peter Davis, the director of HEARTS AND MINDS, will speak after the film relating the film with his new book, "Where Is Nicaragua?"

One Day Only Presentation

MARCH 26 • 7:30
1987   featured at:
PS 41 • 116 West 11th Street
(between 6th and 7th Avenue)

My eight-year-old daughter was killed and my three-year-old son. Nixon, murderer of civilians. What have I done to Nixon so that he comes here and bombs my country? . . . The planes came from over there—no targets here, only rice fields and houses.
**—Vu Duc Vinh
in HEARTS AND MINDS**

Well, the Oriental . . . doesn't put the same high price on life as does the westerner. Life is plentiful, life is cheap in the Orient . . .
**—General William Westmoreland
in HEARTS AND MINDS**

Flyer for the 1975 anti-war film *Hearts and Minds* (revived in 1987 to criticize Reagan's policies.) It features cartoons of Reagan and Nixon and has a scathing quotation on Nixon.

politics of the immediate situation." He wanted "to find out about the Vietnamese," not "Vietnamization" which was the "coverage of the Americans showing the Vietnamese how to run tanks."

"*Hearts and Minds* is the Vietnam film to end Vietnam films, a million dollar Vietnam spectacular" (*Cinéaste*, Fall 1975). The *Nation* called it (April 12, 1975) "an admirably paced, continuously passionate, frequently moving, sometimes shocking, once or twice savagely funny propaganda film…" It contains many shocking scenes: children who have been burned by napalm with their skin falling away; an enemy soldier shot in the head with blood gushing from the wound like a fountain; a New England couple, the Emersons, talking about their son who died on the battlefield: "The strength of our system is that you can rely on President Nixon for leadership." There is a scene of Nixon after the "Christmas" bombing of Hanoi urging a "round of applause for the brave men who took those B-52s and did such a wonderful job." Eisenhower, General Westmoreland, Walt Whitman Rostow and others are edited into the film, all with their special ironies — "Ike" worrying about the loss of tungsten and Westmoreland being more than a little casual about the loss of Vietnamese life. ("Well, the Oriental ... doesn't put the same high price on life as does the Westerner. Life is plentiful, life is cheap in the Orient...").

There are also some comic *cinéma vérité* touches: a high school football coach in Ohio talking about God and Country, shots from the patriotic Ronald Reagan movie *This Is the Army* (1943), and older Americans celebrating the 4th of July (the American Legionnaires and DAR ladies are made to look silly). In short, the Vietnamese come off much better than the Americans who are *cliché*-spouting, self-deluded murderers. And the presidents come off the worst. At least it would seem so in the words of Pentagon Papers leaker Daniel Ellsberg: "Truman lied ... Eisenhower lied ... Kennedy lied ... Johnson lied ... Nixon lied."

Other critical comments:

"[T]he film does not lie. Nevertheless, it manipulates its viewers, as for example when it juxtaposes Westmoreland's notorious statement about the low value Orientals place on human life against scenes of Vietnamese families mourning at the open graves of their beloved dead."— *The Nation*, April 12, 1975.

"It contains probably the most horrendous compilation of war footage ever assembled between two pieces of leader, and for this alone it deserves to be seen, to remind us once more how inhumane a war it really was. It is a film rich in images and details, like the shattered crockery amid the rubble of a bombed out house, or the child's red sandals by the edge of a water-filled bomb crater, or the word 'kill' stenciled on a G.I.'s flak jacket."— *Cineaste*, Fall 1975.

"[A] poor film [because of] its hammerlock on simplicity."— Pauline Kael, *When the Lights Go Down.*

Shampoo (film, 1975)

109 minutes. Directed by Hal Ashby. Written by Robert Towne and Warren Beatty. Produced by Warren Rubecker. Cinematography by Laszlo Kovacs. Edited by Robert C. Jones. Cast: *George* Warren Beatty; *Jackie* Julie Christie; *Lester* Jack Warden.

Shampoo, a black satire of America adrift which had a mixed critical reception but a vast public success, takes place on Election Day, November 4, 1968, and the following two days. Richard Nixon is used as a symbol of the crass materialism that authors Towne and Beatty feel was at the core of American *malaise* after Watergate.

Beatty plays a character named George, a philandering hairdresser to an affluent Beverly Hills clientele. Handsome, charming, not too bright, George is the possessor of a curiously vulnerable naiveté that women cannot resist. To coin a word, he is a *himbo*, a contrast to the film's sly maneuverers, Nixon supporters.

Directed in a brash, free-wheeling style by Hal Ashby, *Shampoo* contains parodies of filmic clichés such as Beatty motorcycling through L.A. with a hair dryer at his
side rather than the more usual phallic symbol of a six-shooter. It also capitalizes on a
famous "inside Hollywood" story, much embellished, no doubt, for prurient interest
that is to be found in at least two books, *Paulette, the Adventurous Life of Paulette Goddard* (1985) by Morella and Epstein and *Opposite Attraction: The Lives of Erich Maria
Remarque and Paulette Goddard* (1995) by Julie Gilbert. The event (sexual in nature,
of course) reportedly took place in 1940 at Ciro's, the popular Hollywood night spot.
As recycled for *Shampoo*, it takes place at a Nixon political banquet while television
commentators report on Nixon's growing strength as he appears on the screen. According to Beatty, as quoted in Terry Christensen's *Reel Politics: American Political Movies
from 'Birth of a Nation to 'Platoon'* (1987), *Shampoo* is "about the intermingling of political and sexual hypocrisy." The film clearly links Nixon to an atmosphere of selfishness
that has permeated the very souls of these characters. For instance, Jackie, the one
woman for whom George expresses any real love, is also the mistress of a crude but
successful businessman who has contributed heavily to the Nixon campaign. At the
end of the film, Jackie goes off with the businessman. Although it lacks true wit, *Shampoo* has some of the bitterness of Jonsonian comedy. Emanuel Levy's *Small Town America in Film* (1991) sums up rather well the impression left by *Shampoo*: "Made in 1975,
a year after Nixon's resignation over the Watergate scandal, the film suggests that
Nixon's hypocrisy and cheating were similar to those in Americans' everyday lives. The
protagonists' lack of concern with larger issues than themselves accounts for the fact
that Nixon was elected in the first place."

What follows are further critical comments:

"The picture is a sex roundelay set in a period as clearly defined as the jazz age."
— Pauline Kael, *Reeling*, 1977.

"[There is] nothing incisive and biting enough to make *Shampoo* a genuine satire;
having neither satirical trenchancy nor some kind of sympathetic immersion in its
characters, the film has no *raison d'être* ... [a] pretentious movie that manages to be
simultaneously slick and inept."— John Simon, *Reverse Angle*, 1982.

"*Shampoo* is disgusting.... it exploits serious subjects and new licenses with nauseating cynicism — not of the society it portrays but of the film-makers. The events
take place on Election Eve and Day in 1968, for no other reason apparently than that
television statements by Nixon and Agnew can (retrospectively) serve as a farcical
sounding-board for the farcical story. But Nixon and Agnew have characters; they are
complex, corrupt human beings. No one in this film is much more than a stockpile of
stock attitudes. Nixon and Agnew tell us something about ourselves: these plastic
Movieland freaks are both uninteresting and unaffecting, even as buffoons."— Stanley Kauffmann, *Before My Eyes*, 1980.

Nixon: From Checkers to Watergate (short subject, 1976)

26 minutes. Directed by Charles Braverman. Color. Distributed by Pyramid Film.

A brief overview through 1976, suitable for secondary schools.

Tea with Dick and Jerry (satire, 1976)

A satire in one act by Erik Brogger, featuring characters modeled on Richard Nixon and Gerald Ford. Presented by the Actors Theatre of Louisville, Kentucky, at the Humana Festival in the fall of 1976. Described as a work in progress with illustration in the Louisville *Courier-Journal-Times* of October 4, 1976. Brogger's agent was the William Morris Agency in New York City. In the 20 years following its original production, the play did not receive further productions nor was it published. See also Brogger's *Basement Tapes* (1983).

The Faking of the President 1974 (satiric film, 1976)

80 minutes. Produced, written and directed by Jeanne and Alan Abel. Spencer Productions. Cast: *Richard M. Nixon* Richard Dixon; *Donald Segreti* Marshall Efron; *Ron Ziegler* Alan Barinholtz.

This low budget film ($100,000) did not fare well, but it had one unique ingredient: Sifting through 250 hours of tapes, with scrupulous re-editing, four editors recorded Nixon's actual utterances to make him guilty of everything critics had accused him of. That gimmick aside, the film had no target audience except chronic Nixon haters and any fans of the Three Stooges who just happened to wander in. Some of the more representative scenes showed Nixon siphoning the gas from Ted Kennedy's car and stealing the flowers from the grave of President Roosevelt's dog Fala to put on the grave of Checkers. Nixon's long-time secretary and loyalist Rose Mary Woods is seen erasing tapes with her feet. Nixon's press secretary Ron Ziegler appears in a Nazi uniform. Few things date more quickly than satire and the events were all at least two years in the past when the film was released.

"Finally, the Abels settle for sticking dirty words in Nixon's mouth (apparently accomplished by some advanced audio mixing machinery), and they segue into childish sex jokes that are irrelevant to their subject…. We've heard it all before and we've heard it better."—*New York Post*, July 16, 1976.

Memory of Justice (feature documentary, 1976)

278 minutes. Directed and written by Marcel Ophuls. Produced by Max Palevsky, Hamilton Fish and Ana Carrigan. Photography by Michael Davis. Edited by Inge Behrens. Paramount. Features (among others): Chief U.S. Consul at Nuremberg Telford Taylor; defendants at Nuremberg — Albert Speer, Admiral Karl Donitz; President, French National Assembly — Edgar Faure; Former member of Hitler's General Staff — General Walter Warlimont; British

Crown Prosecutor at Nuremberg — Rt. Hon. Lord Shawcross; students at Kent State University; students at Duisburg University, Germany; violinist Yehudi Menuhin; and Daniel Ellsberg.

"*Memory of Justice* ... is the investigation of national and individual responsibility in the wake of Auschwitz, Katyn, Dresden, Hiroshima, Algeria and Vietnam. In uniquely revealing interviews with SS men and Resistance leaders, with Vietnam supporters and opponents, with eminent scholars and 'ordinary citizens,' Ophuls probes the question of guilt." — New York Film Festival Program, October 5, 1976.

"Ophuls tries to combine his newsreel and archive film with such material ... as Joan Baez singing 'Where Have All the Flowers Gone' in German, a discussion of Nixon's tapes at Kent State, and a scene of German girls at a swimming pool while the song 'Bel Ami' is heard on the soundtrack. I doubt if the greatest editors around could fit all this footage together and give it rhythm and shape. And Ophuls isn't even a good editor." — Pauline Kael, *New Yorker*, October 11, 1976.

"I could have done ... with fewer of the banal comments of German university students, and could have endured the complete omission of Daniel Ellsberg. (Surely a more enlightening anti–Vietnam voice could have been found.) ...[A]s one who protested the Vietnam war before and after it was popular to do so, I reject the facile parallel between the German Final Solution and Vietnam atrocities. I still think there is substantial difference between a civil-government policy carried out in a routine bureaucratic way, like the Solution, and the madness of military aberration like Napalm and impulsive animality like My Lai." — Stanley Kauffmann, *Before My Eyes*, 1980.

Tracks (feature film, 1976)

Written and directed by Henry Jaglom. Produced by Bert Schneider. Edited by George Folsey, Jr. Rainbow Pictures. Color. Cast: *Sgt. Jack Falen* Dennis Hopper; *Mark* Dean Stockwell; *Stephanie* Taryn Power.

Tracks, a low-budget film, made in 1976 but not released generally until 1979, pleased neither public nor critics. Vincent Canby of the *New York Times*, February 16, 1979, called it a film without "any real center." It concerns an army sergeant (Dennis Hopper) escorting the body of a dead war buddy back to his home town in the East for burial. During the course of the long train journey, he meets a representative group of middle Americans. One passenger (Dean Stockwell) is a member of an angry leftist group pursued by several members of the FBI and CIA who are also on the train. Their presence is meant to further fuel the tension of the script.

The film opens with Nixon's voice announcing the withdrawal of American troops from Vietnam, and the spine of the film is the journey itself and Hopper's being rejected by a pretty girl who is played by the daughter of Tyrone Power. At the end of the film, furious that no one else has attended his buddy's funeral, Hopper defiantly yanks the military gear from the coffin.

An ironic counterpart throughout is Hopper's playing a cassette of upbeat '40s tunes chirpily sung by the Andrews Sisters.

"[F]or all its lack of character development, its careless editing and its plot inconsistencies, *Tracks* has a certain hypnotic power."— Kathleen Carroll, *New York Daily News*, February 16, 1979.

"Henry Jaglom's *Tracks* is rather like an adventurous, avant-garde novel that one admires more for its intentions than for what it actually achieves."— Howard Kissel, *Women's Wear Daily*, February 16, 1979.

Nasty Habits (film, 1977)

A.k.a. *Dirty Habits*. 98 minutes. Directed by Michael Lindsay-Hogg. Written by Robert Enders from the novella *The Abbess of Crewe* (1974) by Muriel Spark. Produced by Robert Enders. Music by John Cameron. Art direction by Robert Jones, edited by Peter Tanner, filmed in Britain at the Elstree Studios and in the United States in various Philadelphia locations, Brut release of a Bowden Productions Ltd. Film. Technicolor/Panavision. Cast: *Alexandra (Richard Nixon)* Glenda Jackson; *Gertrude (Henry Kissinger)* Melina Mercouri; *Walburga (H.R. Haldeman)* Geraldine Page; *Winifred (John Dean)* Sandy Dennis; *Mildred (John Ehrlichman)* Anne Jackson; *Geraldine (Gerald Ford)* Anne Meara; *Hildegarde* Dame Edith Evans; *Felicity* Susan Penhaligon; *Maximilian* Rip Torn; *P.R. Priest* Jerry Stiller; *Monsignor* Eli Wallach; *Mike Douglas* Himself; *Jessica Savitch* Herself; *Howard K. Smith* Himself.

An obvious "send-up" of Watergate, *Nasty Habits* takes place in a convent outside of Philadelphia where life goes on in a quiet way until the old abbess, Hildegarde, is summoned to her place at God's table. Just before going to her reward, Hildegarde calls Alexandra, the nun she prefers above all others, and instructs her in the measures she must take to become the next Abbess of Philadelphia (city of sisterly love?). Hildegarde is about to sign a declaration of intention on Alexandra's behalf when Felicity, a free-spirited young nun, pushes past prioress Walburga; mistress of novices Mildred, and the sports-loving numskull nun Geraldine, who works part-time as the telephone operator ("Thank you for calling the Abbey of Philadelphia — good morning and God bless you").

The disruption so unsettles old Hildegarde that she goes to her eternal rest seconds before putting pen to paper. The mighty power play begins, and there is much tragic-comic drama in the question, "Who will be the next Abbess of Philadelphia?" The question unleashes more intrigues than an Italian court with treachery, betrayal and lust just three of the paths the sisters take.

Alexandra's chief rival is a power-mad nun named Gertrude who is constantly sucking up for photo-ops and headlines, as she speaks in unintelligible guttural rasps while arranging talks that nobody can understand; her trusty Gucci bags and portable phone are always with her as she zips in and out of her private helicopter. When Gertrude steps down for Hildegarde's funeral, Alexandra is frazzled and wants Gertrude to start diplomatizing again. "Don't call me, I'll call you" is the catch phrase *du jour* as Gertrude hits the wild blue yonder for more photo-ops; meanwhile, Felicity is crumpling the starch in Alexandra's wimple. Felicity wants to call the abbey "the love abbey." She's been "having it off" with a young Jesuit named Thomas under the poplar trees, and she wants to "turn the nuns on."

Geraldine Page (Haldeman), Glenda Jackson (Nixon), Sandy Dennis (John Dean) and Anne Jackson (Erlichman) in Muriel Spark's satiric spin on Watergate *Nasty Habits* (1977).

Alexandra begins to experience high paranoia, and the abbey goes hi-tech: closed circuit TV is installed, bugs go into the statue of the Infant of Prague and the libidinous poplar grove. She also begins to curse like a drunken sailor on a three-day pass and sets up toothy, bespectacled Sister Winifred as patsy and snitch to get compromising pictures of Felicity and Thomas, but that is not all Alexandra wants. After she tells Father Maximilian that "your brother Jesuit, Thomas, has been screwing our sister, Felicity," Father Maximilian pledges his support and "a third-rate burglary" is attempted on Felicity's sewing box which reportedly holds Thomas' steamy love letters. The first attempt fails, but on the next night the burglars are caught. The police come in and a cover-up is initiated. It is soon a hot topic in the press and, needless to say, Rome is not pleased.

In spite of the tumult and the shouting, the election takes place, and Alexandra wins in a landslide, but the rumors of bugging, blackmail and sex are so rife that they cannot be contained. Felicity and Thomas appear on the leading Philadelphia talk show and spill the beans about Alexandra and the abbey. Winifred is caught making a pay-off in the men's room at Independence Square. Alexandra cannot decide whether to burn the tapes or not, and she is considering hocking the convent jewels to pay off the blackmail. Winifred is hauled off to the slammer, and her sisters stonewall in well-orchestrated shock. Rome summons Alexandra. She has a press conference before departing and snarls, "You won't have Alexandra to kick around any more."

Although it had its defenders, most critics regarded *Nasty Habits* as a heavy satire that, unlike the helicopter of its bustling Sister Gertrude, could not get off the ground; even its pre-release advertising offended many. The *New York Times* and other East Coast sheets altered their ads for *Nasty Habits*. The original ad featured a picture of a nun with her skirt hiked to her upper thighs with a just-caught look on her face and a tape recorder dangling from her belt. Because of many complaints from nuns and others, a long skirt was air-brushed in.

Nasty Habits' "opening scene [is] a pre-title power play around the bed of the dying abbess (Dame Edith Evans) [in which] director Michael Lindsay-Hogg apes *The Ritz* in getting the comedy off with a death rattle that's a bang" (*Soho Weekly News*, March 17, 1977). Rex Reed pointed out (*New York Daily News*, March 18, 1977) that Dame Edith "looks a bit like Lyndon Johnson in a baby bonnet [and] any resemblance is not only not coincidental but wickedly deliberate."

"The greatest virtue of [Muriel] Spark's novel was its length—100 pages.... But her rather timid satire could not overcome the fundamental problem that most of the actual events of Watergate were so outrageous [that] any work of fiction would seem feeble in comparison," wrote Robert Asahina in the *New Leader* (March 14, 1977). Literary satire does not often translate well on the screen, and Asahina, always a man of few words, summed it up by calling it "downright tasteless." Asahina was not the only critic to find fault with the film's source. *Newsweek* (March 28, 1977) opined, "Spark's idea of setting the Watergate story in a cloister afforded plenty of opportunities to caricature the pious hypocrisy of a panicky Chief Executive, but [Spark]—like the film makers—failed to take advantage of her premise. Without a shrewdly developed plot or a distinctly satiric point of view, the novella read like a bloated short story and, made into a movie, it has only enough comic energy to sustain a brief skit." Unfortunately, the Nixon–Jackson character has a line that foreshadows *Newsweek's* critical comment: "The bloody media will be on our necks in a minute. What we need is a viable story." "It doesn't even sound like a good idea: the Watergate follies done as pure hell in a Roman Catholic nunnery," said the *East Side Express* of New York City (March 31, 1977). Critic John Azzopardi elaborated, "[I]t's not a premise; it's a gimmick, the sort that usually can't be sustained here.... *Nasty Habits* is in the smart-assed school of Britisher put-on, clumsily and incompletely transcribed to an American setting."

Frank Rich, as film and as social critic, always eager to join the Nixon booing section, saw little to praise (*New York Post*, March 19, 1977): "This dumb, dreary movie actually manages to take all the fun out of hating Nixon.... It has no real political point-of-view and no real satirical thrust. Maybe the *Nasty Habits* perpetrators thought they could squeak by on sheer offensiveness—but this film doesn't offend in any way that counts; it never effectively attacks Nixon..."

John Simon (*New York*, March 28, 1977) wrote a very condemnatory review with a somewhat puzzled reference to another critic who was among the movie's few champions. Simon wrote, "*Nasty Habits* is a nasty little piece of goods over which it would be kindest to pass in silence, if only it deserved kindness, and if our most eminent woman critic had not waxed dithyrambic about it. Actually, I think, this most tasteless of movies deserves every kick it can get.... [W]hat is particularly offensive is the transposition of the Nixon gang into a Roman Catholic Convent. What is relevance, desirability, or justification for this? One reason, I suppose, is that Catholics lack the vigilante organizations that other minorities—blacks, Jews, women—so vociferously enjoy. And if you are prejudiced, vulgar, infantile or stupid enough, you can always get a cheap laugh out of nuns using four-letter words, tumbling in the hay with priests, or even just munching a pizza on a bus. And judging by the less than steady but more than sporadic laughter I heard at the screening I attended, there may be a sufficiency of such prejudiced, vulgar, infantile or stupid people to constitute an audience for this muck." Sharing Simon's anger was the *East Side Express* critic (date not given) who parroted Nixon in saying, "Let me make one thing perfectly clear. There is nothing funny about *Nasty Habits*."

The "eminent woman critic" was, of course, Pauline Kael of the *New Yorker* who wrote (February 21, 1977), "Other satires of Nixon have hustled their own political pieties, and they've pointed up his lower-middle-class tone for counterculture audiences.... But even those who voted for Nixon may be able to laugh at *Nasty Habits* because it has a midsummer madness about it." Other (somewhat patchy) praise came from *The Hollywood Reporter* (March 18, 1977): "sophisticated and witty" and from Vincent Canby in the *New York Times* (March 19, 1977): "Half of *Nasty Habits* is very funny. The other half is anywhere from awful to merely poor." *Variety* (October 27, 1976) called it "bitingly funny entertainment which the masses could and should enjoy." Audiences did not enjoy *Nasty Habits* and Glenda Jackson was to have only two more successful films, *House Calls* (1978) and *Hopscotch* (1980). She announced her retirement from acting in 1992 when she entered politics and won a Labor seat in the House of Commons.

"If she went into politics she'd be prime minister; if she went into crime she'd be Jack the Ripper" said Roy Hodge, her ex-husband (quoted in *Halliwell's Filmgoer's Companion*, 1995). For a committed Laborite, satirizing Richard Nixon would be almost as much devilishly good fun as satirizing Margaret Thatcher or John Major.

The Cayman Triangle (feature film, 1977)

92 minutes. Produced and directed by Anderson Humphreys. Assisted by Ralph Clemente. Screenplay by Humphreys and Clemente. Produced by Hefalump Pictures (named for Humphrey's dog). No distributor, Color. Cast: *Richard Nixon* Alexander Humphreys; *Kissinger* Jules Kreitzer; *Jimmy Carter* Ed Beheler; *Scarlett O'Tara* Tian Giri; *Blackbeard* Ryhal Gallagher; *Gen. Eastlessin (Westmoreland?)* Bob Ankrom; *Hot Lips Hector* Emily Hector.

Presented at the Virgin Islands Film Festival in November 1977, *The Cayman Triangle* is apparently a film that went nowhere. *Variety* (November 26, 1977) referred to it as "typical of youthful neophyte productions appealing to the high school and college type of wild satiric trade ... [nevertheless it was] generally amusing, if intermittently labored..."

The plot has something to do with ships being lost in the Cayman Triangle, a stand-in for that more well-known death dealer, the Bermuda Triangle. (Apparently they had free use of the Georgetown streets. That may be the reason.) The entire monkeyshines are an investigation of the Triangle mishaps with heavy-duty American politicos making asses of themselves assisted by Scarlett O'Tara, the hostess in the Oval Office.

Flashbacks to old-time pirates and the variations on a 19th century curse keep the pot and the plot boiling.

Tail Gunner Joe (TV film, 1977)

180 minutes. Directed by Jud Taylor. Written by Lane Slate. Photography by Ric Waite. Edited by Bernard J. Small. Produced by George Eckstein. NBC–TV/Universal. Aired Sunday, February 6, 1977, 8–11 P.M. Cast: *Senator Joseph McCarthy* Peter Boyle; *Paul Cunningham* John Forsythe; *Senator Margaret Chase Smith* Patricia Neal; *Logan* Heather Menzies; *Joseph Welch* Burgess Meredith; *Dwight D. Eisenhower* Andrew Duggan; *General George Marshall* John Anderson; *Drew Pearson* Robert F. Simon; *Harry S. Truman* Robert Symonds; *Richard Nixon* Richard M. Dixon.

Tail Gunner Joe, a film that used the familiar device of a researcher investigating the life and legacy of an influential person as in *Citizen Kane* and *The Prime of Miss Jean Brodie*, was notable for its central performance but received a decidedly mixed press otherwise.

Senator Joseph McCarthy (1909–1957) became a part of 20th century history when, on February 9, 1950, in a speech in Wheeling, West Virginia, he stated that he had a list of 205 Communists who worked in the State Department. In the period after the speech, in what was to become habitual, McCarthy changed the number frequently. Because of these accusations and the hearings given in his name, he was probably the most famous and reviled politician of the 1950s.

Originally a Democrat, McCarthy became a Republican when he saw an opportunity to gain a judgeship in his home state of Wisconsin. He had no platform, no ideology, but he sensed he could capitalize on the anti–Communist mood sweeping the country. McCarthy attacked Truman many times for not supporting the free Chinese forces against the sweeping communist hordes. He had thus taken one of the most complicated issues of his time, mindless of its complexity and its possibilities for endless carnage, and simplistically turned it to his advantage. Yet another catastrophe worked to his advantage. The beginning of the Korean War in 1950 solidified American anti–Communist sentiment, thus opening the door for McCarthy to become entrenched as its spokesman.

McCarthy's power went to his head, and he attacked nearly everyone he did not like or was envious of, including General George C. Marshall, one of the most respected leaders of World War II and the man most responsible for the recovery of postwar Europe. McCarthy had started his attacks in the Truman years and held sway in the early Eisenhower period until Eisenhower, seeing what a liability McCarthy was, surreptitiously maneuvered an investigation of McCarthy's currying favor with the United States Army for a friend of chief consul, Roy Cohn. When this was exposed, the Senate censured McCarthy, and his power was gone.

Tail Gunner Joe dramatizes many of these events. The title is meant ironically since McCarthy lied about his military record. He died at 49, a death that was probably caused by his severe drinking problem which may also have explained his erratic behavior in his days of power.

Variety (February 9, 1977) gave the three-hour film a virtual rave with high praise for Peter Boyle's performance as McCarthy and for the performance of Patricia Neal as Senator Margaret Chase Smith, who made "a great stand" against McCarthy on the Senate floor. *Variety's* only complaint was "that Richard Nixon's influence as a close friend and adviser to McCarthy was passed over (the ex–President was impersonated fleetingly in a scene in which McCarthy physically attacked columnist Drew Pearson in a private club). Overlooked, for example, was Nixon's importance as Vice-President and as president of the Senate in getting McCarthy the chairmanship of the investigative committee which raised such havoc with its chasing of the Red Menace (445 investigations going at once, as the show noted)."

The *Christian Science Monitor* (February 4, 1977) was decidedly negative: "If only people and issues were as clear-cut as this Lane Slate screenplay portrays them. McCarthy was a villain-buffoon, and politicians and newspapermen were cowardly, according to the writer. It's all spelled out figuratively, despite the colorcast, in black and white ... with almost no shadings at all."

Emile de Antonio's 1964 documentary *Point of Order* deals with much of the same material, as does the Broadway musical *Tail Gunner Joe* (1990), a presentation by Adela Holzer, "a Broadway producer and an expert con artist" (*New York Daily News*, May 1, 1994). It lasted one night.

Washington: Behind Closed Doors (TV mini-series, 1977)

12 hours. Directed by Gary Nelson. Written by David Rintels and Eric Bercovici; based upon the novel *The Company* by John Ehrlichman. Photography by Joseph Biroc. September 6–11, 1977, 9–11 P.M. ABC. Cast: *President Richard Monckton (Nixon)* Jason Robards, Jr.; *Frank Flaherty (Haldeman)* Robert Vaughn; *President Scott Anderson (LBJ)* Andy Griffith; *CIA Director William Martin (Helms)* Cliff Robertson; *Myron Dunn (John Mitchell)* John Houseman; *Bob Bailey (Herb Klein, Comm. Director)* Barry Nelson; *Carl Tessler (Kissinger)* Harold Gould; *Elmer Morse (Hoover)* Thayer David; *Sally Whalen* Stefanie Powers.

According to a *New York Times* article (September 13, 1977) by media specialist Les Brown, *Washington: Behind Closed Doors*, was a very popular mini-series that was watched by 80 million viewers, almost did not happen. The series came about when its source, a somewhat glossy commercial novel entitled *The Company* (1976) by Nixon advisor John Ehrlichman, failed to become the best seller that Simon and Schuster had anticipated. As a result, its projected sale to Paramount Pictures fell through, and it was sold to TV at a much lower price. In addition, the book had not been popular enough to trade on its somewhat bland title which too clearly echoed the title of Stephen Sondheim's Tony Award-winning musical of 1970, *Company* starring Dean Jones (soon to star in another Nixon-related picture *Born Again* as Nixon aide Charles Colson). In its transformation for television, *The Company* sported the more provocative super-market tabloids title of *Washington: Behind Closed Doors*.

The resulting TV production was an $8 million, 12-hour series that starred confirmed Nixon-hater Jason Robards, Jr., in a role modeled on a man he had often said he hated. Robards made no attempt to look like Nixon but, like many others, the English critic Clive James was quite taken with Robards' actorly bits of "business"; as James wrote in the *London Observer* (January 8, 1978): "Jason Robards has tricked out the character of Monckton with every nervous spasm and paranoiac twitch that ever

Cliff Robertson as William Martin (based on Richard Helms of the CIA), Robert Vaughn as Frank Flaherty (based on H.R. Haldeman) and Jason Robards as Richard Monckton (Nixon) in the television series *Washington: Behind Closed Doors* (1977).

racked Nixon's chaotic body.... Robards has even succeeded in echoing Nixon's unique slouching walk with arms out of coordination with legs — a physical reflection of the recriminative battle being waged in the spirit."

While it called itself fiction, *Washington: Behind Closed Doors* featured many parallels to the alleged acts of wrong-doing in the Nixon administration: abuse of power, suspicious CIA operations within foreign countries, illegal surveillance, wiretapping,

Jason Robards as Richard Monckton (Nixon) in *Washington: Behind Closed Doors* (1977).

assassination plots, perjury and bribery (the John Mitchell character accepts a campaign contribution saying, "We never forget our friends").

The spine of the teleplay is that Martin (the Richard Helms counterpart), as CIA director, has in his possession a highly explosive report that points to him and the CIA as instruments in the assassinations of heads of foreign states. In order to save the image of the CIA and his own reputation, Martin forms a bond with the Kissinger character, Carl Tessler, chief of the National Security Council. As Karl E. Meyer defines it in *Saturday Review* (September 3, 1977), "the company" is "the in-house phrase for the Central Intelligence Agency ... it suggests the hermetic world of a powerful, largely unaccountable entity that has become a state within a state. Always, the interests of the Company come first, and in this respect the CIA is no different from the White House or the FBI."

According to cameraman Joseph Biroc (*American Cinematographer*, November 1977), the original conception was to film eight one-hour programs, but ABC's enthusiasm for the project was so high that they decided to turn the material into six two hour segments. In order to do so, more material was needed. Only about 30 percent of Ehrlichman's book was retained; the rest is a wild melange of plot for plot's sake. The TV production begins with the announcement that President Anderson (LBJ) will not seek re-election. Although he has not yet been elected, Monckton is clearly the front runner. A Monckton win means that the Primula Report, the assassination exposé, will get out. Meanwhile Martin must fight to keep his position as the head of the CIA. In order to do so, he uses the woman he is in love with (Stefanie Powers) and foreign policy expert Carl Tessler to thwart Monckton's popularity. It does not work, and Monckton is elected in a landslide.

Treachery abounds throughout: Martin lies before a Senate committee on assassination and blackmails Monckton to cover up the murders; the affable press secretary is double-crossed by the Haldeman counterpart played by Robert Vaughn at his steeliest. Marital problems, love affairs and political intrigues, high and low, fill the 12 hours with plot developments that cascade, soap opera fashion, one on top of the other.

Time's perceptive review (September 19, 1977) praised "Robards' extraordinary capturing of the persona of Richard Nixon." Yet, *Time* claimed, "distortions abound.... The miniseries has the *Washington Post* discovering malfeasance long before the Watergate break-in; it did not. The video version of the burglary by White House plumbers of the office of Daniel Ellsberg's psychiatrist becomes a break-in at a St. Louis courthouse; instead of psychiatrists records, the squad is after police records. The fictional Lyndon Johnson orders the CIA to carry out an illegal hunt for any Nixonian dirty laundry before the 1968 election. So far as is known, Johnson did no such thing."

Unfortunately, fabrications are the norm in TV historical dramas. But what of the central character? How true to brooding life is the Robards portrait of Richard Nixon? A channel-surfing Nixon would surely have hated it, but otherwise it received almost universal acclaim. The *Christian Science Monitor* of September 2, 1977 published a representative reaction: "As portrayed by Jason Robards, Monckton is the epitome of self-delusion, of inverted morality, of political paranoia gradually evolving into full-fledged national disaster. Mr. Robards never mimics the former president, yet somehow manages to make him into the ambivalent and inconsistent leader, filled with feelings of insecurity, vanity, high-mindedness interspersed with petty vengefulness which we all observed only recently. But Robards's Monckton is not a one-dimensional villain — as he is written and played, one feels understanding and compassion as well as distaste."

In an impassioned article in *Newsweek* (September 19, 1977), David Eisenhower, defending his father-in-law, cited four main distortions: 1. Nixon's best efforts in office were not "devoted to harassing enemies." 2. Nixon had not "sought election to exact revenge against the Kennedy legend, 'faggot' (a term used by Monckton) Ivy Leaguers and press critics." 3. *The Company* was written by "an aide who had undertaken to purify himself ... Converts have a tendency to exaggerate the magnitude of their past sins." 4. "Nixon may not be a sympathetic figure as a former President and a powerful man brought low. Nevertheless, he deserves protection from reveling in his tragedy, and bullying."

A few days after the *Newsweek* article, the *Christian Science Monitor* editorialized in a piece entitled "Closing the Door on *Doors*" (September 21, 1977) which said, in part. "I do not minimize Nixon's grave abuses of his office. Probably there were two Nixons in the same man during his presidency. But the intolerable offense of *Doors* was that it devoted itself to depicting all that he did was unworthy and purposefully turned the camera away from anything he did that was worthy. What makes these 12 hours of prime-time so harmful is that they filled it with such an indiscriminating mixture of fact and fiction that it was impossible to detect which was fact and which was fiction. Most of the time fiction was made to look like history. Myth and the appearance of fact became constant companions. The line between fantasy and reality was crossed so constantly and so rudely that it was impossible to discern the difference."

Nixon Interviews with David Frost (TV program, 1977)

A series of four 90-minute programs telecast in May 1977 sold in syndication and presented on an ad hoc network that blanketed most of the United States; shown a day later on BBC–TV. The entire series is available on video from the two shops of the Museum of Television and Radio — 22 West 52nd Street, New York, New York 10019-6101 and 465 North Beverly Drive, Beverly Hills, California 90210-4654. All major sections of the telecasts are discussed in "*I Gave Them a Sword*": *Behind the Scenes of the Nixon Interviews* by David Frost (William Morrow and Company, 1978).

"Former President Richard Nixon may not be the most 'lovable man' in the world, as he willingly admits tonight to David Frost on their fifth syndicated interview program — Channel 5 at 7:30 P.M. — but we must agree with him about one thing: 'The greatest concentration of power is in the media.'" — Kay Gardella, *New York Daily News*, September 8, 1977.

Most of the major networks rejected David Frost's proposal for the series, saying either that the price was too high (Nixon was guaranteed $600,000) or that it was "checkbook journalism" (why should they pay an official to talk about what he did in office?). Frost, sensing that there was a vast viewing public available for the series, was able to put together an investment package and line up television syndication and subsidiary rights. A master promoter, Frost leaked some of the interview's content to *Newsweek*, *Time* and *TV Guide* which increased audience potential and resulted in a viewing public of 45 million for the first segment alone. But audience numbers remained high throughout. Frost taped 28 hours with Nixon in the latter's San Clemente office. The original intent was to make four 90-minute segments, but the popularity was so great that a fifth was added from the outtakes. The insight this series gives into the Nixon years is inestimable. It remains one of the major TV documents of its time.

This series of interviews had to have been an agonizing experience for Richard Nixon. Frost asked many tough questions, the toughest of which are re-printed in "*I Gave Them a Sword*," a revealing behind-the-scenes account of Nixon's career as President with its primary focus on Watergate and Vietnam. In the three years since leaving the White House, Nixon had become quite contemplative. He admitted he had let the American people down and that he had really impeached himself.

Win with Wheeler (satiric farce, 1978)

Original title: *Winning Isn't Everything*. A satiric farce in two acts by Lee Kalcheim. Directed by George Abbott. Presented by and at the Hudson Guild Theatre (441 West 26th Street, New York City). Scenery and costumes by Fred Voelpel. Lighting by Annie Wrightson. Limited engagement — November 8 through December 10, 1978. Cast: *Mrs. Florence Wheeler* Bobo Lewis; Bryan

Clark, Forbesy Russell, Marshall Purdy, Steve Ryan, Richard Kuss, Mara Landi, Tom Everett, and Jim Lovelett.

This short-lived production was one of the last directorial efforts of the legendary George Abbott (June 25, 1887–January 31, 1995), who directed such notable stage attractions as *Twentieth Century, Boy Meets Girl, Room Service, On Your Toes, Pal Joey, Where's Charley?, Damn Yankees* and many others. Abbott directed *Win With Wheeler* in his usual slam-bang 1930s style, but in spite of Bobo Lewis' knock-out performance as Florence Wheeler, the tippling wife of a politician with adjustable ethics, the play did not make the hoped-for transfer to Broadway because the train carrying fast-talking political farces 1930s style had left the station long before 1978.

To be sure, *Win With Wheeler* is "not a Nixon play," but any so-called "political comedy" has to have an obligatory Nixon crack or two. Here's a sample:

> FLORENCE WHEELER: He's got to lose. It's the only way he'll learn. He'll be different if he loses.
>
> CAMPAIGN MANAGER: You think *losing* would change him? Look what it did for Richard Nixon. It made him a paranoid winner.

One critic noted:
"Here we are back in the '30s watching a breakneck George Abbott farce with its compulsive schemers, stuffed shirts, a wide-eyed blonde and assorted other zanies. An endearing glimpse of a giddy theatrical past."—*New York Daily News*, November 9, 1978.

(In 1983, at 95, Abbott directed a Broadway revival of *On Your Toes* which ran longer than the original production.)

After the Season (play, 1978)

A drama in three acts by Corinne Jacker. Directed by Marshall W. Mason. Designed by John Lee Beatty. Lighting by Jennifer Tipton. Produced by Arthur McKenzie. Presented July 14, 1978, at the Academy Festival Theater, Lake Forest, Illinois followed by performances at the Brandeis University Playhouse, Waltham, Massachusetts, July 26, 1978. Cast: *Anne Stewart* Irene Worth; *Sen. Crispen Stewart* Charles Cioffi; *Alice Stewart* Sheine Marinson; *Dave Castle* David Rasche.

"Thursday, June 29, 1972: [She] blew her stack, got drunk, told her FBI agent and John's secretary that her husband had every Democrat in Washington bugged, and then decided she'd call a reporter and tell him. The FBI agent got concerned and called John in Washington and got [CPR deputy director] Fred LaRue, who said she starts to do that, unlocked the door, went in and pulled her phone out. She then had a monumental tantrum. Started throwing things at him, demolishing the room. They locked her in. She busted the window with her hand, cut herself badly. They had to get a doctor who had to throw her on the bed and give her a shot to subdue her."—*The Haldeman Diaries*, 1994.

If anyone was the hero of Watergate, that role is usually assigned to Martha

Mitchell, a good-looking compulsive talker whose penchant for saying exactly what she thought to reporters helped to fan the flames of Watergate. To some, she was Cassandra, to others, she was a wacky Joan of Arc, to still others, she was a drunken clown who would not shut up. There is some truth in all of these portraits, but the reality probably lies closest to Cassandra, the king's daughter whose prophecies went unheeded. Martha's more usual behavior, that of Washington's self-appointed madcap hostess, had made her prophecies suspect in the eyes of many.

Nevertheless, Mitchell is the heroine of at least three stage plays, the first and third of which were done with major actresses: Corinne Jacker's *After the Season* (1978) starring Irene Worth, Patricia Cobey's *The Martha Play* (1984) with Crystal Field and David Wolpe's *The Unguided Missile* (1989) starring Estelle Parsons. (Both are discussed later in this volume.)

There are also at least two full-length biographies: *Martha, the Mouth That Roared* (1973) by Charles Ashman and Sheldon Engelmayer and *Martha, the Life of Martha Mitchell* (1979) by Winzola McLendon, a very sympathetic account of her life. She figures in virtually every book that mentions Watergate, probably most prominently in *The Women of Watergate* (1975) by Madeline Edmondson and Alden Duer Cohen. For many years, the actress Diane Ladd, a cousin of Tennessee Williams and the mother of Laura Dern, attempted to make a film of Martha Mitchell's life, but she was unable to gain the financing.

Martha Mitchell died at the Sloan-Kettering Cancer Center in New York City on May 31, 1976, at the age of 57. As her page-one obituary in the *New York Times* (June 1, 1976) stated: "When the Watergate scandal broke, she did not hesitate to turn her barbs on the Nixon Administration, urging its officials to 'tell it like it is.'" On May 31, 1982, in Pine Bluff, Arkansas, her hometown, a life-size bronze bust of Martha Mitchell was dedicated by Ray Jennings, the son of her first marriage. The inscription read: "You shall know the truth and the truth shall make you free."

***

Corinne Jacker was an off–Broadway playwright who had some success in the 1960s and 1970s. Although it had a major star in the Mitchell role, *After the Season* was never produced professionally in New York City, nor was it ever published.

The play is set on an island off the Connecticut coast during a September hurricane. The wind blows, the windows rattle and all sorts of portents hover, but the play, according to *Variety* and *The Christian Science Monitor*, had one interesting character but no life of its own.

The *Monitor*, July 14, 1978: "The problem lies in both plotting and characterization. The drama was inspired by Watergate, in general and Martha Mitchell in particular.... [There is] a Haldeman-Ehrlichman-Dean type of young ad man-lawyer-pol on the make, this one intent on institutionalizing our heroine because she is a menace to the senator and to himself. The only enticing puzzle of the affair is whether the Mitchell character is fit for the institution or for sainthood."

Variety, August 9, 1978 (Irene): "Worth is believable as the self-isolated, half-crazed wife with a compulsion to reveal embarrassing news in phone conversations with reporters and editors. Her characterization expands the play's dimension and theatrical impact."

In sum, *After the Season* is basically a domestic drama with political overtones in a Watergate-themed situation with three characters who have Watergate counterparts.

Born Again (film, 1978)

110 minutes. Biographical film. Directed by Irving Rapper. Written by Walter Bloch from the book of the same title by Charles Colson. Produced by Frank Capra, Jr. Executive producer: Robert L. Munger. Photography: Harry Stradling, Jr. Music by Les Baxter. An Avco Embassy release of a Robert L. Munger Production. Cast: *Charles Colson* Dean Jones; *Patty Colson* Anne Francis; *Richard M. Nixon* Harry Spillman; *Tom Phillips* Dana Andrews; *David Shapiro* Jay Robinson; *Jimmy Newsome* Raymond St. Jacques; *Senator Hughes* Senator Harold Hughes; *Judge Gerhard Gesell* George Brent.

An official car stops at the gates of the Alabama Federal Prison Farm, and two federal marshals accompany a prisoner to the entrance. The prisoner is Charles Colson, probably Richard Nixon's most reviled White House aide. He has been sentenced to seven years in prison for his complicity in the Ellsberg case.

In prison, Colson reviews his association with Richard Nixon, and the pride that he and his wife felt at his being asked to serve in the White House. Life on the Nixon Team becomes very demanding, encroaching upon his personal life, and, prior to the 1972 election, he returns to his private law practice. But the Watergate cover-up soon becomes an international scandal, and he is clearly implicated. During this period of crisis, he experiences a re-birth of religious faith. He denies taking part in Watergate but admits playing a role in the Ellsberg break-in. His friend and law partner Dave Shapiro defends him, but his guilt is clear, and he is convicted and sentenced.

In prison, he makes friends with other prisoners, and he is able to start a Bible study group. However, one prisoner has let it be known that he intends to kill Colson. Some months later, the attempted murder takes place, but members from the Bible study group are able to save him. Colson forgives his attacker. Shortly after, Colson's son Chris is arrested for selling drugs. Because of his good works, Colson is pardoned after serving seven months of his sentence.

"[Colson's] brilliance was undeniable, but it was too often applied to Nixon's darker side, [Nixon's] desire to lash out at his enemies, his instinct for the jugular. I would say that ... Colson was one of the men among [Nixon's] advisers most responsible for creating the climate that made Watergate possible, perhaps inevitable." — Jeb Stuart Magruder, *An American Life: One Man's Road to Watergate* (1974).

(Magruder served seven months for his part in the cover-up and later became senior minister at the First Presbyterian Church of Lexington, Kentucky.)

"In time, perhaps Colson will find serenity and strength through prayer and good works. But he will have to work hard. He seemingly has more to live down than other men at the White House, excepting only H.R. Haldeman and the President himself." — Harriet Van Horne, "Colson the Convert," *New York Post*, June 5, 1974.

In 1974 *Esquire* magazine called critic John Simon and Charles Colson two of the "meanest men in America." John Simon said he wasn't sure he deserved the title but in the future he would endeavor to be worthy of the designation." Charles Colson had *already* changed his ways by December 1973: He had made a "decision for Christ," and *Born Again* is the story of how Colson, one of the "meanest men in America," became the man who chaired the Prison Fellowship and was the recipient of the 1993 Templeton Prize of Progress in Religion.

Dean Jones as Charles Colson and Harry Spillman as Nixon in the biographical *Born Again* (1978).

In a thoughtful essay in the *Wall Street Journal* of August 3, 1994, Colson explained his new purpose in life: "As the House and Senate prepare to vote on the final version of the $33 billion crime bill, the nation's attention is rightly riveted on a crime crisis that has grown to alarming proportions. Yet in today's frenzy to fight crime, no one consults the real experts: the criminals themselves. Prison Fellowship, an organization I helped found after serving time for Watergate-related offenses, decided to do just that. In our newspaper, *Inside Journal*, distributed free to prisoners nationwide, we invited inmates to answer the question 'What could have stopped you from breaking the law?'" Colson's essay discusses their replies in a probing and humane manner.

Although it highlighted several worthy subjects, *Born Again* was not a successful film commercially or aesthetically. It demanded more than the routine marketing that it was given. Its southern regional premiere took place in two locations, Atlanta's huge Fox Theatre and the Atlanta Federal Penitentiary. *Variety* (October 18, 1978) quoted Colson's speech at the latter location: "This is where my heart is. This is why the movie was made so the story of what happened to me can be seen on the screen so others can find meaning in their lives."

The film had little coverage. *Variety's* pre-release review (September 6, 1978) was tepid: "Version of recent history is a turnoff in the screen version of Charles Colson's Watergate undoing and later religious commitment. Slim outlook." *Variety* went on to call it "earnest [and] awkward with"—faint praise—"Dean Jones turn[ing] in a credible performance, whenever the action revolves around religious commitment rather than politics." The review also stated that "Harry Spillman does a fair Nixon imitation, but there's something unintentionally funny about any re-enactment that includes Nixon."

In an interview for this book, Harry Spillman concurred with *Variety's* assessment of Irving Rapper's directorial style which *Variety* described as "functional." Rapper

Harry Spillman in *Born Again*.

(1898–) had been a top director at Warner Bros. in the 1940s with such hits as *Now Voyager, The Adventures of Mark Twain, The Corn Is Green* and *The Voice of the Turtle*. But by 1978 his directorial style had become, in Ephraim Katz's word, "uninspired," and, in Spillman's terms, "over the top" and "Disney." (Dean Jones had been a frequent Disney star.) The melodramatic Warners' style of the 1940s could not be successfully grafted onto a socio-religious film three decades later. Rapper's old pal, Warners' star George Brent (1904–1979), came out of retirement to play the small role of the judge who sentenced Colson.

The Private Files of J. Edgar Hoover (biographical film, 1978)

112 minutes. Directed, written and produced by Larry Cohen. Production design by Cathy Davis. Set decoration by Carolyn Loewenstein. Costumes by Lewis Friedman. Music by Miklos Rozsa. American International. Color.

In discussing his film *The FBI Story* (1959) in his autobiography *Take One* (1974), director Mervyn LeRoy wrote: "If the real history of the FBI is ever written, it will show that J. Edgar Hoover did much to save the things about America we all hold most dear." After Hoover's death in 1972, most people weren't saying that any more. Dozens of books have since been written that show the FBI's clandestine operations, Hoover's talent for manipulation and his sometimes wiggy behavior, for instance, director Samuel Fuller's comment printed in the *Village Voice* of January 17, 1980: "He's sick, cruel, dogmatic, stupid, racist.... Everything I love in a character." After the hotly debated *Official and Confidential: The Secret Life of J. Edgar Hoover* (1993) by Anthony Summers was published, Washington politicians were cracking J. Edgar Hoover jokes in a steady stream. At a press dinner, Bob Dole complemented UPI doyenne Helen Thomas on her attractive new dress, saying that it must be "from the new J. Edgar Hoover collection."

Schlockmeister Larry Cohen (*It's Alive!, It's Alive Again!, It's Alive III: Island of the Alive*) made *The Private Files of J. Edgar Hoover* some time before its delayed release (Hoover and the FBI were still very touchy subjects in the late 1970s, and even after the film's release its distribution remained limited). Like Hoover's life and Cohen's film record, *The Private Files of J. Edgar Hoover* teems with incident. It's clunky; it's junky; it becomes more outrageous by the minute; for just one example, there is a scene early on in which Hoover gives his mother a canary he bought from the Birdman of Alcatraz. Mrs. Hoover examines it and snorts: "Why, it's a sparrow painted yellow. Edgar, you're too gullible." Not for long! The film rattles along like good pulp fiction written by a talented hack. It benefits from the fine sometimes over-the-top performance of Broderick Crawford as America's Number One crime fighter with lots of stage and screen worthies in cameos: Rip Torn (Dwight Webb/Narrator), June Havoc (the canary recipient), Dan Dailey (Clyde Tolson), Lloyd Nolan (Attorney General Harlan Stone who promoted Hoover to FBI chief) and Celeste Holm as a society matron who set herself the Sisyphian task of seducing Hoover.

Nixon (Richard Dixon) appears briefly "in a White House cabal of aides and advisers" (*Sight and Sound*, Summer 1979).

"Hoover [was] the black widow spider of American politics orchestrating everything from the rise of Joe McCarthy to (it's strongly implied) the assassination of Bobby Kennedy and the fall of Richard Nixon" (*Village Voice*, 3/17/80), and the film implies it was "the private files" and Tolson, Hoover's only real confidant, that did it. A narrator (Rip Torn) vouchsafes that Nixon's ruin was "the hand of J. Edgar Hoover reaching back from the grave." (*It's Alive IV?*)

In a highly favorable review, *Cue* (3/28/80) praised *The Private Files of J. Edgar Hoover* for "mix[ing] near-camp with a sinister overview of an evil genius holding dangerous politicians at bay while they all trample the Constitution."

All the President's Men (film, 1978)

136 minutes. Directed by Alan J. Pakula. Written by William Goldman. From the book by Carl Bernstein and Bob Woodward. Produced by William Cablenz. Photographed by Gordon Willis. Edited by Robert L. Wolfe. Music by David Shire. Color. Warner Bros. Cast: *Carl Bernstein* Dustin Hoffman; *Bob Woodward* Robert Redford; *Deep Throat* Hal Holbrook; *Ben Bradlee* Jason Robards; *Howard Simons* Martin Balsam; *Hugh Sloan, Jr.* Stephen Collins; *Bookkeeper* Jane Alexander; *Dardis* Ned Beatty; *McCord* Richard Herd.

Nixon "in a fine use of video tapes of the actual people speechifying or testifying, as glimpsed on TV ... sharpen(s) the teeth" of Alan J. Pakula's *All the President's Men* (John Simon, *New York*, April 12, 1976).

"Watergate" is a name now securely lodged in American, if not world, history. A brief recap of Watergate itself should prove useful in regard to many of the works that will be discussed in the succeeding pages of this volume.

On June 17, 1972, five burglars broke into the office of the Democratic National Committee in the Watergate office complex and hotel. Their mission was to repair a wiretap that had not functioned properly during a previous burglary attempt. The White House claimed no connection with the burglars, but one of them, it developed, James W. McCord, had worked for the CIA and was currently working for CREEP, the Committee to Re-Elect the President. As a result, the DNC started civil suits against the Nixon campaign. The White House stated that the burglary was merely — in press secretary Ron Ziegler's words — "a third-rate burglary." Nevertheless, two of the men who organized the break-in, G. Gordon Liddy and E. Howard Hunt, were found guilty of wiretapping and conspiracy in a federal court. They were given heavy sentences, but there was a provision that the sentences would be reduced if the two men cooperated with the court. (In a secret deal, Hunt was paid to remain silent.)

In March of 1973, McCord told Federal Judge John J. Sirica that some of the defendants had been pressured to remain silent, that others who had testified had not told the truth and that there were some guilty parties who remained free of charges. By this time, Watergate had snowballed into a topic of international interest. Nixon's two chief advisors, H.R. Haldeman and John Ehrlichman, were named in a cover-up, together with the President's counsel, John Dean. All three resigned. Attorney General Richard Kleindienst resigned as well. Nixon then chose Secretary of Defense Elliot Richardson as Kleindienst's replacement. Richardson named Harvard law professor Archibald Cox as Special Watergate Prosecutor, because Richardson wanted a completely independent investigation of Watergate. Around this time, Senator Sam Ervin of North Carolina was chosen to head a new committee, the Senate Select Committee on Presidential Campaign Activities. These proceedings were televised, and watching Watergate became a national pastime. There were at least two intensely dramatic moments: John Dean clearly implicating the President in a cover-up of CREEP, and Alexander Butterfield, Haldeman's deputy, revealing that Nixon had taped all the discussions in the Oval Office. This raised expectations to a tremendous pitch because now Dean's accusations against the President would be proven or disproven.

The Senate investigations revealed that the IRS had been called in to examine the financial dealings of Nixon's political adversaries, that a so-called "plumber's unit" would investigate "leaks," and that a group had burglarized Daniel Ellsberg's psychiatrist's office after this war protester had leaked "the Pentagon Papers" on our Vietnam policy to key journalists. "One of the more bizarre by-products of the Pentagon Papers affair was a plan either to raid or to firebomb the Brookings Institution (where Ellsberg was a fellow) and to pilfer papers there belonging to Leslie Gelb and Morton Halperin, former National Security Council aides" (*The Wars of Watergate: The Last Crisis of Richard Nixon*, by Stanley I. Kutler, 1990).

In the summer of 1973, the Senate committee and Cox sought the White House tapes, but the White House would not release them, citing "executive privilege." In late summer, Nixon appeared on television to discuss Watergate; his statements were ambiguous.

During this period, Vice-President Agnew was found guilty of income tax evasion and fined $10,000. Richardson had pressed the Agnew matter forward because he was worried about the presidential succession. He thought that if Nixon had to leave office, the country would be in worse shape with Agnew at the helm; therefore, Agnew had to go so that a worthier man would be chosen as vice-president and then president, if such were to be the case. Time was important. With Agnew gone, Nixon would be able to choose someone of good reputation as his vice-president and possible successor.

Meanwhile, a tug of war raged over the tapes. Nixon was adamant, ordering Richardson to fire Cox. Richardson refused and resigned. His assistant, William Ruckelhaus, also refused and was fired. Solicitor General Robert Bork was then appointed, and he carried out Nixon's order to fire Cox. These desperate acts became known as "the Saturday Night Massacre." It was now clear that serious wrong-doing had occurred.

A new special prosecutor, Leon Jaworski from Texas, was appointed. The White House agreed to turn over a small number of tapes, one of which, a conversation between Nixon and Haldeman taped three days after the break-in, had a suspicious 18-minute gap.

In February 1974, the House Judiciary Committee voted 4–10 to commence an impeachment investigation. Haldeman, Ehrlichman, Colson, Mitchell (chairman of CREEP) and others were charged with criminal conspiracy to obstruct justice.

On April 29, 1974, Nixon said he would release over a thousand pages of edited transcripts. The public was shocked to see the words "expletive deleted" running throughout the material, but what was much more dismaying to the public was the bitterness and the vengefulness the tapes contained.

In July, the House Judiciary Committee voted to support three articles of impeachment (all three are detailed in Appendix A of Theodore H. White's *Breach of Faith*, 1975). A third of the Republican members sided with the Democrats whose members voted in unanimity. The Supreme Court then demanded that the White House turn over all the tapes that had been subpoenaed. One, the so-called "smoking gun" tape of June 23, 1972, was most damaging. On this tape, Nixon told his aides to instruct the CIA to hinder the FBI's investigation of Watergate. After this tape was played, all members of the House Judiciary Committee, even Nixon's staunchest supporters, stated that they would vote for impeachment.

On August 9, 1974, in a memorable ceremony, Richard Nixon resigned from his presidency of five and a half years. Gerald Ford took the oath of office and delivered his most eloquent line: "Our long national nightmare is over."

To both its benefit and its detriment, the catch phrase "It's all in the details" may be attached rather handily to the film version of *All the President's Men*. At its best, as book and film, it skillfully carries forward an absorbing detective story. At its worst, it is a kind of Bill and Ted's "excellent adventure" in which Bernstein and Woodward perform a few illegal acts of their own to, in journalese, "get that story." As Stanley L. Kutler points out in his definitive *Wars of Watergate*, the team is guilty of "offering bribes, illegally gaining access to telephone numbers, and talking to members of the grand jury." Staying on the negative tack for another moment, surely there is something of an adolescent mentality in pursuing the suggestion that their principal informant be named after the title of a pornographic movie.

In her 1978 book *Lying: Moral Choices in Public and Private Life*, Harvard professor Sissela Bok wrote of "Woodstein's" methodology: "Persons being interviewed were falsely told that others had already given certain bits of information or had said something about them. One of the reporters tried to impersonate [Nixon campaign dirty trickster] Donald Segretti on the telephone, the other lied to Deep Throat in order to extract corroboration of a fact which the witness would have feared to reveal in other ways." Minor points perhaps, but each is a violation of journalistic ethics.

As to the identity of Deep Throat (the Hal Holbrook character), General Alexander Haig said in a TV interview (*Crossfire*, April 24, 1994) after Nixon's death that Deep Throat was probably FBI Assistant Director Mark W. Felt, who was later charged with violating civil rights through break-ins at the homes of members of the radical group the Weathermen in 1972–73. There are other Deep Throat candidates. *Deep Truth: The Lives of Bob Woodward and Carl Bernstein* by Adrian Havill (1993) repeats a claim in *Esquire* in 1976 that journalist and spinmaster David Gergen was Deep Throat. The 1978 film *The Private Files of J. Edgar Hoover* suggests that it was Clyde Tolson, Hoover's friend. But a more likely candidate is General Haig, for whom Woodward was White House briefer when Woodward was a communications officer in the Navy. Yet, with these possibilities considered, it is more probable that, as frequently stated, Deep Throat is a composite of various insiders whom the team interviewed. Building Deep Throat up as a laconic but commanding figure was no doubt part of the mechanics and the art of turning a long piece of investigative reporting into a narrative; this highly effective idea was as close as Woodward had ever gone toward achieving his collegiate goal of becoming a novelist.

Nixon himself appears three times in *All the President's Men*: At the beginning when he is announced to Speaker Carl Albert in the House of Representatives, just past the middle when he is enthusiastically announced as the 1972 Republican presidential candidate and at the end beamingly giving his second oath of office with a solicitous Pat looking on.

Because of its highly controversial subject matter, *All the President's Men* generated long discussions and critiques. We will look at the reactions of three major film critics: Roger Ebert, Stanley Kauffmann and John Simon. The major aspect of the film as noted by both Ebert and Simon was that screenwriter William Goldman was able to take a book that was essentially about a process, the unraveling of Watergate, much of which was known to the public by the time of the film's release, and yet fashion an absorbing 136-minute film.

Goldman's screenplay is very close to the book in its development, and it manages to overcome two of the dangers Ebert foresaw in adaptation (*Movie Home Companion*, 1989): First, that the viewer is "adrift in a sea of names, dates, telephone numbers, coincidences, lucky breaks, false leads, dogged footwork, denials, evasions and sometimes even the truth"; the second danger was that "the movie essentially shows us the same journalistic process several times as it looks closer and closer to an end we already know."

With much to praise in the film such as "a nice touch with the professional lives" of journalists, and "the wizardry of Pakula, his actors and technicians," and his granting it three and a half stars, Ebert felt that *All the President's Men* did not "quite add up to a satisfying movie experience."

Ebert's few cavils meant little. The film had a very favorable public response including a $29 million profit (a very good return for the late '70s), acclaim as the best film of the year by the New York Film Critics, and an Academy Award to Jason Robards as the Best Supporting Actor for his performance as the chipper Ben Bradlee, the *Washington Post*'s executive editor. Still, the film did not receive the superlatives that many felt were its due. An exception was the review of John Simon in *New York* (April 12, 1976), although his praise may have been due in part to his having "despised and loathed Nixon from the very beginning, having no faith whatever in associates chosen by him." For Simon, "the film was an unending concatenation of performances by actors known and unknown, but not a single weak link. [He] was gratified ... and pleasantly aware of being instructed as well as entertained." In the conclusion of what can only be termed a "rave" review, John Simon wrote: "It is worth seeing *All the President's Men* twice; once for everything about it, once more just for the acting."

Stanley Kauffmann (*New Republic*, April 24, 1976) was less enthusiastic than Ebert and Simon: "When the reporters' book about their Watergate investigation was bought for films, a lot of people said it couldn't be made into a film. Well, it couldn't. But on the way to an ultimately static and uncomfortable result, there's some passable acting, by Redford and Hoffman and others, and there's some pleasure in seeing the defeat of — no calmer term will do — an attempted fascist coup." Kauffmann's parting shot was one of fiendish delight: "[The film] gives us the chance to enjoy once again some of the healthiest *Schadenfreude* in 20th century American history."

Another major critic, Pauline Kael (*The New Yorker*, February 21, 1977) was almost as dismissive: "*All the President's Men* is poisonously mediocre and, finally, a celebration of the journalistic benefits of having an informer tucked away in a garage" (a frequent Deep Throat–Woodward rendezvous).

In retrospect, the reviews quoted, which are representative in tenor, certainly were not as enthusiastic as later viewings would suggest. The material does not date, and in spite of some fabrications and "Woodstein"'s minor "dirty tricks," *All the President's Men* has real merit, a tough work on a tough subject that deserves to remain in print and on film well into the 21st century.

Blind Ambition (TV mini-series, 1979)

Directed by George Schaefer. Written by Stanley R. Greenberg. Adapted from *Blind Ambition* by John Dean III and *Mo* by Maureen Dean. Produced by Schaefer and Renee Calente. Executive producer: David Susskind for Time-Life Productions. CBS-TV, Sunday, May 21, 1979, 8–10 P.M., Monday–Tuesday–Wednesday 9–11 P.M. (480 minutes). Cast: *Richard Nixon* Rip Torn; *John Dean III* Martin Sheen; *Maureen Dean* Theresa Russell; *John Ehrlichman* Graham Jarvis; *H.R. Haldeman* Lawrence Pressman; *John Caulfield* Gerald O'Loughlin; *G. Gordon Liddy* William Daniels; *Charles Shaffer* Ed Flanders; *John Mitchell* John Randolph; *Charles Colson* Michael Callan; *Pat Nixon* Cathleen Cordell.

Nixon to John Dean III in the TV film *Blind Ambition*: "Get a good night's sleep and don't bug anyone without telling me."

Two quotations from Rip Torn, *Blind Ambition*'s Nixon, 17 years apart:

> I played Richard III as Nixon back in the late '60s. Then people said I was paranoid about Nixon. When Watergate happened, they said I was prophetic. He's clever, extremely clever, and he's back, of course. I used to say it would take him two years; in fact it's only taken him a

Martin Sheen as John Dean, Rip Torn as Nixon and Lawrence Pressman as Haldeman in the television drama *Blind Ambition* (1979).

little bit longer. — *Women's Wear Daily*, December 28, 1978.

I always had respect for him; he was our president. He kept getting up off the mat, and I liked that part of him. He was also a wonderful family man. I didn't worship him, but I respected him. I believe history will look back kindly on Nixon. He was a tragic figure. — *New York Daily News*, December 3, 1995.

The television version of John Dean's *Blind Ambition* had things going for it: Rip Torn's highly intense and physical performance as Nixon and William Daniel's mesmerizing spaciness as G. Gordon Liddy. Torn, always dressed in "oversized clothing" because he said "Nixon never gave the impression of filling out his suits," had such zany kick-start lines as "I want the most comprehensive notes on everybody who tried to do us in — they're asking for it, and they're going to get it." Liddy's lines were also filled with breathtaking paranoia. Liddy wanted to set up "a pleasure craft" near the 1972 Democratic convention where "the dirty tricks" gang could "without much trouble compromise [Democratic] officials through the charms of some ladies living on the boat." Liddy also wanted to knock out the air conditioning inside the convention hall so that all the Democrats "will sweat" on national television.

If only the rest of the eight hours had as much unintentional humor, *Blind Ambition* would be well worth watching. Unfortunately, in the hope of gaining as wide an audience as possible, the "creative team" melded two books that are related in background but not in tone. As a result, *Blind Ambition* is a broken-backed exercise that has bite in only half of its distended bulk. The *Christian Science Monitor* (May 17,

1979) characterized this hybrid rather well in its neologism "the docu-soap opera," or as *Newsweek* illustrated (May 21, 1979): "The problem is that one of the nation's greatest constitutional crises is played against a banal domestic obbligato that trivializes the show's impact. Then John drags himself home after secretly meeting with Federal prosecutors, Mo (Theresa Russell) petulantly accuses him of being off with other women. He discovers that he is a target of the grand jury. She pouts at having to cancel an outing at the racetrack. He agonizes over being ordered to Camp David. She frets about what dresses to take. As he sinks deeper into the Scotch, she gets off her sudsiest shot: 'When you go to bed you never close your eyes. But you don't see me, John.... You don't *see* me!'" The situation described and the dialogue quoted give a clear indication of the sulking, pouting and whining and incredible mindlessness of the domestic episodes of this patched-together script.

On the plus side, the political side, of Dean's "self-serving version of reality" (*Monitor*, May 17, 1979), the script rattles along at a fairly sprightly inside-the-Beltway clip. Although it's all been served up before and better, there are some rewards along the way, in addition to the star turns by Torn and Daniels. As Dean, Martin Sheen gives a winning performance, but the viewer still doesn't find much to sympathize with when Dean enmeshes himself deeper into deception, not to mention taking money out of a secret fund to finance his own honeymoon. Ultimately, Dean's portrait of an innocent betrayed by a corrupt system is not convincing because Dean is obviously just as guilty as the people he is castigating, and Mo's tactically spaced reappearances, hardly ever without a self-pitying slur and a glass in her hand, just drag down whatever verisimilitude the production manages to occasionally muster up.

The *New York Times* (May 18, 1979) was right on target in saying: "The viewer is told that 'scenes from the Oval Office are drawn from verbatim accounts of White House tapes.' These particular scenes are among the best in the production precisely because they are rooted in fact, not solely on Mr. Dean's interpretation of things, and because Rip Torn captures President Richard M. Nixon perfectly as Superneurotic posing as Everyman." However it is these very scenes that make the viewer even more resentful of Dean's self-proclaimed victimhood, especially when the "prison" for this 1972 "re-election team" has private bathrooms, writing desks and "kitchen privileges" with solicitous Mafiosi dishing up spaghetti. Not exactly Devil's Island! (And half of them got book and movie deals!) On page 249 of the Simon and Schuster edition of *Blind Ambition*, Dean stated that ten of the 15 men who could be indicted by a grand jury as a result of Watergate were lawyers, and of course, Nixon had graduated third in his class from Duke Law School. Watergate had much to do with the great mistrust, if not contempt, that the American public grew to have for lawyers. Because of this, *Blind Ambition* has a singular air of untruth; John Dean and his cohorts deserved greater punishment, at least in Dean's case, than four months in a congenial frat house.

In a drama that is speciously melodramatic to begin with, the highly theatrical performances of Rip Torn and William Daniels almost save the day. As the *Monitor* put it (May 17, 1979): "Rip Torn plays Richard Nixon with a strange blend of caricature, mimicry, and just a touch of humility. Not much, but enough." Overall, *Blind Ambition* had a mixed reception. *Variety* (May 23, 1979) relished its being a "a nostalgia bath for anti–Nixon junkies." The *New York Times* (May 18, 1979) found the material "familiar, perhaps too familiar," but the *Times* found its "final moment ... cleverly frightening. A reporter is heard asking, 'Mr. Dean, could Watergate ever happen again?' As a photograph of Mr. Dean slowly fades from the screen, there is no answer." It is a pity that its few thought-provoking moments are Scotch-taped to the emotionalism of Mo's teenage talk show.

An intriguing footnote to *Blind Ambition* appeared in the *New York Times* of June 15, 1992: "In January, Mr. Dean and his wife, Maureen, filed a $150 million dollar libel suit against Mr. Liddy and the authors and publisher of a 1991 book, *Silent Coup: The Removal of a President.* The book, written by Len Colodny and Robert Getlin, asserts that it was Mr. Dean who thought up the Watergate burglary and the cover-up and that Mrs. Dean had connections to a call-girl ring.... David Kaye, general counsel for St. Martin's Press, which published the book ... said that after reading *Silent Coup,* Mr. Liddy became convinced that its conclusions were correct. Mr. Liddy wrote an afterword to his 11-year-old best-selling memoir *Will,* also published by St. Martin's Press, praising the book, and repeated his praise on his radio talk show in Fairfax, Virginia."

Alexander Haig is not mentioned in the television film, and he is only mentioned once in the text of *Blind Ambition,* but *Silent Coup,* on pages 368 and 369, implies in the strongest terms that Haig was Deep Throat.

David Frost Interviews Henry Kissinger (documentary, 1979)

52 minutes. NBC–TV. Thursday, October 11, 1979. 10–11 P.M.

"Mr. Frost explained his [interview] strategy, 'We want to let Kissinger put his views honestly and effectively. This is informational television not opinion television, but if he does do the facts a disservice, then I have to step in and say, Yes, but ...' One area where Mr. Frost hopes to step in boldly concerns ... the abiding fascination of the Kissinger–Nixon relationship. In [his] Nixon interviews, Mr. Frost drew out the former President, who described his Secretary of State as a kind of egotistical, stubborn, celebrity-hunting intellectual — a neurotic genius in need of a firm hand. 'Ah, but he did it with such humor and deftness,' Mr. Frost recalled. In the memoirs, Mr. Kissinger returns the compliments to Mr. Nixon's 'lonely, tormented psyche.'" — *New York Times,* October 7, 1979.

"In the transcript, which NBC released at Kissinger's request and was also its own decision, Mr. Kissinger describes former President Nixon as 'given to hyperbole.' He also notes that by 1969 secret American bombings of North Vietnamese sanctuaries in Cambodia had become 'part of the landscape.' He acknowledged his own denials of the bombings to news reporters at the time." — *New York Times,* October 11, 1979.

"Time after time, the former Secretary was confronted with [Frost's] challenges to his pronouncements on the sensitive question of Cambodia. Mr. Kissinger said, 'We inherited a tragedy.' Mr. Frost remained unconvinced, insisting that 'you inherited an unwelcome situation.' Mr. Kissinger pushed ahead: 'The Vietnamese engulfed Cambodia.' Mr. Frost quickly parried: 'They didn't bomb the hell out of it.'" — *New York Times,* October 13, 1979.

In this last article, Frost discussed NBC's decision to give reporters unedited transcripts: "We felt we had to do this or the legends and myths would persist forever."

See also: 1995, *Kissinger: An A & E Biography,* and 1996, *Kissinger and Nixon.*

Lady from Dubuque (play, 1980)

A philosophical comedy in two acts by Edward Albee. Directed by Alan Schneider. Costumes by Pauline Trigere. Morosco Theatre. Opened February 5, 1980.

Another "not Nixon play," but in John Simon's terms, "one of the worst plays
about anything, ever." Simon goes on to say that it "is a lot of desperate pretensions
and last-ditch attitudinizing about nothing ... with strategies for stretching out nothing into two acts.... [One strategy is] irrelevant but grandiose political or metaphysi-
cal mouthings" (*New York*, February 11, 1980). Nixon has always been an easy target
for both witty and pseudo-witty playwrights. *Lady from Dubuque* contains the kind
of automatic response laugh line that pseudo-witty playwrights pepper their plays with
when they cannot think of anything truly witty or insightful to say. ("We're too moral
to survive; a real Nixon will come along someday if the Russians don't.")

Irene Worth, star of the Martha Mitchell play *After the Season,* was the title character in this misbegotten enterprise. Stanley Kauffmann stated that Pauline Trigere's
costume for Worth provided the "only drama of the evening." (*Theatre Criticisms* 1983).

First Family (satiric film, 1980)

108 minutes. Written and directed by Buck Henry. Produced by Daniel Melnick. Music by John Philip Sousa as adapted and conducted by Ralph Burns.
African sacrificial dance choreographed by Toni Basil. Warner Bros. release of
an Indie-Prod Production. Color.

This is the story of a late 20th century First Family, the Links — the Missing
branch of the Links, that is. *Variety* (December 31, 1980) stated that they "somewhat
resembled the Gerald Ford clan." The constantly imbibing First Lady lampooned by
Madeline Kahn hints at Mamie Eisenhower, Betty Ford and the assertions made by
Woodstein in their 1976 book *The Final Days*.

The dim-witted First Daughter (Gilda Radner) is kidnapped in the primitive
African country of Upper Gorm. The portrayal of the Africans is on a sub-human level
and is the most dispiriting aspect of this abysmally inept film in which Radner also
does a variation on the famous Nixon line about his mother. Radner says: "I had a dog.
That dog was a saint."

"You keep wondering what could have been in Buck Henry's mind as he wrote
and directed this nonsense."—*Christian Science Monitor*, February 5, 1981.

Hopscotch (film, 1980)

107 minutes. Directed by Ronald Neame. Written by Brian Garfield and Bryan
Forbes, based on Garfield's novel. Photography by Arthur Ibbetson. Music based
on classical themes arranged by Ian Fraser. Produced by Edy and Ely Landau.

Color. Avco Embassy. Cast: *Miles Kendig* Walter Matthau; *Isobel von Schmidt* Glenda Jackson; *G. P. Myerson* Ned Beatty; *Cutter* Sam Waterson; *Mikhail Yaskov* Herbert Lom.

Hopscotch is regarded as something of a comic misfire. The *Variety* review of July 6, 1980, sheds some light on the problem: "In some earlier script versions reportedly, [*Hopscotch*] was serious stuff."

In the release print the basic story line is that Miles Kendig (Walter Matthau) a 30-year CIA "operative," is demoted by his new boss, Myerson (Ned Beatty), an ex-"dirty trickster" and hidebound "company man" of long standing and a scheming bureaucratic martinet.

Kendig seeks revenge after Myerson tells him he will vegetate until retirement by "running a filling station." Kendig's revenge is to write a book exposing all the machinations of the CIA. He is aided in this by his former lover and retired CIA operative Isobel von Schmidt (Glenda Jackson in a role that almost disappears as the film becomes engulfed by chase sequences and explosions).

The action-heavy film has little time to develop character. Next to Matthau and the fading Isobel von Schmidt, Beatty has the best developed part, even though he is something of a cliché as a gun-toting, hard-nosed ultra-right winger who tells his wife when she is about to rent their summer home: "No kids. No pets. No Democrats"— one of the few fairly amusing lines in the script.

Beatty's office is festooned with pictures of his courting of the mighty: Beatty and Nixon ("celebrity look-alike" Richard M. Dixon) and other "celebrity look-alikes" for Kissinger, Ford and Rosalyn Carter.

Variety concluded: "It remains only mildly amusing and climaxes in a finish that isn't worthy of what came before. What's worse, Jackson largely disappears long before the finale, in spirit if not in fact."

Where the Buffalo Roam (film, 1980)

98 minutes. Produced and directed by Art Linson. Written by John Kaye, based on the life of Hunter S. Thompson. Photography by Tak Fujimoto. Edited by Christopher Greenbury. Music by Neil Young. Color. Universal. Cast: *Hunter S. Thompson* Bill Murray; *Lazlo* Peter Boyle; *Martu Lewis* Bruno Kirby; *Richard Nixon* Richard M. Dixon.

"Nixon and the '60s, though they hated each other, were each driven by a fierce relentlessness. Nixon finally died. The '60s go on and on."— Lance Morrow, *Time*, May 6, 1996.

The recipient of the worst reviews in the history of the cinema, *Where the Buffalo Roam* was a film with a 1960s sensibility released in the 1980s. It failed miserably because at least some of its audience had grown up. The film is a series of slapstick routines, but as the *East Side Express* stated (May 8, 1980); "Somehow the viewer needs to know why these things happen, or at least what it all means." *The Hollywood Reporter* concurred (April 1, 1980): "It's a sketchy account of several events in Thompson's life, ranging from the disproportionate sentences handed out in the late 1960s to his antics during the 1972 presidential campaign. There are some funny bits, including a large number of jabs at Richard Nixon, but most of it is overly preposterous low-comedy shtick."

One particular Nixon-Thompson scene was noted by nearly all critics: "Encountering Nixon in the john he regales the startled Chief Executive with his theory of how the United States is divided into two groups, the Doomed and the Screwheads... and the relentless mayhem becomes tiresome chaos rather than liberating comic anarchy, despite occasional, mild epiphanies such as the face of an uncredited actor as Nixon darkening from paranoia to superparanoia as he huddles in a urinal" (Jack Kroll, *Newsweek*, May 12, 1980). Kathleen Carroll of the *New York Daily News* (April 26, 1980) noted the film's desperate attempts at humor by pointing to the same scene: "[Thompson] grabs his interview with Presidential candidate Nixon in a men's room by posing as a reporter from the *Washington Post*; the movie looks like nothing more than an extended sketch from TV's *Saturday Night Live*."

"Writing about *Where the Buffalo Roam* is not really the problem," Richard Corliss wrote in the *Soho Weekly News* (April 30, 1980). "Thinking about it is the problem and sitting through it was the ultimate ordeal. The movie is shrill, dopey, one-note — a hate note to straight America." David Denby in *New York* (May 12, 1980) was even less kind: "This movie ... poses a serious challenge to *A Night in Paradise,* with Turhan Bey as Aesop, as the worst movie ever made about a writer."

Trials of Alger Hiss (documentary, 1980)

164 minutes. Written, directed and produced by Jon Lowenthal. Photographed by Stephen Alexander and others. Edited by Marion Kraft. Sound recording by Richard Breck. Technical advisors: Emile de Antonio, Frederick Wiseman and Marcel Ophuls. Distributed by Corinth Films, 410 East 62nd Street, NY, NY 10021.

As he recounted it in the *New York Times* (January 11, 1981): In 1949, John Lowenthal, a law student at Columbia University, became a research volunteer in Alger Hiss' first trial, a trial in which Hiss was charged with lying to a grand jury. The trial ended in a hung jury. A second trial, a trial for libel, took place later.

One morning in October 1976, Lowenthal, by then a fifty-one-year-old professor of tax law at Rutgers, had a year's leave of absence before him with no challenging project in mind. The Hiss case, wherein Hiss, a former State Department official and later President of the Carnegie Endowment for International Peace, had been accused by the late *Time* editor Whittaker Chambers of being a Soviet spy, had remained a talking point for nearly three decades with vehement partisans on both sides. A lover of controversy, Lowenthal became convinced that the Hiss case was a difficult but worthy subject.

The Trials of Alger Hiss, Lowenthal's baptism by trial and error in filmmaking, took over three years to make and resulted in a financial outlay of over $400,000, much of it Lowenthal's own money (with other interested parties contributing at various times). Whenever money came in, Lowenthal worked on the film, "which meant that shooting had to be scheduled when there was money available to pay for a camera and equipment."

Because there were as many Hiss detractors as there were defenders, Lowenthal had
to play his interviews with the very much alive and tenaciously defensive Hiss against
a champion of Hiss' long-departed accuser Whittaker Chambers. He chose Ralph de
Toledano, Chambers' friend and a former *Newsweek* editor and co-author with Victor
Lasky of *Seeds of Treason: The True Story of the Hiss-Chambers Tragedy* (1950).

One of the reasons that the Hiss case, although over a quarter of a century in the
past, seemed such a viable subject was that in 1975 the Freedom of Information Act
was passed by Congress permitting access to previously unavailable information. The
value of this act for researchers, authors and filmmakers cannot be overestimated. "Since
1976, the FBI has yielded up hundreds of documents relating to the Hiss case as a result
of FOIA suits. The utilization of this material in *The Trials of Alger Hiss* is path-
breaking.... the film underscores the historical importance of the FBI record and the
need to take care that this record is properly conserved" (*Film Library Quarterly*, Volume 13, no. 2, 1980). As presented in the film, the new material suggests that the typewriter claimed by the prosecution to have belonged to Priscilla Hiss may well have been
another typewriter introduced to falsely incriminate her husband. The serial number
on the Woodstock typewriter the FBI introduced suggests a date later than the date of
manufacture of the Hiss typewriter. Therefore, the typewriter used as evidence was
probably not that of either Alger or Priscilla Hiss. Ambiguities such as this and the
audience's own conflict between trust and skepticism make the film fascinating.

Nixon, Hiss and Chambers appear throughout the film. Others are Robert E.
Stripling, the House Un-American Activities Committee's chief investigator; John
Cronin, Nixon's private source at the FBI; Thomas Murphy, the government prose-
cutor, and Claudie, the Hiss' cook.

Was Hiss guilty, or, more to the point, of *what*, and does the United States
government have guilt it *should* share? As Roger Ebert's review (*Chicago Sun-Times*
March 20, 1981) ponders: "Lowenthal's film includes a great deal of footage from the
original HUAC hearings at which Hiss denied knowing Chambers, before eventually
conceding that perhaps he had known Chambers under a pseudonym. Then he remembered giving that man a car, letting him live rent-free in an apartment, buying him
meals, and so on.... I found it impossible to believe that Hiss had not known Chambers in the 1930s. It seemed to me Hiss was perjuring himself. Then, later in the film,
I discovered that the FBI had also apparently acted dishonestly in building its case
against Hiss. For myself, at least, this film left the disturbing impression that both sides
were lying at times. It was a shoddy business, and makes a fascinating film."

The *Nation* (March 8, 1980) and the *Village Voice* (March 17, 1980) were elated
to have another chance to pummel Nixon:

> The visual record is much richer than I expected. We all know, in a
> vague sort of way, that Richard Nixon got his start by pouncing on
> Hiss; here one sees the young, little-known Congressman — already
> self-righteous, already asking the public to admire the selflessness with
> which he carries out his patriotic duty — as he seizes this once-in-a-life-
> time opportunity. — *The Nation*.

> "The Hiss–HUAC contretemps made a political superstar out of com-
> mittee member Richard Nixon, and it's worth the price of admission
> to consider his performance alone. Puffing his chest out for the camera,
> Nixon unctuously brags about how he brought the traitor to bay, then
> stares straight into the eyes of Mr. and Mrs. America and declares: "I

From *The Trials of Alger Hiss* (documentary film, 1980).

believe in congressional investigations. The two antagonists are compelling as well." — *Village Voice*.

After its standard Nixon-bashing which their critic delivered with his usual gusto, the critic's final verdict was that the film was "engrossing, but ultimately unsatisfying. The need is less for films exploring the minutiae of the Hiss (or Rosenberg or Hollywood Ten) trials than for an epic overview analyzing the entire postwar Red Scare, and the purges that accompanied it."

Aside from the questions of patriotism and legal ethics, students of the Hiss case are always struck by one question: What was Chambers' motive for harassing Hiss? Gene Siskel (*Chicago Tribune* March 20, 1981) stated that "the film suggests ... Hiss may have spurned Chambers as a lover." (Prior to his marriage, Chambers had been a practicing homosexual.)

In an ironic coda to the Hiss case, one of Nixon's principal detractors, Garry Wills, author of *Nixon Agonistes* (1970), wrote in the *New York Post* (March 19, 1996): "Now a Soviet cable decrypted by the National Security Agency in 1945 has been released. It describes how an American working for the Soviet Union since 1935 (when Chambers said Hiss began his spying) had attended the Yalta Peace Conference and gone on to Moscow afterward. Only four Americans did that, and no one has any suspicion that the other three might have been spies. The code name for the agent mentioned in the cable was Ales, and it is hard to imagine how this could not have been Hiss.... Difficult as it is for some people, it may be time to admit that Nixon was right. It is time for the left to give up on Hiss."

"The common notion that Richard Nixon cynically 'destroyed' Alger Hiss is insupportable. Hiss destroyed himself..."— Tom Wicker, *One of Us: Richard Nixon and the American Dream*, 1991.

Note: See also *Concealed Enemies* 1984.

Missing (film, 1982)

122 minutes. Directed by Constantin Costa-Gavras. Written by Costa-Gavras and Donald Stewart, based on *The Execution of Charles Horman: An American Sacrifice* (1979) by Thomas Hauser. Photography by Ricardo Aronovich. Edited by Francoise Bonnot. Music by Vangelis. Universal. Color. Cast: *Ed Horman* Jack Lemmon; *Beth Horman* Sissy Spacek; *Charles Horman* John Shea; *Terry Simon* Melanie Mayron; *Kate Newman* Janice Rule.

The fact-based film *Missing* deals with the attempts of Edmund Horman (Jack Lemmon), an American engineer, to learn the details behind the disappearance of his son, Charles, a journalist, captured by a right-wing group in Chile. He is accompanied by his daughter-in-law Beth (Sissy Spacek). Their disappointment grows into shocked disbelief when they realize that the United States had failed to protect Charles once his arrest was known to them. This led Edmund and Beth to further believe that the United States covered up their non-intervention for political reasons.

Missing was a talking point both before and after its release. On the eve of its opening, the U.S. State Department issued a lengthy statement saying that American officials searched scrupulously for Charles Horman, and they refuted any possible negligence or wrong-doing. One of the most chilling scenes in the film occurs at the National Stadium in Santiago when Edmund shouts above the hundreds of prisoners: "Charles Horman, I hope you are out there. This is your father speaking. If you hear me, please come forward. You have nothing to fear." In truth, Charles had been dead for three weeks. Charles had been arrested because he witnessed the rightist invasion on the coast near Valparaiso. He was shot to death because the leaders of the coup were afraid he would expose them. Edmund Horman died on April 15, 1993. He had always said, "I'm not interested in revenge. What revenge can I do? I don't want this to happen to American citizens again."

Missing will remain a controversial film. A passage from *Visions of Empire: Political*

Imagery in Contemporary American Film by Stephen Prince (1992) sheds light on this continuing controversy: "Growing increasingly frustrated with the apparent inability of the American embassy to locate his son, Ed confronts the ambassador and tries to force him to admit that the United States operates a special assistance program for the Chilean security forces. The ambassador denies that any such operation exists, and he is filmed in a close-up with a portrait of President Nixon hanging prominently on the wall behind him. Both he and Nixon almost face the camera, so the composition offers us a nearly direct address by American authorities. Unfortunately, the ambassador is lying.... As the narrative develops, it is implied that American authorities co-signed a kill order with Chilean security officials to eliminate Charles because of what he saw and learned."

In an interview in the *Christian Science Monitor* (February 25, 1982), Costa-Gavras said he did not see *Missing* as an anti–American film. "It's a *pro*–American fact that this film has been made at all. This shows the tradition of freedom and self-criticism in the United States. This is one of the biggest riches of democracy — to see problems, speak about them, and eventually correct them. This is one of the few countries, if not the only one, where such a film could be made and shown freely."

Tom Milne in the *Monthly Film Bulletin* (May 1982) felt that Costa-Gavras claimed rather more than he delivered: "Blaming the CIA for anything and everything has become such a commonplace in both fact and fiction that, by the time Jack Lemmon finally wins through to a solution in his convoluted whodunit — the fact that American military power lay behind a foreign coup — the sense of anti-climax is as acute as if a conjuror promising a brand new trick had proceeded to produce a rabbit out of a hat. That character played ... by Jack Lemmon is also rather too good to be true. Sputtering with true grit and native honesty like a latter-day George Washington, required to express himself in the middle American idiom ... ('I don't want any of your anti–Establishment paranoia'), he is little more than a straw dummy set up to be converted to Sissy Spacek's liberal-leftish viewpoint."

Howard Kissel in *Women's Wear Daily* (February 12, 1982) also felt that the film was too doctrinaire: "Costa-Gavras handles this sensitive subject in the same agitprop style he has handled all his films since *Z*. Everything is so black and white one tends to grow suspicious. Every scene in the American consulate, for example, features prominently a photograph of then President Nixon.... but the device is so obvious — the implication that he is Ultimate Author of All Those Evils — that it only increases one's skepticism. Everything the actors are required to do seems so obvious and manipulative that even Sissy Spacek as the widow of the slain American and Jack Lemmon as his troubled father grow tiresome and predictable in what should be wrenching roles."

An earlier film dealing with the Chilean coup that received higher praise is *The Battle of Chile* (1978), directed by Patricio Guzman. (Stanley Kauffmann: "A grim, intimate, unique record." Pauline Kael: "Aesthetically, this is a major film, and that gives force even to the patterning of its changes.")

Knights Errant (stage play, 1982)

Written by John Hunt with the collaboration of Martin Kaplan. Directed by Geoffrey Shlaes. Scenery by Vicki Paul. Costumes by John Falabella. Produced by Jacquie Littlefield. At the Intar Theater, 420 West 42nd Street, New York, December 1, 1982.

Knights Errant by novelist John Hunt and former President Carter speechwriter Martin Kaplan uses the device of a ghost writer going to La Casa Pacifica to assist Nixon in writing his memoirs. In the process of working on the memoirs, parallels are struck between Nixon's conduct with Hiss and Chambers in the late 1940s and his drowning in the torrents of Watergate in the mid–1970s. As reviewed in the *News-World* of December 2, 1982, the play keeps promising to "show a direct line between the Hiss case and Watergate ... [but] two and a half hours later, after yards and yards of rhetoric, we finally get to the bottom line of *Knights Errant*—we're no wiser about Watergate than when we walked in..."

Only one critic reviewed this play favorably; that minority voice was Jacques Le Sourd of *Gannett Today* (December 2, 1982), who wrote: "Through deft use of testimony before Nixon's House Un-American Activities Committee, and passages from the Nixon memoirs, combined with fictional dialogue that always rings true, Hunt tells the story (two stories really) in considerable detail without getting bogged down in historical minutiae." Le Sourd also praised Harry Spillman's "amazing" Nixon.

In fact, critics were unanimous in praise of Spillman's performance: "Harry Spillman creates a mellowed-out, slightly senile and paranoid Nixon, for whom he's almost a dead ringer."—*News World*, December 2, 1982.

"Mr. Spillman is no double for his real-life counterpart—he needs a jowl transplant—but what really makes him persuasive is his ability to act the part in a low-key fashion, without the spastic arm gestures and icy authoritarian bellowing of the self-caricaturing public Nixon."—*New York Times*, December 2, 1982.

"At the play's heart lies Harry Spillman's fine impersonation of Nixon, jowly, suspicious, nervously jocular, his cheek muscles quivering, and his voice orating. A fine job of caricature reconstruction."—*New York Post*, December 7, 1982.

"Harry Spillman creates a vivid, hypnotic impression of Nixon; he has mastered not only the speech mannerisms but the actual look, as well. And within this impersonation he manages to present a living character whose deeper motivations, along with his more obvious ones, arouse our interest. We feel the need to look into the soul of this tortured man."—Douglas Watt, *New York Daily News*, December 2, 1982.

Will: G. Gordon Liddy (TV film, 1982)

120 minutes. Directed by Robert Lieberman. Written by John Abatemarco from G. Gordon Liddy's autobiography (1980). Produced by the Shayne Company (Robert and Joan Conrad). NBC, January 10, 1982. Cast: *G. Gordon Liddy* Robert Conrad; *Fran Liddy* Katherine Cannon; *Jeb Magruder* Gary Bayer; *John Dean* Peter Ratray; *Bud Krogh* Al Nuti; *Howard Hunt* F. J. O'Neil; *Voice of Richard Nixon* John Byner.

"What doesn't destroy me, makes me stronger."—G. Gordon Liddy, upon his release from prison on September 7, 1977.

The major events of the life of G. Gordon Liddy are presented in the biographical film *Will*, but as Kay Gardella said (*New York Daily News*, January 8, 1982): "There is the overwhelming sense ... that his story is incomplete, that the picture we are look-ing at is a distortion. Some of the fault lies in the fact that the important links to the real story, involving a network of presidential aides are glossed over. Liddy is the pic-ture, but one is never quite sure how he got to such a position of importance and why." The reason may be that this is the shortest dramatization of any of the Watergate-related books.

New York Times critic John J. O'Connor (January 10, 1982) called *Will* "still another smooth example of (a) 'based on a true story' project," but he questioned its purpose: "[m]ore than usual, something about the production rankles. Does the pub-lic really need the autobiography of G. Gordon Liddy, either in book or movie form? What purpose is ultimately served?"

O'Connor's question deserves consideration. Granted, Watergate was a major political scandal, but as filmed, it appears merely as a botched burglary. Little history is learned or served in this production. Its focus is the very bizarre behavior of a very bizarre man. The son of an authoritarian father and a passive mother who was raised in a Catholic household in New Jersey, supervised by a German maid who admired Hitler, Liddy developed into a kind of loopy superman. He *willed* himself to overcome fear by setting goals for himself that no rational person would ever conceive of: killing, cooking and eating a rat, climbing a tree in a thunderstorm, holding his hand over a candle flame for a lengthy period of time and expressing a desire to learn how to shoot someone right between the eyes. His is the oft-told story of the puny child who over-compensates by willing himself to become the most manly of men, all the while pumped up by the theatricalized glorification of German militarism he had heard as a child.

After the bizarre scenes of childhood, *Will* touches Liddy's graduation from Ford-ham Law School, his experiences in the army, the FBI, his appointment as an assistant district attorney in Dutchess County, New York, and his failure at gaining a congres-sional seat. As the United States became more involved in the turmoil of Vietnam, he was attached to the White House for "special duties," then joined the Committee to Re-Elect the President as Counsel. Throughout all these experiences, he retained his perception of himself as a superman and a super-patriot. After Watergate, Judge J. Sir-ica sentenced him to 20 years in prison and a $40,000 fine; some of the severity of this sentence was no doubt caused by Liddy's unrepentant nature and what seemed like a touch of masochism.

The end of the film shows Liddy using his lawyerly skills to compile a case against a warden known for his harsh treatment of prisoners. By doing this, Liddy wins the respect of his fellow prisoners; he is raised on a fork lift truck and paraded around the prison yard. Borne aloft, he begins to sing. It is one of the songs he heard on the Hitler broadcasts in his childhood.

In 1977, President Carter commuted Liddy's sentence to eight years, and he was released in September 1977 after serving 53½ months. He became a writer (a novel, *Out of Control*, 1979, in addition to *Will*) and a very successful call-in talk show host. He is also the "hero" of the two-volume novel *Gordon Liddy Is My Muse* (1990 and 1991) by John Calvin Batchelor. The *New York Times* reviewed both books (Decem-ber 24, 1995), calling them a "sporadically entertaining blur" whose "fictional author ... is a writer of spy thrillers who deeply admires the unabashed macho of President Nixon's former henchman."

A final revealing comment from *New York Daily News* critic Lorenzo Carcaterra

(January 10, 1982): "[What] dominates *Will* [is] the sense of despair that existed during the Nixon years. It was despair that permeated all sides — from the power-puffed Washingtonians to the power-hungry radicals. Looking back, there seems little substantial difference between them; it was simply a question of style."

The jacket of the autobiography says in part: "He is not like you and me, probably not like anyone you've ever known." As another *Daily News* critic, Kay Gardella, wrote, "Thank God!"

The Big Lever (film, 1982)

Subtitled "Party Politics in Leslie County, Kentucky." Not available.

Return Engagement (documentary, 1983)

90 minutes. Directed by Alan Rudolph. Shown at the Embassy 72nd Street Theater. No general release.With G. Gordon Liddy and Dr. Timothy Leary.

"There was a time, after all, when 'tune in, turn on, drop out' was the mantra of a generation." — Jeffrey Ressner, *Time*, April 29, 1996.

Directed by Robert Altman's former assistant, *Return Engagement* is a weird hour and a half gabfest between the supreme guru of the right, G. Gordon Liddy, and the original 1960s "tune in" (to my ideas, forget your parents), "turn on" (to drugs), "drop out" (of society in perpetual drugdom) guru Dr. Timothy Leary.

The film chronicles a week in Los Angeles during which these mighty opposites talked at each other as part of a year's tour of expressing their obsessions and outrages.

As the *London Observer* (September 11, 1983) pointed out: "The title refers to revisiting the '60s and '70s through these emblematic figures, and to the fact that back in 1966 Liddy, as an eager young district attorney in an ultra-conservative New York county, arrested Leary's whole commune several times on drugs charges. The harassment led, so Leary argues, to Liddy being hired as a narcotics expert by the White House, and thus on to Watergate, justifying Leary's claim that the pair helped bring down Nixon."

An Associated Press bulletin of April 19, 1996, entitled "Net Result: death?" stated that Leary, 75, was "actively exploring" committing suicide while logging on the Internet. "I'm very involved in the high tech of dying," he explained.

Leary's involvement became total shortly after.

"By 1963, [Leary] had shared drug experiences with Marilyn Monroe, Allen Ginsberg, Cary Grant, Charlie Mingus, Willem de Kooning, Aldous Huxley, Thelonius Monk and William Burroughs. He had even tripped with one of President Kennedy's mistresses, Mary Pinchot Meyer. Three years later [he] married fashion model Nina von Schlebrugge (better known today as Uma Thurman's mother). Richard Nixon called him 'the most dangerous man in America.'" — *Boston Magazine*, May 1996.

Leaders (TV series, 1983)

A series announced for educational television. Richard Nixon, host. Based upon his 1982 book of the same name. To be produced by Frank Gannon, chief editorial assistant on Nixon's memoirs. Apparently never completed, it was to contain segments on Churchill, de Gaulle, Douglas MacArthur, Shigeru Yoshida, Konrad Adenauer, Nikita Khrushchev, Zhou Enlai and "new leaders in a time of change." Frank Gannon did produce another series entitled *The Real Richard Nixon*, released in 1994 for home video and the History Channel.

Seeing Red: Stories of American Communists (documentary, 1983)

100 minutes. Directed and produced by Julia Reichert and James Klein. Photography by Stephen Lighthill, Sandi Sissel and Martin Duckworth. Edited by James Klein and Julia Reichert. Music by Bernice Reagon and Pete Seeger. Heartland Productions. Among the Communists interviewed: Bill Bailey, Howard "Stretch" Johnson and Pete Seeger. Also appearing: Ronald Reagan, Richard Nixon, Hubert Humphrey and J. Edgar Hoover.

Seeing Red was given a benefit screening at the Entermedia Theater on Manhattan's Lower East Side, the home of a tremendous Jewish population and a thriving Yiddish theater in the early part of the 20th century. The purpose of the benefit was to raise money for the film's national distribution. Introductory remarks were given by Robert Meeropol, one of the sons of Julius and Ethel Rosenberg, and Paul Robeson, Jr. Folk singer Peter Yarrow was also a participant.

The sub-title of the film suggests its development: "a series of portraits — with archival footage of strikers, marches and McCarthy-era politicians (Hoover, Nixon, Reagan, Truman) spewing their Cold War vitriol" (*Village Voice*, March 10, 1984).

Seeing Red did not have a long run in theaters, possibly because the threat of Communism had paled somewhat by the mid–1980s or possibly for the reasons cited in the *Columbia* (University) *Film Review*, Summer 1984: "*Seeing Red* is one of the most brazenly manipulative and intellectually dishonest films I've ever seen. (On the latter charge I grant that the dishonesty may have been unintentional.) It will, though, be a success, critical and otherwise — why, Klein and Reichert even have good old Pete Seeger to draw the folkies in. I'm reminded of the remark on Marx's dictum, 'If religion is the opiate of the masses, then Communism is the opiate of the intellectuals.' The only thing that would have been more despicable than a film celebrating a horde of old Stalinists would be a film celebrating a pack of old Nazis reveling in their gruesome past. I hope I haven't given anyone any ideas."

Basement Tapes (satiric comedy, 1983)

A satiric comedy in two acts by Erik Brogger. Directed by Robert Engels. Setting by Mark Haack. Costumes by Kristina Watson. Lighting by Bonnie Ann Brown.

Stage manager: Kevin Mangan. Produced by Christopher Hart, Mike Houlihan and Eileen McMahon at the Village Gate, 160 Bleecker Street, New York City. Opened September 14, 1983, for a short run. Cast: *Richard Nixon* Michael Laskin; *Gerald R. Ford* Bill Schoppert; *G. Gordon Liddy* David Wohl.

This is the second comedy by Erik Brogger dealing with Richard Nixon and Gerald Ford. The first, *Tea with Dick and Jerry* (1976), was not a success, nor was *The Basement Tapes*, which was co-produced by Christopher Hart, son of playwright-director Moss Hart.

The play is set in the basement rec room of Gerald Ford's Palm Springs home in 1983. It's meant to be a Watergate reunion of sorts, although it is beyond anyone's wildest imagination to think that Gerald Ford would have anything to do with such a maniac as G. Gordon Liddy. (Betty Ford, by the way, is selling Amway products.) Nixon, Ford and Liddy play a game of poker while poker maven Nixon fantasizes about creating a third party called the Reactionary Independents. He'd be President, Gerry would be Vice-President and Liddy's job would be to wound Nixon so he'd get a big sympathy vote. (Chris Hart said Liddy had seen an earlier production in Los Angeles, and "he loved it.")

It was essentially "a character comedy" with gags that played up the eccentricities of the characters, but even by 1983 the chicanerous Nixon, the bumbling Ford and the sado-masochistic Liddy caricatures had been around the block many times. (Brogger has life-of-the-party Liddy drive a nail through his hand for fun.) As Mel Gussow said in the *New York Times* of September 16, 1983, "While it might serve as a 15-minute — or at most an 18-and-a-half minute — interlude on *Saturday Night Live*, Erik Brogger's *Basement Tapes* offers a meager two hours of theater. As political satire, the show is both tired and too late."

Occasionally, the gags were amusing: Ford wants to know if Nixon gets any exercise, to which Nixon replies, "No, I get bad vibes every now and then; that's about it," or the Nixon character will make a reference to a 1977 mini-series and say, "Rip Torn is *not* Richard Nixon." But the theater-going public demands sharper humor than references to old TV shows. Christopher Sharp was on target in *Women's Wear Daily* (September 19, 1983) when he wrote: "The evening only makes us remember how funny the original farce was, a decade ago. That was more in the style of a good English drawing room comedy, with the characters keeping straight faces while they uttered the most absurd excuses. Here it is obvious that the performers are trying to be funny. The result is a trying evening." Putting it more succinctly, *Backstage* critic Gary Stern (September 30, 1983) said, "Instead of an evening of nightmarish confrontations, or exploring the dark recesses of these powermongers' minds, Brogger settles for shtick, one-liners and a tone worthy of a harmless Johnny Carson monologue." He added that Michael Laskin turned Nixon "into a cartoon, missing his demonic, calculating side."

Through an apt comparison, the noted British theater critic Benedict Nightengale, writing in the *New York Times* of September 25, 1983 made several acute observations about the deficiencies of this play: "There is nothing like hearing some other dramatists hold forth on American themes to make one appreciate (Sam) Shepard, even minor Shepard ... Take Erik Brogger's *Basement Tapes* at the Village Gate. On the quaint assumption that something called the Reactionary Independent Party is about to be launched, and at about 20 times the necessary length, this purported satire asserts that Nixon is tricky, Ford, slow-witted, and Liddy a mewling neurotic posing as a Nietzschian superhero. Could one conceive of (Sam Shepard) producing a work so visually and verbally skimpy, so relentlessly rectilinear in its attack on skullduggery in high places?"

And in the plain English of the *New York Daily News* (September 15, 1983), Douglas Watt, "telling it like it was," wrote: "It's really a tacky little show, and the only truly good, well-acted impersonation is that of Bill Schoppert as Ford, to whom he bears an interesting resemblance. Michael Laskin's Nixon is too oppressive, with little indication of the genuine, even boyish, pleasure Nixon took in his eminence."

The Martha Play (play, 1983)

The Martha Play biographical play by Patricia Cobey, directed by Saski Noordhoek Hegt, film sequence by Babette Mangolite, Theatre for the New City, 162 Second Avenue, New York City, December 29, 1983. Cast: *Martha Mitchell* Crystal Field; *Richard Nixon* Gordon Gray; Victor Truro, Tom Howe, Lucrezia Norelli, Robert Zuckerman, and Peter Kisiluk.

The Martha Play had a very short off–Broadway run, and, except for the *Village Voice* (January 3, 1984), very little press coverage. For the purpose of this volume, several attempts were made to reach the author and the stars but without success. This is a pity because Martha Mitchell is a "major minor" character in Watergate and a major "character" in life, eminently stage-worthy, as is Richard Nixon.

As described in the *Voice*, *The Martha Play* is a "biography, almost a docudrama with many peculiarities" which included newsreels and a "home movie" ending with a "close up of Crystal Field's bare buttock" above which "a big hypodermic needle looms." The *Voice* admired Ms. Field's performance, finding her "very comic as the young, romantic *Gone With the Wind*ish Martha, and horrendously realistic as the old, disease-ridden Martha. Bones ache and nerves throb with pain. Very fine — but I did wonder what the connection was between hammy (Miss) Piggy comedy at the start and hospital realism at the end." The form of the play also bothered the critic: Was it "a serious tragedy about the oppression of women," or was it "a satire on all sorts of news shows and political events"?

A final point of confusion was that there were different Richard Nixons in the "home movie" and in the stageplay, nor was it clear how central either Richard Nixon was to the action of the play.

Secret Honor (play, 1983)

Full title: *Secret Honor: The Last Testament of Richard M. Nixon*. A solo drama in one act by Donald Freed and Arnold M. Stone. Presented by Robert Altman and Sandcastle 5 Productions. Originally presented for the Los Angeles Actors' Theater by Diane White and Adam Leipzig. Staged by Robert Harders. Opened November 8, 1983, at the Provincetown Playhouse, New York. Cast: *Richard M. Nixon* Philip Baker Hall.

It is very late at night, Richard Nixon is alone in his well-appointed study. From time to time, he glances at the portraits of Woodrow Wilson, Eisenhower and Kissinger. He begins a tape which is to become an elaborate exercise in self-justification. It takes the form of a legal brief with Nixon sometimes arguing his own case in the third person. He pauses often to re-fill his whiskey glass, to curse his fate and to register concern for the family of his unseen Cuban servant. He remembers the days of his youth when he worked as a carnival barker in order to help his parents pay the medical expenses of the Nixon son who had contracted a fatal illness. He recalls answering an advertisement seeking young men to run for Congress. In doing so, according to the play, Nixon forever put himself in thrall to the Committee of One Hundred, wealthy power brokers who would meet in California's Bohemian Grove. Through these meetings they were able to wield much influence on governmental policy. As the night goes on, he becomes more and more drunk, curses Kissinger and demonstrates his envy of the Kennedys, but his greatest agony stems from his indebtedness to the Committee of One Hundred. They were so manipulative that he lived in fear of their control over him even though he had won a second term by the greatest landslide in the history of the United States. He was afraid the Committee would force him to run for a third term. In order not to have to do so, Nixon *created Watergate*, thereby choosing disgrace rather than continuing the Vietnam war. That was to be Nixon's "secret honor" — being forced from office so that the Committee of One Hundred would no longer have control over him and the war could be ended. The play even intimates that Nixon himself was "Deep Throat." Toward the end of this disjointed exercise in self-excoriation, Nixon picks up the pistol that has been lying on his desk and meditates upon suicide but, *never a quitter,* Nixon remains on the path he has chosen.

Because of Robert Altman's twofold involvement in the film version — as director and as producer — the film version has had by far the greater recognition. The fact that Altman's stage and film careers had both been in eclipse for some time did not dissuade the major theater critics from weighing in for the usual heavyweight Altman showdown.

In a pre-opening interview with *New York Daily News* reporter Don Nelson, Altman said that *Secret Honor* was "not a parody" (probably a reference to *Dick Deterred*) but "real theater." Co-written by Donald Freed, author of *Inquest,* and Arnold M. Stone, *Secret Honor,* Altman pointed out, "is not necessarily factual." To cover some of the controversial hypotheses of the play, Altman and the authors sometimes referred to *Secret Honor* as "a political myth." Altman defended his approach: "Whether it is true or not doesn't make any difference because in art what you try to do is explore various views of things. This is just a view." Furthering this very unorthodox view of Nixon, Altman said that he hoped to present "a very viable point of view in which Nixon in a way is a minor hero. The guy they really get in this play is Kissinger. He really gets his."

In an interview in the *New York Post* some time later, *Secret Honor* star Philip Baker Hall told staff writer Jerry Tallmer that when he watched Nixon's 1952 "Checkers" speech in a fraternity house at the University of Toledo, he found it disturbing, and that many years later when his friend stage director Robert Harders offered him the role of Nixon in *Secret Honor* he found it "fascinating but undo-able." It "floored" him, and he rejected it, but some months later, he decided to re-read it, and then one night just as he was falling asleep, it came to him suddenly that "the whole play ... was ... one ... sentence." This was the approach "to hang everything on," and the two hours in the theater could speed quickly by for him. In playing Nixon, Hall kept the "Checkers" speech in mind because "it was artful ... clever," qualities he needed in playing his role, and he "wondered [how] the American public [could] buy all that crap."

Among the skeptics of the Freed-Stone-Altman premise that Nixon "engineered Watergate" in order to "secretly save the Republic" was critic Howard Kissel of *Women's Wear Daily*, who said that this "rather eccentric hypothesis" should have been "advanced in an essay. Presenting it in the form of a play is the easy way out — you don't really have to prove anything." Kissel praised Hall's performance but concluded that the play itself was not "convincing."

Kissel's review was pretty much in line with David Sterritt's review in the *Christian Science Monitor* of November 30. Sterritt wrote that the play contained much "florid theatricality" and was really "melodrama veering toward psychodrama." It turned Nixon "into a laboratory specimen and the audience into second-hand voyeurs," making it difficult to accept *Secret Honor* as a "historical study." It became "an assault upon the emotions" that promoted its thesis so "bombastically" that it "tired [him] even as it held [him]."

All the New York critics had many of the same reservations, the principal one being that, in spite of some sympathetic vignettes and incisive passages, the play remained essentially a virtuoso acting exercise for Hall (who received generally high praise). For instance, *Variety* noted Hall's "awesome authority." The *Post,* however, having had severe reservations about the play (headline: 'HONOR' WITHOUT SUBSTANCE), was only moderately pleased with Hall's performance, observing that Hall had "avoided drooling."

The two most favorable reviews were those written by Erika Munk in the *Village Voice* (November 15) and Mel Gussow in the *New York Times* (November 11). Munk was quite taken with both the play and the performance. "At times the writing is smart and eloquent, and it reaches inspiration in some wild invective against Henry Kissinger, than whom no one deserves it more." Some of the themes are underscored too heavily, Munk thought, but this "is not fatal because of Hall's performance." To Munk, the character Hall presented was "old, shrewd, funnier than you'd expect, fairly batty, and, as the evening progresses, quite drunk, and [the only critic noting this] neither so brutally sly nor ugly." Munk theorizes that in real life Nixon often functioned as "the loyal servant"—first to his mother, and then to others, possibly the Committee of One Hundred and possibly to Eisenhower. Significantly, Munk's review is entitled "Nethergate," an influence that she feels has echoed throughout his life. Thus, to Munk, *Secret Honor,* in spite of much that is obvious, is a play that succeeds in its ideas and its portraiture.

In his generally positive review, Mel Gussow acknowledged the authors' "blithe rewriting of history"; Gussow calls it "reinterpretive rather than comprehensive." Gussow is willing — it would seem eager — to accept this view of Nixon "because of the bizarre nature of the man and the Byzantine nature of his politics." What Gussow found most appealing was that "both the play and the performance" were "provocative." Hall's Nixon was a rich portrayal of an over-ripe character that had become fetid and was fascinating in its progressive decay. The play also had an open-ended quality that Gussow could respond to: "As directed by Robert Harders, the monologue rambles like a loose spool, working in and around itself until once again we are entangled in the myth of Tricky Dick." For Gussow, it was like watching a curiously amiable act of self-destruction. Gussow was further impressed by the conflicting feelings he experienced while watching this play about a man for whom he had an abiding detestation. In the end, Gussow told his *New York Times* readers that Hall had re-captured "a full measure of the man — his edginess, suspicion, resentment and unconscious humor." Almost to his regret, Gussow left the theater "thinking the unthinkable": Richard Nixon had become "humanized." In Gussow's eyes this was a signal achievement. Yet it remained for Robert Altman's film version a year and a half later to win a fuller audience and a fuller measure of praise.

Summer of Judgment: The Watergate Hearings (TV documentary, 1983)

120 minutes. Host/narrator/writer: Charles McDowell. Directed by Mary Frances Sirianne. Produced by WETA–TV (Washington). Wednesday, July 27, 1983, PBS.

"Looking somewhat somber, reporter/narrator Charles McDowell stood in the hearing room and told the audience how a 'remarkable parade of burglars, fixers and men of standing' came before the investigating committee to tell their various tales, which were sometimes outright lies, to protect then President Nixon.

"By far the most fascinating of the interviews concerned a discussion of how Alexander Butterfield told investigators for the first time about how each conversation inside Nixon's Oval Office was once conveyed through these interviews. The viewer felt the tension ten years later." — *Variety*, August 3, 1983.

"When the hearings began, all three networks were in attendance, televising the proceedings in their entirety. Soon the networks dropped out, leaving only public television in there full-time. WETA in Washington covered all 250 hours, feeding them to other Public Broadcasting Service stations every night. The programs put the then fledgling public television on the map.

"Consider the footage of [Chairman] Ervin, almost all of it. He was an old country boy who was also a constitutional scholar and a Harvard Law graduate. Sometimes he stuttered. Goaded beyond endurance when John Ehrlichman aloofly asked him how he could possibly not understand what was a perfectly obvious point, Mr. Ervin thundered: 'Because I understand the English language. It's my mother tongue.'" — John Corry, *New York Times*, July 27, 1983.

Summer of Judgment: The Impeachment Hearings (TV documentary, 1984)

120 minutes. Host/narrator/writer: Charles McDowell. Produced by Ricki Green, Jim Wesley and Sue Ducat for WETA–TV (Washington), PBS–Channel 13, NYC. August 7, 1984, 11 P.M.

"The 1974 impeachment hearings that forced the resignation of President Richard Nixon are a lesson in government no one should miss.... What makes this program so moving are the emotional interviews with some of the key members of the House Judiciary Committee, who sat in judgment of the President of the United States as millions watched in that July month of 1974.... McDowell points out that [Chairman of the House Judiciary Committee] Peter Rodino would not have been effective without Republican support. That's why he said 'there was something almost Shakespearean to hear pro–Nixon congressmen put politics aside and face the fact that they were in deep constitutional trouble and vote for impeachment. M. Caldwell Butler, a Republican who credits Nixon with his election, can hardly speak as he recalls voting to impeach the President.'"— Kay Gardella, *New York Daily News,* August 7, 1984.

Secret Honor (film, 1984)

90 minutes. Directed by Robert Altman. Written by Donald Freed and Arnold M. Stone, based upon their play. Produced by Robert Altman and Scott Bushnell at and with the cooperation of the University of Michigan (Department of Communications) and the Los Angeles Actors' Theatre. Associate director: Robert Harders. Art director: Stephen Altman. Photographer: Pierre Mignot. Photography: Jean Lepine. Music: George Burt. Music performed by the Contemporary Directions Ensemble (University of Michigan School of Music). Edited by Juliet Weber. Color. A Sandcastle 5 Production. Cast: *Richard M. Nixon* Philip Baker Hall.

No further summary should be needed since, according to Patrick McGilligan's *Robert Altman: Jumping Off the Cliff* (1989), after the play's Los Angeles premiere, the piece "remained substantially the same — the night-long harangue by a wronged Nixon. Altman never had to add or change a word." What then, McGilligan asked, did Altman bring to the new mounting? Co-author Freed's reply was incisive: "Just the courage of filming it — and, naturally, all the expertise that an accomplished director can provide when a stage work is given new life on the screen."

In its transfer to film, many production values were added, highlighting key aspects of the script through effective uses of camera and sound. Because of the many artful choices Altman made in pre-production, *Secret Honor* is one of those rare instances in which a film rendering is considered superior to its stage antecedent. A small-scale work, *Secret Honor* owes something of a debt in its film life to the theater of Harold Pinter. Pinter trademarks such as pauses, repetitions, broken phrases, a sense of menace — things that were not so well-orchestrated (or apparent) in Robert Harders' stage production — were so effectively evoked in the Altman film that Pinter proclaimed it "the best film that's ever been made." (*Cineaste,* September 1985) In fact, as a result of Pinter's enthusiasm, Altman directed two of Pinter's best-known short plays for television: *The Room* with Linda Hunt and Donald Pleasence and *The Dumb Waiter* with John Travolta and Tom Conti.

As Altman stated in an interview in London's *Monthly Film Bulletin* (January 1985), what attracted him to *Secret Honor* initially was that he found it "truthful if not factual." He was not concerned with what "did or didn't happen" because the play "talks

Philip Baker Hall as Nixon in the Robert Altman film *Secret Honor* (1984).

about the White House and the job, rather than the facts of history." In both the stage and screen presentations, Altman wanted to show the chicanery of "power politics" and the accommodations an individual will make in order to attain power. A man possessed of "a political conscience," Altman also wanted to show the effect of conscience upon a man who had compromised his childhood ideals but still believes, at the end, rightly or wrongly, that he chose "secret honor" for "all the little people, Maggie and Jiggs." Although in likelihood we don't accept Nixon's "choice" of "creating Watergate," enough signposts have appeared along the way that we are willing to grant that Nixon, self-deluded or not, at one time, and possibly always, possessed a conscience and fellow feeling.

When the film is over, we are meant to have mixed emotions. In Nixon, we see a terribly flawed but pitiable human being, and yet, as impossible as it may seem to some viewers, the character, in Altman's hands, goes beyond that. Nixon's defiance at the end — the defiance of a weak man who has willed himself to become strong — is both touching and shocking. The viewer has spent time with this man; the viewer has come to know him, his "secret honor" and dishonor. A natural sympathy is extended to him throughout because the creative artists behind the film have shown an undeniable fidelity to human experience.

Concerned about the "facts" of *Secret Honor*, journalist Patricia Aufderheide interviewed both Donald Freed and Altman for the September 1985 *Cinéaste*. Aufderheide asked Freed if he was using drama as a way of making more real a historical process. Freed replied: "I am employing the research tool unavailable to the journalist, my own imagination. Plays, like myths, are a kind of public record keeping. They are open dossiers."

"Is myth preferable to the facts?" Aufderheide inquired.

Freed replied at some length. "There's a half-life to news and journalism. You reach a time in a culture's history when history begins to decompose — Watergate, Vietnam — and that's when you get myth. If myth is allowed to develop organically, it will find its own level, and make a collective record. Myths intend to occupy [a] middle ground to make that collective record."

In her interview with Altman, Aufderheide made the comment, "It seems that most people have forgotten what Watergate was all about." Altman concurred: "We forget our history quicker all the time. It's a serious situation, and I'm afraid the proof of it is that the majority of people who should see this film aren't going to."

"Do you think that's because it has a political subject?"

"No, not exactly. I don't deal in propaganda. I never have; I think this is art. People will understand that the film will force them to re-assess their thinking processes."

"So this film is about unpleasant truths?"

"Not *the truth. A truth. Somebody's* truth." It was not Altman's intention to create an easy relationship with a controversial political figure. He preferred the irreverent satire of Jonathan Swift in political matters. One of the cleverest examples of what Altman brought to the film version is the use of four TV monitors throughout. Through them we see Nixon, the windbag, impressing himself, Nixon, the paranoiac, examining his security system and Nixon, the unraveling personality, whose TV images change as rapidly as his mood swings. Furthermore, the monitors *enlarge the cast.* They literally *people* the film, providing an animated entity that Nixon can play off and play to. The addition of the monitors is probably Altman's most illuminating touch but, oddly enough, it only occurred to him three days before shooting began. He realized that the monitors allowed him "to go deeper." Besides peopling the film and adding a vital area for Canadian photographer Pierre Mignot to play across, the monitors and the tape recorder that Nixon fiddles with also reveal character. He can't get the latter to work and a whiny harpsichord recital begins. As Mel Gussow pointed out in his play review: "He *would* have trouble with electronic equipment." It is a clever touch in the play, but in the film the spooky music and his exasperated expressions in close-up make this Nixon a hilarious comic bumbler.

For some critics, the satire went too far such as Nixon's calling Henry Kissinger "a fat fuck" and Nixon's statement that Kissinger procured young boys for the Shah of Iran. (According to Nixon authority Stephen Ambrose, Nixon when angry, used scatology and sacrilege but never obscenity. As noted elsewhere in this volume, obscenities were not characteristic of the speech of men of Nixon's generation.) Also, Nixon's "playing the China card" to be used later as an entry for investment by his wealthy friends is hammered home more in the film performance than on the stage. *Variety* (July 11, 1984) called it a "putdown of the Presidency." More to the point, shortly after the London premiere in February 1985, *The Observer* commented: "It is America itself, not Nixon, the authors are gunning for." Nixon, as portrayed in the film, was a "pathetic victim of the American Dream, the American Mom and the socio-political Establishment of the East and West Coasts." The English reviewer further noted Hall's "virtuoso" performance and that Freed and Stone had created "a far more sympathetic Nixon" than other writers had done in the past. However, in spite of its merits, the film "doesn't leave you with much at the end."

What fails to impress in London can often succeed in New York. John Herbers, a *New York Times* reporter who had covered Nixon over the years, left the news beat and covered the New York opening since this was a news event as well as an aesthetic one. Possessed of a greater knowledge of Nixon's eccentricities than his fellow reporters,

Herbers was amazed to find himself impressed with the authenticity of the screen Nixon: "There is something eerily fascinating about *Secret Honor*. Perhaps this is because the incredible truth about our 37th President is told in such accurate and telling detail that the outrageous bit (the "secret honor" to end the war) seems just as believable."

Few reporters knew Nixon as closely as Herbers. "The portrayal is accurate down to his uncoordinated physical movements, his low tolerance of alcohol, his list of 'enemies,' his troubled relationship with his mother and his brothers, and his political philosophy. So far, this is the real Nixon, however implausible he has always seemed." In conclusion, Herbers felt that Mr. Hall's mastery of the Nixon mannerisms, rationalizations, voice inflections and world view are so complete that "it seems viewers are indeed in the same room with Richard Milhous Nixon." In spite of the "surprise" fictional ending, Herbers found the film "convincing."

A defense of Nixon as victim came from a most unlikely source, film critic Stephen Harvey in New York's liberal weekly the *Village Voice: "Secret Honor* ... bills itself as a 'fictional meditation' on our most hubris-ridden chief executive." Harvey felt that "ruthless" would be the more appropriate word to describe it, "flecked as it is with a venomous relish Nixon himself would recognize from the days of his campaign to cream Helen Gahagan Douglas." In Harvey's view, the "loathing" portrait that appeared — he particularly objected to the Nixon character calling the Founding Fathers "English shit"— managed "to elicit the one emotion Altman and company could never have intended — sympathy for the poor old devil who prompted their belated scorn."

Confirmed Nixon-hater Stanley Kauffmann, writing in the July 15, 1985, *New Republic*, remained firm in his contempt however. "Little would give me more pleasure than to praise a bitter satire on Richard Nixon because little infuriates me more than his latter-day progress in repainting his image." Characterizing *Secret Honor* as "a lurid fantasy that not only misses the mark" and a "rancid, stuttering mess," the one idea that emerges, that Nixon was the catspaw of "fat cat" investors, the Committee of One Hundred, who were using him to "open Asian markets for them," is "merely childish cartooning," a satire that doesn't work because it is in no way credible biography. Like many other critics, Kauffmann gave Altman high marks for his deft use of the "number of TV monitors" and the lone TV camera that he cuts to throughout the film. Kauffmann found the use of this equipment especially apt, not only because electronics contributed to Nixon's downfall, but, in a larger sense, the equipment implies "a media-wrapped life." Vincent Canby, writing in the *New York Times* on June 7, 1985, called *Secret Honor* "one of the funniest, most unsettling, most imaginative and most surprisingly affecting movies of its very odd kind that I've ever seen." In virtually a rave review, Canby went on to praise in the highest terms the "extraordinary character at its center." Far from being a tragic hero, the character lacks the stature of even the lesser Shakespeare plays, "but he has some of the appeal of— and is as American as — the Duke in *Huckleberry Finn,* attempting to convince us the members of the lynch party that they should elect him mayor." We should not forget that one of Nixon's jobs as a youth was as a carnival barker during which he no doubt heard many a pitch from persuasive snake oil salesmen. In its New York premiere, *Secret Honor* was paired with "the tired old kinescope of *The Checkers Speech* which, Canby felt, "was a mistake." The latter had "become an easy laugh" while *Secret Honor* was "something of a different order. That is, good fiction."

In the *New Yorker* of July 15, 1985, Pauline Kael wrote a gabby, free-wheeling review full of wild enthusiasm. Among other things, Kael called the film "a weird triumph, a nightmare mythology, a seizure, a crack-up, and ... a near-pornographic excess of ... display [that] is transfixing." Throughout all these visions, "Altman keeps the camera dancing," one of the effects of which was to "sustain the illusion of an unbroken harangue by a distraught — and gradually drunken" Nixon. Altman manages to keep this formerly stage-bound work "always in motion," and we have "a roomful of Nixons." To Kael, the film's liveliness and iconoclasm are two of its most delectable qualities. As Kael says: "There's a virtuoso naughtiness about the sureness of Altman's touch" that justifies the "gonzo psychodocudrama" of the "trapped, rancorous man" who "made a spectacle of his Presidency." In no small measure, the merit of the film comes about through Hall's Nixon, who "is practically a werewolf ... horrifying ... an intellectual slob"— and that is "what held" her. Hall's performance is "a stunt," but it works "brilliantly."

Roger Ebert, writing somewhat earlier (November 9, 1984) in the *Sun-Times* after the Chicago opening, had much the same reaction — Hall played with "such savage intensity, such passion, such venom, such scandal, that [Ebert] could not turn away." As a result, the film "created a deeper truth, an artistic truth, and after *Secret Honor* was over," unlike Kael, Ebert "had a deeper sympathy for Richard Nixon than [he] had ever had before."

What Ebert referred to is what Helene Keyssar (*Robert Altman's America*) called "the amazing grace that appears for a moment near the end of an Altman film." The end of *Secret Honor* is passionate and self-exonerating, the self-championing that can stir an audience to enthusiastic partisanship when a subject turns defeat into victory. One of the achievements of *Secret Honor* and one of the ways in which the audience leagues itself with the subject is through the many facets of character that the Hall–Altman duo differentiates for us — and to a much more marked degree than in the stage presentation. For instance, Keyssar points out, the character uses "many voices. Sometimes he speaks as a lawyer, sometimes he speaks as an ordinary American struggling to make his way up the ladder and achieve the American dream." He adjusts his voice and manner to the imaginary audience he is addressing. Sometimes he speaks — usually angrily — to the portraits of the gray eminences on the walls. His progressive drunkenness "frees" the camera to serve as a visual metaphor that disjointedly pans and tracks the many roles Nixon has played and reveals the person he really is when everything is stripped away. In an interview with Keyssar, Altman said: "[T]he people who've hated Nixon have said I'm not sure I like that piece; it makes him almost human. I don't think it's in any sense pro–Nixon, but I think it's good to shake people out of that real hard polarization where he is just some kind of cardboard figure."

Altman's comment demonstrates the quirky kinship he himself felt with Nixon. They were both outsiders. Altman was to Hollywood what Nixon was to Washington. For every Nixon failure (Watergate, Vietnam, wage and price controls), there had been at least one Altman failure (*Health, Brewster McCloud* and *Popeye* to name only three). Altman, who had been on the ropes many times himself, felt a bond with this other "loser," who in Teddy Roosevelt's phrase had put himself "in the arena" time and time again because Hannah Nixon had told him never to be a quitter.

In the film's last minutes, Nixon says: "They wanted me to kill myself. Well, I won't do it. If they want me dead, they'll have to do it."

In the background we hear cries of "Four more years!" as Nixon yells: "Fuck 'em! Fuck 'em! Fuck 'em! Fuck 'em! Fuck 'em! Fuck 'em! Fuck 'em! Fuck 'em! Fuck 'em! Fuck 'em!"

That just might be Altman talking too!

Boys in the Backroom (satiric comedy, 1984)

A comedy in two acts by Andrew Dallmeyer. Directed by Martin Nordal. Produced by the Echo Stage Company. Production manager: Mitchell Mills. Setting and lighting by Leon Di Leone. Actors' Outlet Theater Center, 120 West 28th Street, New York. Opened March 29, 1984. Cast: John Everett, Christiane McKenna, Brian Muehl, Stephen Mulch, Kelly Ray and Kim Waltman.

From the press release of the short-lived New York production: "Dallmeyer's play was originally produced by the prestigious Traverse Theatre for the Edinburgh Festival in 1982. Said Moyce McMillan of London's *Evening Standard*: If you've a taste for scurrilous political satire, a secret liking for dollops of bad taste ... and a total disregard for the sanctities of the American political life, from Rose Kennedy downward, you'll certainly laugh a lot, I'm afraid I did. *Boys in the Backroom* is true political satire, an irreverent re-write of recent history, focusing on some of America's most influential political and financial minds. The play opens on an intimate profile of Hitler's final hours, revealing his possession of the 'Sword of Destiny,' the legendary spear believed to have been used by Longinus to pierce the side of Christ. The sword becomes the modus operandi of the play, and the playwright makes little effort to conceal the true identities of those who brandish it on their rise to power: Dick Fixer, General Riflepower, Howard Huge and of course, the entire Kidney Clan, among others."

"In one scene, Aristotle Onassis pressures Lyndon Johnson to rev up the Vietnam War. It's good for Onassis's business; he ships heroin to the States in the eviscerated bodies of GIs. With the exception of this grisly bit, English playwright Dallmeyer's *Boys in the Backroom* is American politics as a second language, a grade school pageant on the order of 'George chops tree.'... The actors ham heroically, like a team of surgeons who won't give up on a goner.... Kim Waltman — my favorite — has rubber, mobile features and quite transforms himself for each impersonation, among them George Patton, Joe Kennedy and Nixon."— Laurie Stone, *Village Voice*, April 17, 1984.

"*Boys in the Backroom* is a two and a half hour production with enough humor to fill a ten-minute sketch. Screaming actors and a one-level, high-pitched rhythm try to bring humor to this piece but only reveal the emptiness of the entire evening ... McKenna's Kennedy and Mary Jo Kopechne (Ted Kennedy's ill-fated companion on the Chappaquiddick Bridge) are extremely clean, simple caricatures that work because they are built with great care and precision. They are built with a sense of the outrageous that the rest of the production lacks. Waltman's Fixer is extremely well-crafted, [and] even his tiny portrayal of a Reagan aide is memorable."— *Villager*, April 12, 1984.

"*Boys is the Backroom* ... is a scurrilous view of recent events in American political history. It is pointless ... with the exception of Kim Waltman as the Nixon figure Dick Fixer, it's extremely poorly acted. The production values ... are minimal and Martin Nordal's direction is long on the scurrile and short on the subtle. [It offers] not a single insight into the nature of political power in America or its workings. After just a few scenes of [Dallmeyer's] empty caricatures I simply hung in there, waiting for his saga to end. It took 33 scenes to do it, some of them no longer than a simple speech, all of them devoid of depth."— *New York Times*, April 19, 1984.

The Killing Fields (film, 1984)

139 minutes. Directed by Roland Joffe. Written by Bruce Robinson. Based upon the article "The Death and Life of Dith Pran" by Sydney Schanberg, *New York Times Magazine* (January 20, 1980), later published in hardback and paperback by Viking Press Penguin Books, 1985. Cinematography by Chris Menges. Editing by Jim Clark. Production design by Roy Walker. Art direction by Roger Murray Leach and Steve Spence. Music by Mike Oldfield. Produced by David Puttnam for International Film Investors. Color. Released by Warner Bros. Cast: *Sydney Schanberg* Sam Waterston; *Dith Pran* Haing S. Ngor; *Jon Swain* Julian Sands; *Al Rockoff* John Malkovich; *Military Attache* Craig T. Nelson; *Dr. Sudesval* Athol Fugard; *American Counsel* Spalding Gray.

During the slowly unfolding credits, a Voice of America newscaster announces (in part) that "President Nixon will address the nation on the Watergate case in the next few days. His speech will be his first comment since May" on a case that "has nearly paralyzed the White House staff ... and led to intense confrontation. His speech was announced after a Gallup poll indicated Mr. Nixon's popularity has fallen to the lowest point of any American president in the last 20 years." The newscaster then speaks directly to his listeners in Southeast Asia, the locale of the film: "A Supreme Court Judge, William O. Douglas [see section on the play *Mountain* in this volume] has ruled against an appeal by the Administration for a stay of the injunction on further U.S. bombing in Cambodia."

Sydney Schanberg, a *New York Times* foreign correspondent, was sent to Cambodia in 1972 to write about the Cambodian government's conflict with the Khmer Rouge. (The Khmers were the early Cambodians whose civilization reached its height from the ninth through the fifteenth centuries. "Rouge" refers to their re-birth as Communists.) Schanberg's Cambodian interpreter and photographer Dith Pran is a key factor in Schanberg's gaining knowledge of clandestine American aggression in Cambodia. When it is clear that the Khmer Rouge will take over Phnom Penh, the capital which is strategically located on the Mekong River, most educated Cambodians flee, but Schanberg manipulates the good-natured and earnest Dith Pran into staying behind in order to help him get the story of the fall of Phnom Penh for the *Times*. Just before the fall, Schanberg and Dith Pran get Pran's family on to a plane for the United States. After the fall, hordes of Cambodians flood the embassies hoping for sanctuary, but they are taken to the countryside for "re-education"; the Khmer Rouge seeks a return to a peasant society, and they do so by the most brutal means possible. Schanberg and other Western journalists are taken prisoner by a band of indoctrinated Khmer Rouge guerrillas who would think nothing of killing them. After many hours of talks, Dith Pran is able to convince the guerrillas to free Schanberg and his fellow journalists. One of the journalists tries to create a fake passport for Pran, but it does not work, and Schanberg and the others leave. The cities are emptied, the residents taken to state farms where they work 12-hour days, are given little food and suffer every kind of brutality and dehumanization. These developments take us to what is approximately the mid-point of the film.

Besides its strong anti-war theme, *The Killing Fields* is also a film about friendship and how one friend, to his great regret, over-stepped the bounds of friendship, putting another man's life in peril. We now find Schanberg in his attractive New York City apartment. He is playing a Franco Corelli recording of Puccini's "Nessun dorma" as he watches Nixon and scenes of bloodshed in Southeast Asia. We close in on the television set. Nixon, in a left profile shot, is using his right hand to point to various locations on a huge map.

> NIXON: For the past five years as indicated on this map that you see, North Vietnam has occupied military sanctuaries all along the Cambodian frontier with South Vietnam.
>
> NEWSCASTER: As the President spoke, American troops were preparing to move into Cambodia. The decision to invade, like the decision to bomb, was withheld from the Cambodian people.
>
> (Shots of American combat troops in training.)
>
> NIXON: There are no American combat troops or advisors in Cambodia. There will be *no* American troops or advisors in Cambodia. We will aid Cambodia. Cambodia is the Nixon doctrine in its purest form.

"Other than the openings to China and the Soviets ... the NIXON DOCTRINE began to alter the emphasis of American responsibility. With U.S. assistance, those nations faced with threats from leftist subversion were compelled to assume more of their own share of the burden."—Herbert S. Parmet, *Richard Nixon and His America* (1990).

Nagged by remorse and a genuine concern for the friend he let down, Schanberg makes every effort to help Pran. During the film's second hour, the film chronicles the deprivations suffered by Dith Pran, his incredible escape from Cambodia and sanctuary in Thailand. Eventually he is reunited with Schanberg.

The Killing Fields is a tremendously powerful film, surely one of the very best films on the conflict in Southeast Asia. If it has any faults, one of them would be its length, and another would be the somewhat wooden performance of Sam Waterston as Schanberg, but this is a difficult role since the audience resents his shabby treatment of Dith Pran. The film won Academy Awards for Best Supporting Actor (Dr. Haing S. Ngor as Dith Pran), Best Cinematography (Chris Menges) and Best Editing (Jim Clark).

Here's a sampling of critical opinion:

"[T]his movie takes the chance of switching points of view in midstream, and the last half of the film belongs to Dith Pran, who sees his country turned into an insane parody of a one-party state, ruled by Khmer Rouge with instant violence and a savage intolerance for any reminders of the French and American presence of the colonial era. Many of the best scenes of the second half are essentially played without dialogue, as Pran works in the field, disguises his origins, and waits for his chance."—*Roger Ebert's Movie Home Companion*, 1989 edition.

"For all its flaws, *The Killing Fields* is an important, indeed necessary, film.... In the second half, where the film chiefly records Dith Pran's ghastly experiences and resourceful courage in captivity, *The Killing Fields* rises to those heights where our tears flow even as our blood is chilled."—John Simon, *National Review*, December 28, 1984.

At the end of *The Killing Fields*, the two long-lost friends are reunited and Dith Pran later becomes a photographer for the *New York Times*. Ironically, Dr. Haing S. Ngor, who played Dith Pran in the film and had himself been victim of the same horrible deprivations, was later murdered in a robbery outside his apartment in Los Angeles' Chinatown. When told of Ngor's death, Dith Pran believed at first that it might have been retaliation by a segment of the Khmer Rouge, but then discounted it because "the Khmer Rouge has historically never bothered people outside the country" (*New York Post*, February 27, 1996). The autobiography *Haing Ngor: A Cambodian Odyssey* (1988), purchased by Warner Bros. the same year, described how the Khmer Rouge systematically tortured and killed the intellectual elite, indeed all the educated classes in Cambodia. Ngor had had part of a finger cut off, was hung like a dummy over fire for four days, had his head clamped in a vise and an ankle smashed by an axe; twice he was nearly smothered by plastic bags that were put over his head. The Vietnamese invaded Cambodia in 1979; in the melee, he was able to escape to Thailand. In 1989 he arrived in Los Angeles with only four dollars. He was one of 7000 Southeast Asian refugees who tried out for parts in *The Killing Fields*. John Simon's review said of him: "Haing S. Ngor is extremely moving in his earnest, self-controlled way — an amateur actor who approaches his role from harsh experience with absolute histrionic abstemiousness."

In discussing his autobiography with his collaborator Roger Warner, Ngor said he often had difficulty finding the right words to explain some of the incidents of his life. Since he lacked the English vocabulary he needed, he would act out the scenes. Years before, in Cambodia, he acted to save his life. Knowing that all doctors were to be put to death by the Khmer Rouge, he said he was a humble taxi driver. He stuck to his story in spite of incredible suffering. "I am a graduate of the Khmer Rouge School of Acting — without certificate," he said (*Newsday*, February 29, 1988).

Over 250 people attended his funeral. Dith Pran was among them.

Concealed Enemies (TV docu-drama, 1984)

A television docu-drama in two parts (Suspicion and Accusation) by Hugh Whitemore. Directed by Jeff Bleckner. Music by Jonathan Turnick. *American Playhouse*, Public Television, WNET, April 1, 1984, 8–10 P.M.; April 2, 9–10 P.M.; April 3, 9–10 P.M. (See also *The Trials of Alger Hiss* 1980.) Cast: *Whittaker Chambers* John Harkins; *Alger Hiss* Edward Herrmann; *Richard Nixon* Peter Riegert; *Priscilla Hiss* Maria Tucci; *Esther Chambers* Maria Jean Kurtz.

The drama begins in 1948 when Alger Hiss, a well-regarded intellectual and the president of the Carnegie Endowment for International Peace, is accused of being a Communist. The charge is brought by Whittaker Chambers, a disheveled ex–Communist and a senior editor at *Time* magazine. Both are forced to appear before the House Un-American Activities Committee; among its members is a tenacious young congressman named Richard Nixon. Hiss denies the charge, and says he knows no one by the name of Whittaker Chambers. In a later hearing, Hiss admits he knew Chambers more than a decade before under the name George Crosley. (Nixon: "Just like a lawyer! He denies knowing the name, but not knowing the man.") Hiss continues to deny having been a Communist or a Communist spy. In a highly charged speech, Chambers replies, "We are caught in a tragedy of history. Mr. Hiss represents the concealed enemy against which we are all fighting, and I'm fighting.... I testify in a moment of remorse and pity, but a moment of historic jeopardy in which this nation stands. So help me, God, I could do not otherwise."

During an interview on the radio program *Meet the Press*, Chambers repeats his charge that Hiss had been a Communist, thus prompting Hiss to sue Chambers for libel. In an examination prior to the trial, Chambers states that he and his wife Esther met the Hisses two years after Hiss had started to work for the Communist Party. At one point, Chamber says, "My wife and I had a tenderness for the Hisses." Chambers also states that some time in 1937, while Hiss worked in the State Department, Hiss gave Chambers secret documents which Hiss or his wife had re-typed for Chambers to send on to the Soviet Union. Chambers left photostats of these documents in the home of his wife's nephew. He also photographed documents and hid the film in a pumpkin on his Maryland farm. He did this for "future protection." A former State Department worker, Julien Wadleigh also admitted to the FBI that he had given State Department documents to Chambers in the late 1930s. In an attempt to destroy Chambers' character, his bouts with alcohol, a suicide attempt and past homosexual activity are brought forward. Two of the most dramatic episodes in Part II are the search for an old Woodstock on which the documents were re-typed and the checking of the emulsion numbers on the Kodak film. At first, Kodak made a mistake on the date, a mistake which made Chambers appear to be a liar. After this, Nixon shook his head, saying, "Poor Chambers! Nobody ever believes him at first." When a major break in the testimony comes, Nixon is on a cruise ship in the Caribbean. Unhappy to cut short his vacation, he is nevertheless elated to have the evidence that would strengthen their case. Shortly before, Nixon had said, "This is the end of my political career." Alger and Priscilla Hiss then appear before the New York Grand Jury and Hiss is indicted for perjury.

"I opened the questioning by informing Hiss that, since he had raised the possibility of a third party who might be involved in the case — I was referring, of course, to "George Crosley"— the Committee had concluded that Hiss and Chambers should confront each other at the earliest possible time. I told him he would have the opportunity to see Chambers at this hearing. From the beginning, Hiss dropped all previous pretensions of injured innocence, he was on the defensive, belligerent, fighting every inch of the way." — Richard Nixon, *Six Crises*, 1962.

Gifted dramatist Hugh Whitemore (*Stevie, Pack of Lies, Breaking the Code*) told the *Chicago Tribune* (May 6, 1984) that he had "spent four years culling through documents obtained through the Freedom of Information Act, talking to 50 people involved with the case and weaving a teleplay that brings hints of paranoia, adultery and homosexual rage to a case that divided the nation, shaped the Cold War, launched Joseph McCarthy on his hunt for Red sympathizers and started an obscure California congressman named Richard Nixon on a path towards the White House." In addition to interviews and research into documents, Whitemore spent over 60 hours with Hiss in Hiss' lower Manhattan apartment. After serving 44 months in jail for perjury, Hiss (born 1904) was to spend the rest of his life proclaiming his innocence, even into his 90s. His accuser, Whittaker Chambers, died in 1961. He was 60 years old.

Concealed Enemies, a superior example of television drama, is a disturbing work that summons up much of the anti–Communist hysteria of the mid–20th century. The series attempts to be fair. It shows Whitemore's familiarity with Chambers' *Witness* (1952) and Hiss' *In the Court of Public Opinion* (1957) and *Recollections of a Life* (1988). Yet as *Time* (May 7, 1984) notes, "The show's most serious flaw is the congenital problem of many docudramas dealing with controversial events: a dogged inscrutability. Remaining neutral on the issue of Hiss's guilt, the show presents a mass of incidents — some important, some irrelevant, some canceling others out — that are engrossing from moment to moment. But the end result is a sort of dramatic entropy that can be frustrating."

Two of the three leads are well cast. In the *Time* review, Richard Zoglin called Edward Herrmann's Hiss "the quintessence of Ivy League aplomb, but with a hint of arrogance and evasiveness." John Harkins' Whittaker Chambers was even better. John Corry's *New York Times* review (May 6, 1984) said, "Mr. Harkins, a fine actor, gives us the character we know from *Witness*. He has known sin; indeed, he seems obsessed with it. The paradox is that while the judicial system found Mr. Hiss guilty — and a great deal of recent scholarship upholds the verdict — *Concealed Enemies* leaves us in doubt. A man obsessed with sin, after all, could lie; a man free from sin tells only the truth."

Peter Riegert's portrayal of Nixon is disappointing. He told the *Chicago Sun-Times* (May 8, 1984): "I didn't want to make it a caricature. I didn't have a vision, so I tried to invent one. But that's one of the difficult parts of playing anyone that everyone knows." *Time*'s review captured Reigert's Nixon in just a few words: "Reigert maintains a steady scowl but avoids a facile parody." In Reigert's defense, it must be stated that the role is the most under-written of the three leads.

John Corry's lengthy review ended with reference to the ethical and social considerations the mini-series evoked: "*Concealed Enemies* is saying that the Hiss conviction led to, or at least was part of the infamous chapter known as McCarthyism. The message, intended or not, is that if the people were clamoring for Mr. Hiss's conviction were wrong about other things, than presumably they were wrong about Mr. Hiss. It is an improper equation, of course. It implies that if a man's enemies are flawed, we must hold the man blameless. This is simply incorrect, and the real lessons of the Hiss–Chamber confrontation are infinitely more complicated than that."

60 Minutes (TV, 1984)

Interview with Richard Nixon conducted by Frank Gannon (an assistant on *Nixon's Memoirs*). CBS, Sunday, April 15, 1984 7–8 P.M.

"Professional reporters were unhappy that CBS paid $500,000 for interviews conducted by a former Nixon aide who had been an employee of the J. Walter Thompson ad agency. The network brushed the critics aside.... Don Hewitt, executive producer of *60 Minutes* added, 'I saw a Richard Nixon I never saw before.' No serious Nixon-watcher saw a new Nixon, although there were some disclosures — though not about Nixon. One was that Lyndon Johnson had placed microphones in the reception area outside the Oval Office 'so he could listen to what people were saying about him before they came inside.' Another was that Johnson had installed recording equipment under the bed in the White House living quarters. Generally, however, it was the old Nixon saying the usual things.... Watergate 'was wrong.'... On May 9, 1984, he spoke to the

American Society of Newspaper Editors in their Washington convention. It was a triumph. 'I have no enemies in the press whatsoever,' he declared. He even had some journalists who were his friends. But, 'when they give it to me, I give it back, in kind, and that's the way it's going to be.' The editors loved it."— Stephen E. Ambrose, volume III of the biography.

The Life of Einstein (play, 1984)

Written by Norman Leach. Presented at the Duke's Playhouse, Lancaster, England, January 25–February 18, 1984.

Partial List of Characters: Einstein, Nixon, Truman, Queen Victoria, Disraeli, Edison, Rosa Luxembourg, Wallace, Dulles, Bohr, Teller, Stalin, and Churchill.

"[*The Life of Einstein*] encompasses the history of the Western World in this century. Its language varies from the simplest of statements to the complexity of scientific explanations and mocking rhymes spewed from puppet-headed power mongers. Their giant papier-mâché heads are most explicit of the devices used by director David Thacker and designer Shelagh Keegan to sustain interest. Back-projected shots illustrate as the supporting cast of five don jacket, cloak or tie and, adjusting their accent, move through time and space in an odd affirmation of reality."—*Daily Telegraph*, January 26, 1984.

Missing in Action 2 — The Beginning (film, 1985)

96 minutes. Directed by Lance Hool. Written by Arthur Silver, Larry Levinson and Steve Bing. Photography by Jorge Stahl. Music by Brian May. Cannon Films. Color. Cast: *Colonel James Braddock* Chuck Norris; *Mazilli* Cosie Costa.

This is a typical low-budget martial arts "let's-get-the-POWs-outta-Nam" action-thriller. Early on in the film there are several newsreels of Ronald Reagan proclaiming the United States resolve to free all the remaining POWs. The authoritative volume *Vietnam War Films* (edited by Jean-Jacques Malo and Tony Williams) contains the following reference: "Made on a lower budget than its predecessor, Joseph Zito's *Missing in Action* (1984), this prequel may have actually been made before the latter's release. Despite the action man cartoon cinematic format, the opening scenes contain significant items of information neglected in critical analysis. Mazilli's question, 'Why would anyone want to go to Cambodia?' remains unanswered. It specifies Braddock's involvement in Nixon's unlawful and secret aggressive acts."

The *New York Times* (March 2, 1985) called it "primitive but shrewd." *Variety*'s laconic verdict (March 6, 1985) was a "wobbly prequel to Chuck Norris hit."

P.O.W.— The Escape (film, 1986)

89 minutes. Directed by Gideon Amir. Written by Jeremy Lipp, James Bruner, Malcolm Barbour and John Langley. Story by Avi Kleinberger and Gideon Amir. Produced by Menahem Golan and Yoram Globus. Photography: Yechiel Ne'erman. Edited by Roy Watts. Music by David Storrs. Cannon Films. Color. Cast: *Colonel Jim Cooper* David Carradine; *Captain Vinh* Mako; *Sparks* Charles R. Floyd; *Waite* Tony Pierce.

Set in Vietnam during 1973, this is another action thriller dealing with the rescue of POWs, but this time there is the added ingredient of booty taken from prisoners by the double-dealing Captain Vinh who attacks the rescue squad in order to eventually go to the United States with his loot. Colonel Cooper, head of the rescue team, says he will help Vinh with his loot if all the prisoners escape. They all escape but Cooper quarrels with Sparks, another prisoner, over the loot. Sparks escapes in Vinh's Jeep, but Cooper and his men keep the loot and work their way down the river. Cooper hears of another band of beleaguered soldiers and is determined to save them. Meanwhile, Vinh finds Sparks in a bordello and learns of Cooper's plans. In the ensuing confrontation, Vinh is killed as is Sparks. Cooper and his men are rescued by a helicopter.

"The pre-credit sequences show war footage on TV, then track out an image of Richard Nixon anticipating Oliver Stone's 1989 *Born on the Fourth of July*'s video usages of this convenient villain..." — Jean-Jacques Malo and Tony Williams, *Vietnam War Films*, 1994.

Dress Gray (TV mini-series, 1986)

Four hours. Written by Gore Vidal from the novel by Lucian K. Truscott IV. Directed by Glenn Jordan. Produced by Warner Bros.–TV. Sunday and Monday, March 9 and 10, 1986. Cast: *Ry Slaight* Alec Baldwin; *General Charles Hedges* Hal Holbrook; *General Axel Rylander* Lloyd Bridges; *Judge Hand* Eddie Albert; *David Hand* Patrick Cassidy; *Iris Rylander* Alexis Smith; *Colonel King* Lane Smith.

Based upon the sensational 1978 best seller by Lucian K. Truscott IV, *Dress Gray* is of interest to students of Nixon on film, not because Nixon appears or is portrayed, but because much of it is based upon a key member of Nixon's team, General Alexander Haig.

The plot involves a murder and its cover-up at Ulysses S. Grant Military Academy. As a West Point cadet, Truscott (1969) had had several contretemps with Haig after Haig was appointed deputy commander of cadets in June 1968. According to Roger Morris' short but potent biography *Haig: The General's Progress*, Haig "covered up" two West Point scandals, one involving drugs, the other involving cheating. Truscott was a cadet spokesman who challenged Haig on several other issues. Morris relates a major incident with quotations from Truscott: "With Haig coming around the desk, Truscott flung his own defiant rejoinder '...if this is the way you want to play it...' and then Haig exploded, driving himself across the blue carpet until he was inches from my face. His fists were clenched and one of them was raised next to my head. 'You little bastard,' he seethed between gritted teeth. 'I will personally see you out of here one way or another. Now get out of here. Get out of my sight. The next time I see you, it will be at the front gate of West Point, going out.'"

In 1978, Truscott settled accounts somewhat by creating the character of General Charles Hedges, modeled on his old West Point commander. Morris also notes in the same volume that Haig had a talent for showing more than one face in a relationship "as he had once reassured yet ridiculed Kissinger; humored and afterward derided Nixon; allied himself both for and against Haldeman, the NSC staff, the Joint Chiefs…"

Truscott, the grandson of the general who led the Allied invasion of Anzio, had intended to follow the long military tradition of his family, but he resigned his commission in mid–1970 to become a writer. After leaving West Point, Haig went to work for Kissinger. Morris: "What distinguished [Haig] most was not ideology or ideals, but rather the capacity to adapt to the men he served."

The Betty Ford Story (TV film, 1987)

90 minutes. Biographical film based upon Betty Ford's memoirs. Gena Rowlands as Betty Ford.

Essentially a domestic drama showing how Mrs. Ford clashed with her family because of drug abuse and how she gained self-respect through founding the Betty Ford Center. Richard Nixon is seen early on in an excerpt in which he says, "I am not a quitter."

J. Edgar Hoover
(TV biographical drama, 1987)

120 minutes. Directed, written, produced by Robert Collins, based upon *My 30 Years in Hoover's FBI* by William G. Sullivan and William S. Brown. "Showtime Original Movie," Sunday, January 11, 1987, 8 P.M. Cast: *J. Edgar Hoover* Treat Williams; *Richard Nixon* Anthony Palmer; *Lyndon Johnson* Rip Torn; *Franklin D. Roosevelt* David Ogden Stiers; *Dwight Eisenhower* Andrew Duggan; *Joseph McCarthy* Charles Hallahan.

This "Showtime Original Movie" fared poorly. Nixon, played by Anthony Palmer, appears in one scene in which Hoover "beg(s) for job security" (*Variety*, January 21, 1987). This was the only scene that *Variety* considered "well-written" and Palmer's Nixon did not "come close" to capturing Nixon's personality.

J. Edgar Hoover was panned by all television critics. The *Chicago Sun-Times* (January 9, 1987) summed it up fairly well: "*Hoover* is a meandering and unfocused collection of disjointed and often boring vignettes [that] provide neither much insight nor much information … [it] remains unfavorable and unfair both to the late FBI director and all the other historical figures represented."

Nixon in China (opera, 1987)

An opera in two acts (later re-ordered to three acts) by John Adams. Libretto by Alice Goodman. Directed by Peter Sellars. Conducted by John DeMain. Sets by Adrienne Lobel. Costumes designed by Dunya Ramicova. World premiere. Performed by Houston Grand Opera at the Wortham Centre, Houston (October 22, 1987–November 7, 1987), the Brooklyn Academy of Music (December 4–17, 1987), the John F. Kennedy Center for the Performing Arts (March 26–April 5, 1988), and the Netherland Opera (June 2–18, 1988). Cast*: *Nixon* James Maddalena; *Pat Nixon* Carolann Page; *Chou En-lai* Sanford Sylvan; *Mao Tse-tung* John Duykers; *Madame Mao* Trudy Ellen Craney; *Henry Kissinger* Thomas Hammon; *Mao's Secretaries* Mari Opatz, Stephanie Friedman and Marion Dry.

What follows is a summary of scenes:

ACT I, SCENE 1—The airport near Peking; Monday, February 21, 1972, a cold, clear morning . Masses of the Chinese army, navy and air force gather on the field and sing "The Main Rules of Discipline and the Eight Points of Attention." Premier Chou En-lai, heading a band of officials, walks leisurely onto the runway as Nixon's plane, "The Spirit of 76," taxies into view. After a slight pause, the door opens and Nixon stands in the doorway; Nixon slowly descends the ramp; he is followed immediately by Pat in her scarlet coat. Nixon sings of his excitement and the possibility of triumph or failure. As part of a much longer aria, he sings:

> We live in an unsettled time.
> Who are our enemies? Who are
> Our friends?

After pleasantries are exchanged, Kissinger tells Nixon that they must be on their way to meet Chairman Mao.

ACT I, SCENE 2—Chairman Mao is seated in his book-lined study. Several Chinese photographers slip into the room as Nixon, Chou En-lai and Kissinger enter. Mao's three secretaries help him up so that he may greet his visitors. Mao speaks in maxims before which Nixon's customary prolixity founders. Nixon sings in part,

> Fathers and sons,
> Let us join hands, make peace for once.
> History is our mother, we
> Best do her honor in this way.

Amid several heavy jests about the penchant for chasing young girls that is shared by Kissinger and Mao, Mao good-naturedly says, "*Six Crises* isn't a bad book."

ACT I, SCENE 3—Evening of the first day. The Great Hall of the People. Nixon and Pat are on either side of Chou as Chinese and American flags deck the hall. The conversation touches on many subjects and the mood is hopeful throughout. Many toasts are made. Chou sings as part of his toast,

> The virtuous American
> And the Chinese make manifest
> Their destinies in time.

*This was the cast in the recorded version for Nonesuch and the cast for the television production. Edo de Waart is the conductor of these later renderings.

Three shots from the Houston Grand Opera production of *Nixon in China*. Photos by Jim Caldwell/Houston Grand Opera (1987).

Then later, Nixon sings,

> The world watches and listens. We
> Must seize the hour and seize the day.

At the end of the scene, the chorus sings "We marvel now." Nixon, trance-like, sings,

> It's like a dream.

ACT II, SCENE 1— Snow has fallen during the night. It is now February 22, Washington's birthday as Pat points out. The snow continues as Pat, on her own, goes on a sight-seeing tour during which she meets many workers and develops a camaraderie with the guides and journalists. In spite of her naiveté, Pat is a realist.

> Trivial things are not for me.
> I come from a poor family.

Pat visits a glass factory where she is given a glass elephant; she then goes to a model pig farm where she pets one of its denizens, followed by a visit to the Summer Palace where she sings of her vision of the future:

> This is prophetic! I foresee
> A time will come when luxury
> Dissolves into the atmosphere
> Like a perfume, and everywhere
> The simple virtues root and branch
> And leaf and flower.

Pat's last stop is the Ming Tombs. The sky brightens as she taps gently on the leg of an archaic elephant, smiling the while.

Her escorts sing of China's former days. Pat is respectful and reluctant to leave. The day has been full.

ACT II, SCENE 2— A scene of great complexity yet remarkably controlled. Madame Mao, as Goodman states in her libretto, appears in "a dark Sun Yat-sen suit and black-rimmed men's glasses." Madame Mao is seated between Nixon and Pat, who is simply but attractively dressed. Pat is excited. She and Richard are about to see "The Red Detachment of Women," a revolutionary ballet devised by Madame Mao, the former actress known as Chiang Ch'ing. In the opera, three girls are bound to posts. The rest of the scene becomes surrealistic as the Nixons, naive westerners, lean forward in their anxiety at the plight of the three young women who are threatened by the villain Lao Szu (the actor playing Kissinger plays this role as well). One of the girls is beaten insensible. Kissinger sings,

> This is the fate
> Of all who set
> Small against great.
> Leave it to rot.

A tropical storm comes up. The Nixons stand above the body of the beaten girl, their clothes drenched. Nixon sings,

> What would I do without you, Pat?

The weather clears as Party Representative Hung Chang-ching appears with his scouting mission. Dick and Pat raise the beaten girl to her feet. Pat sings,

> Thank God you came. Just look at this!
> Poor thing! It's simply barbarous!
> 'Whip her death!' he said. I'd like
> To give his God-damned whip a crack!
> Oh Dick! You're sopping!

The girl escapes and liberates her village. Many ambiguities occur here at the end of the act (originally the middle scene of a three scene second act). Like the ballet that the scene depicts, the ideologies are bizarrely jumbled and filled with high emotion and great theatricality. The scene ends stunningly with Madame Mao singing,

> At the breast
> Of history I sucked and pissed,
> Thoughtless and heartless, red and blind,
> I cut my teeth upon the land
> And when I walked my feet were bound
> On revolution.

Act II, Scene 2 is the set piece of the opera. It is total theater followed by the most clearly defined contrast.

Act III is a study in introspection, almost an extended reverie for all the leading characters. It is the Nixons' final night in China. The Nixons, Chou and the Maos appear in their respective bedrooms. Dance rhythms of past times weave through the score as the characters reminisce. They think of how ordinary their pasts have been, all sharing their regrets and longings. A pop tune begins, and Chiang Ch'ing says to Mao, "We'll teach these motherfuckers how to dance." (These lines appear in the libretto but are not on the recording.)

The night passes, filled with memories, buoyed by the adventure that is just now coming to an end. The opera ends quietly with Chou, the idealist, thinking of the work yet to be done.

> At this hour nothing can be done.
> Just before dawn the birds begin,
> The warblers who prefer the dark,
> The cage-like birds answering. To work!
> Outside this room the chill of grace
> Lies heavy on the morning grass.

The first complete run-through of John Adams's minimalist opera *Nixon in China* was given by American Inroads in May 1987 at San Francisco's Herbst Theater. (Two scenes had been done earlier at New York's Guggenheim Museum.) The San Francisco instrumentation was two pianos and a synthesizer. The September 1987 issue of London's *Opera* called the Inroads production "a pseudo-historic-quasi-satirical opera-in-progress." With its expectations high, *Opera* said: "It will all be terribly daring, terribly mod, terribly chic, terribly up-to-date. It may also be provocative. It may even be fun." So much for the potentialities of Peter Sellars's staging, but what of the music? *Opera* took the dimmest of views: "repetitive twaddle ... primitive piffle ... doodledy instrumental meanderings compounding a precarious line between caricature and pathos."

Fortunately, Sellars's staging and a full orchestra did in fact work wonders and *Nixon in China* played to many favorable, even rave, reviews at its premiere at the Houston Grand Opera and in later performances in Brooklyn, Washington, Amsterdam,

Edinburgh and Germany as well as on American television. It is one of those rare occasions in art, like Edward Albee's return to critical favor with *Three Tall Women*, in which an unpromising artistic event, when realized in production, astonishes its critics and forces them into re-evaluation.

The idea for the work came from "boy wonder" Peter Sellars. The "thirty something" John Adams immediately rejected it. "I thought it would be ridiculous for Nixon to sing," Adams said, but Sellars persisted with a zealot's vision and Adams finally relented. Sellars then chose one of his Harvard classmates, young Alice Goodman, to write the libretto. The result, Adams thought, was "brilliant," and he "cut almost nothing of the finished poem." In an *Opera News* interview in October 1987, Adams went on to say, "Alice and I created our own Nixon, and we fell in love with him. We've focused on his more heroic aspects. He's such an interesting character because he is so vulnerable. We didn't try to make saints out of these people or to rehabilitate them. We tried to make each character speak as eloquently as he or she could." A key example is Pat Nixon's touching aria in Act II in which her middle class values are treated sympathetically, especially in prosaic lines like

> The sirens wail
> As bride and groom kiss through the veil,
> Bless this union with all its might,
> Let it remain inviolate.

Adams continued: "In today's so-called classical music, we've lost track of the vernacular ... We hardly need another opera on a Shakespeare play or a Greek myth."

Alice Goodman wanted to write "a heroic opera" in which some or all of the characters are quite ordinary and yet "every character is as eloquent as possible." Written chiefly in couplets, Goodman's libretto is an accomplished work of poetry in its own right. Among the few dissenters in this regard was Paul Moor of *Musical America* who called Goodman's work "a curious, episodic, largely iambic tetrameter libretto" which seemed "woefully inadequate." *High Fidelity*, on the other hand, with the majority, went so far as to call the libretto "a masterpiece [that creates] a richly intimate portrait of a politician most of us remember only from his questionable public words and actions." The portrait may or may not be accurate, but that is beside the point. *Nixon in China* does not aim for biographical scrupulousness, and the Adams–Goodman rendering endows Nixon with many qualities — "among them [the] ambition, pride, idealism, vulnerability [and] *naiveté* that make for a viable operatic protagonist."

For the most part, Adams and his colleagues succeeded, and the Nixons appear winningly middle class and middlebrow throughout. When the Nixons are overcome with a romantic reverie it is to the accompaniment of a Glenn Miller saxophone quartet, the kind of music they danced to in the early days of their love. "There's a spot where John wrote in three muted trumpets for them," said John DeMain, Houston Grand Opera's Music Director. "I mean it's real sweet. It's Sammy Kaye ... a lot of fun." This kind of period touch is important to the fullest realization of the characters. In the October 1987 *Ovation,* Adams commented, "We're not having fun at Nixon's expense." The Nixons and the Maos are demythologized in high and good spirits. For instance, another but much more modern musical element is the Motown harmony that peppers Mao's three "right on" secretaries, referred to by Sellars in rehearsals as the Maoettes. Oddly enough, Mao is never "camped up," but Madame Mao frequently is, especially during her Broadwayese "show stopper," *I Am the Wife of Mao Tse-tung.*

In the original German production this aria included a striptease, making former actress Chiang Ching an even more notorious First Lady than former actress Evita Peron.

Kissinger's portrait, that of a basso not so profundo, includes such benighted utterances as "I'm lost," "Please, where's the toilet?," "Who, me?" and:

> I'm here to liaise
> With the backroom boys
> Who know how to live
> And me, I contrive
> To catch a few crumbs
> The ringleaders' names
> The gist of their schemes
> Loose change.

Certainly having Kissinger appear as the villain in Madame Mao's ballet *The Red Detachment of Women* makes him not only a figure of comic menace, but it is also the creative team's comment on American foreign policy under Nixon. As delivered with a thick "Churman" accent, Kissinger cannot but become a caricature "heavy" circa 1943 Hollywood.

With its grab bag of sources, *Nixon in China* verges close — especially in Madame Mao's bravura and the Kissinger "send up" — to *Saturday Night Live* sophomorism and late-night TV monologues. In short, the entire opera is an incredible blend of originality, pop culture clichés and audacity, but in spite of its undergraduate élan, it remains a very moving work. Seldom, if ever, have small town American WASPs and their middle class values ever been presented so sympathetically in opera.

More than anything else, what the opera strives for is an endearing innocence. As James Maddalena, the opera's first Nixon, said: "We're talking about a man from an American culture that is 200 years old sitting next to Mao and Chou, whose culture goes back thousands of years. Europeans have this idea about us that we are like children in our attitudes. But I think it's nice to be a little naive and just a little idealistic. We all have this beautiful *naiveté* that is really American, and I think this comes out in Nixon."

"What is charming about the Nixons," said Paul Griffiths in London's *Musical Times* of the HGO premiere, "is that they never understand themselves." Nixon thinks that he is "shaping time" and that his words to Mao are of extreme importance. Literally, he and Pat are kids "in a China shop," little people going about the world's big business, and in the next scene, Pat visits a glass factory where she is given a glass elephant. She sings, "I come from a poor family" and goes on,

> This little elephant in glass
> Brings back so many memories
> The symbol of our party, prize
> of our success, our sacred cow
> Surrounded by blind Brahmins, slow
> Musclebound —

— like the Nixons, "slow, musclebound," out of their element, given a playful tap in Goodman's libretto when Mao tells Nixon "*Six Crises* isn't a bad book," like a master teacher indulging an insecure student eager for praise. Other critics such as Kyle Gann (writing in the *Village Voice*) had high praise for the dexterity of Alice Goodman's "ravishingly poetic libretto" which in turn Adams "fragments ... into Gertrude

Steinish enigmas. Treatment of the English language, disgracefully handled in most American operas, is here the focal point that unites musical and textual ideas." These voyaging innocents and their inscrutable hosts, Gann says, "are caught up in world events they can nuance, but not control"; they are borne along by a rush of music like a stream of passing time.

To counter Nixon's innocence, Adams, Goodman and Sellars were also drawn to Nixon's "dark recesses" where his idealism was at war with his ambition, his desire for "a place in history." This was, as Sellars said, "Nixon's greatest moment, and at the time he sensed it too. When he first steps off the plane in Peking, he sees himself as an Apollo astronaut setting foot on the Moon. There's a certain poignancy and hero-ism about it and a touching sentiment as well," but his ego is not that far away. It shows from time to time.

To Sellars, Pat was the focal point of the opera. "Her contact with China was the most interesting spiritual exchange of the trip." To any careful student of the opera, Pat is far more than the cheery little dearie personified by her contemporary June Allyson in so many 1940s and 1950s MGM films. "Far more interesting than Nixon's conversation with Mao is the look in the eyes of the Chinese people as they are look-ing at Pat and the look in her eyes as she is looking back at them."

In one of the most scathing of all *Nixon* reviews, Jonathan Lieberson in the Jan-uary 21, 1988, *New York Review of Books* said Pat's character was "predictably virtuous, haunted by the poverty of her childhood and by memories of slipcovers and longing to be in California" after which he castigated the entire enterprise for "its comic-strip imagery and glossy colors and its snapshot version of history — so many of which seem torn out of the pages of fashion magazines."

Nevertheless, a much more favorable press overpowered the nay-sayers. "Rhyth-mically shimmering, meltingly lyrical and colorfully orchestrated," said William Albright in the Spring 1988 *Opera Canada* of the Houston premiere, words he repeated almost verbatim in the April 9 *Opera News*. In both publications, Albright had high praise for the performances of James Maddalena and Carolann Page. ("Pat's poignant, soaring aria about an idyllic future of the world was gorgeous.") Albright was also impressed with Chou's "flowingly noble soliloquies" and Madame Mao's "fiercely spiky, Queen of the Night-shaded coloratura outbursts." Echoing the general sentiments of the premiere, *Variety* concluded its November 2, 1987, review with "At its best, *Nixon in China* is an exciting, volatile, thought-provoking experience." In an impish mood, Manuela Hoelterhoff of the *Wall Street Journal* chortled: "What could be more divine, or at least pleasant, and good for the Nixon name? There is little in the libretto by Alice Goodman that would make Julie Nixon cry. This Nixon has no sweat spots, and nobody trills [an aria called] *Watergate*."

The first performance outside the United States occurred on June 2, 1988, in Amsterdam at the Holland Festival. According to *Opera* (London, November 1988), it was "an unqualified success." Critic Michael Davidson went on to say, "With clar-ity, empathy, and humor, *Nixon* reveals the vulnerability of those who shape history. Alice Goodman's masterly libretto poetically sketches the awesome gap between emo-tion and belief, between the personal and the public."

Davidson said further, "Each character had distinctive vocal style," a point empha-sized by many discerning critics, notably Allan Kozinn in *Grove's Dictionary of Opera*, Volume III: "The musical characterizations ... are often quite striking, and Adams's text settings for Richard Nixon in particular reflect his speech patterns recognizably."

Both Nixons were "totally believable" in performance, and Trudy Ellen Craney "made a meal of Madame Mao's coloratura flights." Sanford Sylvan was an "eloquent" Chou.

Rodney Milnes was *Opera's* critic when the HGO production became a last-minute addition to the Edinburgh Festival on September 1, 1988. His review cited the music's enrichment of the characters: "Adams's 'enhanced minimalism' is certainly capable of characterization. Nixon, Mao and Chou are precisely fixed by the very singable music they are given, even if the characterization is at odds with one's perceived ideas of the people themselves (Nixon an essentially innocent, would-be sly, overgrown schoolboy, Mao a tired cynic, Chou a visionary idealist)." Milnes felt that Carolann Page's "beautifully sung Pat Nixon triumphed over derivative music and purposefully wan characterization," and Maddalena's Nixon was "full of arresting dramatic detail."

On December 10, 1990, the German premiere took place in Bielefeld. There had been some question whether Germany would allow the production to go forward because of the slaughter of Chinese students in Tiananmen Square by Communist hard-liners the previous year. When performed, German audiences did not care for the music or the directorial interpretation which had become heavy satire. Although, to be sure, a gentle satire does permeate the work, some of the staging ideas at Bielefeld would have given even Peter Sellars pause. For instance, in addition to Madame Mao's strip-tease, in the final scene designer Gottfried Pilz had Chou appear on the fuselage of the Spirit of 76 in the lotus position while the Maos created a love nest on the plane's left wing. During the concert piece *The Chairman Dances* earlier in the evening, Madame Mao had seduced the Chairman behind the stuffed furniture holding the Nixons. Kissinger, who, as noted, is presented for comic effect throughout, was so upset he had to go to the bathroom. *Nixon* has much that in the wrong hands can, as the British say, "go over the top." This production apparently went farther than the astronauts.

In one of his early interviews, Adams stated that the meeting of Nixon and Mao in Act I, Scene 2 is the emotional and philosophical center of the work, yet to many critics the last scene which constitutes the entire third act has higher claims in this regard. Act III, as Adams says, "is about age and love." We see "the two most powerful couples" in the world confronting these two most vital aspects of living, and both we and they are forced inward. Nixon and Pat speak of the chaos and the curious cohesiveness created by World War II, and Mao speaks of mythology's "eternal charm."

To some, this muted ending was a disappointment, but in a brilliant essay entitled *Inner Landscape* in the July 1989 *Opera News,* Patrick J. Smith states that the collaborators' initial intention was to have a farewell banquet scene paralleling the last scene of Act I. After much discussion, they decided to present "an interior" scene which would occupy the entire 33-minute final act. In this way, the audience would come to know the characters on a more personal level. Nevertheless, this well-intended change drew considerable criticism, even from the opera's champions. In spite of disapproval from some quite influential quarters, Smith became convinced on re-hearing and re-viewing that this decision was the right one because it is a character-revealing contrast to the material that has preceded it. Smith felt that "*Nixon* needed some insight into the personages as men and women — and, more important, as men and women together." Underscoring this point, here the dance rhythms steal in, stirring the characters and the audience — no matter that for the majority their only knowledge of World War II will be that found in history books. Collective memory, through the art of the creators and performers, is seductively at work here. The dance music, so evocative of the youth of the two middle-aged couples, allows them to enter what Michael Steinberg in his liner notes for the Nonesuch recording calls "the inner landscape of their minds."

A curious aspect of the original production is that the last scene — so filled with private thoughts — appears to take place in a dormitory, an odd refutation of the intimacy that seems called for. With its contrastingly softer mood, a kind of free association occurs, linking all the major characters. A case could be made for either open or area staging of this scene that in its conception is so close to chamber opera. Hugo von Hofmannsthal's libretti for Richard Strauss are worthy ancestors here. There is a loveliness of spirit as Nixon sings about being a naval officer in World War II and opening a hamburger stand at his post in the Solomon Islands "where he served free hamburgers and Australian beer to grateful flight crews who had eaten little besides lamb for weeks" (Stephen E. Ambrose, *Nixon: The Education of a Politician 1913–1962*). The World War II Nixon created by Goodman sounds close to the real Nixon of the 1940s and Thomas Heggen's Mister Roberts, a comparison, according to Ambrose, often made by the men in Nixon's former company.

> Done to a turn;
> Rare, medium, well, anything
> You say. The customer is King.
> Sorry, we're low on relish. Drinks?
> This is my way of saying thanks.

"This is my way of saying thanks" is such a graceful way of the opera's saying goodbye to Richard and to Pat, who has encouraged him so charmingly in his reverie.

Finally, Chou sings of his need to work, and the opera ends in the very early morning of the Nixons' last day. It ends as it began, in the early morning.

With any new artistic work there is always the question, "Will it last?" No matter what its artistic worth, *Nixon in China* will always have its detractors. The reason of course lies with the man himself. It is very clear that in spite of President Clinton's admonition at Nixon's funeral that judgments of Nixon should be based on "the totality of his life," for some, skepticism, even derision will always be present. This criticism was present at *Nixon in China*'s very beginnings. Witness Will Crutchfield's Sunday in the *New York Times* after *Nixon*'s opening at the Brooklyn Academy of Music: "Problematic is the creators' dogged avoidance of comment on the whole Nixon. Ms. Goodman, who was a teen-ager when Mr. Nixon's presidency ended, went about 'relentlessly ignoring everything published after 1972 except for the Nixon and Kissinger memoirs.' This blinkered view of history is a delicate problem." "Why?" one might ask. If art had always served history, Shakespeare would not have written *Richard III*. Yet none but "blinkered" historians lament that he *did* write it, and surely David Edgar glories in this Shakespearean transmogrification since it forms the basis of one of the cleverest parodies in 20th century political theater (Edgar's own *Dick Deterred*, a work previously discussed in this text).

Quite predictably, in the years following the San Francisco concert version, the verdicts have ranged wildly between witty slams such as Donal Henahan's comment in the *New York Times* that *Nixon in China* "works to redefine boredom," or another clever Henahan comment such as "Mr. Adams does for the *arpeggio* what McDonald's did for the hamburger, grinding out one simple idea into eternity. At one point when something musical threatens to take shape, it turns out to be a quotation from Wagner." But there are also verdicts like those of the critic of the *Village Voice* (December 29,

1987): "*Nixon in China* ... may miss being the Great American Opera, but not since [the Virgil Thomson–Gertrude Stein] *Mother of Us All* (1947) has an opera come so close to one's fondest hopes for what American opera could be."

Richard Nixon will probably never gain a higher public persona than in this remarkable work of modern musical theater. In spite of some adverse criticism, this opera holds an assured place in late 20th century American opera. In a highly laudatory review dated December 6, 1987, John Rockwell of the *New York Times* stated, "*Nixon in China,* while not perfect, is a stirring creation, full of charm and wit, and, in the end, beauty. Unlike so many new operas, grimly earnest or shinily trendy, this one is likely to last."

In an early interview, John Adams said that *Nixon in China* was "not just an entertainment." Andrew Porter in the *New Yorker* gave a significant endorsement to Adams' high aims when he wrote that *Nixon in China* is "a successful and stirring musical drama ... [it] needs to be heard with critical ears; it does not do our thinking for us."

Nearly ten years after its first performance, Alex Rose of the *New York Times* (April 7, 1996) wrote: "[*Nixon in China*] is too good, too beautiful, too necessary [to drop] from sight. Nixon is dead, but he still lives vividly in people's minds. Alice Goodman's libretto looks back at Nixon from a distant, nonjudgmental vantage point. It seems to emanate from some point in the future. It does not fall into the traps of Oliver Stone's recent Nixon film and the filmmaker's eternal obsessions. The opera's strongest claim is its clarity, simplicity and shocking elegance."

Above the Law (film, 1988)

99 minutes. Directed by Andrew Davis. Written by Steven Pressfield, Ronald Shusett and Andrew Davis. Story by Andrew Davis and Steven Seagal. Photography by Robert Steadman. Edited by Michael Brown. Music by David M. Frank. Color. Warner Bros. Cast: *Nico Toscani* Steven Seagal; *Delores "Jax" Jackson* Pam Grier; *Sara Toscani* Sharon Stone; *Father Gennaro* Joe V. Greco; *Zagon* Henry Silva.

Richard Nixon supplies the title of this film in a clip that appears just after an anti–Vietnam riot: "My friends, let me make this clear, Abraham Lincoln said this is a nation of laws, and no one is above the law, no one is below the law, and we're going to enforce the law, and Americans should remember that if we're going to have law and order."

Above the Law is the story of Nico Toscani, played by Steven Seagal in this, his debut film. Shots of Seagal's own childhood start the film on an almost domestic note; his light, breathy voice, so out of character with his corporeal self, tells us that at 17 he went to Tokyo to study with the martial arts "masters." These points from Seagal's own life lend an authenticity to and create a rapport with the central character. From then on, it is Nico Toscani's story, an idealist in a world of official corruption. When he was 22, he was recruited into the CIA at a party at the American Embassy in Tokyo. He goes to Southeast Asia and quickly becomes disillusioned with United States policies when he learns that some of the CIA operatives were involved in drug smuggling and the torture of the Vietnamese.

Years later, as a Chicago cop with a breezy, down-to-earth sidekick (Pam Grier), he stumbles upon weapons-running and drug dealing by some of his former CIA associates who are also planning to assassinate a senator who is investigating them. Good guy that he is (a family man, loving son, churchgoer, half of the police team with a beautiful but "strictly business" partner), Nico fights off the baddies and saves the senator, but the unusual thing about *Above the Law* is that it is one of the few action films that is not chauvinistic. Produced at a time when secret arms deals to anti–Communist rebels in Central America were a hot topic, this is one aspect of the film that the *New York Daily News* critic praised (April 8, 1988): "This flat, sloppily directed action-thriller turns out to be a very timely message movie as Toscani, in a voiceover narration, denounces the lawless activities of certain government agencies." This was a sentiment also expressed in *Newsday* (April 8, 1988) whose review began: "Something about *Above the Law* doesn't *feel* right. Something seems oft-kilter ... out of place..." and ends with: "What separates *Above the Law* from all the other [action-thrillers] is political viewpoint. Getting a left-winger to behave this way — breaking arms and legs with his fist, chopping down assassin teams with his feet, standing up to automatic weapons with a smile — I'm telling you, this could do more for the liberal image than Fritz Mondale and Paul Simon combined."

Born on the Fourth of July (biographical film, 1989)

145 minutes. Directed by Oliver Stone. Written by Oliver Stone and Ron Kovic as adapted from Kovic's autobiography of the same name. Produced by A. Kitman Ho and Oliver Stone. Photography by Robert Richardson. Music by John Williams. Color. Universal. Cast: *Ron Kovic* Tom Cruise; *Charlie* Willem Dafoe; *Mrs. Kovic* Caroline Kava; *Donna* Kyra Sedgwick.

Ron Kovic's powerful autobiography came out in 1976 shortly after his 30th birthday. It was a *cri de coeur* as well as a revealing and compelling social document. Soon after its publication, Oliver Stone bought the screen rights and turned it into a screenplay, but the project collapsed when the financing suddenly fell through. He did not give up. After the success of *Platoon* in 1986, Stone was able, with Kovic as co-author, to re-work the script, gain the financing and turn *Born on the Fourth of July* into a popular film that grossed over $70 million.

Richard Nixon dominates the end of Chapter VI in Kovic's book when he gives the acceptance speech at the 1972 Republican convention. (The autobiography: "It was the night of Nixon's acceptance speech and now I was on my own, deep in his territory, all alone in my wheelchair in a sweat-soaked marine utility jacket covered with medals from the war. A TV producer I knew from the Coast had gotten me past the guards at the entrance with his press pass. My eyes were still smarting from tear gas.") What follows in both the book and the film is riveting. Kovic shouts throughout Nixon's speech, which is edited into *Born on the Fourth of July* three times. The first shot is Nixon's formal acknowledgment of the nomination; the second is the segment that refers to the angry groups (shouts in the background) "that make us a divided country." Nixon's last appearance in the film contains the somewhat forced irony of Nixon's saying that the Vietnam veterans must have "the honor and respect they deserve" as Kovic is accosted by outraged Nixon supporters.

Like most Stone films, this film is a polemic, and for some critics, like Pauline Kael, it had more than its share of false notes: "Kovic's book is simple and explicit; he states his case in plain, angry words. Stone's film yells at you for two hours and 25 minutes" (*New Yorker*, January 22, 1990).

The film creates a picture of a youth of incredible *naiveté*, fed on gung-ho John Wayne movies and bourgeois guilt-inducing platitudes. In the book, this somewhat simplistic philosophy is honestly rendered. The reader feels that this *was* Kovic's life, even though the reader wonders how any young man could have been unaware of the social upheaval after Kennedy's assassination and the many persuasive voices on both sides of the Vietnam issue. To Kael, who was obviously familiar with the book, "the falseness starts during the opening credits, with the dusty, emotionally charged Fourth of July celebration in 1956 — Ronnie's tenth birthday.... [Stone] uses slow motion to mythologize the drum majorettes. Even the kids' baseball game is a slo-mo elegy. A lyrical glow fuses sports and kids playing soldier and civic boosterism and imperialism. And John Williams' music is like a tidal wave. It comes beating down on you while you're trying to duck Robert Richardson's frenzied camera angles. So much rapture, so soon, I was suffering from pastoral overload before the credits were finished."

David Ansen in his perceptive *Newsweek* review (December 25, 1989) also pointed out how the film is primed with easy targets: God, patriotism, an anything-to-win wrestling coach, a docile father, a repressive and uncompromising mother and the glorification of war by chauvinistic louts. (In one of the domestic scenes, General Westmoreland is heard in a background TV interview.) Ansen wrote, "The movie is a tirade against the authoritarian macho mentality that led us into Vietnam, but Stone fights back with his own brand of emotional authoritarianism. The problem is clearest in the opening encapsulation of Kovic's flag-waving, baseball-playing childhood. It's trying so hard to be archetypal it ends up feeling unreal."

Surprisingly, Nixon supporter Pat Buchanan treated the film very respectfully (*New York Post*, January 31, 1990), calling it "a powerful antidote to shallow jingoism, a stark reminder that even 'good wars' exact a terrible toll that falls heaviest on the bravest." Feeling that the film treated Nixon unfairly, Buchanan wrote: "Kovic and Stone assault Richard Nixon, but it was John Kennedy and Lyndon Johnson who marched us in, and by the time of that '72 convention 90 percent of U.S. troops were home, the draft was ending, and we were bombing the North only to protect U.S. forces left behind, to get our POWs back, to give Vietnam the chance for which Ron Kovic had fought."

Noting how Stone's films usually divide both audiences and critics, David Ansen concluded his *Newsweek* review with: "Stone's aesthetics of hysteria can take you only so far: it's the cinematic equivalent of heavy metal, awesome fragments buried in a whole lot of bombast. This movie offers you two choices: you can be overwhelmed by it, or do battle with it. Either way it leaves you drained."

It was a film that was well-received by Stone's peers: Stone won the Academy Award as Best Director; David Brenner and Joe Hutshing won the Academy Award for Best Editing. Although he did not win, Tom Cruise was nominated as Best Actor in a performance that was praised by nearly every major critic with the exception of

Pauline Kael. David Denby (*New York*, December 18, 1989) called the film an "often powerful and heartbreaking piece of work, dominated by Tom Cruise's performance."

The Unguided Missile (play, 1989)

Written by David Wolpe. Directed by Fred Kolo. Presented by the American Place Theater, Wynn Handman, director, 111 West 46th Street, New York City. Cast: *Martha Mitchell* Estelle Parsons; *John Mitchell* Jerome Dempsey; *Alan Webster and others* Nick Searcy; *Mike Madden and others* Barry Cullison; *Sherri Peterson* Lezlie Dalton; *Cathy Ried and others* Mary Jo Salerno.

By 1989, interest in Watergate was at a low ebb, and *The Unguided Missile* was fortunate in being presented for a limited run at a subscription theater. At such a theater, a Watergate-related play could have a short run and not be considered a failure. No matter what its weaknesses were as dramatic literature, it gave Estelle Parsons an opportunity for a stellar performance — which she delivered.

A worthy play that contained some weaknesses, *The Unguided Missile* had a mixed reception. One of the more negative reviews was that of the *New York Times* (February 13, 1989): "Speaking her mind during the depths of Watergate, Martha Mitchell was either a virago-gone-haywire or a protector of democratic principles. David Wolpe's play *The Unguided Missile* bolsters the first description, while making it clear that Mrs. Mitchell kept her tunnel vision fixed firmly on the interests of herself and her husband, John Mitchell, the indicted former Attorney General.... It is unclear whether Mr. Wolpe intends to spoof his protagonist or present a sympathetic portrait of her.... The most theatrical character is off-stage and that of course is Richard Nixon, 'King Richard' as Mrs. Mitchell calls him. She hopes that he will rescue them, but he will not even answer his telephone."

John Simon's review in *New York* (February 27, 1989) was somewhat more favorable: "I don't think Wolpe has succeeded more than superficially, but even that puts *The Unguided Missile* a cut above the current offerings that are about nothing at all. The evening is helped by the genuinely felt and honestly and knowingly executed Martha of Estelle Parsons, an actress almost completely devoid of mannerisms and affectations. There is something naked about this performance that I find bracing and touching."

Like the two other Martha Mitchell plays referred to in this volume, *After the Season* and *The Martha Play*, *The Unguided Missile* was not a play destined for a long stage life and was, therefore, never published.

U.S. vs. Nixon (documentary, 1989)

20 minutes. Directed by John G. Young and Patrick Fitzsimmons. Produced by Susan Elkov Green for Guidance Associates, Communications Park, Box 3000, Mt. Kisco, NY 10549.

"This short program is well narrated and occasionally supported by appropriate video clips. However, most viewers will probably be overwhelmed by the attempt to present such a complicated case with its Watergate overtones in this brief 20-minute format."— *Choice* (Association of College and Research Libraries), May 1989.

"Compensated for its often grainy footage, [*U.S. vs. Nixon*] fascinatingly navigates through the legal maze that pitted the executive and judicial branches against one another and threatened the Constitution's viability in 1974. The comprehensive, smoothly narrated program incorporates excerpts from the Watergate hearings and Nixon's news conferences, traces precedents for the Court's undivided decision, and notes the importance of the justice's unanimity."—*ALA Booklist*, March 15, 1989.

Unauthorized Biography: Richard M. Nixon (TV, 1989)

Written and narrated by Barbara Howar. Produced by Peter Bull and Jonathan Kaplan. Channel 9, New York City, 8–10 P.M., March 8, 1989.

LBJ apologist and occasional journalist Barbara Howar created a two-hour "biography" that even the liberal *New York Times* called "a hatchet job" (March 8, 1989) with graphics "employed to make Mr. Nixon look sinister, sordid and smarmy.... The program seems designed to confirm the charges of the political right that television is in the grip of a left-wing cabal. Even those who share Ms. Howar's evident dislike of Mr. Nixon may be put off by her relentless animadversions."

Howar's unauthorized biography "is not criticism, it is a diatribe, advocacy journalism at its most blatant and worst." Howar's contempt for her subject, in the end, backfired and reflected more poorly on her than it did on Richard Nixon. As the *Times* review concluded: "On exhibition in these two hours is merely the ability of the medium, when unenhanced by journalistic imagination or sophistication, to do some kicking around."

Nixon: The American Experience (TV biography, 1989)

180 minutes. A three part biography written by Geoffrey C. Ward. Produced by Elizabeth Deane. Narrated by Will Lyman. Part I: "The Quest," produced and edited by David Espar. Part II: "Triumph," produced and edited by Elizabeth Deane. Part III: "The Fall," produced by Marilyn Mellowes. A production of WGBH–TV, Boston, in association with Thames Television, Channel 13, 8–11 P.M., October 15, 1989.

"[I]nsecurity led him ... a secure Nixon almost surely ... would never have been President at all."— Elliot Richardson, Nixon's attorney general.

An extremely well-researched documentary that touched upon the milestones in Nixon's life and career: Hannah and Frank Nixon, his brothers, sports, hard work, school plays, college, law school, meeting Pat, the Navy, early law practice, rough early campaigns, the Hiss case, the Rosenbergs, McCarthy, the Fund, Checkers, ambiguous relationships with Ike, Kennedy, California defeat, the boredom of life in a New York law firm, the triumphs and failures of his five and a half years as President, his slow and steady return to the public arena — all very well done, possibly too much (almost the entire last hour) devoted to Watergate. It also captures very well the unending state of siege that war protesters created outside the White House. There are several penetrating comments from former high level White House official Roger Morris, who resigned over the invasion of Cambodia. (Morris' 1990 *Richard Milhous Nixon: The Rise of an American Politician* is one of the four or five truly outstanding books on Richard Nixon.)

Here's a sampling of critical opinion:

"When all is said and done and written, it is likely that Richard Nixon and not Elvis or Reagan will dominate the landscape of the second half of America's 20th century as no other personality. If you doubt this, if you still hate the man too much to accept this notion, please watch the three-hour edition of '*The American Experience*' called 'Nixon.' This is as full-blown a television portrait as we have seen. Although it does not touch on the post-presidential years and devotes too much time to Watergate, it still makes a fascinating program." — *Chicago Tribune*, October 15, 1990.

"The safe conclusion offered here is that 'his legacy remains ambiguous.' Lately, in what seems an effort to polish up his legacy, Mr. Nixon has been presenting himself on talk shows and elsewhere as an elder statesman willing to share his wisdom with his latest successor in the White House.... If tonight's program cannot quite illuminate the corners of an intriguing mind, it does suggest that for all his moody introspection, Richard Nixon never confronted his own character." — *New York Times*, October 15, 1990.

The Final Days
(TV docu-drama, 1989)

180 minutes. Written by Hugh Whitemore. Based on the book of the same name by Bob Woodward and Carl Bernstein. Directed by Richard Pearce. Music by Cliff Eidelman. Photography by Fred Murphy. Produced by the Samuels Film Company for AT&T, ABC–TV, Sunday evening, October 29, 1989, 8–11 P.M. Cast: *Richard M. Nixon* Lane Smith; *Fred Buzhardt* Richard Kiley; *Gen. Alexander Haig* David Ogden Stiers; *Leonard Garment* Ed Flanders; *Henry Kissinger* Theodore Bikel; *James D. St. Clair* Richard Venture; *Elliot Richardson* James B. Sikking; *Alexander Butterfield* James Edgcomb; *Gerald Ford* Alan Fudge; *Ron Ziegler* Graham Beckel; *John Dean III* Gregg Henry; *Archibald Cox* George Wallace; *Tricia Nixon Cox* Amanda Wyss; *Julie Nixon Eisenhower* Ann Hearn; *Rose Mary Woods* Diane Bellamy; *Pat Nixon (a non-speaking role)* Susan Brown.

The TV film of *The Final Days* is one of the few instances in which the dramatization of a work was superior to its source.

Lane Smith as Nixon in *The Final Days* (1989).

The teleplay opens in 1973. Watergate and its ramifications are spreading farther and farther while the Nixon White House attempts damage control. Haldeman and Ehrlichman have resigned and Fred Buzhardt has been engaged as Nixon's legal counsel for Watergate. During this time, Nixon has maintained an active Presidency highlighted by a visit from Leonid Brezhnev (1906–1982), former chairman of the Politburo and President of the U.S.S.R. in 1977. In the film, Brezhnev takes Nixon for a death-defying ride through the narrow hilly roads surrounding Camp David. (These are the film's only light-hearted moments.)

The Nixon circle suffers acute agitation when Alexander Butterfield, a Nixon aide, discloses the existence of a taping system inside the Oval Office. The revelation causes tumultuous international reaction, prompting a demand for the release of the secretly recorded material. The object of the greatest speculation is the "smoking gun" tape which would implicate Nixon himself in an attempted cover-up.

The negative reactions to Watergate and a possible cover-up are unrelenting. Nixon faces tremendous pressure on every side, and a holding action becomes less and less tenable. Buzhardt listens to the tapes and discovers an 18½-minute gap in one of them. Rose Mary Woods, Nixon's secretary and die-hard loyalist, takes the blame for the damaged tape as the White House becomes a house of cards with the staff increasingly unable to function; talk of impeachment or resignation becomes the norm in daily conversation.

Nixon withdraws more and more into himself, even when members of his family, particularly his daughter Julie, try to draw close to him. During this period of tremendous anxiety, the Supreme Court rules that Nixon must relinquish 64 tapes, and the House Judiciary Committee passes three articles of impeachment. An anguished Nixon, in spite of pleas from his family to fight on, makes his fateful decision, becoming the only man to resign the Presidency.

As with *All the President's Men*, "Woodstein"'s first collaboration, the second created some doubts about its uncredited sources and its fabricated dialogue. An example of the criticism appeared in *George*, the magazine founded by JFK, Jr. (June/July 1996): "John Osborne, *The New Republic*'s respected White House-watcher, pronounced the unsourced rendition of Nixon's *Gotterdammerung* 'on the whole, the worst job of nationally known reporting that I've observed in 49 years in the business.'" An example of the lack of Woodstein's responsibility occurs on page 166 of the original edition of *The Final Days* which states that "on several occasions members of the household staff came upon [Pat] in the pantry of the second-floor kitchen, where the liquor was kept, in the early afternoon. Awkwardly, she tried to hide her tumbler of bourbon on the rocks." Clearly, no direct source is cited in the text or in the end matter of the book. Meanwhile, the damage has been done, "legitimizing" a drunken Pat in the media. As recounted in Julie's touching 1986 book on Pat: "*Saturday Night Live*, a popular late night television program, portrayed my mother as a drunken slob." On the same page of the biography, Julie wrote: "July 7 [1976] had been a traumatic day. In the morning she had read part of *The Final Days*, which, despite my father's protests, she had borrowed from one of the secretaries in his office." That night she had a stroke. According to Adrian Havill's book on Woodstein, *Deep Truth* (1993): "When Richard Nixon learned that AT&T was sponsoring the $7 million TV project, he publicly switched both his home and office phones to competitor MCI and suggested his friends follow his example. [Nixon aide] John Taylor wrote a letter to AT&T chairman Robert E. Allen, saying, 'Perhaps you should change your corporate slogan to 'reach out and smear someone!'" A group of Nixon supporters attended the 1989 stockholders' meeting of ABC and protested the anticipated misrepresentations of the docudrama. As Havill points out, "the prayer scene between Richard Nixon and Henry Kissinger" was of particular importance to them. "When Bob and Carl had written about the final days of Nixon's presidency, they had described Nixon as remaining on his knees after the prayer, sobbing, then beating his fists on the floor and moaning, 'What have I done? What has happened?' The scene had been included in both Richard Nixon's and Henry Kissinger's memoirs.... But while it was true that both Kissinger and Nixon had written about the scene, admitting they had prayed together, and that Nixon had wept, both denied the carpet pounding and the quotations." White House advisor (1969–1974) Leonard Garment wrote an "op-ed" piece in the *New York Times* of October 30, 1989:

"*Final Days* is a cartoon, of course. Worse, it is littered with false pictures, false sequences and words that were not spoken by the people who speak them. In fact, the show's dramatic climax — Richard Nixon collapsing, in tears, in front of Henry Kissinger on the carpet of the Lincoln sitting room — is fiction. There was no out-of-control sobbing, no beating of fists on the rug. Mr. Nixon has said, in his memoirs and elsewhere, that the account is false. So has Mr. Kissinger, as recently as last week in a conversation with me. To pretend otherwise, in order to make Mr. Nixon seem pathetic and bizarre, is contemptible." Another Nixon supporter, William F. Buckley of *National Review* (December 8, 1989) reacted to this controversial scene quite differently: "[Leonard Garment] flatly denies the moving scene in which Nixon and Kissinger descend to their knees, under the prodding of Nixon, to seek divine help, a scene that ends with Nixon prostrate on the floor in tears. To which one can only say: Perhaps it didn't happen, but if it did, it adds to every inclination to esteem the man, Richard Nixon; the victim of the most lethal of all Richard Nixon's enemies, Richard Nixon."

Nixon made some attempts through legal "saber rattlings" to halt the broadcast. As quoted from a news story in the *New York Times* of September 22, 1989, Nixon's lawyer, William E. Griffin of Bronxville, New York: "In two letters to ABC and to AT&T in June, Mr. Griffin described the Woodward and Bernstein book as 'attack journalism' at its worst, wildly distorted in some places, purely fictional in others. He also asserted that 'not a single source for any of the damaging allegations it contains has ever been made public by the authors.'" In an unusual move, the *Times* published an editorial (October 31, 1989) that was basically in support of Nixon's claims: "*The Final Days* had several merits, including a more three-dimensional view of Richard Nixon than previous treatments offered. Still, there is room to object to its skimpy labeling, a one-sentence statement that the film is a 'dramatization' of the book by Bob Woodward and Carl Bernstein. Parts of the film were based on the transcripts of the Nixon tapes and hence authentic. Parts derived from other books. Parts were fictional dialogue. Yet viewers knowing of the transcripts may have assumed the rest as solidly based. It wasn't; even the original book cited so few sources that its methodology was roundly criticized. Viewers needed forceful warnings about the varied authenticity of its source materials.... Print and screen journalists have a duty to the truth and to their audiences."

Although aspects of the work seemed specious, there was unanimous agreement on the high quality of Lane Smith's performance. As William F. Buckley stated in the previously cited essay: "If there is a prize out there for artistic impersonation, it should go to Lane Smith." Unqualified praise also from John Leonard (*New York*, October 30, 1989): "In *The Final Days*, we're asked in the belly of the whale to identify with the whale, Nixon, impersonated by Lane Smith.... And Smith is marvelous — wounded, moody, maudlin, flummoxed, spastic — an automatic Emmy." The *Chicago Sun-Times* (October 27, 1989) was almost as enthusiastic: "*The Final Days* explores more than just the facts. It is a poignant study in human frailty.... Smith delivers a passionate effort, capturing the often-parodied mannerisms and elliptical speech patterns of Nixon while never resorting to caricature." The *Village Voice* (October 31, 1989) was in the amen corner on Smith's performance: "Smith has the sweep and color of action painting. His Nixon is not without a certain nobility of ambition, particularly on the international stage, but he is also lying, devious and ruthless." In spite of the negative aspects of the character, *Variety* (October 26, 1989) focused on Lane's "eschewing caricature ... but suggesting a vulnerability. Nixon becomes a victim of circumstances, even if they're of his own making. He comes across as a figure from a classic tragedy…. Smith's finest moments are when Nixon recovers from a blunder and when he delivers his farewell speech to the White House staff— an intimate portrait of Nixon that's touching." Even higher praise came from the *Chicago Tribune* (October 27, 1989): "Lane Smith gives a remarkable performance. It is one of nuance and sensibility, a delicate but successful juggling act that enables us to observe many of the dimensions of a complicated man."

In a lengthy interview in the *Los Angeles Times* (June 4, 1989), given while the film was in production, Lane Smith pointed out that he was given the role only one week before shooting began, and he had very little time to prepare. He found an old Nixon tape and worked on the voice and the mannerisms. As Smith expressed it: "I got the physicality of Nixon. He's so specific in what he does, but you have to get it to the point where it's second nature to you, and then not overdo it. I stay pretty much in character the whole time I'm here, I stay in the physicality. I'll show you," he said, noting that in the dress codes of the '30s and '40s, men wore their pants very high up. "All of a sudden I saw pictures of Nixon with his pants up to here," he said, demonstrating. "So you put your pants up there, and it's a little tilt back, and all of a sudden, it's just *there*." Smith also illustrated the wave Nixon used from the helicopter on the White House lawn as Nixon "throws his hand away almost. His wrist, it's limp, but it's not effeminate. And I think part of that physicality is that there's so much emotion there." Smith did not watch tapes of Nixon's final speech, but he delivered it beautifully. "I called on the very most private things that have occurred to me," Smith said, "[T]he loss of a great love, and the isolation, when things totally turned against me." Many fine actors have played Richard Nixon but no actor has been closer to the very core of his nature than Lane Smith. In the fall of 1989 with the much-deserved praise for *The Final Days* at its height, Smith, Bernstein and Hugh Whitemore talked of turning the material into a stage piece. It did not come to pass, but, given the merit of the work, it would appear a worthy project although probably not a commercially successful one. Of course, Smith's performance would not have been so riveting had not Whitemore's script been of such high quality. It should be noted that the script always had a human dimension without the easy villains so typical of political drama, and it should be further noted that Whitemore kept Nixon's private life private. There was no "behind the bedroom door" prurience as in the Woodstein book and Oliver Stone's 1995 film.

Unfortunately, *The Final Days* did not find its audience. As Adrian Havill wrote in *Deep Truth*, *The Final Days* finished a dismal 58th out of 77 rated programs. It received a 17 percent share of the audience, the worst showing of any ABC Sunday movie that season.

Other critics noted:

"[A] formidable performance by Lane Smith."— James Warren, *Chicago Tribune*, July 24, 1989.

"Smith blows you away with his Nixon … brilliant."— Kay Gardella, *New York Daily News,* July 24, 1989.

"*The Final Days* is a docudrama so stunning that it brings new luster to that much abused form. The two-way punch of this movie … is Hugh Whitemore's superb script and a magnificent performance by Lane Smith as Nixon."— Ann Hodges, *Houston Chronicle,* July 21, 1989.

"Lane Smith seems to have rented Richard Nixon's body, soul and pathos. If you think you've seen all the Nixon imitations you'll ever want to see in this life, wait until this airs ... You'll be riveted." — Gene Seymour, *Philadelphia Daily News*, July 28, 1989.

Speeches of Richard Nixon (video, 1990)

55 minutes. Produced by MPI Home Video.

This contains the Checkers speech, historical overview of U.S. commitment to Vietnam, the trip to China, Nixon's speech to the Soviets, Q and As on Watergate, his final press conference and many more including the seldom-televised conclusion to his 1962 "Nixon kick-around" speech which is well-stated and dignified. A valuable compendium and readily available from the producer: MPI Home Video, Dept. 1500, 15825 Rob Roy Drive, Oak Park, IL 60452, or from the shops at the Museum of Television and Radio, 25 West 52nd Street, New York, NY 10019 or 465 North Beverly Drive, Beverly Hills, CA 90210.

Mountain (biographical drama, 1990)

In two acts. Written by Douglas Scott, Directed by John Henry Davis. Produced by K and D Productions in association with Lucille Lortel. Set by Phillipp Jung. Costumes by David Woolard. Lucille Lortel Theater, 121 Christopher Street, New York City. Opened April 5, 1990. Cast: *William O. Douglas* Len Cariou; *various female roles* Heather Summerhayes [Cariou]; *various male roles, including Richard Nixon* John C. Vennema.

Mountain is a highly documented yet absorbing stage biography of William O. Douglas (1898–1980) whose 36½ years as an Associate Justice of the United States Supreme Court are herein sketched tellingly, as are many more personal aspects of his audacious, purposeful life. To be sure, there are many well-aimed Nixon barbs:

> DOUGLAS: I first met Nixon in the '30s. He was a student at Duke University and I gave a lecture there at the law school. Years later, he came up to me, in that patented way of his, and told me how important to him that lecture of mine had been.
>
> NIXON: Justice Douglas — I just want you to know that your lecture inspired my own political career.
>
> DOUGLAS: I do believe that hearing that compliment was the most upsetting moment of my life.

Mountain repeats a popular gag of the 1980s: "Did'ja hear what Bob Dole called our last three Presidents — Carter, Ford and Nixon? Called 'em, 'See No Evil. Hear No Evil. And ... Evil.'"

Here's a sampling of critical opinion:

"A mountain of fascinating material has yielded a weightless play." —*New York Times*, April 6, 1990.

"You realize that the construction of the play is artful indeed, and most artful in concealing its very artfulness. Some questions remain unanswered, no doubt; but there is enough revelation to chew on contentedly for a good long time." — John Simon, *New York*, April 16, 1990.

"John C. Vennema play[s] a reasonably believable array of foreigners (and an adequate Richard Nixon)..." — *Show Business*, April 11, 1990.

"John C. Vennema, whose characters include FDR, Richard Nixon and Brandeis, does a fine job bringing understated humor to his roles..." — *Variety*, April 11, 1990.

Richard Nixon Reflects: An American Interests Special (TV, 1990)

PBS, May 4, 1990. Host-interviewer: Morton Kondracke. 9–10:30 P.M.

Richard Nixon Reflects, a one-hour interview (1990).

"In Nixon's first extended interview since those with David Frost in 1977 and *60 Minutes* in 1984, *Richard Nixon Reflects* also explores the former president's thoughts about the Communist world past, present and future; domestic politics from Eisenhower to Bush; the media; and Watergate. Commenting that the Watergate wire-tap was far from unusual, and that George McGovern had no chance of winning the election, Nixon adds: 'I should have knocked it off right there [at the beginning] and said, 'Let's find out who did this and let them walk the plank.' Eighteen years later, he maintains he doesn't know who authorized the burglary." — *Christian Science Monitor*, May 3, 1990.

"Regardless of your political disposition, this interview with Kondracke remains an endlessly fascinating historical document. Since his resignation at the height of the Watergate crisis, Nixon has written extensively about his years in office and the scandal that destroyed his political career. And while virtually all memoirs penned by world leaders are invariably tinged with self-justifications for their mistakes, Nixon in his late years has begun to face his failings with remarkable candor." — *Chicago Sun-Times*, May 4, 1990.

Resurrection of Richard Nixon (TV, 1990)

TV interview, *Nightline*, ABC News, 11:30 P.M. July 19, 1990.

The opening day of the Nixon Library. Volume III of Ambrose's biography calls this Nixon's "Last Laugh, July 19, 1990." In addition to *Nightline* (shown later), "some of the biggest names in the news business were there: R.W. Apple of the *New York Times*, Barbara Walters and Tom Brokaw." As Ambrose describes it: "By 6 A.M. on the morning of July 19, 1990, there were thousands of people standing in line, waiting to join the midday celebration and to welcome Dick Nixon home to Yorba Linda…. Banners, streamers, helicopters, cops, massive publicity, loudspeakers, Secret Service, limos, movie stars, and the rest…. There were more than 1000 reporters present, plus television cameramen and broadcasters from all over the world…. It was the first time four Presidents had appeared together in public … It was the first time ever that four First Ladies were together. It was Pat Nixon's first public appearance in ten years."

As Ambrose said on *Nightline*: "He has been, for 16 years, running for the office of elder statesman, and now he's made it. This library represents his final resurrection, his total recovery from his disaster of 1974."

Point Break (film, 1991)

122 minutes. Directed by Kathryn Bigelow. Screenplay by W. Peter Iliff. Based on a story by Rick King and Iliff. Produced by Peter Abrams and Robert L. Levy. Photography by Donald Peterman. Edited by Howard Smith. Music by Mark Isham. Art direction by Pamel Marcotte. Stunt coordinator: Glenn Wilder. A Largo Entertainment presentation, released through Twentieth Century–Fox. Color. Cast: *Bohdi (Reagan)* Patrick Swayze; *Johnny Utah* Keanu Reeves; *Pappas* Gary Busey; *Tyler* Lori Petty; *Roach (Nixon)* James LeGros; *Nathaniel (LBJ)* John Philbin; *Grommet (Carter)* Bolesse Christopher.

Kathryn Bigelow's *Point Break* is a buddy-chase-surfer-crime movie with pseudo-philosophical overtones *viz.* Bohdi, the antagonist played by Patrick Swayze, is named for the Buddhist tree of enlightenment. Action movie fans who dabble in eastern religions will no doubt attach great significance to this teasing bit of nomenclature.

The plot deals with four surfers who rob Los Angeles banks as a group called "The Ex-Presidents" wearing masks of Nixon, Carter, LBJ and Reagan. A rookie policeman with the improbable all–American name of Johnny Utah is set on their trail, but first he has to learn surfing. Predictably he falls in love with Bohdi's surfer girlfriend Tyler. In a bid for audience sympathy, we learn that the "Ex-Presidents" never harm anyone, and they only rob banks to support their sport of surfing — which means that they check into the world's best surfing areas from season to season. When Johnny Utah tracks Bohdi to a beach in Australia, instead of turning him in, he lets him go free to catch that "last wave" and probably — here is the pseudo-profundity of which the film is so fond — become one with nature. Just prior to this final confrontation on the beach, "LBJ," "Carter" and "Nixon" have all been piled up in the carnage that was their last robbery.

"[The] tale rattles on long after audience lost interest in the fate of the murderous sun-bleached desperadoes, and reaches numerous crests of absurdity. At one point Swayze postulates that the people out there 'crawling along the freeways in their tin coffins' are depending on him and his fellow robbers to prove people can still buck the system. Not likely, dude." — *Variety*, July 1, 1991.

"The director is Kathryn Bigelow, whose previous protagonists have been bikers, vampires and a female cop. Is she Hollywood's Leni Riefenstahl or just its Margaret Thatcher?"—*London Observer*, November 24, 1991.

Air America (film, 1990)

112 minutes. Directed by Roger Spottiswoode, produced by Daniel Melnick, written by John Eskow. *Cast:* Mel Gibson, Robert Downey, Jr., and Lane Smith.

Nixon appears during the credits delivering a speech that the film itself will contradict with bitter irony.

Air America (is) "an air-headed serial comedy that sets out to both twist and trivialize the exploits of Air America pilots flying missions in Laos during the Indochina war. This drivel is scripted with all the subtlety of an *Animal House* cast reciting passages from Jane Fonda's Hanoi Diaries."—*Wall Street Journal*, August 23, 1990.

"Lane Smith marvelous as Richard Nixon in *The Final Days* adds ironic humor to the casting."—*Variety*, August 15, 1990.

Assassins (stage musical, 1991)

Music and lyrics by Stephen Sondheim. Book by Jerome Weidman. Directed by Jerry Zaks. Sets by Loren Sherman. Costumes by William Ivey Long. Musical direction by Paul Gemignani. Presented at Playwrights Horizons, 42nd Street, New York City. Actors playing assassins and would-be assassins: *John Wilkes Booth* Victor Garbor, *Giteau, assassin of Garfield* Jonathan Hadary; *Czolgosz, assassin of McKinley* Terrence Mann; *"Squeaky" Fromme, a would-be assassin of Ford* Annie Golden; *Sara Jane Moore, another would-be assassin of Ford* Debra Monk; *Lee Harvey Oswald* Jace Alexander; *John Hinckley, Jr., would-be assassin of Reagan in 1981* Greg German; *Zanfara, would-be assassin of FDR* Eddie Korbich; *Sam Byck, would-be assassin of Richard Nixon* Lee Wilkof.

John Simon's *New York* review (February 4, 1991) states that "*Assassins* gathers up the men and women who have killed or tried to kill American presidents and aims to figure out what they had in common, what made them do it. The answer seems to be that they were all losers of one kind or another, genuinely deprived or imagining themselves cheated by society, and bent on getting even or somehow making a mark. So what else is new? To be sure, one could write a searching, perhaps even moving, show concentrating on one such person but it would have to be compassionate, analytical, philosophical. *Assassins* is none of these.... The show is particularly condescending to the little Jewish fellow, Samuel Byck, who tried to crash a commercial plane into Nixon's White House..."

Linda Winer of *Newsday* (January 8, 1991) hated the show, enjoyed the performances: "*Assassins*, which opened last night at Playwrights Horizons with the inevitable hope for a Broadway move, is a bad idea, fuzzy headed and, despite a lovely cast, unremarkably executed.... The cast is excellent. Lee Wilkof—an Eric Bogosian style ranter — as Sam Byck, the New Yorker who tried to crash a hijacked plane into Nixon's White House was … outstanding."

The *Village Voice* (February 1, 1991) was struck by the effectiveness of Wilkof's performance: "Slouching around in a Santa Claus suit, babbling into a tape recorder, he becomes a repellent mirror image of the Nixon he hoped to kill. The real Byck killed himself, and two innocent bystanders, when his attempt to hijack a 747 and crash it into the White House was thwarted, but his ravings as recorded in the script are those of a discombobulated suburbanite; only the wild-eyed scruffiness of Lee Wilkof's performance conveys the potential danger behind them."

Actually, the *Voice* began with the theme that was implied, if not stated in virtually all of the reviews: "The only real question about *Assassins*, which I doubt even its creators could answer with complete confidence, is why it exists."

JFK (film, 1991)

188 minutes. Directed by Oliver Stone. Written by Oliver Stone and Zachary Sklar. Based on *On the Trail of the Assassins* by Jim Garrison and *Crossfire: The Plot That Killed Kennedy* by Jim Marrs. Photography by Robert Richardson. Edited by Joe Hutshing and Peitro Scalia. Designed by Victor Kempster. Music by John Williams. Produced by A. Kitman and Oliver Stone. Color. Warner Bros. Cast: *Jim Garrison* Kevin Costner; *Liz Garrison* Sissy Spacek; *David Ferrie* Joe Pesci; *Clay Shaw* Tommy Lee Jones; *Lee Harvey Oswald* Gary Oldman; *Jack Martin* Jack Lemmon; *Willie O'Keefe* Kevin Bacon.

Oliver Stone's controversial *JFK* grossed $195 million at the box office and had high revenues as well from video sales, rentals and the marketing of the 593-page screenplay published by Applause Books.

Stone's film was based upon two sources, *Crossfire: The Plot That Killed Kennedy* by Jim Marrs and *On the Trail of the Assassins* by former New Orleans District Attorney Jim Garrison, whose obituary (*New York Times*, October 22, 1992) outlines the theory of Mr. Garrison's book: "Announcing that he had 'solved the assassination,' Mr. Garrison accused anti–Communist and anti–Castro extremists in the Central Intelligence Agency of plotting [Kennedy's] death to thwart an easing of tension with the Soviet Union and Cuba, and to prevent a retreat from Vietnam." Garrison tried his theory in a New Orleans court in 1969 and failed, but he continued to press the theory among card-carrying conspiracy addicts like Oliver Stone, who in 1991 turned the theory into a film that a *New York Times* editorial (December 22, 1991) called "history by default … a fiction so cunningly disguised that audiences will accept it as fact."

For starters, Stone offers sweeping shots of the *zeitgeist*, one of which is a 1960 Kennedy–Nixon debate in which Kennedy looks predictably more presidential than Nixon, who was recovering from a very painful bout with phlebitis. Nixon is also mentioned in speeches on page 72 (in a speech by a loopy right-winger played by Kevin Bacon) and on page 178 in a typically theme-driven Oliver Stone philippic in which Garrison (Kevin Costner) says in part: "Let's ask the two men who have profited the most from the assassination — your former President Lyndon Johnson and your new president, Richard Nixon — to release 51 CIA documents pertaining to Lee Oswald and

Jack Ruby.... All these documents are *yours*— the people's property — you pay for it, but because the government considers you children who might be too disturbed to face this reality, because you might lynch those involved, you cannot see these documents for another 75 years."

John Simon's review (*National Review*, March 2, 1992) was less an assessment of the film's aesthetic merit than a comment on Stone's veiled intention to issue "a clarion call for the release of documents ordered sealed until 2020— [to start] a political process that will lead to truth and justice and better government." But for all Stone's high-mindedness of purpose, "There is, to be sure, an aura of arrogance and sensationalism about the filmmaker that invites skepticism and dismissal."

Tom Wicker was another skeptic who, in a long piece in the *New York Times* (December 15, 1991) wrote: "Oliver Stone treats matters that are wholly speculative as facts and truth, thus rewriting history."

Nevertheless, audiences flocked to the film, accepting — even savoring — what Terrence Rafferty (*The New Yorker*, January 13, 1992) called "the movie's hysterical manner and its slipshod handling of the facts [that] actually have the effect of diminishing the credibility of the case for conspiracy. The clearest sounds we hear in *JFK* are those of Oliver Stone shooting himself in the foot."

Photo-Op
(performance art/mock opera, 1992)

Composed by Conrad Cummings. Libretto by James Siena. Directed by Bob McGrath. Performed by the Ridge Theater, La Mama's Annex, 74 East Fourth Street, New York City. Cast: *Candidate One (Soprano)* Margaret Bishop; *Candidate Two (Baritone)* Larry Adams.

"[*Photo-Op*] is a sly and wry orgy of sophistry, self-serving pseudologic and double-speak. The two candidates ... sing out their formless platforms — a delightful intertwining of rhetorical balderdash and frank intent.... Sinister Secret Service men hiding behind mirrored sunglasses weave around the audience-as-delegates. Other touches include a bomb-sniffing canine, an assassin lurking on the scaffolding and sideline news anchors gesticulating their vacuous commentary. Richard Nixon looms larger than life, his flailing arms seem to conduct the quintet of musicians before him." —*New York Post*, June 3, 1992.

Watergate: The Secret Story
(television documentary, 1992)

120 minutes. Anchor: Mike Wallace, produced by Jill Fieldstein, Marice Murad, Andrew Lack. A CBS/*Post–Newsweek* co-production. Wednesday, June 17, 1992, 9–11 P.M.

Other than the Watergate hearings themselves and the 1994 BBC Discovery Channel production *Watergate: The Corruption of American Politics and the Fall of Richard Nixon*, Mike Wallace's *Watergate: The Secret Story* is the most valuable television treatment of Watergate's origins, investigations and aftermath.

A few of its more revealing statements follow. The first deals with the possible reason for the break-in: The rumor that the Democrats had information on a prostitution ring that might prove embarrassing to John Dean. In this television production, convicted Watergate felon E. Howard Hunt gives *his* reason: "The account books of the Democratic National Committee ... could conceivably reflect the entry of foreign funds. And for that reason, we had been authorized to try to get photographs of these pages — in fact, all of the pages of the account books — and bring them back for future exploitation by the White House."

One of the points that is seldom discussed in the post–Watergate years is that in the late 1960s and early 1970s, Washington was literally under siege by war protesters. The paranoia index inside the White House accelerated daily. Mike Wallace: "At one point, more than 100,000 demonstrators marched toward Richard Nixon's White House where troops from the 82nd Airborne were billeted in the basement." Charles Colson: "It was a legitimate siege.... You had buses all around the White House — cordoned off ... and a couple of buses got turned over. And then the tear gas hit, and there was a west wind, and it swept across the White House." Mike Wallace: "And it wasn't just the anti-war movement ... there were the militant Black Panthers and the radical left and leaks to the press that Nixon felt were sabotaging his foreign policy..."

Washington was often in a state of hysteria and every facet of American life experienced tremendous unrest, but, according to Wallace, it was not the turmoil in Washington and the rest of the country that led to Watergate, it was "Richard Nixon's fear of losing [the 1972 election]. By the spring of 1971, it was becoming clear that he could turn out to be a one-term president. His popularity had plunged to its lowest since his election, and the Democrats smelled blood."

From then on, Nixon desperately tried to cover up everything dealing with the break-in. Nixon advisor Leonard Garment felt that the impeachment process was "tremendously accelerated" by Nixon's firing Watergate special prosecutor Archibald Cox. "[A] huge media din took place at that point. They treated this thing as if it were World War III breaking out. I mean, everything else was drowned out."

As the investigation drew closer to the truth, we hear an audiotape of Nixon talking to Haldeman about pay-offs: "I just don't know how it is going to come out, though. That's the whole point, and I just don't know. And I was serious when I said to John at the end there — I said, 'Goddamn it. All these guys that participated in raising the money and so forth have got to stick to their line — that they did not raise this money to obstruct justice.'"

In an early press release, CBS hinted that the identity of "Deep Throat" might be disclosed — and it would not be either Alexander Haig or Henry Kissinger. Wallace stated that Richard Nixon had once said that Mark Felt, the deputy director of the FBI, was Deep Throat. A few minutes later, Wallace said, "There is one person we have come to believe who best fits the description of Deep Throat — and that is L. Patrick Gray, 76 years old now, former assistant attorney general. He started as a Nixon loyalist but according to our sources, ... came to loathe dealing with all the president's men."

In a final conversation with Mike Wallace, Charles Colson muses, "One of the interesting footnotes of history, I suppose, is why I went to prison. I went to prison because you interviewed me, Mike, and in the course of a *60 Minutes* interview, you asked me how I could be a Christian and still defend the kinds of things that Richard Nixon did and said in the White House that were being disclosed on the tapes.... I called up my lawyer the night after I did the broadcast and said, 'David, I want to plead guilty.' He said, 'You're crazy.' And the next week we negotiated with the Watergate prosecutors. I told them what I had done. We did not plea-bargain. I told them I wanted the sentence determined by the court. And that was it. I went to prison."

In the program's last few minutes, there is a file tape of Nixon's final speech, the words which have become so familiar: "Always give your best, never get discouraged, always remember others may hate you. But those who hate you don't win unless you hate them. And then you destroy yourself." After the tape played, Mike Wallace said, "But he was himself, a president who hated." Leonard Garment replied, "He was and he knew it, and that's why he said that."

On the day of the telecast, the *New York Times* raved: "It's a story, full of sound and fury, that signifies a great deal about the possible abuses of political power and the readiness of a privileged cadre entrusted with guarding the law to flout it."

Hoffa (film, 1992)

140 minutes. Directed by Danny DeVito. Produced by Edward Pressman, DeVito and C. Chubb. Written by David Mamet. Jack Nicholson as Hoffa.

The film claims that Nixon pardoned union boss Hoffa in order to get the endorsement of the Teamsters. Hoffa had been convicted of pension fraud and served five years.

"Mamet and DeVito's handiwork offers no clear perspective on the life of this man who created the country's most potent workers' movement but was felled by his own arrogance and amoral methodology." —*Film Journal*, January 1993.

Charlie Rose: Pat Nixon Remembered (TV panel, 1993)

60 minutes. Host: Charlie Rose. Guests: Patti Matson, a member of Pat Nixon's staff; Sarah Booth Conroy, *Washington Post* columnist; Mike Wallace, television commentator and Ray Price, former Nixon speechwriter. Wednesday, June 23, 1993, PBS–TV, Channel 13, New York City.

Pat Nixon died in her sleep at 5:45 A.M. Tuesday, June 22, 1993, at her home in Park Ridge, New Jersey, just hours after celebrating her 53rd wedding anniversary.

Four people who had known Pat Nixon met with Charlie Rose to share their memories three days before the funeral (held at 10:00 A.M. Saturday, June 26, 1993, in Yorba Linda). Ray Price recalled the "love, devotion, and loyalty" she gave her husband and her desire to "fight to the end" on Watergate. He also cited *The Final Days*, "that fiction masquerading as non-fiction," as the cause of Pat's earlier stroke. Mike

Wallace remembered taping Tricia's tour of the White House and how every few minutes she would run to another part of the White House to talk to her mother. Patti Matson reminded the others that Pat was born before the television age, and although she had been a successful teacher, had acted in many plays and even appeared in a Hollywood film, she was not comfortable with television. But she was "superb" in groups and had appeared before groups on many occasions. Sarah Booth Conroy recalled her sense of humor. Pat was "good company," but her last Christmas in the White House was very poignant "because she said there was a little nest in the Christmas tree, and that meant that the next year would be a lucky time for them."

The program ended with many still photographs, among them — Pat talking to Big Bird, good-naturedly partaking in exotic rituals, visiting children's hospitals and beaming at Tricia's wedding.

Red Channels (play, 1993)

A stage play in two acts by Laurence Holder. Directed by Fred Newman. Produced by Diane Stiles, Castillo Cultural Center, 500 Greenwich Street, New York (September 23–October 23, 1994). Note: originally produced in the fall of 1993 as a workshop at the Theatre for the New City, 155 First Avenue, New York. Cast: *Richard Nixon* David Nackman; *Joseph McCarthy* Roger Grunwald; *W.E.B. DuBois* Doug Miranda; *Bob Burns* Jeff Aron; *Sheila Harcourt* Gabrielle Kurlander; *Hal Porter* Grant Banks; *Paul Robeson* Emmitt H. Thrower.

A note from the program: "The play is a fictionalized compression of events occurring over the time period of 1950–1954. It is set in Washington, D.C., Harlem and Greenwich Village, New York City."

What Nixon aide John Taylor said he feared about the TV adaptation of *The Final Days* (*Deep Truth*, page 200) — that Richard and Pat Nixon would be played by Pee-Wee Herman and Madeline Kahn — almost occurred in the off–Broadway play *Red Channels*. In this unintentionally funny social drama, set in the "Commie chasing" 1950s but written with 1930s Warner Bros. overtones (breakaway furniture included), Nixon was played by a Pee-Wee lookalike who performed such un–Nixonite acts as fondling the breast of a dumb blonde and rasping out such un–Nixonite lines as "You're a real bitch, Sheila." In *Red Channels*, Nixon, the Red hunter, even stoops so low as to use Sheila as sex bait to catch Communists. (It sounds like a revue sketch but it *wasn't*, and the cast could not understand where the laughs were coming from.) The play was presented on a revolving stage, each segment of which was so tiny that the actors were constantly nose to nose and toe to toe, thus making breast fondling almost unavoidable. The protagonist, a character named Hal Porter, must choose between accepting a plum stage role or betraying two black social leaders, Paul Robeson and W.E.B. DuBois, who opine endlessly and to very little purpose. In this play, the occasional Nixon hanky-panky is a welcome relief. At least, *he* has a sense of humor. *Theater Week* (December 27, 1993), one of the few publications to review it, called it "a compelling re-creation of McCarthy-era confrontations, viewed from the experience of two important black intellectuals," a euphemistic way of saying it was all talk. While he was not true to life — neither was the play — this Nixon made the evening bearable.

Angels in America, Part I: Millennium Approaches, Part II: Perestroika (play, 1993)

"A gay fantasia on national themes" by Tony Kushner. Directed by George C. Wolfe. Sets by Robin Wagner. Costumes by Toni-Leslie James. Lighting by Jules Fisher. Music by Anthony Davis. Walter Kerr Theater, New York City, May 3, 1993. Cast: *Ray Cohn* Ron Liebman; *Ethel Rosenberg* Kathleen Chalfront; David Marshall Grant, Marcia Gay Harden, Jeffrey Wright, Joe Mantello, Stephen Spinella and Ellen McLauglin.

Christopher Hitchens in the May 1993 issue of *Vanity Fair* called this seven-hour work "a huge diorama onto which to project American discontents." This was Kushner's second play to be produced in New York. His first, *A Bright Room Called Day*, was described by the *New Yorker* (November 30, 1992) as a play "which drew explicit parallels between Germany in 1933 and America under Reagan. It flopped in New York."

Angels in America, which won both the Tony Award and the Pulitzer Prize for 1993, was written over a five-year period with the assistance of an NEA grant. As characterized briefly in the *New York Times* of November 21, 1993, the play is "a radical vision of American society, politics and religion set against the AIDS epidemic and the Reagan years." While Nixon does not appear, the author clearly intends that Nixon is to be indicted together with other Republican presidents for the malaise of late 20th century America. Kushner in a *Newsday* interview of May 6, 1993: "You could say the whole Nixon-Reagan-Bush era was a backlash to the '60s, in part because the '60s were successful. They changed this society. [Despite] all of that counter-revolution, the world didn't go back to the '50s, or wherever [conservatives] thought it should go. They lost because history doesn't go back. You can only create the illusion that it's going back. I think there will be a lot of ugliness."

Donald Lyons on Part I: "[Kushner's] agenda is brutally and artlessly familiar: to indict conservative governments of the United States for the sins of anti–Communism and (don't ask how, please) responsibility for AIDS."—*New Criterion*, June 1993.

Donald Lyons on Part II: "[Part II] adds nothing of significance, rather exposing the whole enterprise's pretensions."—*New Criterion*, January 1994.

"Kushner's writing testifies to the strength of the American theater."—*Theater Week*, December 13, 1993.

"As a tearjerker, *Angels* is a success. It is a universal story about emotional courage and the power of love. A gentle young man named Prior contracts AIDS and his partner Louis questions whether he has the fortitude to watch him die. This is a moral dilemma with equal relevance to straights and gays. [But] *Angels* ... is engaging agitprop. Mr. Kushner is just another liberal prophet of doom. He is the Paul Kennedy of the playwrights, spewing the rhetoric of decay and decline. That may be what the theatrical elites talk about at intermission, but it's not why ordinary folks go to the theater."—Melanie Kirkpatrick, *Wall Street Journal*, May 13, 1993.

"I have never seen a play more full of pretension, folderol, flim-flam and glitz, nor one so puffed up with its own importance."—Thomas Monsell, *New York Guardian*, July 1993.

Nixon's Last Trump (dialogues, 1994)

Three highly amusing dialogues (purportedly by Oliver Stone, E. Howard Hunt and James S. Rosen, the biographer of John Mitchell) and two essays. *Harper's Magazine*, August 1994.

Three wickedly funny conjectural dialogues between Richard Nixon and H.R. Haldeman that might have been on the fabled 18½ minutes that disappeared into the heavenly ether. Oliver Stone's contribution is almost a parody preview of his Nixon film with Nixon fixated on "the Bay of Pigs" thing, saying that CIA Director Helms "will jump like he was in an electric chair" when Haldeman mentions it. The next dialogue, written by convicted Watergate felon and spy novelist E. Howard Hunt, is a very clever mock "inside view" which ends with Nixon saying to Haldeman: "Ummm. I've waded through shit before, but this time I'm not gonna get dirty, Christ! Brief Ron [Ziegler], number one, then find out what Colson, Ehrlichman and Mitchell know. Tell them to keep their ******* mouths shut. Just keep a lid on things, Bob, clamp down hard. I'm depending on you. Contain." The last dialogue trots out, with lip-smacking prurience, the story that John Dean wants to see "the trick books ... of one of these call-girl rings." Haldeman says: "Maybe he thought he'd find some familiar names." Nixon (laughing): "Like Mo?"

NOTE: In regard to the missing 18½ minutes, the *New York Times* of January 13, 1995, featured a story the first paragraph of which stated: "The White House lawyers for President Richard M. Nixon secretly told a judge that Mr. Nixon's secretary, Rose Mary Woods, intentionally caused the 18-minute gap in a crucial White House tape recording, a newly disclosed document asserts.... She has always denied being the culprit in one of the biggest remaining mysteries of the Watergate case.... Repeated efforts to reach Miss Woods tonight (January 12) were unsuccessful."

The Precedent (play, 1994)

Historical drama by David Wesner. Directed by Barbara Wesner. Produced by the off–West Broadway Theater Company, Lamb's Little Theater, 130 West 44th Street, New York City. Unpublished.

Richard Nixon does not appear as a character. The play takes place between 1641–1649 in and about Whitehall Palace, London. As described in *New York* (November 21, 1994): "*The Precedent* links the downfall of a king blinded by his own ambition into thinking he's infallible to the downfall of a modern president tripped up by some similar ideas and a few missing minutes of taped conversation." The author, David Wesner, played Charles I, a parallel figure to Richard Nixon. In an interview that appeared in the program, Wesner said:

> Both men had advisors who played key roles in their demise. Both men asserted that they were — as the supreme leader of the land — above the law. To his dying day, I do not think that President Nixon believed he was guilty of committing a crime. He never apologized or in any way

recanted for what he did. And he always felt that history would re-member him kindly. Which it has! When he died the country mourned deeply for his passing. He was remembered as a President who accom-plished a great deal. Similarly, I have read that the moment the axe fell on Charles, the entire country went into mourning, believing they had done the wrong thing. But all I remembered about him was that he had been beheaded. The same is true of President Nixon. He always wore a scarlet letter for having been forced to resign mid-term. His tenure was "cut-off" as well. When President Nixon left office, he said, "I'm no crook." When Charles was being tried, he said, "I'm no criminal."

The Naked Truth (play, 1994)

A satiric comedy in two acts by Paul Rudnick. Directed by Christopher Ashley. Setting by James Youmans. Presented by the WPA Theater (Kyle Renick, artistic director), 519 West 23rd Street, New York City. Opening night: June 16, 1994. Cast: *Nan Bemiss* Mary Beth Peil; *Cassandra Keefer* Valerie Pettiford; *Alex DelFlavio* Victor Slezak; *Sister Mary Loyola, Bonnie Barstow, Electra Katzman* Cynthia Darlow; *Dan Barstow, Jonathan Welker Father Middlebury* Peter Bartlett; *Sissy Bemiss Darnley* J. Smith Cameron; *Senator Pete Bemiss* John Cunningham; *Lynette Marshall* Debra Messing.

Paul Rudnick's poorly received comedy *The Naked Truth* was a satire on artistic freedom, not its excesses but hypocritical reactions to works in the manner of Robert Mapplethorpe and other "push the envelope" innovators.

Rudnick's inspiration was a Mapplethorpe opening that he could not forget; he discussed his reaction in a *New York Post* interview on the day of the play's opening. Well-dressed art lovers "were chatting and holding hors d'oeuvres and standing in front of these pictures of explicit sado-masochistic activity. And, of course, there were pic-tures of flowers and vases that seemed filthier than anything. These people would never *dream* of admitting to being shocked, but how far could you push it? It was this ripe comic situation that stayed in my mind for a real comedy of manners."

Besides the free-spirited photographer and his lesbian ex-con assistant, the char-acters included a Republican senator who was also a presidential hopeful; Nan, his uptight Republican wife who sidelined as a charity maven; Sissy, his uptight married Republican daughter; and the senator's centerfold girlfriend Lynette.

The title deals with a photograph of a penis which Sissy mistakes for "a big lonely tree." Needless to say, proverbial uptight Republican attitudes become much more free-flowing as the evening progresses, especially in the Sissy of J. Smith Cameron whom Clive Barnes called a "special delight" in his post-opening review (*New York Post* June 17, 1994). In another *Post* article, Stephen Schaefer wrote: "The show's unabashed scene-stealer is ding-a-ling socialite Sissy, a ringer for Tricia Nixon in her White House days." John Simon (*New York*, July 11, 1994) did not find Sissy a "ding-a-ling" at all "but a drolly devious figure amusingly played by J. Smith Cameron." Stylish performances could not save the play, however. Influential *Time* critic William A. Henry III summed it up (July 4, 1994): "It has nothing fresh to say about the culture wars, Republican hypo-crisy, women's self-imposed lack of liberation or any of its other thematic targets."

A proposed transfer to a Broadway house by film producer Scott Rudin (*The Addams Family*, *Sister Act*) did not take place. Using a new title, Paul Rudnick revised this satire on arts subsidies for a production at Robert Brustein's American Repertory Theater in Cambridge, Massachusetts, with a hopeful eye on a second New York production. Ben Brantley in the *New York Times* of June 29, 1996, said that it was "still in need of serious revision."

The Critic (cartoon, 1994)

A television cartoon series in syndication. Segment broadcast February 9, 1994.

In this segment of the well-received but short-lived cartoon series dealing with a pudgy, balding, kvetchy film critic who looks suspiciously like critic Roger Ebert, the hero has had a series of domestic *contretemps* with his mother, a malevolent Katharine Hepburn wannabe. Cooling off in a tacky French restaurant, he is spotted by fellow diner Richard Nixon. Nixon surveys the critic and says, "Excuse me, but I've lost my appetite. My mother was a saint." The unruffled critic replies, "I guess she was unimpeachable." Nixon storms out, snorting: "Bald-headed schnook!"

The Inkwell (film, 1994)

110 minutes. Directed by Matty Rich. Written by Tom Ricostronza (real name: Trey Ellis) and Paris Qualles. Produced by Irving Azoff. Music by Terence Blanchard. Edited by Quinnie Martin, Jr., Buena Vista release of a Touchstone presentation. Color. Disney. Cast: *Drew Tate* Larenz Tate; *Kenny Tate* Joe Morton; *Brenda Tate* Suzanne Douglas; *Spencer Phillips* Glynn Turman; *Lauren Kelly* Jada Pinkett; *Evelyn* Mary Alice.

Twenty-something Matty Rich's second directorial effort *The Inkwell* was, unfortunately, a social comedy misfire, but it was probably the first film to deal seriously and respectfully with the black middle class.

The story takes place in 1976 in "the Inkwell," a black summer colony on Martha's Vineyard. Essentially a coming-of-age story with echoes of *Summer of 42*, *Dirty Dancing*, *Porky's* and other hits, the film follows the misadventures of Drew Tate, a personable but very immature 15-year-old. The secondary focus is on Drew's father, very well-played by Joe Morton, and Drew's affluent Republican Uncle Spencer who salaams to his portrait of Richard Nixon on the wall of his attractive summer home. The Nixon portrait yields a lot of comic mileage, little of it mocking. Some of the more amusing lines are (after some fisticuffs): "I learned one thing today — black Republicans can fight," and "Any brother who can put Richard Nixon on his wall *has got to know how to deal*."

What follow is a sampling of critical opinion:

"[A] serious comedy dashing for a foothold." — *The New York Times*, May 11, 1996.

"Much of the humor derives from pitting Drew's former Black Panther father against his starchy, Republican uncle: Malcolm X vs. Martin Luther King debates plummet into infantile name-calling."—*Hollywood Reporter*, January 27, 1994.

"[D]espite all the missteps, predictability and general clunkiness, there's a certain sweetness behind the story and its handling that elicits viewer sympathy and goodwill. It's also nice to see a broadening of the range of black stories on the screen, and this one certainly takes audiences to a destination never before visited."—*Variety*, January 31, 1994.

Jackie Mason: Politically Incorrect (satiric commentary, 1994)

Written and created by Jackie Mason. Produced by Jyll Rosenfeld at the Golden Theatre, 252 West 45th Street, New York City. Opened April 5, 1994.

This hugely successful one-man show had a year's run at one of Broadway's most attractive houses. Two of Jackie Mason's targets were Nixon and Clinton. Mason: "Nixon *did* lie, but he hid lies. He had a twitch. Nixon had a conscience. Clinton has none."

"There is a unifying thrust, a focus, a structure: an attack on both liberal hypocrisy and conservative apathy, and on the climate of political correctness that makes it impossible to attack anyone but WASPs."—John Simon, *New York*, April 18, 1994.

Forrest Gump (film, 1994)

140 minutes. Directed by Robert Zemeckis. Written by Eric Roth from the novel of the same name by Winston Groom. Produced by Wendy Finerman, Steve Tisch and Steve Starkey. Photographed by Dan Burgess. Edited by Arthur Schmidt. Music by Alan Silvestri. Designed by Rick Carter. Paramount. Cast: *Forrest Gump* Tom Hanks; *Jenny Curran* Robin Wright; *Lieutenant Dan* Gary Sinise; *Bubba* Mykelti Williamson; *Mama Gump* Sally Field; *Voice of Richard Nixon* Joe Alaskey.

Forrest Gump is a film that took its young producer, Wendy Finerman, nine years to bring before the public, but from the first preview the public response was overwhelmingly positive. Forrest is a "feel good" character to whom, in spite of his lack of intelligence, the audience can respond, a warm-hearted Alabama boy with an I.Q. of 75 who journeys, Everyman-style, through the *zeitgeist* of the 1950s, '60s and '70s: race tensions, athletic stardom, Vietnam, the Moon landing, war protests, the opening to China, AIDS, Watergate, the technological revolution, the jogging craze, meeting Elvis, John Lennon, Chairman Mao, JFK, LBJ and Nixon. Forrest (as in dense) and Gump (as in gumption) is usually a passive wayfarer but, holy fool that he is, whenever he steps in *merde*, he always comes up covered with diamonds. In the case of Watergate, however, Forrest is Richard Nixon's nemesis. Forrest meets Nixon when he returns to Washington after, as a member of the United States ping pong team, their visit to China. Nixon (the real Nixon clipped into the film but speaking with Joe Alaskey's voice) says, "So you are enjoying yourself in the nation's capital, young man?" The always respectful Forrest says, "Yes, sir." Nixon then suggests "a much nicer hotel" than Forrest's current choice; the one Nixon has in mind is "brand-new, very modern," and he'll have his "people take care of it." The next shot is of Forrest watching a third-rate burglary in progress in the opposite wing of his "much nicer, brand-new, very modern" hotel. Forrest is on the phone: "You might want to send a maintenance man over to that office across the way. The lights are off; they must be looking for a fuse box or something. Those flashlights — they're keeping me awake." Some of this is in voice-over as we then see shots of Nixon's final address and his last helicopter wave.

Forrest Gump was faulted by some of the more serious critics such as Stanley Kauffmann (*New Republic*, August 8, 1994) who called it "hogwash." He went on to say that he could "easily see how ... people might be offended by its smug unreality." David Sterritt (*Christian Science Monitor*, July 7, 1994) in a review headed '*Gump' Takes Optimism Too Far* wrote that the film "rings dreadfully hollow most of the time." In a Sunday re-cap (July 31, 1994), echoing some of the political correctness of the day, the *New York Times* hinted that the film was "dangerously retrograde." Audiences, however, loved it, allowing it to gross over $100 million in less than a month. Some of these more "serious" critics did not give the audience enough credit for separating fact from fantasy. *Forrest Gump* presented what millions of people had lived through in a charmingly irreverent way — Forrest "mooning" LBJ, a concerned Nixon recommending a nice little hotel called Watergate. Forrest's story did not make a definitive social statement. Forrest is really a Candide whose adventures panorama, in comic counterpart, the upheavals of about 35 years in the last half of the 20th century. His life is a picaresque adventure, and Forrest isn't any more "real" than James Bond, Edward Scissorhands or, reaching much higher, the ghost of Hamlet's father. Forrest strikes a deeply responsive chord in the audience because he is a sweet, idealistic and idealized character with whom the audience, in their fantasy lives, can identify. When Forrest says, "I'm not a smart man, but I know what love is," the audience accepts that because he is the better part of themselves, the lucky, lovable *mensch* they'd all like to be.

Other critics noted:

"[It is] a smart, affecting, easygoing fable with plenty of talent on both sides of the camera. The key ingredient is Hanks, the one actor whom the mass audience trusts as an exemplar of equality. He can sell a tough subject to tough customers because they know the film will not be so much about issues as about the decency with which his character faces up to them.... The neat thing about Forrest is that he can symbolize so many people.... He's E.T. with a little Gandhi thrown in." — *Time*, August 1, 1994.

"*Forrest Gump* is a sort of updated, hip version of a Frank Capra movie. Capra's heroes were no great shakes in the brains department either, but at least they didn't make the point that being slow-witted was a big social and moral advantage. The good news is that the central Frank Capra message is in this movie too — that character and courage can prevail over all obstacles." — John Leo, *U.S. News & World Report*, August 8, 1994.

"It would be easy to mock this movie, with its shameless use of popular music to signal time and mood changes, its limited historic view, its sentimentality. But, like Forrest Gump, the character, the movie is true to itself. It does not waver from its fairy tale format, which — for those willing to accept its terms — turns Forrest's life into a charming and poignant fantasy." — Julie Salamon, *Wall Street Journal*, July 7, 1994.

"Much of this movie has a lulling dreaminess to it, a near-poetry of innocence pierced by sadness..." — David Denby, *New York*, August 8, 1994.

Diplomacy and Conspiracy: The Two Sides of Richard Nixon's Presidency (documentary, 1994)

60 minutes. *Twentieth Century* series. Host: Mike Wallace. CBS–TV.

This edition of *Twentieth Century* devoted one-third of its time to what it called "the high watermark of the Nixon presidency," the opening to China. It praised Nixon mightily for this endeavor, saying that only Nixon could have done it, its success having been based upon his militant anti–Communism which, in effect, made him the only man worth talking to. Wallace called it "a week that changed the world." Many of the scenes recreated in John Adams' opera *Nixon in China* (1987) appear before us in their reality: Pat and Dick deplaning in China just in time to coincide with prime-time American television, the lavish Chinese banquets, the meetings with Mao, shots inside the Great Hall of the People, a scene from the ballet *The Red Detachment of Women*, the ping pong team shown in *Forrest Gump*, Pat visiting the pandas at the zoo, the Nixons at the Great Wall of China, inside the Forbidden City and finally, the promise of future cultural exchanges and the hope of better diplomatic relations.

The major portion of this absorbing hour program was devoted to how the Vietnam War led indirectly to Watergate and "conspiracy," the second half of the program's title. Egil Krogh, head "plumber," said the 1969 inauguration started the paranoia inside the Nixon administration when war protests flared up at the edges of the inauguration ceremony. In order to counter the growing anti-war movement, Krogh said the "administration stepped over the line" after Nixon said he wanted to plug leaks and to protect documents such as the "leaked" Pentagon Papers. In reality, it was undoubtedly the desire of a win-at-any-price and tightly focused re-election team that caused Watergate.

Diplomacy and Conspiracy is a very worthwhile piece of television journalism, but its development is not even-handed. For instance, there is virtually no reference to Henry Kissinger or to any other diplomatic effort during Nixon's time in office. Nevertheless, the program contained some shots and short interviews that had not been shown before, or, if so, rarely.

Watergate (TV series, 1994)

Series consultant: Fred Emery. Director: Michael Gold. Producers: Norma Percy and Paul Mitchell. Narrator: Daniel Schorr. Brian Lapping Productions for the

Discovery Channel and the British Broadcasting Corporation. Sunday, August 7, 1994, 9–11 P.M. and Monday, Tuesday, Wednesday, August 8, 9 and 10 from 9–11 P.M.

"These were 'the aging ex-jailbirds' who did the time because in different ways they had done the crime for the President. Yet now, a generation later, they seemed not just at peace with themselves about what had once been painful humiliation, but actually pleased with the celebrity status conferred by association with such a famous moment in history. They exuded the sleek contentment one sees in Rembrandt's Dutch burghers..." — Russell Baker, *New York Times*, August 13, 1994.

In a piece for the *Christian Science Monitor* of August 12, 1994, narrator Daniel Schorr wrote: "There are still caves to explore for new Dead Sea Scrolls in the 42 million pages of documents and the 4,000 hours of Nixon tape in the hands of the National Archive. (All the tapes released in the investigation of Watergate amount to only 60 hours.)" Nevertheless, the small number of tapes did not prevent Fred Emery from creating a damning indictment of political wrong-doing. Like many another Englishman, both left and right, he is fascinated by American politics. Quite ironically, Richard Nixon was equally fascinated by British politics and British political coverage. The *Variety* of June 28, 1982 quotes from a Nixon letter to the BBC which states that the BBC "has earned the widest possible reputation for credibility and integrity." More or less, depending upon the biases of television critic, these two qualities were brought to the fore in the Discovery Channel/BBC co-production of *Watergate: The Corruption of American Politics and the Fall of Richard Nixon* which is also the title of Emery's exhaustive companion volume published in July 1994 by Times Books/Random House.

In an "op-ed" piece in the *New York Times* of July 19, 1994, Emery previewed the television series and the book by making three main points: "First, it is clear that long before Watergate, Mr. Nixon wallowed far more in campaign detail and dirty scheming than he would have had us believe from his pretense of being preoccupied with diplomacy. Second, his involvement in the cover-up was virtually immediate. And third, as early as April 1973 — before the Senate Select Committee on Watergate began its television hearings — he sensed that he was doomed, and contemplated resignation more seriously than has been appreciated."

This series has been released as a three-volume set (for information, call 1-800-922-7800).

Volume I: *A Third Rate Burglary*
Nixon declares war on his "enemies," A secret White House police force takes shape. The President's men get caught in a "third-rate burglary." A cover-up begins.

Volume II: *The Conspiracy Crumbles*
Dean spills the beans. The Oval Office taping system is revealed. The Special Prosecutor is fired. The Vice-President is forced to resign.

Volume III: *The Fall of a President*
Damaging evidence against the President. Impeachment approaches. The President is forced to resign.

Here's a sampling of critical opinion:
"Implicit in *Watergate* is the possibility that the best and the brightest have been in fact the worst and the dimmest. You may leave this tough five-hour account

convinced that confinement to the Beltway strangles common sense as well as honesty." — *The New York Times*, August 6, 1994.

"Narrator Daniel Schorr ... keeps referring to a 'chilling' memo, a 'chilling' taped conversation. There's a kind of innocence, as well as self-righteousness, in such language. People go into politics because they crave power, and to act shocked when they manipulate power for their own ends is to play hypocrite. People forgive the misuse of power when it is done in service of things they support. As Nixon's defenders often said, this sort of thing didn't begin with Watergate — as the federal government grew larger and larger throughout the 20th century, the presidential temptation to use its expanding power was irresistible for Kennedy and Johnson too — and they might have done worse things. They just didn't get caught." — John Podhoretz, *New York Post*, August 5, 1994.

"Watergate was all about — not a 'third-rate burglary' but a subversion of democratic politics. And then one imagines Nixon later on, as in a play by Samuel Beckett, alone at night in a dark wing of the White House listening to his incriminating self on tape." — John Leonard, *New York*, August 1, 1994.

"[T]he relentless focus on the events surrounding Watergate and the subsequent fall of the President is unforgiving. It is, in the words of one British reviewer, like watching 'a slow motion replay' of an accident. The sheer weight of the condensed chronology of criminal misdeeds, as well as the program's careful reconstruction of the atmosphere of political suspicion and paranoia that characterized the time, leads a viewer to the inevitable conclusion that Nixon was an architect of the cover-up." — *New York Times*, May 16, 1994.

"In the face of passionately partisan points of view, the show's persistence in corroborating facts is well-nigh heroic. Let the narrative mention a check written by Howard Hunt, and you'll see that check in a close-up. If someone refers to an important memo, you'll often see that section of the text highlighted. When there is nothing real on hand to illustrate a point with, the show will often stage something ... such touches may not mislead in any factual way, but they do contribute to the program's primary faults: a melodramatic style and a doggedly incriminatory tone. The narrative is impressively well organized and well informed, but its litany of catchy, condemnatory phrases and its ominous music and flashy editing techniques all create a souped-up effect. It's the wrong tack for a topic like this, which doesn't need dramatization, since it already *is* dramatic." — Alan Bunce, *Christian Science Monitor*, July 29, 1994.

"Mr. Emery ... has written [a] book ... [that] stands on its own as a comprehensive account of this century's most notorious political scandal, from the earliest discussions in which Nixon aids contemplated illegal buggings and break-ins to Nixon's resignation after it became evident that he had sought to cover up White House crimes." — *New York Times Book Review*, July 3, 1994.

Richard M. Nixon: His Life and Times (documentary, 1994)

60 minutes. Produced by William Abrams. Capital Cities/ABC Video, P.O. Box 3815, Stamford, CT 06905-0815.

This video, while not up to the level of the 1990 *American Experience* film or the 1996 A & E biography, is of some value. Its prime deficiency is a jumbled, tabloid newspaper quality with some pretty hard-hitting digs within a rather slapdash, uneven progression. It is not a well-unified entity, but it benefits at the beginning from the use of Nixon's own voice as we see some vintage Nixon photographs. Predictably, Peter Jennings, one of the many narrators, manages to make more anti–Nixon statements than any of his fellow speakers who include Sam Donaldson, Barbara Walters, Harry Reasoner and Howard K. Smith.

The Real Richard Nixon (video series, 1994)

Richard Nixon interviewed by Frank Gannon and Jesse Raiford, producers for Raiford Communications. Music by Homer Byington. Interviews directed by Roger Ailes. Consultants: Susan Naulty and Jonathan Aitken. Editor: Steve Wheeler. Raiford Communications, Inc., 928 Broadway, Suite 500, New York, New York 10036, or PBS Home Video, 1-800-645-4PBS, or the Richard Nixon Library and Birthplace, 18001 Yorba Linda Blvd., Yorba Linda, California 92686, 1-714-993-5075.

Volume I   *Early Life*   (66 minutes)
Volume II   *Pat*   (50 minutes)
Volume III   *Twenty-Eight Days*   (85 minutes)

VOLUME I— Before being released on video, *The Real Richard Nixon* appeared on the History Channel. It presents a great deal of the biographical material that is available in other films and videos, but is in itself a good introduction. It offers some fresh glimpses of Nixon's psyche such as his analogy between politics and poker, long before these two seemingly disparate pursuits were allied in the show tune "Politics and Poker" on Broadway in *Fiorello*. Nixon: "Some of the things you learn in poker are very useful in politics — when to bluff, when to call and when to be unpredictable is one of the chief qualities any politician can have."

VOLUME II—*Pat* is a lovely film of which Gannon should be proud. It seeks to finally show the courage and public service of Richard Nixon's staunchest loyalist, always in his shadow but always urging him on. It touches upon the deaths of her parents during her school years, her outstanding academic achievement at USC, her fierce desire to be independent, her early interest in acting, her beauty, her work with children, her good will missions to countries in South America and Africa, her love of gardening, her encouragement of civic volunteerism at every level of community life.

In a *Newsday* article (December 17, 1995), Joseph Gelmis interviewed Frank Gannon about the series and about Pat. Gannon stated that the series was filmed in 1983 for 38 hours over a period of ten months. Some of the footage was sold to Mike Wallace for *60 Minutes*, but Gannon had "no money to go into post-production" with the rest. Trained as a historian (he has a Ph.D. from Oxford), Gannon had been a White House Fellow and had helped Nixon with his memoirs. During that time, he came to know the Nixons rather well and with the deaths of both Nixons, the unedited hours of interviews seemed too valuable a record not to bring before the public. "For Gannon, the most hurtful inaccuracy in [Oliver Stone's] *Nixon* is its depiction of a 'loveless marriage held together by political expediency. Mrs. Nixon is presented as a sex-starved alcoholic.... [Pat] was a vivacious, beautiful, funny, vital woman who made some enormous sacrifices and ended up misunderstood."

In a *New York Post* article of 1995, Gannon, in effect, calls Oliver Stone an opportunist and a coward in his rendering of Pat Nixon: "Scene 117 opens with the directions: 'NIXON is really drunk now ... PAT's voice cuts in. She's standing at the doorway. She's been drinking too...' In the middle of the scene, Nixon shouts, 'You're drunk.' Pat laughs, 'Yeah, I am.' There are no footnotes. Audiences will leave *Nixon* with images of Pat Nixon, several sheets to the wind, slurring her words while she wanders around the White House in her nightgown. Readers [of the screenplay], however, might consider this undocumented portrayal of a strong and private woman as a cowardly act by someone who should — and, judging by the absence of any footnotes, did — know better." Even six months after the release of Stone's *Nixon*, Chris Matthews on his TV show *Politics* said, "Oliver Stone has a screw loose," after Stone reviewed Matthews' book *Kennedy and Nixon* for a Los Angeles newspaper.

VOLUME III— While *Twenty-Eight Days* lacks the dramatic drive of Lane Smith's superb performance in *The Final Days*, the "real Nixon" supplies some drive of his own as we see him, in spite of his vaunted sense of control, register a myriad of emotions: anger, regret, bitterness, gratitude and serenity pass before us as Nixon discusses what had to be the most painful month of his political life. Yet his view is wide-ranging, and he offers telling vignettes of some of the people who affected his life in various ways: His parents, his grandmother, his football coach, Pat, Julie, Tricia, Rose Mary Woods, Bebe Rebozo, Herb Stein and world figures such as Ike, Churchill and MacArthur. Thanks to the low-key atmosphere that Gannon establishes throughout the series, Nixon attains in these three films an air of contemplation that is not present in his other interview films.

At the end of the last film, Nixon recites a poem that was sent to him by his old friend Clare Boothe Luce, "The Ballad of Sir Andrew Barton":

> I am hurt, but I am not slain:
> I'll lay me down and bleed awhile,
> and I'll rise and fight again.

In a generally favorable review, the *New York Times* (December 22, 1995) called the series "a carefully orchestrated but oddly affecting effort by the former President to come across as a regular fellow."

Death of a President: NBC News Special Report (TV, 1994)

Documentary with Tom Brokaw (anchor), Ron Ziegler, Frank Gannon, Charles Colson, George McGovern and Alexander Haig. NBC, 11:37 P.M.–12:00 A.M. April 22, 1994.

In the days between Richard Nixon's death and funeral, all the major television networks and CNN devoted generous air time to the passing of the 37th President. With the exception of Jules Witcover's sarcastic comments as mourners filed by the flag-draped coffin in the Nixon Library at Yorba Linda, the television coverage of Nixon's death was respectful and often touching. The plane in flight bearing the coffin, the close-ups of many deeply affected mourners and the conduct of Nixon's children and grandchildren as well as the dignity of the ceremony itself had a quiet eloquence that was appropriate to the man who led the country in times of great turmoil, sometimes wisely, sometimes unwisely.

It would not be possible to recap the dozens of television hours devoted to Richard Nixon's dying and death, but if one program were to be chosen, it would be best to choose one that remains accessible to the public. NBC's *Death of a President* is available on tape and transcript from Burrell's, 75 East Northfield Road, Livingston, New Jersey 07039 (1-800-876-3442).

From the transcript:

> TOM BROKAW: "Good evening. Former President Richard Milhous Nixon, who had more lives than his enemies wished and not enough for his family and friends, finally gave up tonight. He's dead at the age of 81. He died in New York's Cornell Medical Center of complications from a stroke on Monday, thus ending a life of great triumphs, great controversies and great disgrace. For five decades, from the '40s to the mid-'90s, few Americans were as well known, as prominent; few Americans generated such strong emotions as Richard Milhous Nixon.

> NIXON (file tapes): "A man cannot sit in his own jury. However, if I were to present the case before the jury of history, I think this is what I would say: The instant historians, understandably, are obsessed with Watergate. They hardly see anything else about me, and they rate me very low. I understand that ... But there's also a more positive part.... I'm the president who opened relations with China after 25 years of no communication; I ended a war in Vietnam in which there were 550,000 Americans there when I came in and none when I left. I ended the draft. I negotiated the first arms control agreement with the Soviet Union. I initiated programs in the field of the environment and hunger and cancer and drugs that I think are very sound building blocks for the future. These are positive achievements. They must be there along with the negative ones...."

Some other further highlights of the program were Frank Gannon's repeating Nixon's comment to Gary Wills in 1968 wherein Nixon described himself as "an introvert in an extrovert's game" which Gannon called "a brilliant piece of self-analysis."

Ron Ziegler commented on Nixon's ability to "absorb" conflicts in "his public career in a very dignified, courageous way" and "to accomplish many new and additional things after a defeat or shortcoming or disgrace..."

Charles Colson spoke of the inhospitable atmosphere in Washington when Nixon was first elected: "*The Washington Post* said the Nixon administration coming to Washington was like the Nazis occupying Paris..."

One of the speakers was George McGovern, the senator from South Dakota who was Nixon's 1972 Democratic opponent:

McGOVERN: I think [Nixon] is quite right that his position is going to improve.... Watergate will remain obviously as the stain on the Nixon presidency. But I do think the opening to China and the steady improvement of relations with the Soviet Union will give Nixon a fairly high place in history. He was pretty good on domestic policy as well. We sometimes forget that, but during the late '60s and '70s I headed, for example, the Select Committee on nutritional programs, all of which had the support of President Nixon.

ALEXANDER HAIG: "Every foreign leader that I knew over the span of 20 years regarded him as our best president."

Brokaw concluded the broadcast by saying that "for so many Americans [Nixon] was both a heroic, a tragic and ultimately still an enigmatic figure."

What follows are excerpts from two televised eulogies:

HENRY KISSINGER: "During the final week of Richard Nixon's life, I often imagined how he would have reacted to the tide of concern, respect, admiration and affection evoked by his last great battle. His gruff pose of never paying attention to media comment would have been contradicted by a warm glow and the ever-so-subtle hint that another recital of the commentary would not be unwelcome. And with-out quite saying so, he would have conveyed that it would mean a lot to him if Julie, Tricia, David and Ed were told of his friends' pride in this culmination to an astonishing life..."

BOB DOLE: "One of his biographers said that Richard Nixon was 'one of us.' And so he was. He was a boy who heard the train whistle in the night and dreamed of all the distant places that lay at the end of the track. How American. He was the grocer's son who got ahead by work-ing harder and longer than everyone else. How American. He was a stu-dent who met expenses by doing research at the law library for 35 cents an hour while sharing a run-down farm house without water or elec-tricity. How American. He was the husband and father who said that the best memorial to his wife was her children. How American.... The tens of thousands who have come to Yorba Linda these past few days are the people from whom he had come, no longer silent in their grief. The American people love a fighter, and in Dick Nixon they found a gallant one.... May God bless Richard Nixon and may God bless the United States."

Here's a sampling of critical opinion:

"I have long had a soft spot for [Nixon], thinking him attacked more for quirks of personality than for errors of policy."—Robert Scheer, *Los Angeles Times*, April 26, 1994.

"Nixon clearly sensed that social disaster would occur if disadvantaged families did not somehow get 'a piece of the pie.' So he refused to rant and rave about 'reverse discrimination' when cities and corporations began affirmative action programs to give jobs and work contracts to blacks and minority firms. Nixon seemed to sense the need to make amends for 300 years of racial discrimination in America.... He seemed always to regain a sense of the fairness and justice this society needed to remain internally strong."—Syndicated columnist Carl Rowan, April 27, 1994.

"[The last] 20 years of Mr. Nixon's life could have been spent in angry, disappointed seclusion. But, tenacious to the end, he created a new, and ultimately a well-regarded, life by becoming a scholar. America's Lazarus became again a confidant of the great and the mighty."—James Perry, *Wall Street Journal*, April 25, 1994.

The *New York Times* (April 29, 1994) reviewed the funeral itself "as if it were a television program." This opened the door for some cracks about the mortality of the former presidents in attendance:

"The setting and the direction struck an often stirring note of Americana. There was the frame house where Richard M. Nixon was born; the men and women of the armed forces, too young to have their own memories of the Presidency they had been ordered to commemorate, going smartly through their routines; the music from the patriotic repertory, and especially the current First Couple and the four living former Presidents and their wives in the front row like a Norman Rockwell sketch for a new Mount Rushmore.

"Those four, across whom the camera frequently panned, may have been in the mind of the Reverend Billy Graham, who has evidently never met a President he didn't like or couldn't certify as heaven-bound, when he said his closing sermon, 'I think today every one of us ought to be thinking about our own time to die.'... Watching the former Presidents, two of whom have used up their allotted Biblical span and two of whom are on the verge, a viewer could imagine them imagining their own final television specials, with the 21-gun salute, the flyover and the eulogies."

Nixon on Nixon (TV documentary, 1994)

Biography series, Peter Graves, host. Program advisors: Bill Harris and Michael Cascio. Archival assistant: Sandy Quinn. A & E Network, May 3, 1994.

Because it was assembled shortly after his death, *Nixon on Nixon* retained much of the respectful air that was part of the days of mourning. It was very informative and narrated by carefully selected voice-overs from Nixon's own speeches and file interviews.

Nixon discusses his mother, his football team, the Voorhis and Douglas campaigns, Checkers, his relationship with Eisenhower, the Caracas riots, the kitchen debate, the 1960 and 1962 defeats, Tricia's pleas that he run in 1968 ("You have to run; otherwise, you'll have nothing to live for"), TV anchor John Chancellor on the trip to China ("one of the most stunning developments that anyone in my generation can remember"), Watergate ("Why didn't we clean it up right then when we could have?") and resignation ("Tricia put her arms around me and said 'For the good of the country, you must not resign.' I said, 'I hope I haven't let you down,' but I knew I did").

At the end, we see Nixon as a little boy. Nixon voice-over: "The doctor said I had the strongest voice of any baby he delivered." In conclusion, host Peter Graves said, "He had grown to greatness by his strong voice."

Blacklist: Hollywood on Trial (TV documentary, 1995)

90 minutes. Written and directed by Christopher Koch. Photography: Erich Roland. Executive producer: Lewis Bogach. Produced by Christopher Koch Productions and American Movie Classics. Narrated by Alec Baldwin.

"[Kirk Douglas] had arranged to meet then Vice-President Richard M. Nixon, who had been a member of the HUAC committee which subpoenaed the Hollywood Ten, in his offices at the Capitol. Douglas hoped, first, to get a statement from Nixon condemning the blacklist or failing that to get a statement supporting a producer's right to employ whoever [sic] he wished should that producer publicly break the blacklist.... Nixon refused a statement pointing out that the blacklist was an industry problem which the industry itself should consider without governmental interference." — *Additional Dialogue, Letters of Dalton Trumbo*, 1942–1962, edited by Helen Manfull.

Narrated by Alec Baldwin in an almost funereal voice, *Blacklist: Hollywood on Trial* covers much of the material in the almost similarly named 1976 documentary *Hollywood on Trial*, a success at the 1976 Cannes Festival which nevertheless did not have a large scale commercial release. This earlier film, according to the *London Observer* (October 8, 1978), "let the Hollywood leaders off pretty lightly, and [was] perhaps rather too ready to accept the good faith of the publicity-seeking committee."

The later film featured actors well known in the 1990s such as Joe Mantegna, Rob Reiner, Morgan Freeman and Martin Sheen playing members of the Hollywood Ten of blacklisted writers and directors: Alvah Bessie, Herbert Biberman, Lester Cole, Edward Dmytryk, Ring Lardner, Jr., John Howard Lawson, Albert Maltz, Samuel Ornitz, Adrian Scott and Dalton Trumbo. One of the principal interviewees was Marsha Hunt, an MGM player of the 1940s who had great difficulty finding work because of her association with members of the Hollywood Ten, although she had never been a Communist sympathizer herself.

The blacklist was treated in dramatic form in another 1976 film, *The Front*, directed by Martin Ritt, starring Woody Allen and Zero Mostel.

Richard Nixon appears in the 1995 film twice — at the beginning near the Ronald Reagan and Walt Disney segments and just before the final credits.

America's War on Poverty: My Brother's Keeper (TV documentary, 1995)

Written, directed, produced by Leslie D. Farrell. Music by Brian Keane. Edited by Betty Ciccarelli. Photography by Chin. Wednesday, January 18, 1995.

"...gritty, often horrifying, occasionally triumphant." — *Variety*, January 16, 1995.

"Under the Nixon Administration, grants to states for services rose from $346 million in 1968 to $500 million in 1972. Through the Housing and Community Development Act of 1974 housing opportunities for the poor were expanded." — PBS *Series Viewer's Guide*, 1995.

Crocodiles in the Potomac (comedy, 1995)

Written by Wendy Belden. Directed by Suzanne Bennett. Produced by the Women's Project Productions (Julia Miles, Artistic Director), Theatre Row Theatre, 424

A flyer for the Off-Broadway play *Crocodiles in the Potomac* (1995).

West 42nd Street, New York City, October 19–November 12, 1995. Cast: *Bev Lehr* Kristin Griffith; *Jacquie Crayton* Gretchen Egolf; *Becky Lehr* Tristine Skyler; *Constantine Xanthos* Firdous Bamji; *Richard Nixon* Brad Bellamy.

Wendy Belden's comedy *Crocodiles in the Potomac* is a spaced-out domestic comedy with political satire also very much on its wayward mind. It has something of the campiness of John Waters' *Hairspray* and though not as good-natured and much coarser-grained it has some of the girlish fun of Amy Heckerling's *Clueless*. (Sample dialogue: Jacquie: "I know my rock and roll facts." / Becky: "You do not. Look at you. You wear a bra, for Christ's sake.")

Instead of Waters' Baltimore, we have Washington in the hot and eventful August of 1974. The story centers on three adolescents. The leading character, Becky, is the daughter of a liberal Democrat and a bottle-nipping single mother who is a sort of ZaSu Pitts with attitude. In one scene Becky's mom tells off the United States Senate. Becky's best friend Jacquie is the daughter of an ultra-conservative senator who has no time for Jacquie because of the pressures of Watergate. Becky and Jacquie become pals with Constantine, a foreign student who flirts with Marxism and all sorts of ill-focused idealistic causes. His father is a Greek diplomat so he can afford to fool around with noble causes for a while. Becky's home life is obviously a mess, but graduation looms, and she desperately wants to go to "a good school." With the help of Jacquie's starchy father, Becky gets a job as a congressional page, surely, she thinks, an open sesame to the best groves in academe. One steamy August night when Becky and Jacquie are squabbling, as usual, and Constantine is ranting about the injustices of the world, something eerie happens. Richard Nixon wanders in, and Constantine yells: "You ruined my country." Richard Nixon sucks his cheeks in thoughtfully and says: "Let me guess, Greece?" Which is followed by other straight-faced near–Nixonisms. As the *New York Times* put it: "The one moment of inspired writing comes at the end, with the startling appearance of Nixon in the teenager's home. He seems to be talking with the other characters but in fact is delivering a halting, frequently interrupted and deluded monologue that is amusing, unsettling and a good reminder of the air of unreality that hung over the whole nation at the time."

Nixon enjoys talking to Becky and Jacquie, and they help him to rewrite history. As the author explains (*Women's Project Dialogues*, Fall 1995):

> While writing the play, I felt very strongly about employing two women to send Nixon to his exile [in a station wagon with a bad alternator!]. It's my answer to the Oliver Stone-style, Draconian approach to dramatizing history. As a kid in D.C., what I saw of history was small moments, people crowded outside the White House gates before the resignation, for instance. I wanted to pay attention to women and to details, and to allow Nixon's fall to occasion a mother-daughter resolution. [In the play] the mother gives the daughter the keys to the car in the end — to take Nixon back to the waiting helicopter."

The *Village Voice* (October 3, 1995, generally pleased, called it "a frolic with a druggy cameo by Nixon."

American Presidents — Character Above All — A Lecture Series — Richard Nixon (TV, 1995)

93 minutes. Lecture by Tom Wicker, from the LBJ school of the University of Texas at Austin (78713). Transcript from C-Span in the Classroom, Education Services, 400 North Capitol St., N.W., Suite 650, Washington, D.C. 20001 (800-523-7586); broadcast on C-Span March 11, 1995.

Much of the content of this lecture appears in Wicker's tough but fair 1991 volume *One of Us: Richard Nixon and the American Dream*. Both the book and the lecture examine the many paradoxes of Richard Nixon's character (e.g. his strong anti–Communism and his paradoxical defense of J. Robert Oppenheimer; his extreme isolation and his longing to be "in the arena"; his reliance on and his mistrust of Henry Kissinger). A specific outline of the lecture with time lengths for each topic is as follows:

Introduction, Nixon as a pioneer in TV use	5 minutes
Campaigning as Nixon's greatest strength; deliberately played down his intelligence	4 minutes
Lack of rapport with the public	7 minutes
Nixon's understanding of the working class; his resentment of the wealthy	8 minutes
He did not trust the ordinary voter; Nixon as a loner	5 minutes
Nixon's achievements as President: opening to China, EPA, SALT, revenue sharing, Family Assistance Plan, greater school integration, the OMB	5 minutes

The marked contrasts in personality of his parents and their effects upon his personality	3 minutes
Anxieties within the White House	5 minutes
Watergate and the Resignation; How will history regard him?	2 minutes

Kissinger: An A & E Biography (documentary, 1995)

60 minutes. Narrated by Walter Isaacson. Based on material from Isaacson's *Kissinger: A Biography* (1992) published by Simon and Schuster. This program was telecast in 1995 and in succeeding years, New Video Group, 126 Fifth Avenue, New York, New York 10011.

An absorbing and informative career and personal overview of Nixon's last Secretary of State, and, in his own right, a figure of world significance who, with his parents and brother, was a refugee from Nazi Germany in 1938. The film discusses Kissinger with Nixon in many instances and describes their uneasy relationship, including the famous final "prayer scene" which both mentioned in their memoirs. The script also illustrates Kissinger's love of celebrity and his ability to attach himself to useful mentors. Nixon does not come off too well, nor does Kissinger because in Isaacson's view both were "rather devious"; they both loved secrecy. In Nixon's case, it was disastrous.

Kissinger and Nixon (TV drama, 1995)

120 minutes. Directed by Daniel Petrie. Written by Lionel Chetwynd. Based on the book *Kissinger: A Biography* by Walter Isaacson. Produced by Daniel Blatt, Jon Slan, Judith James and Lionel Chetwynd. Photography by Rene Ohashi. Production design by Karen Bromley. Music by Jonathan Goldsmith. Turner Television Network, December 10, 1995. Cast: *Henry Kissinger* Ron Silver; *Richard Nixon* Beau Bridges; *Alexander Haig* Matt Frewer; *H.R. Haldeman* Ron White; *Le Duc Tho* George Takei; *Charles Colson* Tony Rosato; *President Thieu* Henry Chan.

"It would be difficult to imagine two societies less meant to understand each other than the Vietnamese and the American." — Henry Kissinger, *Foreign Affairs*, January 1969.

The television film *Kissinger and Nixon* is based on the middle chapters of Walter Isaacson's 1992 Kissinger biography which, according to Kissinger associate Peter Rodman (*National Review*, January 29, 1996), is "an extremely shallow and cliché-ridden book." The film dramatizes the six month period of the Paris peace talks from June 1972 to January 1973 when Kissinger and Nixon were often at odds about how to end the Vietnam War honorably.

Nineteen seventy-two was Nixon's third run for the presidency, and a landslide victory was predicted, the effects of which would have an impact on Southeast Asia. The core conflict of this dramatization is Nixon's desire to gain peace *after* the 1972 election because he believes that by ending the war before the elections he will be accused of using a peace settlement simply to get votes. Kissinger, however, follows the urgings of Le Duc Tho, the North Vietnamese leader, who fears that with a landslide victory Nixon will heighten the war. What ensues is a stealthy cat and mouse game in which Kissinger and Nixon play off each other with a keen eye on the media and media spinmasters. In essence, the film is less about finding peace than it is about the egos of two extremely complex men both of whom have large doses of *chutzpah* and paranoia.

After the credits and the cautionary words "All history is subject to interpretation," there is a brief narration accompanied by stock footage of the war. The first scene of the dramatization itself takes place as Le Duc Tho addresses the North Vietnamese Politburo in regard to President Thieu of South Vietnam: "If we can persuade the Americans to do what the Soviets and the Chinese have done to us — withdraw support — we will see the end of Thieu. In the forthcoming election, Richard Nixon is expected to gain a vast victory. It will embolden [Nixon] to, in his words, *get tough with us*. On the other hand, if Henry Kissinger can deliver to his president a peace with honor, it will be hard for even Nixon to refuse. We will force their hands by not insisting that Thieu be ousted in return for the promise that the Americans will withdraw all troops from all regions of Vietnam. With the Americans gone, the days of our final liberation of the South will be numbered.... We will avoid embassies, ignore their State Department and use back channels. I will deal directly with Kissinger. He will deliver."

The angry tone of the Nixon character is set in his first scene as he discovers through an intelligence "intercept" that Kissinger is working through back channels without the President's knowledge. Kissinger is able to placate somewhat Nixon's claim of Kissinger's over-reaching. In the first of a series of sports metaphors that dot Nixon's speeches throughout, Nixon says he "doesn't like the receiver calling plays the quarterback doesn't know." (Note: The Vietnamese are given to animal metaphors: "We must be slyer than the fox.")

Nixon always appears angry with Kissinger and (with his cronies) belittles Kissinger behind his back. The antagonism is an undercurrent throughout the entire work, presenting the White House as a viper's nest of envy, back stabbing and sycophancy. Nixon calls Kissinger (behind his back) "an elitist suck-up," and Kissinger, not overhearing, but no doubt intuiting, returns the compliment by calling Nixon "the madman in the Oval Office." Much of the script deals with the question of who has been leaking aspects of the peace negotiations to the media. The question really should be "Who *hasn't?*" There are scenes of Kissinger confiding in "Scotty" Reston, respected *New York Times* columnist, and scenes of Nixon and his cronies chortling after they've planted some leaks of their own. There are also scenes in which both Kissinger and Nixon subtly bribe two-star General Haig with two more stars if he will become a kind of double duty snitch. In an equivocating scene, the Haig character implies that some of the leaks may have come from two of Nixon's speechwriters, Pat Buchanan and William Safire.

There is little question that the tone of the script presents both Vietnamese leaders as honorable men — in some ways more honorable than the President of the United

Beau Bridges as Nixon and Ron Silver as Kissinger in the television drama *Kissinger and Nixon* (1995).

States and his national security advisor. President Thieu, in particular, is presented as a pawn with whom the United States dealt badly. It is this realization that gives the Nixon character one of his few humanizing moments. While both Vietnamese leaders are presented with dignity, it is Thieu who agonizes over the fate of his people and the weak hand he has been dealt. In several absorbing scenes of parallel action, Kissinger talks about his Vietnam plans to the *New York Times* while Nixon and his cadre of Haldeman, Colson and Haig plan how to hold the reins on Kissinger.

The script, not always clear in its intentions, sends mixed signals. For instance, at one point, producer–author Chetwynd has Nixon say: "I won't be a party to jamming anything down Thieu's throat." The line suggests an attempt at even-handedness in its portrayal of Nixon since an outright villain would turn the entire proceedings into a melodrama. Yet in the end that is what is accomplished as *Newsday* (December 10, 1995) pointed out: "Nixon comes out as the villain in the story, talking like a hyper-ventilating coach at a dysfunctional cow college." Nixon: "The American people want us to score a *winner*!" and to Kissinger: "All right! You put your deal to 'em, but make it *tough*!" After many discussions, the opposing Vietnamese leaders do not come to terms as quickly as Kissinger's machinations seemed to promise. With a misguided belief in his success, Kissinger made the mistake of stating "Peace is at hand." The statement was premature. Nixon: "I plan to leave office a winner. This is all your fault, Henry. This 'peace is at hand' crap." Nixon decides to force an agreement by bombing North Vietnam. General Haig, who in this script does not appear as much more than a boot-licker, urges: "Stand tall, Mr. President." Nixon replies: "When people see this bombing ['the Christmas bombing'] end the war, they'll see how right I am." After Kissinger leaves, Nixon says: "I knew [the American people] would catch on to Kissinger sooner or later." Graphic shots of the bombing follow, forcing the weary negotiations to begin anew.

In January 1973, the United States and North Vietnam signed the Paris Peace Agreement. It contained three provisions: The withdrawal of all American troops, the return of U.S. prisoners and a cease fire. But while the war ended for the Americans, the internal conflict continued and by April 1975, the North Vietnamese had captured Saigon. At the end of the film one of its themes, that of the Americans watching a political clock during an election year, is underscored when President Thieu muses: "Our allies are motivated by the great game of power politics."

In an angry letter to the *Wall Street Journal* (December 22, 1995) shortly after the telecast, Kissinger called *Kissinger and Nixon* "the Jane Fonda version of history." In a television interview with Chris Matthews, Nixon speechwriter Ray Price called it "a travesty"; he was bristling, no doubt, at such Nixon attributions as "I'll fire the son of a bitch [Kissinger] and end the war myself" and "The American people will not sell an ally down the river. They'd rather keep on bombing." Loony and "over the top" as it was, if one didn't place too much faith in its "facts" and its "interpretation," *Kissinger and Nixon* was absorbing television. Isaacson's Kissinger biography suggests that Kissinger sometimes romanticized himself as the Lone Ranger. John Ehrlichman, quoted in the same book, says Nixon would have cast him as Tonto.

What follows is a sampling of critical opinion:

"Daniel Petrie's resourceful direction and pacing of Lionel Chetwynd's intense account of the Vietnam negotiations in 1972 and 1973 and this drama urgency as Richard Nixon and his national security adviser vie for personal glory. Beau Bridges' own strong personality soaks through the overdone Nixon makeup, but Ron Silver's Kissinger is indeed a study; here's backstage at the palace."—*Variety*, December 11, 1995.

"I have to confess that until watching Mr. Bridges, I was ignorant of the fact that it was always cocktail time in the Nixon Oval Office. But kicking around the mighty is an American sport, and if you're willing to settle for pointedly unfair portraits of a pair of the century's movers and shakers, *Kissinger and Nixon* should satisfy."—*New York Times*, December 9, 1995.

"[T]he movie ... could not have been more flattering if [it] had been written by Henry the K himself. [It] portrays Nixon as a besotted drunk, a great oversimplifier. But [when] the story kicks in, [it] is a fascinating tale of intrigue, a study of the differences between policy and politics."—*Newsday*, December 10, 1995.

"[A] tight, polished drama with a crackling pace.... Above all, this film traces the story of two massive egos in conflict. As seen here, the president and his national security adviser may share the same ideology, but it's clear they don't understand each other, don't trust each other."—*Wall Street Journal*, December 18, 1995.

"What astonishing performances Dan Petrie manages to elicit from Silver and Bridges. They sound so precisely like the tapes in our heads that there's an eerie echo, a symbolic styling of gutturals and slur."—*New York*, December 11, 1995.

Richard III (film, 1995)

Directed by Richard Loncraine. Written by Ian McKellan and Loncraine. Based on a stage production by Richard Eyre from the play by Shakespeare. Photography:

Peter Biziou. Production designer: Tony Burrough. Editor: Paul Green. Music by Trevor Jones. Produced by Lisa Katselas Paré and Stephen Baylay. Released by United Artists. Technicolor. Cast: *Richard III* Ian McKellen; *Queen Elizabeth* Annette Bening; *Duchess of York* Maggie Smith; *Clarence* Nigel Hawthorne; *Edward IV* John Wood; *Lady Anne* Kristin Scott Thomas; *Rivers* Robert Downey, Jr.

This is not a "Richard Nixon film," but that did not keep critics from reviewing it as if it were.

Each of Richard Milhous Nixon's three names has an ironic relevance to his life. The Irish surname of Nixon means "he faileth not" in Gaelic; his middle name is that of his maternal Quaker grandparents; and his given name was meant to encourage within Nixon the valor of Richard the Lion-Hearted. Unfortunately, for much of his political life, Richard M. Nixon's more usual role, to many critics, is that of the unhistorical villain Shakespeare imagined as Richard III, a parallel noted by Sir Laurence Olivier as early as 1955. Two of the obvious later manifestations of Richard Nixon as Richard, Duke of Gloucester, are Rip Torn's performance in *The Bearding of the President* and David Edgar's clever parody *Dick Deterred*, both discussed earlier. The campy 1995 British film of Shakespeare's play (Al Jolson sings the finale) offered confirmed Nixon-haters an easy opportunity for further demonizing the recently departed former President in this re-setting of Shakespeare in a fascistic 1930s England.

"If Europe in the '30s seems too remote, consider Richard of Gloucester as the evil twin to Richard of Whittier. As a satanic conniver, McKellen combines the darkest dreams of the 37th President and his Secretary of State. He has the hunched posture of the cartoonist's Nixon, the brutal statecraft of the conspiracy theorist's Henry Kissinger. This movie is the fetid, enthralling goods, the *Nixon* that Oliver Stone didn't dare to make." — *Time*, January 15, 1996.

"Nixon's world has passed. What remains is the character of Nixon, as eternal as Richard III: a persona more amenable to interpretation by a dramatist than by a politician. The more pretenders try to imitate him, the more they falter. In comparison, he appears bigger than ever, larger than life…. 'It's like Elvis,' said John Sears, who served as a technical adviser on Oliver Stone's movie. 'Nixon isn't dead either.'" — Sydney Blumental, *New Yorker*, October 2, 1995.

"[E]vil is not elusive or charmingly seductive (even charismatic), but may be readily identified by those with any moral insight in such powerful figures as Richard III or Richard Nixon…" — Hugh M. Richmond, *Shakespeare in Performance: King Richard III*, 1989.

"Because of his name, Richard Nixon has often been likened to Richard III…. He's more like the shifty, hypocritical Bolingbroke, who managed to get rid of Richard II while protesting he really didn't want to. Bolingbroke became Henry IV, a character who has two plays named after him yet stars in neither of them — just the kind of thing you feel could have happened to Nixon, a star of history with the personal magnetism of a bit player." — Lloyd Rose, *The Washington Post*, December 24, 1995.

A congratulatory note to William F. Buckley:

"Just a word of congratulations on the first issue of *National Review*, though … Nixon do(es) rather remind me of Richard III." — Sir Laurence Olivier, *National Review*, December 21, 1995 (reprinted).

(It should be noted that Olivier was an old hand at role-playing-as-revenge: In his great 1955 film of *Richard III*, Olivier settled a long standing grudge against the American stage director Jed Harris by playing Shakespeare's archvillain in makeup that was Harris to the life.)

Nixon (film, 1995)

190 minutes. A Buena Vista (Disney) release from Hollywood Pictures. An Andrew G. Vajna presentation of an Illusion Entertainment Group/Cinergi production. Produced by Clayton Townsend, Oliver Stone and Vajna. Directed by Oliver Stone. Screenplay by Stephen J. Rivele, Christopher Wilkinson and Oliver Stone. Photography: Robert Richardson. Editors: Brian Berdan and Hank Corwin. Music: John Williams. Production design: Victor Kempster. Art direction: Donald Woodruff, Richard F. Mays and Margery Zweizig. Set decoration: Merideth Roswell. Costume design: Richard Hornung. Cast: *Richard M. Nixon* Anthony Hopkins; *Pat Nixon* Joan Allen; *Alexander Haig* Powers Booth; *E. Howard Hunt* Ed Harris; *J. Edgar Hoover* Bob Hoskins; *John Mitchell* E.G. Marshall; *Ron Ziegler* David Paymer; *John Dean* David Hyde Pierce; *Henry Kissinger* Paul Sorvino; *Hannah Nixon* Mary Steenburgen; *John Ehrlichman* J.T. Walsh; *H.R. Haldeman* James Woods; *Clyde Tolson* Brian Bedford; *Charles Colson* Kevin Dunn; *Murray Chotiner* Fyvush Finkel; *Julie Nixon* Annabeth Gish; *Harold Nixon* Tony Goldwyn; *"Jack Jones"* Larry Hagman; *Nelson Rockefeller* Ed Herrmann; *Martha Mitchell* Madeline Kahn; *Johnny Roselli* Tony LoBianco; *Richard Nixon at 12* Corey Carrier; *Frank Nixon* Tom Bower; *Richard Nixon at 19* David Barry Gray; *Manolo Sanchez* Tony Piana; *Trini Cardoza* Dan Hedaya; *Gordon Liddy* John Diehl; *Tricia Nixon* Marley Shelton; *Confrontational Student* Joanna Going.

At first it was thought a detailed content analysis scene by scene would be of assistance to anyone researching Richard Nixon as a figure in the popular arts. A problem arises, however; a detailed analysis of so lengthy a script, with its many flashbacks, reordering of time and the necessity to introduce to the reader every minor character in so sprawling a work would not in reality assist the reader in understanding the portrait of Richard Nixon created by Oliver Stone. For these reasons, only the key scenes of plot and character development are included.

On the screen: "This film is an attempt to understand the truth of Richard Nixon, 37th President of the United States. It is based on numerous public sources and on an incomplete historical record." A further note explains that incidents "and characters have been condensed" and some scenes "have been conjectured."

"What shall it profit a man if he shall gain the whole world and lose his own soul?"— *The Book of Matthew.*

SCENE 1— June 17, 1972, Watergate Hotel, the night of the second and crucial break-in by the plumbers. Hunt states there were four attempts to break into the Democratic National Headquarters at the Watergate. At the end of the scene a radio report announces the capture of the burglars.

SCENES 2–4— The White House. 1973. The President receives an envelope of tapes from White House Chief of Staff Haig. Haig: "Those are the ones ... the lawyers feel ... will be the basis of the ... procedures." Nixon refers ironically to suicide. Haig leaves. Nixon belts a Scotch and starts playing the tapes.

Pat and Richard Nixon as played by Joan Allen and Anthony Hopkins in Oliver Stone's *Nixon* (1995).

SCENE 5— President's office. 1972. A damage control meeting. Nixon, Ehrlichman, Haldeman.

SCENE 6— Oval Office. 1971. The aftermath of David Ellsberg's giving over the Pentagon papers. Colson says to Nixon: "Just whisper the word to me, sir, and I'll shoot him myself." Nixon goes back to his memories of the Hiss case through which the screenwriters present a foreshadowing. Nixon: "It's the lie that gets you."

SCENE 7— Ellsberg's psychiatrist's office. 1971. Night. G. Gordon Liddy and three assistants. No dialogue.

SCENE 8— President's office. 1972. Nixon agrees to pay hush money to Hunt.

SCENE 9— Nixon, wallowing in self-pity, fumbles with pills and Scotch.

SCENES 10–13— Chart Nixon's early political career.

SCENES 14–18— Childhood in California. Family relationships established.

SCENE 20— Defeat in California Governor's race, 1962.

SCENE 23— Highly surrealistic; some highlights: "You won't have Nixon to kick around any more"; the Beast; Pat and the Checkers speech.

SCENE 24— A Fifth Avenue, New York City apartment. 1963. Seeds of a political return: Nixon meets Rockefeller and Kissinger.

SCENES 25–27— Scenes with Texas fat cats filled an air of menace and sleaze. Nixon leaves Dallas hurriedly as JFK's plane arrives. Scene 29 ends with the note: "Nixon takes one last look up at his fate written in the soft white clouds over Texas as in Scene 30 documentary footage shows the arrival of JFK and Jackie."

SCENES 31–38—Very short scenes dealing with Nixon's childhood, the funeral of Kennedy, the swearing in of Johnson.

SCENES 39–42—On the campaign trail for 1968 including a short but telling revelation of Pat's love for him.

SCENES 43–44—Establishes J. Edgar Hoover as a very behind-the-scenes operator.

SCENE 45—TV studio. A scene written for the film that is not based on fact. A black member of the audience tries to embarrass Nixon.

SCENES 46–49—Scenes at the La Costa Country Club and the racetrack. Scenes with a gangster named Roselli who's got something on Nixon; scenes that present Hoover and Tolson as two "old queens" with the strong implication that Hoover will make sure that "another radical" (Robert Kennedy) will not follow JFK into the White House. Nixon seems in tacit agreement to anything Hoover has in mind. We see "Beast" imagery again. The horse that Hoover is betting on "emits a devil's fire."

SCENES 50–52—Follow-up scenes to meeting Roselli at the racetrack in the second of which Nixon says, "We felt the invasion wouldn't work unless we got rid of Castro." Scene 52 is the murder of Robert Kennedy, a "radical" who won't follow "another radical" into the White House.

SCENES 53–54—The motif of death, no doubt suggested by Fawn Brodie's highly critical *Richard Nixon: The Shaping of His Character*. Brodie discusses the deaths of Nixon's brothers Harold and Arthur at great length and how Richard tried to be "three sons in one" to please his parents. The deaths of his brothers, both of whom were well liked (according to the film), provided the financial means for his education. The deaths of the well-liked Kennedy brothers also cleared Nixon's path for the White House.

SCENES 55–56—Arizona sanitarium and Nixon home. 1933. Scenes dealing with the death of his older brother Harold from tuberculosis. Mrs. Nixon says to Richard: "God has chosen thee to survive." Richard: "What about happiness, Mother?" Mrs. Nixon: "Thou must find peace at the center, Richard. Strength in this life. Happiness in the next."

SCENE 57—1968 Republican convention. A rousing Nixon speech. The crowd is with him. As an ironic counterpoint, we see a B-52 dropping napalm in a jungle.

SCENES 60–62—Scenes dealing with the escalation of the Vietnam war. Secretary of State Rogers: "It'd be a disaster for us, Mr. President. There's a lot of sympathy out there for Cambodia, a tiny Buddhist nation."

SCENE 63—Aboard the Presidential yacht *Sequoia*. News of student unrest. Nixon's startling decision to go to China. Nixon: "I can do this because I've spent my whole career building anti–Communist credentials." At the end of the scene, very angry, he threatens to "drop the big one."

SCENE 64—Shortly after on board the *Sequoia*. A very introspective scene in which Hopkins says some of Nixon's own words, words that have appeared in virtually every Nixon biography: "I think that's when it starts. When you're a kid. The laughs and snubs and slights you get because you're poor or Irish or Jewish or just ugly." These lines and the lines that follow in this long speech are among the most character-revealing Nixon ever uttered. At the end he says he cannot send condolences to the parents of the students killed at Kent State University.

SCENES 65–68—Dealing primarily with civil unrest, Nixon's defense of his China trip to the CIA; quoting Yeats' "The Second Coming" as continuity of the beast imagery.

SCENE 69—A domestic scene to imply that the Nixon marriage is asexual, not so subtly suggested by the screenwriters' use of Pat's adolescent nickname "Buddy," a term no one used after Pat's high school days.

SCENE 70—A short scene that further enshrines JFK through the speech of Manolo, Nixon's valet.

SCENE 71—The Lincoln Memorial just before dawn. One of the most important scenes in the film: THE NATURE OF THE BEAST IS REVEALED TO NIXON.

SCENES 72–74—The contrast of Hoover's chicanery and the preparations for Tricia's wedding.

SCENE 75—Nixon has a tirade about the Pentagon papers: "This administration is a Goddamn disaster."

SCENE 76—Backtracking. Hunt and Liddy and the creations of the plumbers.

SCENE 77—The break-in at Daniel Ellsberg's psychiatrist's office.

SCENE 78—Nixon in China with Mao; this scene has some humor.

SCENE 79—The bombing of Hanoi.

SCENES 80–86—Varied scenes of reaction to China trip, the machinations of the Texas fat cats, the death of Hoover, an assassination attempt on George Wallace which clears the field for Nixon in the 1972 election.

SCENES 87–91—January 1973 and other points in 1973. Nixon: "I can therefore announce that our long and tragic involvement in Vietnam is at an end." This is followed by scenes in which Nixon and advisors discuss the break-in at the psychiatrist's office, the firebombing of the Brookings Institution and the planting of left-wing literature in the apartment of Arthur Bremer, George Wallace's would-be assassin. In the order cited, Ehrlichman's *Witness to Power* and Emery's *Watergate* accuse Nixon himself of these schemes.

SCENES 92–94—A fictionalized scene with Hunt and Dean which Dean says took place "in spirit." Dean: "How the hell do you have the temerity to blackmail the President of the United States?" Hunt: "That's not the question, John. The question is: Why is he paying?" The last two scenes, both of which are very short, follow up this Dean-Hunt dialogue with a Dean speech to a passive, ruminative Nixon.

SCENE 95—A return to the immediately preceding scene after a shot of tape recorders. Nixon tells Dean to write and sign a full report on all he knows about Watergate. Dean senses he is being made a scapegoat and refuses.

SCENES 96–100—Scenes leading up to the resignation of two of his closest associates, Bob Haldeman and John Ehrlichman. (Ambrose TV interview: "He threw them overboard one by one.")

SCENE 101—A bitter scene between Pat and Dick. Pat: "Dick, sometimes I understand why they hate you."

SCENES 102–104—Dean goes before the committee and talks about the cover-up.

SCENE 105—Inside the White House with Soviet Premier Brezhnev on SALT II (Strategic Arms Limitations Talks). Brezhnev feels Nixon is "a man with little time left."

SCENES 106–110—Basically domestic scenes, in one of which Pat learns that "for the past three years Nixon has recorded virtually every conversation he has had ... even members of his own family." Scene 110 shows in the Bethesda Naval Hospital after he collapsed with pneumonia and phlebitis. We also have voice-overs of Special Prosecutor Cox "broadening his investigation" and of evidence being put forth on Vice-President Agnew being guilty of bribery.

SCENES 111–116—The Watergate web grows tighter.

SCENE 117—A bitter scene between Pat and Dick about the tapes. (In this scene Pat Nixon's character is drunk, a condition she never attained according to virtually everyone who knew her.)

SCENES 118–123—The fight for the tapes. (In many of the scenes after the hospital, Nixon flashes back to his past.) His claim of "executive privilege" is denied. "The House Judiciary Committee ... voted seven to eleven to recommend impeachment to the full House."

SCENE 124—A long scene with Haig and Kissinger. Haig and he know they must prepare for the end. Haig leaves the resignation to be signed. Kissinger comes forward. Kissinger: "History will treat you more kindly than your contemporaries." Nixon: "That depends on who writes the history." The famous scene of Nixon and Kissinger praying together. Kissinger says impishly: "This is not going to leak, is it?"

SCENE 125—Nixon is completely abject. Pat gives him a mother's love as "she slowly leads him up the grand staircase—into the shadows of history."

Last dialogue scene—Nixon delivers his last speech.

SCENE 127—Pat and Dick walk to the helicopter. Voice-over, then shots of Nixon's funeral. "Shenandoah" sung in the background, flashbacks of Hannah and Frank Nixon. A smiling 12-year-old Richard Nixon looking into the future.

NOTE: The video of *Nixon* released on July 9, 1996, has an additional five scenes (20 minutes) that were cut from the film. Stone stated that at least one of the scenes might be "off." "I'm not into details like that," he said.

True to his record of controversy (*Born on the Fourth of July, JFK* and *Natural Born Killers*) Oliver Stone stunned the public with his portrayal of the lives of Richard and Pat Nixon in *Nixon: An Oliver Stone Film*. Political analyst Chris Matthews succinctly called the highly annotated screenplay "a fraudulent use of sources. Zero history. Packed with lies." On two TV interviews (December 20 and 21, 1995) on America's Talking Network, Matthews, Nixon scholar Stephen E. Ambrose and Nixon speechwriter and law professor Ben Stein discussed the film heatedly.

Their principal bones of contention: The film insinuates that Nixon, while Vice-President under Eisenhower, was party to an assassination plot against Cuba's Fidel Castro. (Ambrose: "There were no assassination plots while Eisenhower was president.") The film also implies that Nixon had something to do—it seems deliberately ambiguous in the script—with the deaths of John and Robert Kennedy. (Stein: "It is an absolute blood libel to say that Nixon had anything to do with the deaths of the Kennedys.")

Other objections raised by this highly informed trio were the film's treatment of Pat Nixon, J. Edgar Hoover and the filmic Nixon's frequent use of obscenity. Briefly noted:

> MATTHEWS: They even tore into Pat Nixon and made her look like a lush.

> STEIN: The portrayal of Pat Nixon is obscenely false. Her speech about Alger Hiss is obscenely false.

> MATTHEWS: The treatment of J. Edgar Hoover as a raging queen is the most juvenile stuff I've ever seen in a major movie. It is irresponsible. [It's] the kind of rant you hear from schizoids on street corners who say they have receivers in their teeth from the CIA.

> AMBROSE: I've heard the tapes. I can remember Ron Ziegler [Nixon's press secretary] saying about a "Hell!" or "Damn!", "My God! What are people going to think when they see 'expletive deleted'?"

The *New York Times* (December 19, 1995) was among the first to voice protest: "Perhaps the most controversial element of the film is its suggestion that Nixon took part in planning a Castro assassination attempt that unwittingly fed forces that later brought about the assassination of President Kennedy."

There is considerable agreement, as many of the excerpts to follow will show, that in spite of some very moving moments dealing with Nixon's childhood and young manhood and a superb performance by Joan Allen as Pat Nixon, this is clearly a theme-driven work; it has an axe to grind. In real life, Nixon had many critics and there is no question that he deserves many of the criticisms, but Stone's film, which he called "an interpretation," may, as Stone admits, become a "misinterpretation" in the minds of some audience members. When questioned in the above *New York Times* article about the charge that President Johnson (in *JFK*) was responsible for the assassination of President Kennedy, Stone replied "with a 'Hey, it's only a movie' defense, saying: 'I am not responsible for the interpretation that the audience takes away. Sometimes it is misinterpreted.'" In the front matter of the *Nixon* script, Stone has a useful cover line: "Of course, there's license and speculation, but they are based on reasonable assumptions which we've discussed with highly reliable technical advisers who lived through the history we're recounting in the film." In regard to the many "reasonable assumptions" peppered throughout the film, Matthews and Ambrose called Stone "a liar" and "a fraud" respectively.

In a 1987 interview in *Film Comment*, Stone said in regard to the U.S. invasion of Cambodia: "If you want to protest, let's get a sniperscope and do Nixon." Eight years later with Nixon safely in his grave from natural causes and no threat of law suits — one cannot sue for the rights of the dead — Stone was able to "do" Nixon. It came out as a mixed bag critically and the box office reception was even more dismal than the last film in his Vietnam triptych, *Heaven and Earth*; yet, for both sound and unsound reasons, the Nixon portrait was often curiously involving in spite of some weighty objections to the eponymous performance. In the first paragraph of his *New York* magazine review (January 8, 1996) David Denby called Richard Nixon "the most wretched man who ever lived" ended his second paragraph with, "Yet there's a generous soulfulness here, an intimacy with defeat and rage, and a strain of shocked pity, particularly in the scenes between Dick and Pat. I was often moved."

Putting the performances aside, a December 24, 1995, *New York Times* editorial stated: "The real star of *JFK* and *Nixon* is Mr. Stone's psyche.... This brilliant film maker has harnessed his great story telling ability to an infantile political intelligence." According to film critics and political pundits, Stone's obsession is that the CIA, the FBI, the Mafia, the defense industry, Texas fat cats, oily Cubans and Wall Street form an all-encompassing veil of malevolence which Stone calls "the Beast" and this malevolence controls the world and holds humanity in thrall.

The idea owes a small debt to the Altman play and film *Secret Honor* and its shadowy cabal of wealthy entrepreneurs who supposedly bank-rolled Nixon in his early political career. *Nixon* also owes much to Stone's privileged but isolated childhood as the son of a wealthy Wall Street broker; and there is no small debt to Stone's 1960s sensibility and his virtual deification of JFK as the only man worthy to be president of the United States. (Ambrose: "Jack Kennedy was Stone's hero. If only the Camelot hero had lived, everything would be perfect in America. Stone's thinking is *that* juvenile"—AT Network, December 20, 1995.) In comparison, Nixon is the poor boy at the party, the one who has no power to charm, only the power to attack and manipulate. In addition to the *New York Times* editorial writer, many of the film's detractors pointed out aspects of Stone's own mindset in the film's treatment of Nixon. "Stone is no stranger to truculent self-pity. Nixon, moreover, may be the only politician whose paranoia matches his own" (J. Hoberman, *Village Voice*, December 26, 1995).

Nixon is without question a thesis film. (Ambrose: "Stone has an agenda. He wants a revolution in America.") With the seeds planted long before, Stone had been playing with the ideas of the script prior to Nixon's death in April 1994. Nixon's death freed Stone to move forward quickly. His early casting choices were odd: Tom Hanks, Jack Nicholson, Dustin Hoffman and Warren Beatty. All passed, regarding it, no doubt, as a highly dubious venture, but even odder was Sir Anthony Hopkins as the final choice. There was nothing in Hopkins' appearance or his speech pattern that could possibly suggest Richard Nixon. In fact, the Nixon–Hopkins speech is often a yammer that is out of character with Nixon's speech which was typically Californian, very clear and uninflected. Nor did Hopkins' usual approach to character building seem promising for so well known a figure. Hopkins has discussed acting as a series of "errors" that are to be corrected. According to critic Michael Medved (*New York Post*, December 20, 1995): "Anthony Hopkins ... neither sounds nor looks like the all-too-familiar Nixon. Hugging his own elbows, with his head pulled unnaturally into his shoulders, he more closely resembles a bad Ed Sullivan imitator." *Variety* (December 12, 1995), not so downbeat, said: "In his consummately actorly way, he convinces the viewer ... [but] one never forgets that this is an actor giving his best impression of a terribly famous man."

Mannerisms aside, the lack of depth in Hopkins' performance is not all his fault. The script has a non-linear development and underwent several drafts before and during production. Also, the script had to step lightly in treating the figures of the Nixon circle who were still alive (Rose Mary Woods, Spiro Agnew, John Ehrlichman, General Alexander Haig and Henry Kissinger).

Newsweek's cover story (Dec. 11, 1995) a week and a half before the release of the film contained a highly detailed one-page article by Ehrlichman in which he pointed out several blatant factual errors as well as the faulty footnoting in the published script, a script that the *Independent* (London, December 3, 1995), well in the minority, called "superb." Ehrlichman: "I fear this history *manqué* may become a cultural Cliff Notes to the Nixon era. That would be a shame." According to Ehrlichman, not only were many of the facts wrong, but those advisors from the Nixon circle who were hired by Stone, John Dean, Alexander Butterfield and John Sears were not close enough to Nixon to know anything beyond their own limited spheres. Dean, Ehrlichman said, "probably saw Nixon in person fewer than 15 times over three years," and Butterfield was "Nixon's office gofer" while Sears "had a brief tenure." None, in short, could speak authoritatively on the Nixon presidency. They were merely a kind of safety valve to lend ostensible authenticity to the script.

Stanley Kutler, whose *The Wars of Watergate* is frequently cited in Stone's footnotes (inaccurately, Kutler complains), wrote, "[Stone] doesn't get the history right. He just wants us to *think* he did" (*New York Post* December 18, 1995). In his introduction and interview Stone had said many times, "There is no intention here to revise history." Yet, as Prof. Ambrose, no Nixon idolater himself, has said repeatedly, Stone "has an agenda ... he hates America." Stone wants his own vision of the second half of the 20th century to prevail. In spite of his disavowals, Stone is re-writing history. He had Warner Bros. "legitimize" *JFK* by sending out *JFK* study guides. He had the Disney Corporation do the same for *Nixon* (*Wall Street Journal*, February 13, 1996). Such practices do not seem far removed from the great German and Soviet propaganda machines; the only difference is that despite Stone's talent he is no match for Leni Riefenstahl and Sergei Eisenstein artistically — and, fortunately for the public, Stone lives in a free society where his ideas can be challenged. "Taken together, *JFK* and *Nixon* represent Mr. Stone's effort to rescue John F. Kennedy from the facts of his short life. Mr. Stone was too young to live in Camelot, so he serves by laundering its legend" (*New York Times* editorial, December 24, 1995).

Maureen Dowd's essay "Nix *Nixon*—Tricky Pix" on the op-ed page of the *New York Times* (December 21, 1995) is particularly insightful: "Perhaps every society gets the mythmaker it deserves.... A culture that confuses celebrity with value, historical knowledge with repressed memory, gets Stone. Artful falsehood is more dangerous than artless falsehood, because fewer people can see through it. [Stone] gloms on to whole big sections of recent history and filters everything through one unproven prism: That JFK wanted to withdraw from Vietnam and that he was murdered for it by the System.... Oh, for the day we won't have Oliver Stone to kick around anymore."

Shortly before, *Newsday* columnist Martin Schram was invited to a pre-release screening of *Nixon*, Oliver Stone was interviewed by John Powers of the *Washington Post*. Stone asked Powers: "'Why do they hate me so much? Do you think it's me they hate — or my work?' The answer, of course, is probably both. We hate to be deceived; we hate the deception and deceiver; just before the lights dimmed, he asked his audience to grant one request: 'I ask your tolerance.... Although many of you bring much baggage in your suspicions of Richard Nixon — and of me — I ask you to suspend your judgment.'" Schram's conclusion: "IT TAKES ONE TO KNOW ONE" (*Newsday*, December 27, 1995).

While Dowd and Schram and many others attacked the film on intellectual and historical grounds and had serious questions about Stone's intentions, John Simon (*National Preview*, February 12, 1996) attacked Stone's artistic integrity: "Oliver Stone's *Nixon* is very small, and not especially new potatoes. Stone and his sundry writers and consultants cannot make up their minds about what to think of Nixon: conspirator or political wizard, flawed superman or inflated opportunist, marked by a hapless childhood or unlucky loser in Washington's intriguing derby? Object for pity, terror, or grudging admiration. This is not the same thing as creative ambiguity, where the filmmaker sees all sides of a man and presents him in the paradoxical and total round. Rather, it is a matter of vacillation, inconsistency trying to have it too many ways — not multivalent wisdom but shapelessy fuzzy thinking... Excess is like mother's milk to Stone. Better yet. Like liquor to a drunkard."

In his *New Republic* review (January 22, 1996), Stanley Kauffmann wrote: "The film does not become an artistic whole; it remains the examination of characteristics." The *Times* (London) wrote: "Hopkins impersonates but never becomes the tormented politician, and Stone outdoes himself in tiring razzle dazzle. It lasts a very long three hours" (February 21, 1996).

Like the *New York Times*, *Newsday* devoted a great deal of coverage to *Nixon*. "Special correspondent" Dimitri K. Simes of the Nixon Center for Peace and Freedom wrote: "After Stone reportedly deleted, from earlier scripts, clear references to Nixon giving the go-ahead for the assassination of John F. Kennedy and George Wallace, the plot ceased to hold together. The references — removed after complaints from Nixon's alleged co-conspirator, former CIA Director Richard Helms, who, unlike Nixon, is still alive and could have sued for libel — were totally without foundation but were central to Stone's initial effort to explain what the 37th president 'really' had to hide during Watergate. Further, the characters — particularly Anthony Hopkins as Nixon — are unpersuasive.... Stone's *Nixon* is so fundamentally flawed it cannot be taken seriously." (January 24, 1996) One month prior to Simes' article, *Newsday* published a not particularly insightful but generally favorable review headed by three stars.

There were few raves for *Nixon* and no lines at box offices. On January 30, 1996, Elaine Dutka of the *Los Angeles Times* wrote: "It was one of the higher profile movies of the season. But in a month of release, Oliver Stone's *Nixon* has taken in only $13.2 million at the box office — far less than the Walt Disney Studios and the filmmaker had anticipated." In a later portion of the article, film historian Richard Schickel gave what he considered one of the reasons for the film's failure: "Oliver Stone is a masterful, kinetic filmmaker who made the mistake of throwing in some cockamamie stuff about Nixon and the Kennedy assassination. Instead of talking about entertainment, the critics focused once again, on 'a filmmaker's obligation to the Truth!'"

Dave Kehr of the *New York Daily News* (December 20, 1995) summed up the entire enterprise in very strong language: "The thin line between tragedy and farce is crossed, re-crossed and finally obliterated in Stone's *Nixon*, a film that bears the same relationship to traditional movie biography that LSD does to aspirin. Stone's Nixon resembles no living person so much as the cocaine-crazed Al Pacino in the Stone-authored *Scarface* of 1983. This Nixon turns out to be a Kennedy conspiracy buff and the notorious 18 minutes of tape are said to contain his theories on the subject — Stone creates a Nixon who fits snugly into his portrait gallery of screwball American martyrs: Jim Morrison (*The Doors*), Jim Garrison (*JFK*) and fictional outlaws Mickey and Mallory (*Natural Born Killers*)." Because of its obvious polemics, *Time* (December 18, 1995) called *Nixon* "a $43 million term paper" whose "Nixon was a tragicomic figure [who] doesn't need Stone's demonizing or mythologizing touch. His saga is familiar from a quillion docudramas and *Saturday Night Live* skits."

To re-enforce the polemics, Stone featured, as usual, endlessly cascading shots of the 1960s, other documentary and pseudo-documentary footage, the White House shot at odd angles with threatening clouds racing above it, a (mostly) non-linear story line, ominous music and artless borrowings from other sources, such as a dinner scene with Pat and Richard that echoes the breakfast scene in *Citizen Kane* with Orson Welles and Ruth Warrick. There is also much artless theme-driven dialogue such as Pat's saying "I remember Alger Hiss. I know how ugly you can be — you're capable of anything" (p. 289), or the theme-driven lines, their red lights flashing, Nixon gives to a co-ed at the Lincoln Memorial, dealing with the Beast (p. 222):

> NIXON (to Haldeman): She understands something it's taken me 25... years in politics to understand. The CIA, the Mafia, the Wall Street bastards...
>
> HALDEMAN: Sir?
>
> NIXON: ... "The Beast." A 19-year-old kid. She understands the nature of "the Beast." She called it a wild animal.

As any glance at the cast list would indicate, *Nixon* featured a cast of highly accomplished actors, among whom Joan Allen's portrayal of Pat won unanimous praise. Among those who acquitted themselves particularly well were Mary Steenburgen as Mother Nixon, Tony Goldwyn as Harold Nixon, David Barry Gray as Nixon at 19, Fyvush Finkel as Murray Chotiner, Nixon's first campaign manager, Paul Sorvino as Kissinger, Ed Harris as E. Howard Hunt and Corey Carrier as Nixon at 12. Good actors all! In addition to adverse criticism, Hopkins received praise as well: "Once the initial period of adjustment is overcome, Hopkins *is* Nixon. It's not imitation, it's alchemy. Hopkins grants us access to Nixon's wounded soul, in a way that probably the real man never could. He captures the physical awkwardness, the staccato rages, the chilling emotional repression and bad-salesman's bluster. It's a daredevil performance that teeters on the edge of buffoonery without ever falling over" (*Newsweek* December 11, 1995). High praise as well from the *Christian Science Monitor*: "Anthony Hopkins' superb portrayal ... seamlessly blends Nixon's physical traits with the actor's own interpretive brilliance" (December 20, 1995).

Much has been written by critics and by Stone himself that Nixon's life is like a Shakespearean tragedy. There are many reasons why this is *not* so, the first of which is the supreme articulation of his dilemma given to each tragic hero by the world's greatest dramatic poet. The second is the purging of emotion and the cleansing of the spirit at the end of the hero's story. At the end of Nixon's life and at the end of the film there is an acceptance of Nixon's very human failings and an acknowledgment of many of his accomplishments, but in both regards, a puzzle and a remoteness remain. This is not so with Lear and Hamlet and other great Shakespearean heroes. In Nixon there is a sense of incompleteness, there will be a sense of something inexplicable and not quite whole, a deep hurt, forever inside. A third point, a minor one, but one that should be remembered by those who call Nixon a figure of Shakespearean proportions is that Shakespeare's heroes are all patrician whereas Nixon, in spite of his high intelligence, always remained *bourgeois*. In fact, although he decried it at times, he was often able to use his humble background to good political advantage.

While his life is not of Shakespearean dimension, there is one great playwright whose works have some uncanny parallels to the life of Richard Nixon. He also has some correspondences to Ibsen's master builder Solness who used the work of others to advance himself, who was often cold to his wife, a man who reached far beyond his grasp and fell to his doom because of it. He has some correspondences to Ibsen's John Garbriel Borkman, the title character in one of Ibsen's plays about "the coldness of the heart," a man who is forced to live in isolation because of a crime he committed years before. Nixon also had some of the sternness and idealism of Ibsen's Brand and some of the power of deception and "covering up" and self-serving of Bernick in *Pillars of Society*. He also has some of the dreaminess and self-delusion of Peer Gynt, "the life lie," as Ibsen called it. True to the model of an Ibsenite figure, not *hero*, man must be *in* society, not *above* it. Being above it or attempting to be above it is always an illusion and leads to failure. In a sense, Ibsen's plays are morality plays as, in another sense, Nixon's life is a morality play, not a tragedy. It lacks the stature to be a tragedy, but it *could* be an Ibsenite social drama. If, however, we were to seek a parallel figure to Nixon in a social comedy, the muddled, obsessive middle-aged men of Moliere would not be off the mark.

"Narrating [the film's] epilogue, [Stone] points out why history books will give Nixon more respect than his contemporaries did, lists the number of ex–Presidents and

First Ladies who attended his bizarre state funeral, counts the books he wrote, and poses the question: Was Nixon as bad as everyone thinks? All of this anticlimactic bilge is accompanied by the Mormon Tabernacle Choir singing a beatific "Shenandoah." Is this supposed to be funny [or] is Mr. Stone getting the last cynical laugh?" (*New York Observer* December 25, 1995).

The effects of the film are meant to last long after the final strains of "Shenandoah" have faded away. In an impassioned *New York Post* (January 23, 1996) article entitled "Not the Nixon I Knew," Henry Kissinger wrote: "Oliver Stone's *Nixon* raises an issue that goes far beyond the film's fairness to Richard Nixon: the responsibility of the motion picture industry itself.... Truth, as John Stuart Mill argued, in the end prevails in the competitive marketplace of ideas. But what if public discourse becomes warped by powerful engines of myth, big budgets and outright falsehoods?"

A final word from Chris Matthews, a no-bones-about-it centrist Democrat and no Nixon idolater (America's Talking Network, *Politics*, December 20, 1995): "This movie is full of crap. Richard Nixon comes off as a mensch in spite of it."

In spite of its box office failure, in the spring of 1996, Graphic Zone issued an enhanced CD of the *Nixon* soundtrack. This was a spinoff of a CD-ROM biographical project from Graphic Zone begun before the release of the film. This material did even less well than the film.

Here's a sampling of critical opinion:

"Where *JFK* discoursed on history as conspiracy, Oliver Stone's de facto follow up explores character as destiny, copying *Citizen Kane* in its life-spinning search for the soul of Richard Nixon. What results is far too sympathetic to please liberal tastemakers, who may be too offended to acknowledge that the three-hour film is tremendously involving, with a humanity and a humor that mark definite strides in Stone's already remarkable work. Then there's Anthony Hopkins' uncannily convincing Nixon and a constantly surprising supporting cast that includes Joan Allen, Paul Sorvino and James Woods. Not perfect, surely, but as challenging and ambitious as Hollywood moviemaking gets."—*New York Press*, January 31, 1996.

"[Hopkins gives] a hauntingly brilliant Nixon interpretation."—*Vanity Fair*, September 1995.

"Oliver Stone's 191-minute sprawl over the life and times of the ex-president is uncharacteristically subdued and almost melancholy. Anthony Hopkins gives a commanding central performance—it's a small paradox to have this most magnetic of actors playing a thoroughly un-charismatic man.... He has the gestures down pat: the hunched shoulders, the stiffness of manner, the sudden disconcerting flashes of teeth—as one character remarks, it's as though his smile and his face are never in the same place at the same time."—*The Independent* (London), February 22, 1996.

"[T]he script is, on balance, sympathetic."—*Premiere*, December 1995.

"*Nixon* is mesmerizing even when it rambles incoherently, cramming its confusing indictment of the 37th President of the United States with everything from Tricia's Rose Garden wedding to the shameless manipulation of 58 million television viewers with the corny Checkers speech."—*New York Observer,* December 25, 1995.

"It's one thing for Stone to create imaginary events in which a public figure participates. To a great extent that's what docudramas consist of. Thus, while scenes of Nixon's private life with his wife Pat, have understandable protests from Nixon's daughters, they're within bounds. So are scenes of Nixon alone, sloshing down drink after drink and listening compulsively to the tapes that doomed his presidency. And so are scenes of Nixon's strange relationship with his mother, even one in which Nixon as a boy asks her to treat him as a 'faithful dog.' These may not ring true — to me, they don't — but Stone is free to speculate about Nixon's private affairs. He's not entitled to rewrite history. Stone himself says so. 'There is no intention to revise history,' he writes in a note on the first page of the screenplay. Yet that's exactly what he does in … a 1968 TV appearance before a studio audience assembled by his presidential campaign staff.… What Stone has done is falsify an historic event. It's like doing a movie bio of Lincoln and changing the words of the Gettysburg Address."— Fred Barnes, *National Review*, January 22, 1996.

"This film is not just a disservice to history but a disservice to the United States of America."— Stephen E. Ambrose, "Brinkley," December 24, 1995.

"This is sophomoric Marxism circa 1950. The gross simplification of how and by whom the United States is run misses the complexities of the system and assigns to the unseen and scarcely defined Beast an evil intent … without a single piece of evidence of serious thought or study by Stone."— Stephen E. Ambrose, *Journal of American History*, March 1996.

"Stone knows that an artist has to stand against censorship of any kind. He just doesn't yet see that artists have to be accountable too."— novelist John Grisham, *Vanity Fair*, July 1996.

Gore Vidal to Oliver Stone as quoted in the *New York Post* (July 2, 1996): "I'd never work for you. You distorted Kennedy; you distorted Nixon, and you lack the one quality a director needs most — talent!"

Forbidden Hollywood
(satiric cabaret, 1996)

Created and written by Gerard Allessandrini. Produced by John Freedson, Harriet Yellin and Jon B. Platt at the Triad Theater, 158 West 72nd Street, New York City. Cast: Fred Barton, Toni DiBuono, Michael McGrath, Christine Pedi and Lance Roberts.

With the dearth of new Broadway shows in 1996, Gerard Alessandrini, creator of many *Forbidden Broadway* revues, was forced, happily so for audiences, to create a new series entitled *Forbidden Hollywood*.

One of the sketches of the first edition was a send-up of Oliver Stone's *Nixon* with the real-life husband and wife team of Michael McGrath and Toni DiBuono as Richard and Pat Nixon. To the duet of Lerner and Loewe's "I Remember It Well" from *Gigi*, they reminisced about Tricia's wedding, the Bay of Pigs, washing Hoover's wigs, praying for peace and bombing Hanoi and Watergate, after which Pat announced that she was Deep Throat. The sketch was amusing, but since the film was a box office failure, it did not have the impact of the parodies of more popular films like *The Bridges of Madison County* and *Pulp Fiction* that a majority of the audience had seen and could relate to.

Nixon Audio Tapes (1996)

"Nixon fans! Let down by Oliver Stone's historic drama? Take heart: Nixon's coming back, in glorious monaural. Yes, every word Richard Nixon ever recorded from February 1971 to July 1973. Not just Watergate's biggest hits ... but the whole enchilada: 3,200 hours of secretly recorded Nixon White House tapes. After an expected settlement is reached, they will slowly be released." — *New York Times*, March 31, 1996.

Nixon Audio Tapes (1996)

(The actual 37,000 hours of secret tapes, available for listening at the National Archives, College Park, Maryland.)

Thanks to the indefatigable Stanley J. Kutler, Fox Professor of American Institutions at the University of Wisconsin and author of the definitive Watergate history *The Wars of Watergate* (1990), all 37,000 hours of secret Nixon tapes from the White House, his office in the old Executive Office Building and at Camp David were made available to the public. Only 63 hours (enough to lead to the certainty of impeachment) had been released prior to the November 1996 release of 201 hours of tapes related to Watergate. The entire span of tapes covers 1971 through July 1973.

The 1996 decision came 21 years after Congress demanded that the tapes were to be made public. Kutler sued for the remaining tapes in 1992. In 1993, Nixon was granted a court order protecting whatever personal conversations that might have been recorded.

The final agreement was reached through "a monumental breakthrough" arrived at by Nixon's estate, Professor Kutler working through an advocacy group called Public Citizen and the National Archives. "Mr. Kutler said the archives had engaged in a 'cover-up' by refusing to acknowledge the existence of hundreds of hours of tapes" (*New York Times*, April 13, 1996).

After resigning the presidency, Nixon fought tenaciously to thwart public scrutiny of the remaining material, but as of November 1996, the public had the opportunity to hear what for over two decades only the discussants and a few archivists had heard. The tapes were to be made public in segments accompanied by 27,000 pages of notes citing dates, locations, participants and topics. Two hundred seventy hours from the White House Cabinet Room had a release date of April 1998, the remaining segments "by the turn of the century ... [with some] deletions that may be made on the ground of national security and privacy" (*New York Times*, April 13, 1996).

"John H. Taylor, director of the Nixon Library and Birthplace and co-executor of the estate, said that the Nixon daughters took the lead in the decision, 'not only because they believe in disclosure, but also [because] historians will be apt to conclude that the achievements far outweigh the tragedy.'" — *Newsday*, April 13, 1996.

Character Above All
(TV panel discussion, 1996)

Directed by David Deutsch. Produced by Robert Wilson for MacNeil/Lehrer Productions. Moderator: Jim Lehrer. Executive producer: Al Vecchione. PBS–Channel 13, New York, 9–10 P.M., May 29, 1996. Taped at the House of Burgesses, Williamsburg, Virginia.

Panelists: Ben Bradlee, Peggy Noonan, David McCullough, Hendrik Hertzberg, Robert Dallek, Stephen Ambrose, Michael Beschschloss, Tom Wicker and James Cannon.

In reply to Lehrer's question "What is Presidential character?", David McCullough said, "The courage of one's convictions." Stephen Ambrose added, "Trust is also critical."

A few of the observations made about Nixon, all of which leave questions in the mind of the viewer:

> McCULLOUGH: If Nixon had only gone before the public and said "I'm sorry," he would have stayed in office.

> AMBROSE: Dick did not have respect for others. You've got to have respect for the people you've left behind. I don't think Nixon had that.

> PEGGY NOONAN: Nixon said only two kinds of men run for Presidency: One who wants to be big, and one who wants to do big things.

> TOM WICKER: Nixon cut a lot of corners, but I find it very hard to believe that he was an evil man.

"An hour with nine such close observers is bound to be illuminating, if not, as it turns out, blindingly so.... The exception to the happy talk is Richard M. Nixon: the best anyone says of him is that he wasn't evil. Well, nobody's perfect."—Walter Goodman, *The New York Times*, May 29, 1996.

Richard Nixon: Man and President An A & E Biography (documentary, 1996)

100 minutes. Narrated by Jack Smith. Written by Alan Goldberg. Produced by Lisa Zeff and Goldberg. ABC News production and the A & E Network; available from the New Video Group, 126 Fifth Avenue, New York, New York 10011.

A very good Nixon overview, artfully and richly illustrated, this features excellent musical accompaniment and a dignified narration with the pluses and the minuses in just about the right places with the right emphases. The segments dealing with "the kitchen debate" and the California defeat are particularly illuminating. Stephen E. Ambrose contributes mightily.

Nixon's Nixon (play, 1995–1996)

A full-length play in one act by Russell Lees. Directed by Jim Simpson. Sets and lighting by Kyle Chepulis. Costumes by Daniele Hollywood. Sound by Mike Nolan. Projections by Abigal Simon and Tal Yarden. Productions supervisors: Laura Kravets Gautier and Ira Mont. Presented by the Manhattan Class Company, Robert LuPone and Bernard Telsey, executive directors. "Made possible in part with public funds from the National Endowment for the Arts and the New York State Council on the Arts." MMC Theater, 120 West 28th Street, New York. Acting edition published by Dramatists Play Service, 440 Park Avenue South, New York 10016. (Opened October 4, 1995, re-opened March 13, 1996). Cast: *Richard M. Nixon* Gerry Bamman; *Henry Kissinger* Steve Mellor.

> KISSINGER: You have to be an actor.
>
> NIXON: God, yes. This job, you have to be. On the world stage and so on.
>
> KISSINGER: The press. To be properly duplicitous —
>
> NIXON: You've got to portray — you've got to believe —
>
> KISSINGER: The true statesman, he's a chameleon. He shades his opinions, even facts, to draw in and seduce his opponents, occasionally, I even convince myself.
>
> NIXON: It's more than that, Henry. It's that ... the burdens of the position. If you show your true self, you're standing there with your fly wide open. If you show your true self, your weaknesses are all.
>
> KISSINGER: You've got to wear the proper Greek mask.
>
> NIXON: Yes.
>
> KISSINGER: You've got to be larger than life.
>
> NIXON: That's it exactly. Because you've got to play the great man of the state. You've got to play the wise leader, the brilliant schemer. The ruthless murderer. But with no backstage. The mask gets stuck.

According to several biographers, notably Bruce Mazlish in his *In Search of Nixon: A Psychohistorical Inquiry* (1972), Richard Nixon had "role-playing ability." He was an amateur actor in such well-known plays as Ayn Rand's *The Night of January 16th*, John Drinkwater's *Bird in Hand*, George Kelly's *Philip Goes Forth* and Kaufman and Woollcott's *The Dark Tower*. Nixon, so say his detractors, carried these abilities over into his personal and political lives. *Nixon's Nixon* is a very good example of this theory being put to trenchant satiric use.

The puzzling title of Lees' trim two-hander was used earlier as a reference to Nixon's slippery second banana Spiro Agnew on page 585 of Herbert Parmet's formidable *Richard Nixon and His America* (1990), which also states that Nixon "is familiar as an American version of that ancient Roman conspirator Catiline," the hero of Ibsen's first play, a blank verse tragedy in three acts. As noted elsewhere in this volume, an examination of many of the major Ibsen plays will suggest Nixon as a parallel figure to several of Ibsen's leading male characters, particularly Solness and John Gabriel

Robert Vaughn as Nixon in *Nixon's Nixon* tryout.

Borkman, but there are many other correspondences an interested reader can find as well. Nixon himself shows familiarity with Ibsen by referring to Peer Gynt, a character to whom he corresponds in ambition and self-delusion. Nixon cites Peer Gynt in two of his later books, *In the Arena* (1990) and the posthumously published *Beyond Peace* (1994).

In an interview for this book, Russell Lees said he was unaware of Parmet's use of the term and simply meant his title to suggest Nixon as a player of many political and social roles since that is the device that motivates the latter portion of the play which has Nixon and Kissinger pretending to be the world leaders who took part in the Nixon–Kissinger triumphs. Lees also stated that much of the coarse language of the play was made up. "The transcript's use of 'expletive deleted' gave me lots of room," he said. This statement sheds light on Stephen E. Ambrose's criticism of the coarse language in Oliver Stone's *Nixon*. Middle-class men of Nixon's generation used mild scatology and sacrilege in anger. They did not use obscenity. The extremely coarse language of *Nixon* is the language of Oliver Stone and his fellow writers, not Richard Nixon. (This is also true of Russell Lees.)

The play begins at 10:00 P.M., August 7, 1974, in the Lincoln Sitting Room of the White House. The play has no intermission and the action is continuous during its 80-minute length. As the lights come up, Nixon, his back to the audience, is grandly conducting a tape of Tchaikovsky's Fifth Symphony. He is in a deep quandary about his future and is unaware that Henry Kissinger, whom he has summoned, has entered the room. Kissinger and he are to discuss Nixon's possible resignation. To Nixon, resignation means humiliation; to Kissinger, it means the almost certain loss of prestige if Nixon's successor, Ford, dismisses him as Secretary of State and appoints the far less experienced Alexander Haig in his place. Therefore, each man has something at stake, and, in both cases, it is their place in history. If nothing else, this scrappy, masculine play is about two colossal egos who drink too much, yell too much and slaver over their past glories even as they know those glories are fading — so much so that as they hunger for the past, they re-live their triumphs with Brezhnev and Mao in what becomes a bittersweet riff on recrimination peppered with ribald humor and bracing self-knowledge. Each character has many poignant as well as nastily comic moments e.g. Nixon's grandiose idea of running for Pope as Kissinger tries to hold the reins on Nixon's marathon drinking — although the drinking, even by 1996, was fast becoming a pseudo-historical cliché. Yet, in the larger-than-life, highly theatrical terms in which the play is written, the drinking is true to the wickedly funny heart that beats within this deliciously wayward play. Toward the end of the piece, the dynamic of the play goes way over the top, *Dr. Strangelove* fashion, as the two inebriates decide to create an international crisis, so that Nixon can leave office as a hero. Their self-deluded elation is short-lived, however, and the play ends on a note of dignity and reflection.

Nixon's Nixon is often presented as surrealistic farce, as it was, for the most part, in its two New York productions. But while the script is often bitingly clever, it also has a human dimension. All of Nixon's scar tissue is in the play, as it should be in a satire, but Lees brings forth enough of the man, in spite of Nixon's politician's mask, to have him step aside, take a hard look at himself and accept self-knowledge. In doing so, Lees created a play that entertains, reveals and prompts thought — three very tall orders for any 80-minute play. Nixonphiles will be appalled at its language, its drunkenness and its often grotesque air. True, there are things to be appalled about — in the play and in the life — but judged in terms of the author's vision, *Nixon's Nixon* has a clarity and leanness of form that places it among the four or five works of true artistic merit in this volume that annotates over 100 plays and films. Whatever one thinks of Richard Nixon, this highly accomplished work will, like Richard Nixon, have more than one life.

After several staged readings, the last of which was at Mitzi Pazer's Playwright's Theater of the Hamptons (Long Island) starring the Nixon of Robert Vaughn (himself a Ph.D. in political science), the play was presented in New York at the 99-seat MCC Theater in the Chelsea district for a short run in the autumn of 1995. It reopened at the larger Westside Theater on March 12, 1996. In spite of an excellent press, it closed in May, prompting its new producer, Gerald Schoenfeld, chairman of the Shubert Organization, to say: "*Nixon's Nixon* was never able to attract an audience, for reasons which I cannot understand." Possibly the theater-going public in New York, never a pro–Nixon town, already sated with Hopkins' Nixon and Bridges' Nixon, was unwilling to support another Nixon, no matter how great its artistic worth. *Nixon's Nixon*, definitely among the very best works dealing with Nixon, did not have the success it deserved. It should also be noted that both New York productions — actually the same production but in two different venues — were snappily directed by Jim Simpson.

What follows is a sampling of critical comments:

"You can judge a country's culture by its political satire: how witty, how widespread, how devastating. On this scale, American culture ranks somewhere between Outer Mongolia and Burkina Faso. Which is why *Nixon's Nixon* is welcome, even if it's longer and less focused than it might be..." — John Simon, *New York*, October 16, 1995.

"[A] blissfully funny and sometimes cruel fiction..." — Vincent Canby, *New York Times*, March 13, 1996.

"Transcendent icon that he was, Nixon has long been a lightning rod for cheap humor. Often, the name alone is enough to illicit an easy laugh. Lees resists any such temptation, and the result is a droll and savvy triumph. Nixon and Kissinger have never been better." — Sam Whitehead, *Time Out New York*, October 11, 1995.

"The Nixon of *Nixon's Nixon* is a rounded portrait: a powerful President, a formidable statesman, a wily politician, a foul-mouthed adversary, a wounded animal loathing himself as the instrument of his destruction and a father heart-wrenching in his acknowledgment of his betrayal of his daughter Julie, who had come to his defense." — Lawrence Van Gelder, *New York Times*, October 14, 1995.

"*Nixon's Nixon* helps to answer the question Russell Lees puts in Nixon's mouth: 'What will they say of me in a hundred years?'" — *Backstage*, October 13, 1995.

"Director Jim Simpson creates such breathtaking rhythms of speech and movement that Nixon and Kissinger are never just two suits on a sofa; words and actions ripple gently like a stream through confessions of boyhood wounds, or sear and char like a defoliant as two naked egos go for broke. Of this pathological liaison playwright Lees has crafted not a political cartoon but a double portrait in the tradition of Goya or Grosz..."—Margaret Spillane, *Nation*, December 11, 1995.

"The MCC Theater production of Russell Lees's satire, which proved an off–Broadway hit last fall, has transferred for a commercial run to the larger Westside Theater/Downstairs. And thanks to Lees's acerbic vision, Jim Simpson's directing, and the subtly exaggerated portrayals of Gerry Bamman (Nixon) and Steve Mellor (Kissinger), *Nixon's Nixon* continues to be sharp, funny, political theater."—Alexis Greene, *Theater Week*, April 1, 1996.

"Mr. Nixon wanted to become Richard the Great. He wanted nothing short of world peace and a prosperous, happy America. He was brought down by his own hubris, his own actions, by his own character. This is tragedy. Whenever Mr. Nixon lapsed into self-description, he talked about struggle. It was struggle that gave meaning, not victory. Given that he never abandoned the struggle, it can be assumed that he died a happy man, a man at peace with himself."—Stephen E. Ambrose, *Wall Street Journal*, April 25, 1994.

As the reader can see, much of the cleverly developed spine of *Nixon's Nixon* is suggested by the real Nixon's ability to play a role, to, as Kissinger says in the play, "wear the proper Greek mask." Nixon himself had always been an avid and wide-ranging reader. He had read Shakespeare, Ibsen and the Greek tragedies. Four years before his death, Nixon said: "Two thousand years ago, Sophocles wrote, 'One must wait until the evening to see how splendid the day has been.'"

D.C. Follies (TV satire, 1996)

60 minutes. Written and directed by Christopher Koch. Comments by Robert Klein. AMC "Special," October 15, 1996.

An amusing look at campaign politics.

"The ground covered includes negative campaigning and fawning journalists. There are candidates who entertain: Truman and Nixon on the piano, Clinton on the sax. And in the sharpest segment, there are candidates who parade their household pets: Roosevelt had Fala; Nixon had Checkers; Dole had Leader: Clinton had Socks."—*New York Times*, October 15, 1996.

Humble Birth: Key to the Presidency (TV panel, 1996)

60 minutes. Chicago Humanites Festival. Bill Kurtis, moderator. WBBM-Chicago. Original date: October 18, 1996.

Panel of historians: Stephen E. Ambrose (biographer of Nixon and Eisenhower), Roger Ferrell (biographer of Truman and Harding), Robert Remini (biographer of

Jackson) and Ed Burke, author of *Inside the Wigwam*, a study of all the national conventions held in Chicago.

Ambrose: "I think Ike and Dick were born in the nineteenth and twentieth century equivalents of a log cabin. This was poverty. His father put it up with his own hands. There was Bible reading every night in both homes. It was Dick Nixon's fate to spend his early career in hand to hand combat with Jack Kennedy."

Bob Hope ... Laughing with the Presidents (TV variety show, 1996)

60 minutes. Directed by Daniel Helfgott. Written by Gene Perret, Martha Bolton and Daniel Helfgott. Produced by Linda Hope. Appearances by Julie and David Eisenhower. NBC, November 23, 1996.

"The clips assembled here form a kitschy mosaic of American pop culture images from the Second World War to the present. Covering more than 50 years of Hope's hijinks with 11 presidents, *Laughing with the Presidents* has more than enough material to interest members of all generations."—*New York Daily News*, November 21, 1996.

Book Notes (TV author interview, 1997)

60 minutes. Brian Lamb, host. Robert Ferrell, guest. C-SPAN, January 12, 1997.

Professor Ferrell and Brian Lamb discussed Ferrell's recently published biography of Warren Harding. In discussing the presidency, Ferrell stated that Nixon should have gone to jail because of Watergate.

Nixon in China Act III (concert performance, 1997)

EOS Festival II "Minimalism and the Baroque," concert at Alice Tully Hall, Lincoln Center, New York City, January 22, 1997. James Maddalena of the original Houston Grand Opera cast appeared again as Nixon. Juliana Gondek was Pat.

Investigative Reports: Secret White House Tapes (TV documentary, 1997)

60 minutes. Written, produced, directed by Carol Fleisher. William Doyle, co-writer and producer. Bill Kurtis, executive producer and host. A & E Network, March 29, 1997.

"President Nixon, whose mistrust of the world at large ran deep, had voice-activated recording equipment installed all over the place. The famous tale of his tapes, including the famous 18½ minute gap (which the program attributes to the President's technical incompetence), is briskly retold.

"The narration, delivered by Bill Kurtis, can be portentous, but historians and former officials provide context, and effective use is made of newsreels. With Nixon's departure, the microphones were ripped out, leaving some scars on the walls of the Oval Office, and so far as is known, they have not been replaced. Still, the next time you're invited to sleep over in the Lincoln Bedroom, you might want to be careful of your pillow talk."—*New York Times*, March 29, 1997.

Retrospective on Watergate (TV panel, 1997)

60 minutes. Sponsored by the American Bar Association at the Boca Raton Resort and Club. C-SPAN. Recorded February 7, 1997; broadcast March 31, 1997. Available from American Bar Association, 750 North Lake Shore Drive, Chicago, Illinois 60611.

Among the panelists: Leonard Garment, Bob Woodward, Ben Bradlee. Among their comments: "Watergate created a culture of distrust" (Garment). "We are all somewhat prisoners of Watergate" (Woodward). "There's more cover-up now than there ever was before" (Bradlee).

Saturday Night Live (TV variety, 1997)

One minute sketch, NBC, April 12, 1997.

Nixon as cartoon Superman. Checkers as cartoon Robin.
Nixon to Checkers as they shoot off into the sky: "I am not a crook. I'm a killing machine. Checkers *away!*"

"Nixon": The Film as History and Commentary (TV panel, 1997)

60 minutes. Sponsored by the American Historical Society at the New York Hilton. Available on tape from Film and History, Popular Culture Center; RR3; Box 80; Oklahoma 74020. Recorded January 4, 1997, and broadcast on C-SPAN II on Memorial Day, May 26, 1997.

Basically a Q and A with Oliver Stone, who did not present a smooth or convincing defense of the merits of *Nixon* as a work of art or as a commercial venture.

Stone: ...Nixon's "daughters certainly haven't told the truth.... We're not saying (Nixon) was an alcoholic. We're just saying he didn't drink very well."

The Cold War (TV panel, 1997)

45 minutes. Panel discussion with Julie and David Eisenhower and Sergei Khrushchev. University of California at Irvine; Hugh Hewitt, host. Broadcast on C-SPAN at various times in June 1997.

Julie Nixon discussed her father and his role in ending the cold war, with additional comments from her husband and the son of Nikita Khrushchev.

Hardball (TV interview, 1997)

30 minutes. Political commentary. Chris Matthews, host. G. Gordon Liddy, guest. CNBC, June 16, 1997.

"It's been 25 years since the Watergate break-in — but G. Gordon Liddy is still playing hardball. The difference is that he's doing it on TV. Tonight ... Liddy returns to the Howard Johnson's hotel where, on June 17, 1972, he watched from a balcony as burglars broke into the Democratic National Committee headquarters at the Watergate Hotel across the street. Liddy tells Matthews on tonight's show (8:30) that some good may have come from the break-in." — *New York Post*, June 16, 1997.

(On June 18, Matthews had Bob Woodward as his guest. The identity of Deep Throat was one of the topics. Matthews suggested David Gergen.)

Campaign Financing and Watergate (TV panel, 1997)

180 minutes. Panel discussion with Senator Fred Thompson, journalist Elizabeth Drew, political analyst Charles Lewis, others. Fred Wertheimer, formerly head of Common Cause, moderator. Newseum, Arlington, Virginia. C-SPAN, July 2, 1997. Part of a series.

Discussions of the parallels of Nixon's 1972 campaign with Clinton's 1996 campaign. Follow-up John Dean and Charles Lewis — one of five programs during the week of June 3–July 5, 1997, observing the twenty-fifth anniversary of the Watergate break-in. The July 3, 1997, segment dealt with effect of Watergate on later political reporting. Many Nixon clips were peppered throughout. The series offers an absorbing, if familiar, overview.

Elvis Meets Nixon
(TV "mockumentary," 1997)

90 minutes. Teleplay directed by Allan Arkus. Written and produced by Alan Rosen. Narrated by Dick Cavett. With: Rick Peters as Elvis Presley and Bob Gunton as Nixon. Sunday, August 10, 1997, 9 P.M.

Nixon's meeting with Elvis is certainly a good idea for a comedy, but Alan Rosen's script doesn't work; there is too much padding.

"Nixon is seen in all his isolated insecurity, peering out the window at anti-war protesters. Only someone as out of touch as Nixon would have thought Presley was the guy to restore his image with rebellious youth whose chant was John Lennon's 'Give Peace a Chance.' Bob Gunton's imitation carries a curious undertone of Jack Benny. The film moves toward broad caricature when he's around, so it's lucky that the Nixon scenes are minimal." — *New York Times*, August 9, 1997.

George Wallace (TV biography, 1997)

4 hours. Directed by John Frankenheimer. Written by Paul Monash and Marshall Frady based on *Wallace* by Frady. TNT, August 24 and 26, 1997.

Students of Richard Nixon's political strategies would do well to view the film. (Nixon does not appear.) Gary Sinise and Mare Winningham give outstanding performances as Wallace and his first wife, Lurleen, as does Joe Don Baker as former Alabama Governor Big Jim Fulsom.

"Every president from Nixon to Clinton based his successful campaigning on some key elements of the Wallace political cannon." — *Weekly Standard*, August 18, 1997.

Jackie: An American Life (play, 1997)

A play written and directed by Gil Hoppe, originally produced as *Jackie Through the Looking Glass* in 1990. Somewhat revised, *Jackie* was produced by the Poet's Theater, Cambridge, Mass., on January 9, 1992. Further revised, it played for six months in Boston, arriving on Broadway at the Belasco Theater on November 10, 1997. Cast: *Jackie Onassis* Margaret Colin; *JFK* Victor Slezak; *Aristotle Onassis* Thomas Derrah; *Tina Onassis* Gretchen Egolf; *Richard M. Nixon* Derek Smith.

In an appropriately 10-minute sketch JFK and Nixon, who appears to be having convulsions, enact the first of the 1960 debates. Much is made of the fact that Nixon's clothes do not fit properly. The only amusing scenes are those between Aristotle and Tina Onassis.

"Christina Onassis, who once described her American stepmother as the kiss of death, appears in the play as Cassandra fortelling doom on the Onassis household; Jean Kennedy is played in drag, and Teddy is an oversexed Little Lord Fauntleroy. Even last year's auction gets spoofed with an auctioneer offering items retrieved from under her sink, including washing powder and one yellow glove that might have been used by the former first lady."—*Newsday*, August 3, 1997.

Of the Poet's Theater production in 1992, *Variety* wrote: "At its best, *Jackie: An American Life* is wickedly on-target and hilariously merciless. But there's a lot more worst than best in playwright/director Hoppe's new work, which needs cutting, redirecting and recasting."

JFK: A Musical Drama (musical, 1997)

Scheduled for Broadway production during the 1997–1998 season.

"Authors Will Holt and Tim Sawyer are planning to bring their new show *JFK: A Musical Drama* to the Great White Way later this season, the *Post* has learned. The JFK show — described as a documentary-like revue of the late president's life — has already played in limited runs at the Goodspeed Opera House in Connecticut and Dublin, Ireland."—*New York Post*, September 21, 1997.

The Ice Storm (film, 1997)

112 minutes. Directed by Ang Lee. Written by James Schamus. Based on the novel by Rick Moody. Director of photography, Frederick Elmes. Edited by Tim Squyres. Music by Michael Danna. Fox Searchlight Films. Cast: *Ben Hood* Kevin Kline; *Elena Hood* Joan Allen; *Jane Carver* Sigourney Weaver.

"The movie is set in the early seventies. Nixon, seen on TV, sweats and lies, and two families are falling apart. The husband and father (Kevin Kline) in one of these families, the Hoods, is having a tepid affair with Janey Carver, the wife and mother (Sigourney Weaver) in the other; at the same time, Ben Hood's 14-year-old daughter, Wendy (Christina Ricci), who likes to expose herself, is fooling around under the covers and in bathrooms with Janey's two sons."—*New York*, October 6, 1997.

"Over a few days, as President Nixon's sweaty, beleaguered visage flickers on the television screen, the Hoods veer closer to full-blown emotional crisis, reflected literally in the wife-swapping party and symbolically in the freeze that descends on their universe, turning it treacherous."—*New York Times*, September 21, 1997.

"Vittorio De Sica was once asked why so many of his films dealt with adultery, and he replied that, if you take adultery out of the bourgeoisie, there is no drama left. *The Ice Storm* is a desperate confirmation of that belief, here laced with early adolescent sexual heat. Watergate, for all we get the flashes of Nixon on TV and the comic use of a Nixon mask in one scene, has absolutely nothing to do with the texture or intent of the picture: it's just a portentous decor."—*New Republic*, October 13, 1997.

Nixon Tapes
(audio tapes, 1997)

"Nearly a quarter century after their existence was revealed, 201 hours of secretly recorded tapes from the Nixon White House have been transcribed for the first time. They show the darkest side of the former President, and they strongly suggest that Mr. Nixon's guilty knowledge of the Watergate's scandal, crimes and consequences arose earlier and ran deeper than previously known.

"These tapes, identified by an Act of Congress as evidence of Mr. Nixon's abuse of power, were kept from the public by the former President through 22 years of litigation, from his resignation until after his death.

"They are now transcribed by Stanley Kutler, the University of Wisconsin historian who sued for and won their release last year. His work will be published next month as *Abuse of Power: The New Nixon Tapes* (The Free Press)."—*New York Times*, page one, October 31, 1997.

An excerpt:

Nixon: "If I walk out of this office, you know, on this (expletive) stuff, why it would leave a mark on the American political system. It's unbelievable ... But the other thing is — the other thing, if they ever want to get up to the impeachment thing, fine ... My point is that if they get to that, the President of the United States, my view is then *fight like hell*."

Nightline — Nixon Tapes
(TV series, 1997)

30 minutes. Ted Koppel, host. Guests: Stanley I. Kutler and George Lardner (*Washington Post*).WABC-TV, Tuesday, November 18, 1997, 11:35 P.M.

A program of readings of the just-released Nixon tapes with Nixon pungently read by the on-target Lane Smith. Koppel repeated the line often used to characterize Nixon: "Even paranoids have enemies." Koppel concluded by saying that the "new" tapes argue well for the release of "the three thousand plus hours that remain."

Music of American Politics
(cassette and CD, 1997)

The many songs include "Happy Days Are Here Again," "I Like Ike," "The JFK Song," and "The Ballad of Richard Nixon." Performed by Joe Glazer. Available from Collector Records, 1604 Arbor View Rd., Silver Spring, Maryland 20902, (301) 652-0393.

Epilogue

"The life of Richard Nixon has become a lens through which we may see the many paradoxes of human nature. Nixon's life is not just complicated; it represents the collision of human potential and human deficiency.... The end of life brings the final synthesis of man and experience. Nixon looked back and forward with critical discipline. He passed his lessons to me so that I might pass them to others. He prepared me for my future while preparing the future to be without him. At the final passage, Nixon had a true sense of what his life — and the history through which he lived — had meant."

— Monica Crowley, *Nixon Off the Record* (1996)

Index

227